Modern American
Counter Writing

Literary Criticism and Cultural Theory

WILLIAM E. CAIN, *General Editor*

For a full list of titles in this series, please visit www.routledge.com

Contested Masculinities
Crises in Colonial Male Identity from
Joseph Conrad to Satyajit Ray
Nalin Jayasena

Unsettled Narratives
The Pacific Writings of Stevenson,
Ellis, Melville and London
David Farrier

**The Subject of Race in American
Science Fiction**
Sharon DeGraw

Parsing the City
Jonson, Middleton, Dekker, and City
Comedy's London as Language
Heather C. Easterling

**The Economy of the Short Story in
British Periodicals of the 1890s**
Winnie Chan

Negotiating the Modern
Orientalism and Indianness in the
Anglophone World
Amit Ray

Novels, Maps, Modernity
The Spatial Imagination, 1850–2000
Eric Bulson

Novel Notions
Medical Discourse and the
Mapping of the Imagination in
Eighteenth-Century English Fiction
Katherine E. Kickel

**Masculinity and the English
Working Class**
Studies in Victorian Autobiography
and Fiction
Ying S. Lee

Aesthetic Hysteria
The Great Neurosis in Victorian
Melodrama and Contemporary Fiction
Ankhi Mukherjee

**The Rise of Corporate Publishing
and Its Effects on Authorship in
Early Twentieth-Century America**
Kim Becnel

**Conspiracy, Revolution, and
Terrorism from Victorian Fiction
to the Modern Novel**
Adrian S. Wisnicki

City/Stage/Globe
Performance and Space in
Shakespeare's London
D.J. Hopkins

**Transatlantic Engagements with the
British Eighteenth Century**
Pamela J. Albert

**Race, Immigration, and American
Identity in the Fiction of Salman
Rushdie, Ralph Ellison, and William
Faulkner**
Randy Boyagoda

**Cosmopolitan Culture and
Consumerism in Chick Lit**
Caroline J. Smith

**Asian Diaspora Poetry in
North America**
Benzi Zhang

**William Morris and the Society for
the Protection of Ancient Buildings**
Andrea Elizabeth Donovan

**Zionism and Revolution in
European-Jewish Literature**
Laurel Plapp

**Shakespeare and the Cultural
Colonization of Ireland**
Robin E. Bates

Spaces of the Sacred and Profane
Dickens, Trollope, and the Victorian
Cathedral Town
Elizabeth A. Bridgham

**The Contemporary Anglophone
Travel Novel**
The Aesthetics of Self-Fashioning in
the Era of Globalization
Stephen M. Levin

**Literature and Development in
North Africa**
The Modernizing Mission
Perri Giovannucci

**The Tower of London in English
Renaissance Drama**
Icon of Opposition
Kristen Deiter

**Victorian Narrative Technologies in
the Middle East**
Cara Murray

Ruined by Design
Shaping Novels and Gardens in the
Culture of Sensibility
Inger Sigrun Brodey

Modernism and the Marketplace
Literary Culture and Consumer
Capitalism in Rhys, Woolf, Stein,
and Nella Larsen
Alissa G. Karl

**The Genesis of the Chicago
Renaissance**
Theodore Dreiser, Langston Hughes,
Richard Wright, and James T. Farrell
Mary Hricko

**Haunting and Displacement in
African American Literature and
Culture**
Marisa Parham

Misery's Mathematics
Mourning, Compensation, and Reality
in Antebellum American Literature
Peter Balaam

**The Politics of Identity
in Irish Drama**
W.B. Yeats, Augusta Gregory
and J.M. Synge
George Cusack

**Female Embodiment and
Subjectivity in the Modernist Novel**
The Corporeum of Virginia Woolf and
Olive Moore
Renée Dickinson

**Ethics and Politics in Modern
American Poetry**
John Wrighton

Modern American Counter Writing
Beats, Outriders, Ethnics
A. Robert Lee

Modern American Counter Writing

Beats, Outriders, Ethnics

A. Robert Lee

Routledge
Taylor & Francis Group
New York   London

First published 2010
by Routledge
270 Madison Avenue, New York, NY 10016

Simultaneously published in the UK
by Routledge
2 Park Square, Milton Park, Abingdon, Oxon OX14 4RN

Routledge is an imprint of the Taylor & Francis Group, an informa business

Typeset in Sabon by IBT Global.
Printed and bound in the United States of America on acid-free paper by IBT Global.

Library of Congress Cataloging-in-Publication Data
Lee, A. Robert
  Modern American counter writing : Beats, outriders, ethnics / by A. Robert Lee.
    p. cm. — (Literary criticism and cultural theory)
  Includes bibliographical references and index.
  1. American literature—20th century—History and criticism. 2. Beat generation.
3. Dissenters in literature. 4. Counterculture in literature. 5. Cultural pluralism
in literature. 6. Ethics in literature. 7. Literature and society—United States—
History—20th century. I. Title.
  PS228.B6L44 2010
  810.9'0054—dc22
  2009039061

ISBN10: 0-415-99811-5 (hbk)
ISBN10: 0-203-85808-5 (ebk)

ISBN13: 978-0-415-99811-6 (hbk)
ISBN13: 978-0-203-85808-0 (ebk)

Para Pepa como siempre

Contents

Acknowledgments   xi

   Introduction: Counter Writing   1

PART I   Beats

1   Beat Canon, Beat Shadow Canon   9

2   Beat Speaking Women: Diane di Prima, Joanne Kyger,
    Anne Waldman   44

3   Black Beat: Performing Ted Joans   58

4   Beat International: Michael Horovitz, Andrei Voznesensky,
    Kazuko Shiraishi   70

PART II   Outriders

5   Gonzo Scripts: Hunter S. Thompson   87

6   A View of One's Own: Joan Didion   99

7   Pirated Words: Kathy Acker   111

PART III   Ethnics

8   Ethnics Behaving Badly: Texts and Contexts   125

9   Home and Away: US Poetries of Immigration and Migrancy   147

10 Out of the 1990s: Latino/a Un-bordering in US Fiction   161

11 A Western East: America's China Poetry in Marilyn Chin,
    Russell Leong, John Yau and Wing Tek Lum   174

12 Insider, Outsider: Japanese America Writing Japan   183

13 Bad Boy, Godfather, Storyteller: Frank Chin   198

14 Manila Tropics: Jessica Hagedorn   212

15 Black South, Black Europe: William Demby   223

16 Rearview Mirrors: Gerald Vizenor   235

Notes   247
Index   277

Acknowledgments

Any number of debts lie behind this volume, all of them built up over a considerable timeline and mix of geographies. The Beat chapters have a point of origin in my experience of the 1960s as political and cultural change-era both from a base in Britain and then first-hand in the United States as I made my first extended stay in universities from Princeton to Virginia to California. The pioneer work done in Beat and other American literature by Eric Mottram under London University auspices was inspirational. Much subsequently, and in the course of visiting professorships that have taken me to Northwestern, the University of Colorado and Berkeley, I would have the opportunity to enjoy friendships and compare notes with Anne Waldman, Anselm Hollo, Ron Loewinsohn, Kazuko Shiraishi, and the late Ted Joans, along with Beat scholars like Ann Charters, Jennie Skerl, Maria Anita Stefanelli, Larry Smith, Kurt Hemmer, and the contributors to my edited essay-collection *The Beat Generation Writers* (1996).

The Outriders sequence, and its contexts, reflects a host of discussions about America beyond the mainstream. I think back with gratitude to the analysis and backs-and-forth of talk with Richard Kostelanetz, Gerald Graff, Jeff Rice, Susan Castillo, Andrew Hook, Joe Lockard, John G. Cawelti, Sanford E. Marovitz, Robert Pois, Juan Antonio Suárez, Barry Lewis, Peter Dempsey, and the late Laurence B. Holland, Harold Cruse, and Harold Beaver.

My interests in ethnicity, or more exactly the literatures and cultures of ethnicity, has benefited infinitely from a host of creative writers and scholars in whose company I have been able to try out ideas and approaches: Gerald Vizenor, Ishmael Reed, John A. Williams, Frank Chin, John Yau, Gary Pak, Carter Revard, Jim Barnes, Patricia Clark-Smith, Rex Burns, and the late Louis Owens and Leon Forrest, together with scholars like Werner Sollors, Barbara Fields, Ling-chi Wang, Sau-ling Cynthia Wong, Helmbrecht Breinig, Wolfgang Binder, Evelyn Hu-DeHart, Joseph Skerrett, Lane Hirabayashi, Epifanio San Juan Jr., Marco Portales, Arnold Krupat, Gunter Lenz, Bernadette Rigal-Cellard, Hans Bak, Theo D'Haen, Ole Moen, Deborah Madsen, Elvira Pulitano, Javier Coy, Carme Manuel, Rocío Davis, Dorothea Fischer-Hornung, and Yu-cheng Lee.

In Japan, my present base, I owe a round of appreciation to my Nihon University colleagues, Kimitaka Hara, Takeshi Sekiya, Ichitaro Toma, Yuko Noro, Takeshi Onodera, Tomoko Kanda and Stephen Harding; also, for their great support and friendship, to Mark Gresham, Nicholas Williams and Shoko Miura, along with Dorsey Kleitz, David Ewick and James Vardaman.

Portions of some of these chapters have known earlier lives but have undergone substantial revision and updating. My thanks for permissions to Palgrave-Macmillan and Blackwell. It would be remiss not to say how much I have benefited from the editorial good spirits of Erica Wetter and Elizabeth Levine at Routledge and from the first-class compositor work by Eleanor Chan at IBT Global.

Josefa Vivancos-Hernández, as always, has been the necessary anchor.

Introduction

I . . . prefer rather to hang myself in my own halter than swing in any other man's swing.

        —Herman Melville, Letter to Evert A. Duyckinck (1849)[1]

She is a splendid example of a woman writer who made it from the margins; also, just as important, a writer who always demonstrates how vital counter-cultural impulses are to the very existence of any worthwhile tradition.

        —Lorna Sage, "Obituary for Angela Carter" (1992)[2]

"What are you rebelling against?"
"What'd ya got?"

        —Marlon Brando as Johnny Strabler in *The Wild One* (1953)[3]

Modern American counter writing. Counter to what? Counter in what sense? Even more plainly, whose and what authorship? The short answer would be fiction, poetry, life-writing and drama, and a plenitude of discursive work, pledged to un-write, more aptly to re-write, the one or another agreed America. Each of these nomenclatures, Beats, Outriders, Ethnics— the last a term carefully to be interrogated, is meant to indicate considerably diverse groupings, writers in no absolute sense ideologically or in any other way bound to each other. Rather, these are terms to point up affinities, a shared disposition through resources of word or narrative to stir anti-bodies, upset apple-carts. In this they offer not simply some adversary measure, but writings that by definition counter totalization of America as assumed consensual order or frame, and most especially of the kind Walter Lippmann almost a century ago called "manufactured consent."[4]

American literary-cultural dissidence, to be sure, not to say the history and politics behind it, can look to its well enough known lineage. "Hanging in my own halter," in Melville's resonant formulation, has been nothing if not its own tradition, whether rogue Puritanism from Michael Wigglesworth to Henry David Thoreau, Anne Hutchinson to Margaret Fuller, or a contemporary incarnation from 1960s New Journalism to the present-day Bad Subjects cyber-group. The literary work created under Beat, Outrider and Ethnic auspices, in like spirit, bespeaks yet other seams of dissidence, writing against the grain, words against the wind.

Beat creative output, in this respect, looks to the visionary bardism of Whitman, his call-to-arms of open road life-encounter and matching open poetics of extended breath-line, with the likes of William Carlos Williams and Charles Olson in the heritage. Outrider imagining likewise looks to its own distinctive legacy in American literature, whether the Melville of *The Confidence-Man* (1857), the Twain of "What is Man?" (1906), the Ambrose Bierce of war stories like "An Occurrence at Owl Creek Bridge" (1891) and *The Devil's Dictionary* (1906, 1911) or the Nathanael West of *Miss Lonelyhearts* (1933) and *The Day of The Locust* (1939).[5] Ethnics, ethnicity, has a precedent (and unlikely WASP) advocate in the Randolph Bourne of "Trans-national America" (1916), his early, prophetic and welcoming insistence on America as implicated in a national dynamic of cultural pluralism.[6] More than a little cannily he anticipates much current debate, not to say accompanying contention, as to multiculturalism—mainstreams against peripheries, canons against "ethnic" mosaics of language, history and literary voice. The debate has had its notable proponents. Arthur M. Schlesinger's *The Disuniting of America: Reflections on a Multicultural Society* (1992) gives one characteristic emphasis, Lawrence W. Levine's *The Opening of the American Mind: Canons, Culture, and History* (1996) another, with Ronald T. Takaki's *A Different Mirror: A History of Multicultural America* (1993) providing a timeline and canvas.[7]

Postwar America, with the 1960s as axial decade, can claim a lien on all these several and yet allied traditions, the challenge, each writer to their own idiom, of mounting both affirmation and critique of America's latest modernity. In this sense Counter Writing overall, and its apportioning into Beat, Outrider and Ethnic, should not be taken to mean *the* counter-culture, nor the 1960s as somehow extending rights of sway or style into the well over half a century since World War II. Rather it is meant to serve more inclusively as a portmanteau term of focus, that of America imaginatively inscribed at contrary and often enough mutually contending angles. All the names in play in the present study, novelist and poet, essayist and life-writer, and however different the fashioning, can be said to act on this impetus, American counter-voices given to the making of American counter-texts.

The Beats, from their late 1940s-1950s outset through the 1960s and down into the ensuing century, and to approbation or otherwise, continue to carry some of America's best known literary counter-insignia. That is not to say that all the critical returns are settled history, the judgments done and dusted. To that end the historic roster of Allen Ginsberg, Jack Kerouac, Gregory Corso, William Burroughs and Lawrence Ferlinghetti, or rather their best-known prime work, invites renewed appraisal, respective re-readings. "Howl" (1956) is thereby read through Ginsberg's letter of 1956 to Richard Eberhardt, *On The Road* (1957) through Kerouac's Sal

Paradise as subject-narrator, Corso's *The Vestal Lady of Brattle* and *Gasoline* (1955, 1958) through their hugely inventive play of image, Burroughs's *Naked Lunch* (1959, 1959, 1962) as dystopian-carnivalesque dark comedy, and Ferlinghetti's *Pictures of the gone world* (1955) and *A Coney Island of the Mind* (1958) as spatially configured word-paintings.[8]

If, however, these have become the canonical texts, what of the further Beat circuit, that which might be called the shadow canon? As a kind of counter-weight, the opening essay also takes bearings on a complementary Beat chronology of other key writings—John Clellon Holmes's *Go* (1952) to Joyce Johnson's *Door Wide Open* (2000), LeRoi Jones/Imamu Amiri Baraka's *Preface to a Twenty Volume Suicide Note* (1961) to Herbert Huncke's *Guilty of Everything* (1987, 1990), with considerations in-between of texts by Michael McClure, Diane di Prima, Irving Rosenthal, Bonnie Bremser, and Harold Norse.[9] Even allowing that this double-critique gestures towards the fuller Beat gallery, there still remains more of the different tiers and geographies of achievement. It is precisely to meet this end that the three essays which follow come into play.

First, women's authorship under Beat or Beat-connected auspices are centered in a trio of names, those of Diane di Prima, Joanne Kyger and Anne Waldman. Each, unmistakably, writes to their own drummer, to their own muse: di Prima as early poet-bohemian, editor, dissident and political radical, Kyger as wry ironist, Buddhist, free-verse virtuoso, and Waldman as St. Marks and Naropa veteran, Ginsberg lifetime friend, landmark editor and anthologist, and in the form of nearly fifty published collections Beat poetic fertility writ large. Black Beat, Afro-Beat, has a wholly necessary place in the landscape, rarely more engaging than in the minstrel-surrealist person of Ted Joans. If Beat took to jazz and blues, Joans carried the legacy in his very being, born on a Mississippi riverboat, trumpeter, onetime room-mate of Charlie Parker, Paris and Africa traveler, and a round-midnight visitor to Harlem and other music haunts with none other than Jack Kerouac. Nor was Joans alone—he had literary company in LeRoi Jones/Imamu Amiri Baraka, Bob Kaufman and A. B. Spellman. Beat as international signature has had its writer sentinels across several continents. Michael Horovitz, Andrei Voznesensky and Kazuko Shiraishi carry the register of Beat in Britain, Russia and Japan. But their poetry, Blake-affiliated in Horovitz, Soviet-dissident in Voznesenky, and Tokyo-located jazz and sex bad-girl in the early Shiraishi, equally does duty for Beat as the larger global round.

Outriders, again and of necessity an elastic term, are personified in three kinds of luminary—Hunter Thompson, Joan Didion, and Kathy Acker. Gonzo "doctor of journalism" by his own coining, Thompson established his cachet with two seminal works, each a theatrical departure from past journalistic conventions of distance and objectivity. Both *Hell's Angels: The Strange and Terrible Saga of the Outlaw Motorcycle Gangs* (1996) and *Fear and Loathing in Las Vegas: A Savage Journey to the Heart of the American Dream* (1971), in line with the writing and essay-collections that followed, established him as a rare, urgent, and truly one-off and hugely enjoyable participant-reporter—politics to sports, Nixon to the TV evangelists.[10] Joan Didion, by contrast, has been meticulousness itself, a cool and for some glacially deliberative voice since she made her discursive mark with the writings that led to *Slouching Towards Bethlehem* (1968) and *The White Album* (1979).[11] In no way, however, does that lessen her claim to outsider status or the acuity of bearings taken from quite another kind of angle on America as both domestic and hemispheric culture. In Kathy Acker, the postmodern as punk enters the reckoning. Gender, patriarchy, power as sexuality, language as pre-edited authoritarian code, and a Burroughsian view of modernity as the power-politics of domination and submission, runs through the fiction that followed in the wake of *Politics* (1972) and *The Childlike Life of the Black Tarantula* (1973).[12] Plotlines little exist, vocabulary runs into unsparing sexual riffs, violence is frequent. Little wonder she was early to acquire rogue status, that of a highly literate author-pirate. Outsiders each in their fashion, Thompson, Didion and Acker serve as measurers of the times.

Ethnics, a term too long or by rote taken to signify periphery, is underwritten throughout by the assumption that America's minorities may be so by demographic number but that does not mean a minority literature. Powers of textual imagining know no limits, whatever the sources of cultural time-and-place. In that spirit the opening essay in the sequence, "Ethnics Behaving Badly," offers a *tour d'horizon*, a lay-of-the land, of the imaginative range of "ethnic" counter-texts starting from the inveterately singular example of Zora Neale Hurston and moving through a gallery to include Ishmael Reed and Darryl Pinckney, Gerald Vizenor and Leslie Marmon Silko, Oscar Zeta Acosta and Richard Rodriguez, and Monica Sone and Max Yeh. The emphasis in this voluminous but still selective range of Black, Native, Latino/a and Asian American texts falls upon contrarian verve, the substance and fashioning of "ethnic" inscriptions of America.

A quartet of maps follow. "Home and Away" looks to a multicultural roster of verse in its bearings upon America as immigrant and migrant history, the poetic voicings of a plurality of peoples variously caught up in diaspora, exile, the memory of ocean crossing, and the displacements brought about by transformations of border (especially the southwest and Caribbean) and the search for livelihood. "Out of the 1990s" is meant as a period-evaluation, the recognition of the one decade's virtuoso storytelling, novel and story, across the Chicano, Puertorriqueño, Cuban American and other Hispanic spectrum. "A Western East" gives focus to Chinese American poetry, the work of Marilyn Chin, Russell Leong, John Yau and Wink Tek Lum as subtly created registers of image in the ways China has made its way into the America of California, New York and Hawai'i. In "Insider, Outsider" the writing of Japan from within Japanese American literature comes into play, Japan itself as no simple unitary Chrysanthemum cultural or political order, and Japanese America, likewise, as its own consortium of richly diverse literary mirrors.

These each have a follow-up in specific authorships. Frank Chin has long acquired the sobriquet of battler-royal, a fierce polemicist in the cause of a masculinist Chinese America. His flurries against Charlie Chan and Fu Manchu stereotype, and against film and media passivity images of both Chinese and Chinese Americans, along with Maxine Hong Kingston, Amy Tan and David Hwang as supposed purveyors of prejudicial assimilation and exotica, have kept him to the forefront of controversy. His writings, whether the essays of *Bulletproof Buddhists* (1998) or the fiction of *The Chinaman Pacific & Frisco R.R. Co.* (1988), *Donald Duk* (1991) and *Gunga Din Highway* (1994), are here given an overview not just for their counter-stance, however, but also their resourcefulness of craft.[13] In Jessica Hagedorn, American letters has another seeming Bad Girl, a Filipina American novelist, poet, performance artist, and the anthologist of *Charlie Chan is Dead* (1993), whose un-respect for cultural cliché as to US-Philippines relationship takes the form of inventively calibrated irony.[14] She writes with a keen flair—Manila, New York and California, colonialism and power, Imelda and the movies, each plaited into the postmodern counter-narrative of *Dogeaters* (1990), *The Gangster of Love* (1996) and *Dream Jungle* (2003).[15]

William Demby has rarely had his full deserts, in part because of the ascendancy of Ralph Ellison and James Baldwin, Toni Morrison and Alice Walker, Jones/Baraka and Maya Angelou. Yet his three novels each bespeak great invention, and a willingness to strike against usual writ—respectively the hill south as somehow always bucolic in *Beetlecreek* (1957), black fiction as required naturalism-realism in *The Catacombs* (1965), and New York as black northern city though in truth deeply southern in memory, history, and language in *Love Song Black* (1978).[16] Gerald Vizenor has been a Native American literary force-field, as prolific as counter-imaginative. Much known for his neologisms, postindian, survivance, transmotion, and the like, he has logged up a huge bibliography of novels, stories, discursive essays and drama. But from the outset his turn has also been towards poetry. His two most recent works, *Almost Ashore: Selected Poems* (2006) and *Bear Island: The War at Sugar Point* (2006), give confirmation, lyric and haiku in the one, a verse history of "the last Indian war" in the other, both in common with his other writings to be thought species of imaginative contradance.[17]

This volume, I hope, will be seen as more essay-collection than monograph (and in this respect I have allowed occasional overlaps of reference to stand). It seeks to draw together writings of shared animus, an America articulated in counter-voice, and yet given to wholly discrete imaginative shapings of idiom. Beat, Outrider and Ethnic, of necessity, are approximations, less category than contour or route-marker. Each itself invites qualification, an insistence upon specificity and nuance. But there should be no doubt of how the authorship involved makes for a postwar literary treasury, sustained vitality, the counter reading and writing of America to compelling effect. Such, at least, has been the conviction arising out of my own close-encounters with the texts in play—and their expression as critique. For these I owe genuine pleasure and debt, unique pathways into an America if at once an Atlantic away from my own upbringing in England and a Pacific away from my current academic berth in Japan, then rarely less than close to hand.

Part I

Beats

1   Beat Canon, Beat Shadow Canon

The beat generation can be seen as an aspect of the worldwide trend for intellectuals to reconsider the nature of the human individual existence, personal motives, the qualities of love and hatred, and the means of achieving wisdom. Existentialism, the modern pacifist-anarchist movement, the current interest of Occidentals in Zen Buddhism, are all a part of that trend. The beat generation is particularly interesting because it is not an intellectual movement, but a creative one: people who have cut their ties with respectable society in order to live an independent way of life writing poems and painting pictures, making mistakes and taking chances—but finding no reason for apathy or discouragement. They are going somewhere . . .

> —Gary Snyder, "Notes on The Beat Generation" (1960)[1]

The stakes are too great—an America gone mad with materialism, a police-state America, a sexless and soulless America prepared to battle the world in defense of a false image of its Authority. Not the wild and beautiful America of the comrades of Whitman, nor the historic America of Blake and Thoreau where the spiritual independence of each individual was an America, a universe, more huge and awesome than all the abstract bureaucracies and Authoritative Officialdoms of the World combined. Only those who have entered the world of Spirit know what a vast laugh there is in the illusory appearance of worldly authority. And all men at one time or another enter that spirit, whether in life or death.

> Allen Ginsberg, "Poetry, Violence, and
> The Trembling Lambs," (1959)[2]

Beats. The Beat Movement. How best to re-engage with its one and several measures? How to give fresh eye and ear to a postwar repertoire of verse, fiction and performance that in its time and place stirred headlines as another America? Admirers, then and still, contend not only for a luminous gathering of literary-cultural energies but life-style in kind, the self unfettered, the spirit freed. To the un-persuaded the Beats will for ever smack of the easy shot, antics more than art, not to say a careerist shrewd regard for the market. Either way, and well over a half-century on from the bow first made in the late 1940, continued into the 1950s, and with an apogee in the 1960s, Beat remains un-erased, nothing if not unfinished business.

First has to be the founding circuit of texts, all long installed as canonical Beat fare—Ginsberg's *Howl and Other Poems* (1956), Kerouac's *On The Road* (1957), Corso's *The Vestal Lady on Brattle* (1955) and *Gasoline*

(1958), Burroughs's *The Naked Lunch* (1959, 1962), and Ferlinghetti's *Pictures of the gone world* (1955) and *A Coney Island of The Mind* (1958).[3] Each, from a current vantage-point, has filters to be negotiated, notably the encrustations of fame, even notoriety, and for all their one-time generational shock of the new, the danger of having eased into familiar writ. A yet further complication, moreover, arises. Beat's core players, its strike-force, have long tended to exert the pre-emptive effect. The upshot has been to relegate whole tiers of Beat-related authorship into a species of nether or shadow canon. Selective names in this regard, and for all that they can exert claims on other than Beat grounds, look to John Clellon Holmes, LeRoi Jones/Imamu Amiri Baraka, Barbara Probst Solomon, Michael McClure, Diane di Prima, Irving Rosenthal, Bonnie Bremser/Brenda Frazer, Harold Norse, Herbert Huncke and Joyce Johnson.[4] Each bespeaks singularity, a discrete power of imagination, yet each in their own degree a liveliest cross-path into Beat's literary orbit.

Even so, an iconic status attaches to Ginsberg's *Howl* and Kerouac's *On The Road* as Beat's respective first and best celebrated calling-cards. The one offers "holy litany," the would-be visionary hymn to life in the face of corporation and dollar appetite, Cold War and atomic bomb. The other, with Sal Paradise as chronicler and Dean Moriarty as re-configured Neal Cassady, relays the serial male companionship of road, jazz and sex within the novel's itineraries from New York and New Jersey into Denver, California, New Orleans, The South and Mexico. Both serve as legendary countercultural anthems, whether the Eisenhower years defied for the sense of life as gridlock—the politics of McCarthyism, Wall Street as all-encompassing ethos, the Cold War—or, as each took on its own kind of notoriety, the 1950s into the 1960s as a generational change-era in social culture.

Beats, beatniks, hippies. The transition is long familiar. The Ginsberg-Kerouac inaugural years were creative, literary, "Howl" in City Lights format, *On The Road* as Viking Press bestseller. In their wake came Beat as style, "liberated" youth, drop-out, the Village and Berkeley as key locations, diffuse ventures across the highways and into communes. The legacy would then move on to the drug-flower children of Haight-Ashbury, the Summer of Love in 1967, and Woodstock in 1969 with Jimi Hendrix and Janis Joplin, the both of them Beat-influenced. Beat's trace, or overlap, at the same time was said to have been seen in the Free Speech Movement, the sexual revolution—not that Beat and feminism made for a nexus, the Chicago Democratic Convention protests of 1968, and the various Vietnam and Cambodia protests.

Yet Beat into Beatnik and beyond, along with the drugs heritage of pot, LSD and the heavier regimens, did not always sit easily in all original Beat quarters. Kerouac notably inveighed again the morphing into flower-power hippiedom (in his "Letter to Myself," written in November 1960, he speaks disparagingly of having become the media's "bloody King of the Beatniks").[5] The still subsequent transition, Beat as emerging media and market commodity, could prompt Burroughs in the 1980s to some vintage drollery ("Kerouac opened a million coffee bars and sold a million pairs of Levi's to both sexes. Woodstock rises from his pages").[6]

As America's more public history evolved, Nixon and Watergate, the Carter and Reagan-Bush eras, the Clinton and Bush Jr. presidencies, through to the Obama White House, the 1960s and with it Beat and related counter-culture, could hardly avoid becoming part of period myth. The upshot has been both a sense of distance, and yet, paradoxically, an augmentation of interest. However construed, true or fake liberation, new American Renaissance or passing parade, the sheer spiritedness of both players and texts clearly has remained a draw. Both separately and compositely each writer-figure, each historic poem, novel, play, film or act of life-writing, together with work not so historic, wins latest reader-listeners. To say that Beat has found a historical place in modern American cultural formation is far from saying it has gone out of fashion, become moribund, or devolved into anachronism. The 1955 San Francisco Six Gallery readings under the orchestration of Kenneth Rexroth, especially Ginsberg delivering "Howl," remain legend, as does City Lights as bookstore-publishing anchor, cinema like *Pull My Daisy* (1959) and *Easy Rider* (1959), and a Beat journal history stretching from *City Lights Journal* (1963–66) to *The Beat Review* (2007–).

The writings themselves manage the unusual feat of inspiring both huge popular followings and dedicated rolls of scholarship. It would be impossible to ignore the ever lengthening bibliography of monographs, essay-collections, reference-books, journal special issues, film, screen and print documentaries, bio-pics, web-sites, translations, DVDs and CDs. Archives, at Boulder's Naropa and Stanford, or at the New York Public Library and the Library of Congress, continue to expand. Beat literature regularly enters the curriculum, High School to college. Beat conferences and panels convene with regularity, whether MLA, City Lights and Berkeley, or as in 1994 the NYU Beat conference under the co-chairing of Allen Ginsberg and Anne Waldman. Among international capitals London, Paris, Amsterdam, Rome and Tokyo, each with their Beat heritage, play host to ongoing commemorative festivals. Interest may well take different focus and shape, but the momentum clearly remains un-slowed.[7]

Enthusiasm continues to vie with reservation. In his insider-participant flourish, *Tales of Beatnik Glory* (1975), Ed Sanders, classicist, verse historian and founder-composer of the Fugs, mooted the Beat phenomenon as nothing short of a break-through in American consciousness, the very dawn of the New Aquarius.[8] He affirms the mantra to have been one of liberation, the awakening of self through Zen, drugs, and however male-privileging, un-cosseted sexuality. Where once a consensual America in the wake of World War II had found its best-known symptomatic expression in the gray flannelled suit, suburban nuclear family, home-making and the cocktail hour, along with bobbysoxers as precursors to teenagers, the ethos had become the self of free space and, with the 1960s, the exhilarations coded in sex, drugs and rock and roll. The Beats would point not only to road and commune, but open relationship, ubiquitous pot, and a sound wrap to graduate from jazz to pop, Afro-America's Charlie Parker, say, to California's The Doors. Dress likewise moved on—button-down shirts and tweed jackets for men or all-black female attire yielded to bell-bottoms, shades, long hair as statement. As to literary texts they were no longer to be met with in silent library sessions or college-course classroom intimacy. The call had gone up for performance, the festival, campus, or coffee-house reading as participatory theatre.

At the opposite reach were the gate-keepers, the guardian sentinels warning of an America at risk of cheap-thrill surrender of mind. In "The Know-Nothing Barbarians," written for *Partisan Review* in 1958 with due echoes of Matthew Arnold's *Culture and Anarchy*, Norman Podhoretz, Allen Ginsberg's one-time classmate, would indict "a movement of brute stupidity and anarchy know-nothingness."[9] For Robert Brustein, likewise, Beat and its wave-effects amounted to nothing short of "the cult of unthink."[10] As to the America of postwar Main Street, the small-town and rural hinterlands of the Midwest or South, Beat could hardly not seem other than aberrant, a fringe, especially in sexual behavior, and to be warned against by conservative parent and church or school authority.[11]

Whichever the bearing, and as an encyclopedic history like David Halberstam's *The Fifties* (1993) confirms, Beat's standing as totem and taboo assumed near mythic status.[12] For true believers Ginsberg's "Howl" still signifies break-through illumination, a transcendental spirituality fused of Whitman and Manhattan, Zen, Veda and Torah. At the same time it still faces dismissal as mere incantation, even dirty-word graffiti. *On the Road*, for its part, is still greeted as a pathway into America's untapped existential wellsprings, life taken at speed and in spontaneous narrative to match. But the slaps it once received also still sting, notably from Truman Capote in 1959 on David Susskind's show, *Open End*: "None of them can write. Not even Mr. Kerouac. . . [It] isn't writing at all—it's typing."[13] In common with Beat's other ranking texts, both poem and novel so continue to stir contention, either a rebirth or decline of America's postwar authorship.

Other mixed responses come into play. It has not gone un-noted that if Beat's call was to creative-spiritual new heights a no doubt wry postscript arises in two notable recent manuscript sales. Kerouac's original 120-foot taped scroll of *On The Road*, un-paragraphed, and with its true-named characters and edgier sexual material, was sold at Christie's Manhattan auction for $1.9 million in 2001 to Jim Irsay, the present-day owner of the Indianapolis Colts, a display-item shown across the US with a 50-year anniversary exhibition during 2007. Ginsberg's papers went to Stanford University for $1million, recognition, though many thought it opportunism as much on the part of the academy as by the poet and his estate, towards a Beat movement whose best-known writings and its usual suspects it had once viewed with little disguised condescension.

With the deaths of Ginsberg and Burroughs in 1997, and Corso in 2001, a number of quarters decided Beat had pretty much reached its close, memorial silhouette more than live substance. Yet on almost every showing such has proved anything but to hold. The 50th anniversaries of "Howl" and *On the Road* have been widespread, a line of read-ins, media documentaries and bookstore displays. In Kerouac's case there has been not just the reprint of *On the Road* but his other fiction in the Library of America, typical laudings like that in *Newsweek* in 2007—"The novel that launched the Beats, the hippies and designer jeans turns 50," and a promised screen adaptation with script by Roman Coppola and directed by Walter Salles of the screen documentary *The Motorcycle Diaries* with its 2004 portrait of Che Guevara.[14]

Beat canon. Beat shadow canon. This greatly diverse archive of voice and writing serves to remind that Ginsberg, Kerouac, Corso, Burroughs and Ferlinghetti, with Neal Cassady as "gone" poster boy and Gary Snyder as Buddhist and ecological spirit, together with their fellow literary makers, were never less than a genuinely wide, more inclusive gallery. If the presiding names and texts invite their respective re-evaluation, so in kind, do Beat's fellow writers, the recognition of connecting other imaginative contours—Diane di Prima and women Beat figures, an African American tradition, early contemporaries like Holmes and Solomon. This is also to be reminded that for all Beat's challenge to American cultural politics, Beat as way of life and being, it was also and at all times a literary efflorescence, its main impulses those of the fashioning imagination—word, voice, image, narrative, style, the text spoken and written.

* * *

Despite the intensely demanding fame he'd had to deal with for more than forty years, he'd kept the world both intimate and transcendent.

—Robert Creeley, Foreword, Allen Ginsberg (1997),
Death & Fame: Poems 1993–1995[15]

The one-time taboo accorded Ginsberg's "Howl," the controversies of language, un-abashed homoeroticism and drug reference, has infinitely contributed to keeping the poem in view. But that hardly plays true to the whole achievement. No serious anthology, or history, of postwar US verse would now consign "Howl" to some literary exclusion zone simply on the grounds of notoriety. Detractors go on insisting upon dishevelment, the upshot of a mind fatally shrill or divided. But those who hold the poem in altogether higher regard look to a stunningly spoken mantra, the dispelling of America perceived as corporation dollar greed, consumerism or bomb, and the un-life of establishment authority Ginsberg calls Moloch.

Six decades on, and even more than at first airing and publication, "Howl" refuses to be denied.

The terms in which "Howl" has won its place have grown familiar: Beat anthem, incantation, confession, private vision of public malaise, in all Ginsberg's homily or hex for the times. Yet an oddly underused route-way lies in the letter he sent to Richard Eberhardt in 1956.[16] Commissioned by the *New York Times Book Review* to write the piece that became "West Coast Rhythms," Eberhardt had met Ginsberg ahead of time and spoken admiringly of his imaginative energy even if he had misgivings as to what he said was the negativity of "Howl."[17] The considerably detailed response it prompted from Ginsberg, replete with line diagrams and a near scholarly show of sources, opens avenues both into the poem's force of vision and its organizing prosodic measure.

In countering the notion that he had written only despair, or mere confessional psychodrama with its own avid sexual seams, Ginsberg gave emphasis as he saw it to the near-Buddhist ethos of compassion:

> Howl is an "affirmation" of individual experience of God, sex, drugs, absurdity etc. Part I deals sympathetically with individual cases. Part II describes and rejects the Moloch of society which confounds and suppresses individual experience and forces the individual to consider himself mad if he does not reject his own deepest senses. Part III is an expression of sympathy and identification with C.S. (Carl Solomon) who is in the madhouse, saying that his madness is basically his rebellion against Moloch and I am with him, and extending my hand in union.
>
> —Ginsberg, Letter to Eberhardt (1956)[18]

On this account the poem can indeed be said to pitch for affirmation. The impetus runs through Part I's sympathy for "individual cases"—be they "angelheaded hipsters" (9) or his own mother Naomi, Part II's recoil at society as conformist writ ("Moloch the incomprehensible prison . . . running money . . . Robot apartments!/invisible suburbs!" [21–2]), and Part III's arrival at the final beatification of those under psychiatric hospitalization like Carl Solomon in Rockland Hospital ("I'm with you in Rockland/ where we are great writers on the same dreadful typewriter"[24]). The "best minds of my generation" (9), a designation Ginsberg has said was meant ironically, have been called upon to contest the America of Moloch. This image of the reborn Canaanite fire-god he attributes, high on peyote, to seeing San Francisco's St. Francis Drake Hotel electronically lit up against the night-sky. The regime to hand, money-driven, sexlessly phallic ("granite cocks! monstrous bombs" [22]), is one to ravage the spirit, the malign nexus of corporation and military oppression.

Solomon's specific regime at Rockland elicits the poem's "mercy" both for him and for the cadre of "twenty-five-thousand mad com/rades all together singing the final stanzas of/ the Internationale" (25). The apprehensive compassion ("ah, Carl, while you are not safe I am not safe" [25]), the ironic utopian politics ("the Hebrew socialist revolution against the fascist national Golgotha" [25]), and the oceanic coast-to-coast dream of brotherhood ("in my dreams you walk dripping from a sea-/journey on the highway across America in tears/to the door of my cottage in the Western night" [26]), together with the elegiac "Footnote to Howl" ("holy the hallucinations" [28]), provide the ligatures for the poem's beatificatory resolve. To this end, both in "Howl" and in the Eberhardt letter, Ginsberg explicitly situates himself in the company of Poe, Hart Crane, Pound, Apollinaire, Lorca, Rimbaud, Cézanne, Fenollosa, Snyder, Olson, Creeley, Kerouac, Burroughs, Huncke, along with the Torah, Plotinus and St. John of the Cross. Each, for him, offers visionary precedent, a lament which progresses into his own affirming *gloria in excelsis*.

The Eberhardt letter equally gives the poem's overall architectonic— "The "form" of the poem is an experiment. Experiment with uses of catalogue, the ellipse, the long line, the litany, repetition, etc." Read alongside the like-minded letter Ginsberg wrote to John Hollander, his one-time classmate and fellow-poet and after Hollander's unfavorable review of *Howl and Other Poems* ("a dreadful little volume") in *Partisan Review* for Spring 1957, there can be no doubt of a serious concern with design, metrics, sequence.[19] His debts to Whitman's breath-line catalogues in the making of his verse-paragraphs and to William Carlos Williams's free verse variable foot (for all that he advances his own notions of meter) win due mention. The poem, he makes clear, is conceived as the forward press throughout all three sections out of a "fixed base" for each successive verse-paragraph. The effect is epic litany hinged by each repeated initial word or phrase ("who . . . ," "Moloch . . . ," "I'm with you . . . ," "Holy. . . ,"), and aimed to achieve a gathering and emergent whole. Within the three constituent parts this propulsive movement is to be met what Ginsberg calls "elliptical" displays of local image (he himself instances "hydrogen jukebox"—one could add celebrated coinages like "Blake-light tragedy among the scholars of war" or "the lamb stew of the imagination"). These "strophes," as he terms them, each "spoken with one breath" and of "equal rhetorical weight," are to be understood as building into the gathering serial whole.

The unfolding bardic vision of "Howl," in other words, calls upon quite unmistakable prosodic self-awareness—little as Ginsberg has tended to be given credit for it, the deliberateness of image, the controlling measure, the overall frame. Is there not even a reflexive note that calls such components in a line like "the noun and dash of consciousness"? The notion of "Howl" as having been idly thrown into being, the mere "negative howl of protest" mentioned in the opening page of the letter to Eberhardt, falls by the wayside. The poem, assuredly, will never win over all-comers. But it does radical disservice to think it some mere operatically pitched homily, any more than T.S. Eliot's famous gloss of "The Waste Land" as some personal grumbling. Whatever the fierce visionary immediacy of "Howl" Ginsberg never drew on less than a meticulously deliberated poetics.[20]

*   *   *

How inseparable you and the America you saw yet was never there
to see . . .
— Gregory Corso, "Elegiac Feelings American for
the dear memory of Jack Kerouac"(1969)[21]

"My whole road experience" (9). "The purity of the road" (121). "The road is life" (191). "Road kicks" (212). "Holyboy road, madman road, rainbow road" (229). Can it be doubted that *On The Road* gives the most encompassing implication to its key motif? Literal as may be Route 66, or a given New York, Denver or California interstate, or the Pan-American Highway into Mexico, or indeed the Hudsons, Fords, Cadillacs and long-haul trucks that serve to ferry Sal Paradise and Dean Moriarty on their Beat odysseys, the novel throughout insists upon the road as always inner encounter and awakening. Was not this life taken at the hilt, itinerant, weathered, ever at the edge of new revelation, and delivered in a prose style alive in its own spontaneity? Yet beyond the coast-to-coast or US-Mexico frenetic drives, beyond the hotrod escapades and hitching, beyond Dean's readiness for every manner of exhilarated roistering or sexual adventure, even beyond the bouts of talk and writing, the America of Kerouac's road at every turn implies an enciphered spirituality, the call of the numinous.

To this end the role accorded Sal Paradise as narrator-participant, not that it has gone unexamined, invites considerable emphasis.[22] For as much as Sal is caught up in the energy that Dean embodies, and whatever his would-be *disponibilité*, he also plays the autobiographer fretful at his own hesitations. "I shambled after as I've been doing all my life" (7) serves early notice, a disposition he acknowledges as hanging-back yet eager for action, impetus. "My whole life was a haunted life, the life of a ghost" (15) he confides, as though stationed always at the one remove. Not unfairly he has been compared to that other custodial amanuensis, Nick Carraway, Fitzgerald's compelled and often enough bedazzled witness in *The Great Gatsby* to the dust and dreams of Gatsby as spectacle.

Sal's sense of margin takes on repeated emphasis—the New Jersey writer dependent on his aunt, the addled California camp-guard, the travel-bureau car companion to Dean, the spectator to the city and drug ground-zero of Time Square and where Kinsey's team surveys the sexual habits of Elmer Hassel and Carlo, and the would-be sex-roué in Mexico. At other times he speaks of being drawn to the life of a Tex-Mex *campesino*. But in fantasizing these new stations of self he illuminates all the more those to be found in the road as life-horizon under Dean as presiding if blemished avatar. The willingness to trade in his identity for another, and yet the holding-back, gives just the right added degree of magnification to the story. This authorial self-positioning could not better work to the novel's advantage.

At the outset Sal edges close to road anti-hero, rained-upon, addled as to whether New York's Bear Mountain gives the best route west, and obliged to start again. He can be the bop-enthusiast in Chicago's jazz clubs but he hardly equals Dean with his "gone" listening ("Dean was in a trance" [79]). His parochial sense of scale highlights "the great hugeness" (32) of the Midwest and Plains and Colorado's "rolling wheatfields" (33). This is the city-boy released into American land-space yet whose insignia he finds in the ice cream and apple pie splurges and the heady ride with the Minnesota brothers delivering farm machinery. All, to be sure, is not always euphoria, as in his near-depressive dismay at the cowboy-chic "Wild West Week" or his sense of the brooding opera of *Fidelio* in Central City, a west of kitsch and drift. His vacillation as to where his journeying is headed, or actually signifies, gets reflected in the "damned good question" (20) put to him by the Iowa carnival-owner, namely "You boys going to get somewhere, or just going?" (20).

Even so he has his exultations, nowhere more so than in the feelings that seize him mid-travel. "As we crossed the Colorado-Utah border I saw God in the sky" (165) he avers. The road becomes subject to Dean's "euphoric driving," (209) in which he sees Dean at the wheel as though transfigured, "a burning shuddering frightful Angel" (236) who "looks like God" (259). Of Mexico City Sal writes "We'd made it . . . from the afternoon yards of Denver to these vast and Biblical areas of the world" (274). It is this same style of monitoring that registers Dean's "yea-saying overburst of American joy" and produces the celebrated rhapsody that has these adventurers transpose into "fabulous roman candles . . . mad to live, mad to talk, mad to be saved" (7).

Sal also provides the lens for other estimation—Carlo Marx's "nutty surrealist low-voiced serious staring talk," Old Bull Lee's "critical anti-everything drawl" or Elmer Hassel's "hip sneer" (9). It is Sal who speaks early of Dean as "simply a youth tremendously excited with life" (6), and then, in a footfall of Dostoevsky, as also "the Idiot, the Imbecile, the Saint of the lot. . . .the HOLY GOOF" (176). Dean, under Sal's construing, can be a Gene Autry, the front-range westerner but also the feckless drifter indicatively possessed of the bandaged thumb broken in a fight with his wife or "ragged in a motheaten overcoat" (280) in the nighttime closing New York scene. In Mexico, if Sal sees Dean as beatific ("Dean's face was suffused with an unnatural glow that was like gold" [259]) he also finds himself obliged to face Dean's treachery in leaving him sick with fever ("When I got better I realized what a rat he was" [276]). Sal it is, too, who acts as Beat's very lexicographer—to be defined as "the root, the soul of Beatific" (177).

Illness, start and finish, shadows him. His Mexican fever complements the initial "serious illness" and "miserably weary split-up" (3) from his wife. It is an illness which plays into how the East, for him, has become cultural fatigue, to be contrasted with the health of Rocky Mountain Denver or golden horizon California. Other settings take on the promise of redemption, whether the Nebraska towns passed-through with "unreal but dreamlike rapidity" (209), or Bull Lee's Louisiana farm, or jazz Chicago and New Orleans, or Mexico's Latin sexuality of border and brothel, or even the brute cityscape of Los Angeles's Central Avenue. The west in general, its roads and sightlines, nonetheless can equally flatter to deceive, mocked by cowboy chic billboards, casual violence and hard-scrub labor. Sal's relationship with his Mexican lover Terry gives a reminder of an agri-worker migrancy quite the opposite of Beat's exhilarated road travel. Likewise he finds himself obliged to acknowledge Dean's thieving, the dangers built into his car speeding, and the compulsive philandering for which Dean receives due chastisement from Galatea Dunkel ("You have absolutely no regard for anybody but yourself and your damned kicks" [176]). Sal weighs all of these highs and lows, ever watchful, yet inescapably, ever also self-watchful.

Across the board *On The Road* thereby serves as a kind of existential ledger, the observer inextricably implicated in his own observations. Sal gives his judgments as to Dean's capers with Marylou, Camille and Inez even as he concedes his own dismay at the relationship with Rita. If he is drawn to his own male bonding with Dean he also guards his distance as Dean performs his sexual feints in the motel with the gay pick-up driver (infinitely more graphic in Kerouac's first draft). Each hot-rod escapade sees him as ancillary more than main player, the lead invariably taken by Dean. With Carlo, or Remi Boncoeur, or Ed and Galatea Dunkel, he is more at ease as listener than colloquist ("it was a great forum we were having" he observes of an early talk-fest with Carlo [120]).

For always there is Sal's custodial judgment, be it to Dean's excited outpourings, Carlo's discourses, or Bull Lee's laconic pronouncements. Yet drawn as he is to each and to the road's promise of action he is always, and equally, to be met with as the "author" looking over his own shoulder. Little wonder that Dean, however disingenuously, initially seeks him out at his aunt's New Jersey home to teach him writing. Through him, and however vicarious his role in the Beat trajectory around him, Kerouac is able to give *On The Road* both its invitational pace, the great riffs of prose with their diary-eye acuity of observation, and also the contemplative notes that accompany it. If, as his narration makes emphatic, Sal takes his bearings in others, he at the same time reflexively actualizes their lives in his own, a process which gives interiority as much as road eventfulness to the novel.

Gilbert Millstein's historic 1957 *New York Times* review began the process whereby *On The Road* achieved its standing as iconic Beat text—the travel and kicks, Dean as hipster-existentialist, the inscriptive fluency. "*On The Road*," he argued, "is the most beautifully executed, the clearest and the most important utterance yet made by the generation Kerouac himself named years ago as 'beat,' and whose principal avatar he is."[23] This hardly has won over all quarters, especially those in accord with Capote's vaunted charge of typing. But Millstein can generally claim to have had far the better of it, his recognition both of the visionary plenty disclosed in the routes and trysts of *On The Road* and in the role of Sal as persona of its compositional savvy, precisely Kerouac's writer-surrogate in the execution of word and line, measure and frame.

"Words are Buddhas" reads a line in Kerouac's "Bath Tub Thought" in the posthumous City Lights gathering *Pomes all Sizes* (1992).[24] Off-the-cuff, a snippet as may be, it even so throws an important light on *On the Road*. It points to the religio-existential spirit of the novel, the transcendent call to the road-as-illumination (it also implies Kerouac's sense of his text for all its spontaneity as also highly concentrated in its crafting). A 1960 observation further underlines the point. Speaking of "my true-life novels about the 'beat' generation" he designates himself "a strange solitary crazy Catholic mystic."[25] This combination may also lie behind Kerouac's letter to Ginsberg of May 10 1952 which otherwise could easily be taken for mere vainglory: "On The Road is a very great book, but I may have to end up daring publishers to publish it . . ."[26]

*　*　*

Gregory Corso is the last voice of the original Beat rebellion . . .

—Lawrence Ferlinghetti,
Woodstock Journal (September 2000)[27]

The cover notes for City Lights's reprint of Corso's first two volumes, *The Vestal Lady of Brattle* and *Gasoline*, could hardly come more emblazoned in Beat garland. Ginsberg gives laudatory mention to "refinement of beauty out of a destructive atmosphere," together with an affectionate caution, "Open this book as you would a box of crazy toys." Burroughs speaks of Corso as "a gambler" and of his life's "reverses," but also of his "vitality and resilience." Kerouac invokes the Lower East Side "tough young kid" yet also "the one & only Gregory the Herald." Together they offer a frame, Beat cross-lights, through which to remember Corso's bow into poetry.[28]

In one sense Corso has appeared always the junior partner, with New York's reformatories and jails his Harvard or Columbia. In fact he was quite the equal of the others in originality, his poetry full of rare contrarieties, an arresting dissonance. His early prison-cell reading, Shelley pre-eminently, left indelible footprints, the poet as inspired wild-child. As *Mindfield: New and Selected Poems* (1989) infinitely confirms, each best-known poem carries this sense of life met at an angle, both serious yet at times anarchically whimsical and surreal-tinted.[29] These, typically, include "Marriage," with its colloquial tease as to responsible courtship and family ("All the universe married but me!"); "Bomb," with its mushroom-cloud format and

allusions to "Death's jubilee"; "America Politica Historia, In Spontaneity," his march-of-the-Presidents poem ("Mad beautiful oldyoung America
has no candidate/the craziest wildest greatest country of them all"); and
"Columbia U. Poesy Reading—1975," his verse synopsis of Beat history
("ours was a history with a future") with its "messenger" self-identifica-
tion ("Gansesha, Thoth, Hermes") and encomia to Kerouac, Burroughs
and Ginsberg ("a subterranean poesy of the streets enhanced by the divine
butcher"). Both *The Vestal Lady on Brattle* and *Gasoline* could not better
have given indication of imaginative route.

   Vestal Lady clearly offers a mixed regime. It includes terse, imagistic
vignettes like "Thoughts on a Japanese Movie" (62), "Greenwich Village
Suicide" (67) and "My Hands are a City" (69). The title-poem "The Vestal Lady on Brattle" (61) looks to its spinster's lonely self-contemplation
and implied Boston witch-legacy. Poems of place come into view like the
dark, Calvinist-hued "In The Tunnel-Bone of Cambridge" (72–3) and its
companion-piece "Cambridge, First Impressions" (103–5). No poem, however, better shows Corso at early strength than "Requiem for 'Bird' Parker,
Musician" (88–92), his quite monumentally heartfelt tribute set in chorus-
form and seamed in jazz-hipster imagery. It opens with a "prophecy," that
of Death as the *"nowhere bird"* (88) with its remembrance of Parker as
"BIRD" (the name capitalized throughout) and *"a room/in which an old
horn/ lies in a corner"* (88). Four tributary voices play into the ensuing
colloquium, four riffs on Bird's music, life and death. His memorial horn
is said to have been irresponsibly put aside ("like where's the horn, man,
where?" [88]). His very presence has become an absence ("like where's
BIRD?" [88]).

   This is the Charlie Parker to be thought in jazz-speak the "weirdy monk"
(89), "goner than sound" (89), and whose playing "broke the barrier" (89).
The poem becomes not only a hosanna to Bird's musical genius, his ear
and pitch ("he blew his horn to the sky/made the sky fantastic!"[89]), but
an elegy to his heroin-addict's too ready dice with death ("the draggy bird
ran death into BIRD's throat/and the whole building rumbled/when BIRD
let go his horn/and the sky got blacker . . . blacker" [91]). Bird's symphonic
trumpet riffs, the very flights of his musical genius, are to be remembered as
one "long crazy note" (91). These orphic allusions and images play one into
the other, after-sounds, mourning echoes, equivalences in their own turn of
Bird's own dazzling horn improvisation. It makes for vintage Corso.

   It was, however, with *Gasoline* that Corso made his mark, thirty-plus
poems full of travel and city sight and sound, jazz-figures, painters and
their canvases, and his own stock of wry, comic visions and sense-data. The
volume's geographies span the Atlantic. "Ode to Coit Tower" contrasts this
Californian "idiotic colossus" against "stocky Alcatraz weeping on Nep-
tune's table" (17), a summoning of Shelleyian imagination over mere man-
built "height," and in which "Truth's divine dialect" is to be set against
"absurd Babel" (19). "Vision of Rotterdam" gives a wry imagining of the

Dutch port reborn from war "amid a madness of coughing bicycles" (23). "Paris" again calls up the era of liberation, a "Childcity," an "Aprilcity," its poets "beautiful Baudelaire/Artaud, Rimbaud, Apollinaire" (54). It stands "Newyorkless," with the Seine and Tour d'Eiffel the historic markers of a metropolis freed of occupying German yoke and "Mama War" (54).

Jazz virtuosity wins its celebration in "For Miles," the Bee Bop-to-Fusion "poet" whose sound ("true & from within/a confession/soulful & lovely" [50]) is to be recalled in a set "when you & bird/wailed five in the morning some wondrous/yet unimaginable score" (50). The tribute is intimate, hugely felt, the language of heart. "Uccello" reflects another direction to Corso's temperament, his astute visual sense. The poem clearly has in view the 14th Century master's San Romano three paintings, the animating command of perspective with its battlefield troops and horses, banners and insignia. Corso celebrates Uccello's grasp of committed life in the face of death ("You'd think it impossible for any man to die/each combatant's mouth is a castle of song/each iron fist a dreamy gong"[35]). "Pictorial war," in Corso's reflexive shaping, seeks to refract, if not re-enact, Uccello's rich visual junctures of sight and (as it were) sound, itself also a spoken painting.

Corso's invention of a first-person speaking self can look to two well enough known pieces. "The Mad Yak" speaks in the voice of sacrifice, animal for poet, perhaps, linked. Milk, bones ("They want to make buttons of my bones"[48]) and tail ("How many shoelaces will they make of that!"[48]) become litany, an evisceration. A near Buddhist compassion holds, the yak as gallows-humor secret sharer. In "I Am 25" the "I" is all impatience with the establishmentarian turn of older poets ("Especially old poetmen/who speak their youth in whispers"[42]). The fear of losing edge, the necessary vitality of contra-stance ("a love a madness for Shelley/Chatterton/Rimbaud"[42]), runs throughout. The pitch is kept playfully both fond and unfond ("I HATE OLD POETMEN!" [42]). The speaker, Hermes-like, even assumes the role of messenger-burglar out to renew the force of poems discarded or renounced by their begetters—"Then at night in the confidence of their homes/rip out their apology-tongues/and steal their poems" (42) The duty of true poetry, runs Corso's implication, is to de-familiarize, un-settle agreed norms. "What you once were, thru me/you'll be again" (42) runs the insistence. It would be hard to escape the Beat rowdy-ism and drugs, the many fissures and collisions, in Corso's own history. But, from *The Vestal Lady on Brattle* and *Gasoline* onwards, there can be no mistaking the better challenge of his poetry, the contrary wit, the inventiveness of image.

* * *

Burroughs started out in the 1940s as a founding member of the "Beat Generation" . . . a movement for which Jack Kerouac became

the mythologizer, Allen Ginsberg the prophet, and Burroughs the
theorist.

—Ann Douglass, Introduction, *Word Virus:*
The William Burroughs Reader (1988)[30]

Ann Douglass's notion of saturnalia does no injustice to *Naked Lunch*. The
world Burroughs calls interzone, a grid or hive of endlessly mutating control systems, he discharges quite exactly as though serio-comic farce. Mary
McCarthy, in her review for *Encounter* in 1963, and at the Edinburgh
Festival, famously spoke of the text as "vaudeville," "a musical-comedy
inferno."[31] J.G. Ballard, introducing a modern re-issue, speaks of "a ban-
quet you will never forget," "comic apocalypse."[32] Other fellow-writers
from Kathy Acker to Alan Moore, Angela Carter to Thomas Pynchon,
bear yet further witness to Burroughs's dark, satiric-comic virtuosity. Each
has given tribute to Burroughs as dark vaudeville master, the begetter of a
multi-novel mythography extending across *The Soft Machine* (1961), *The
Ticket That Exploded* (1962), *Nova Express* (1964), *Dead Fingers Talk*
(1973) and well beyond. Collectively they develop a satiric anatomy of the
world as *l'univers concentrationnaire*, a supply-and-demand junk dispensation visited on humanity by political hegemonies, corporations, religions,
medical and media bureaucracies. Burroughs's tunnel intelligence and mor-
dancy of wit at best goes on being likened to that of Swift or Céline.

   Naked Lunch serves as founding installment whose lodestone is always
the ultimate fix of control. Whether, quite, it has been the "endless novel
which will drive everybody mad" supposed in Ginsberg's "Howl," there
can be no denying its potency. The interpretation of modernity as line-
matrix, a cybernetic web or simulacrum, and to which the Wachowski
brothers's *Matrix* screen trilogy (1999–2003) with its virtual as against
actual war-of-the-world replete in programs, dial-ins, hackers and virus
pays homage, has increasingly looked prophetic.[33] To this end his vaunted
use of the cut-up, literally disordered narrative, adds further dynamic to a
vision of the world hooked to controller-images. The effect is to situate Burroughs not only as a necessary voice of dissent but at the very headwaters
of the postmodern turn.

   Naked Lunch's rite-of-passage into publication has itself long become
legend. This takes in the 1950s Yage Letters to Ginsberg (the novel at the
time provisionally called *Interzone*), the early excerpts published in *Black
Mountain Review*, *Yugen* and *Chicago Review*, Maurice Girodias's Olympia Press edition of 1959, and the US censorship obstacles before the eventual Grove Press edition of 1962. Equally well known has been Burroughs's
own situating lexis: *the algebra of need, the sexuality of power, word virus,
the singing telegram, cut-up, fold-in*. To this end his "ATROPHIED PREF-
ACE. WOULDN'T YOU?" supplies more than just a few appended bearings, not least *the naked lunch* as the title phrase suggested by Kerouac and
glossed by Burroughs as *"what is in front of [the] senses at the moment of*

writing" (174). For it both diagrams, and re-enacts, the world being put into view throughout the novel and offers a species of *ars poetica*. In how he invokes teller and telling, tale and reader, Burroughs issues a kind of narrative health-warning, namely, to expect nothing in the way of stock literary convention.

Pitching his teller as mock-ancient bard ("Now I, William Seward, will unlock my word horde," [180]), Burroughs at the same time plumps ineluctably for modern-postmodern authorship ("I am a recording instrument . . . I do not presume to impose 'story,' 'plot,' 'continuity' " [174], or "The writer sees himself reading to the mirror as always"[175]). The teller speaks as though of a world gleaned through some synaptic radio-wave—"This is Revelation and Prophecy of what I can pick up without FM on my 1920 crystal set" (180). The upshot, he assures, "is a blueprint. A How-to Book" (176). *Naked Lunch*, that is, not only carries Burroughs's assault on governing power-structures, its report offers the means to de-encode, and subvert by parody or obscenity to the degree necessary, those very self-same structures.

Telling, for its part, foregoes linear cause-and-effect in favor of narrative as interchangeable, a simultaneity—"You can cut into *Naked Lunch* at any point" (176) or "This book spills off the page in all directions, kaleidoscope of vistas" (180). In this is to be found Burroughs's assault not only on political, military, sexual and media power-structures but the very syntax by which English or other western language coerces reality into subject-verb-object units or addictive binaries. Communication, Burroughs's text suggests, has become more or less subliminal, rote, the purview of senders out to co-opt perception by both directing and yet eviscerating meaning within static and infinitely repeatable dead word-constructions ("'Things go better with Coca Cola," "Have a nice day," "Winning the War"). In accord Burroughs makes his telling resemble that of the addict's quick-change episodes, the one "fix" replaced by the next. At a more intellectual level this also reflects his own longtime interest in non-hierarchical register, Mayan or Chinese or the wall pictographs of ancient Egypt, together with his interest in the non-sequential logic-system of Korzybski as against the linearity of Aristotle.[34]

As to tale, the novel's plot-line happenings, they operate as though a hallucinatory mirror world of interrogation, brainwashing, agents, all given over unsparingly to "sex and pain" (173), "thermodynamics" (176), and in its every iconographic loading, "needle scars" (182). Burroughs's sense is of the "broken image of Man" (136), a human order hooked to one or another constructed reality with its infected media and word. To this end he deploys the supplier-user-junk equation, a fatal circuit of control and dependency. Equally to this end, he can affect a perversely lyric Gothicism—"The black wind sock of death undulates over the land, feeling, smelling for the crime of separate life" (176). The remaining player-component lies in the "Gentle Reader," the mock-decorous naming deliciously belied by the drugs, sex, ejaculation, and hanging and other punishment graphics of the reading-experience to hand in which "the Word will leap . . . with leopard man iron claws" (180).

Not a few of the novel's routines have become satiric lore in their own independent right. How not to warm to the opening Chandler-ism of "I can feel the heat closing in, feel them out there making their moves . . ." (17)? What better gargoyle cast to encounter than Dr. Benway, The Vigilante, Bradley the Buyer, A.J., Dr. "Fingers" Schaefer and the Lobotomy Kid, the cops Hauser and O'Brien, Burroughs himself in the mask of Agent Lee, together with the Factualists, Liquifactionists, Mugwumps, Senders and the rest? He lowers a sublimely disrespectful eye upon the control-circuit of corporate managers, shrinks, say-anything politicos, Pentagon officer-soldiery, medical bureaucrats and society-women *fashionistas*.

Each hallucinatory sex or junk vignette carries Burroughs's coruscations of wit, from "talking assholes" to sperm-filled water-pistols impregnating society matrons. Dr. Benway runs his Reconditioning Center in Freeland (likely Sweden) as though comic Kafka in which scalpels can be wielded in some medical freefall and young interns play bullfighting *espontáneos*. At Interzone University a session on Coleridge's "Ancient Mariner" turns the poem into psychiatric case-sheet. The Mark-Mary-Johnny sex-hanging charade takes its unblinking swipe at the obscenity of capital punishment. The "Dr. Berger Mental Health Tour" reveals its dubious purpose to be that of brute reversal of gay sexual orientation. A. J.'s restaurant and aphrodisiac antics target *haute bourgeois* manners. The good ol' boy Southern sheriff scenes, and their race-venom, could not be better lampooned in their dry-as-dust Texas twang. *Naked Lunch*, thereby, amounts to contra-narrative, an unyielding satiric multi-screen.

Even so, and whatever the often spectacularly funny swerves, hostile critique has far from been assuaged. Does not the text bespeak paranoia in which context Burroughs's New York later bunker retreat and flirtation with scientology is usually mentioned? Is there not pathology to the view of the body as little more than ectoplasm, vein, jism, genitalia and bodily vent? What of the taste for sex and hypodermic extravaganzas or the not so hidden whorls of misogyny—all to good satiric purpose? Burroughs himself has insisted that the novel's routines of staged sado-masochism, fake blue movies, drug and medical irrealism, or cockroach and other insectoid vista, amount to hard-boiled comedy and act wholly within and upon the spirit of the text as a whole. Yet in all the haze about obscenity in *Naked Lunch*, so trenchant a vision, and its wholly-to-purpose voicing, has not always been quick to win informed acknowledgement.

*   *   *

Ferlinghetti's has been an important accessible "voice" . . . who has had a real effect in his support of open-field New American Poetry. His links—personal/poetic—to the Beat generation are legendary.

—Anne Waldman (2006)[35]

Pictures of the gone world (1955), Ferlinghetti's debut verse-collection, gave notice as much of his typical poetics as directions of interest. The very title was indicative: poetry as picture, the world as "gone world" in his own Beat-inflected idiom. Ferlinghetti's open style thus installed itself early, knowledgeable, allusive, yet light-of-touch in satire and surrealism. The career since has been voluminous, not to say enduring, a ply of writer-painter, City Lights publisher-bookseller, internationalist (and from his early days Francophile), translator, and the libertarian activist of verse like "Tentative Description of a Dinner Given To Promote the Impeachment of President Eisenhower" (1958) with its accusing trope of Ike-as-golfer at the helm of a world at nuclear cliff-edge.

Were contours-in-small needed of Ferlinghetti's life and literary credo two poems in particular do duty. "Autobiography," first published in "Oral Messages" in Part II of *A Coney Island of the Mind* and "conceived specifically for jazz accompaniment" (along with pieces like his much acclaimed "I Am Waiting" given over to the desidera of "a rebirth of wonder" [49] and Wordsworthian "intimations/of immortality" [52]), operates as autobiographical roll-call, the "sheaves of grass" (66) in his own creative formation. The companionable first person conjugations ("I am leading a quiet life/in Mike's Place" [60] or "I have heard the Gettysburg address/and the Ginsberg address" [61]), along with each Ginsberg allusion ("I too have ridden boxcars boxcars boxcars" [61]), work to shared purpose. They situate the speaker in actual and literary American time, observer and bard.

"Adieu à Charlot" (*Second Populist Manifesto*)" (1978) invokes "the collective subjective" in the name of life over conformity, a writer-litany to include Whitman and Poe, Lorca and Rimbaud, Bob Dylan and Neal Cassady. Most of all it confirms Ferlinghetti's reverence for Chaplin, the begetting genius to whom he and Peter Martin paid historic tribute in the naming of their own City Lights. That film and the other Chaplin screen classics he sees as conjuring poet from tramp ("the little Man is all of us"), the very figure of the promissory human spirit. In a poem gamesome in its own right (lines like "the halitosis of industrial civilization"), and full of call for a rebirth of idiom ("How many Ginsberg facsimiles/and carbon-copy Keseys/still wandering the streets of America . . .?"), Ferlinghetti pitches for committed new creativity in the face of familiarity or cliché. Chaplin's bowler and the baggy pants he hitches up have become silent-film allusions of fondest recall. But as much as they emblematize the past screen they also, for Ferlinghetti, retain their still necessary beckoning to fresh imagination.

This premium upon visibility could not more mark out *Pictures of the gone world*, the *flâneur* style of observation re-embedded in the leisurely spatial lay-outs of each poem with their shifting line indentations and want of page numbering. Whether one sees a linkage back into Jacques Prévert's *Paroles*, which Ferlinghetti took upon himself to translate, together with Paul Eluard and other French virtuosi of the surreal, or into the abstract expressionism of Pollock and Kline, or into the Open-Form of Robert

Duncan and Charles Olson, this verse-sequence achieves it own unique momentum. From the invitingly liminal opening of "Away above a harborful/of caulkless houses/among the charley noble chimneypots . . ." (No. 1), with its "wetly amorous" woman hanging out her morning's laundry against the (likely California) "reachless seascape spaces," through to close-observed scenarios like "People kept coming in and looking/at the half-alive fish on ice. . ." (No. 36), there can be no mistaking the visual imperative, the poet-as-eye.

"A POEM IS A MIRROR WALKING DOWN A STRANGE STREET" reads "Not too long/after the beginning of time . . ." (5), the perfect Ferlinghetti mantra—an echo of Stendhal's "A novel is a mirror being carried along a highway." The note is all for accessibility, the private-in-public, and above all, the visual. Almost every one of the forty-five pictures acts on these cues, each a form of sighting (the same poem speaks of the painter's "hungry eye" and gives a found-poetry list of "one hundredandsixtythree people all talking/and waving and laughing and eating and drinking. . . . ."). Infinitely to the point as the poems range from New York and California to London, Paris and Rome, street to gallery, is the manner in which painter-allusions work into and against each different city or household scene, typically "Sorolla's women" (No. 8), "Picasso's acrobats" (No. 24), and "the Hopper house" (No. 37).

Poetry as painting, and poet as painter, meets an especially key articulation in No. 28, a Beat sutra as it were, a form of brief meditation, to ponder the imaginative alliance in play. "Each poem a picture" runs its key line, "an exhibition upon a blank wall/made of concrete chaos." This making-over of "picture" from "chaos," and as the poem goes on to say, "meaning" from "the inarticulate," offers Ferlinghetti in characteristic mode. In effect all of the component poems in *Pictures of the gone world* can be said to draw upon this perceptual process, the poem's sight-into-word, the poet's exhibited painting of the world.

In this respect it little surprises that *A Coney Island of the Mind* opens with yet another painter reference ("In Goya's greatest scenes we seem to see/the people of the world/exactly at the moment when/they first attained the title of 'suffering humanity'" No.1 [9]). In the Foreword's brief explanation of how he borrowed the volume's title-phrase from Henry Miller's *Into the Night Life* Ferlinghetti speaks of his poems as "a kind of circus of the soul," a yet further gesture to inward life given public display. Each best-known poem in the twenty-nine-part sequence can be said to operate in this manner. "In Goya's scenes" the view is of humanity still caught out by "false windmills" albeit in the modernity of "bland billboards/illustrating imbecile illusions of happiness" (9). In "The poet's eye obscenely seeing" (No. 3) there is a listing of "kissproof world of plastic toiletseats tampax and taxis" as "fatal shorn-up fragments/of the immigrant's dream come too true/and mislaid/among the sunbathers" (13). "Sometime during eternity" (No. 5), as famous an early Ferlinghetti poem as any, the vista yields its Beat-iconographic Christ "looking real Petered out" (16).

This emphasis upon world and picturing, the one image kinetically layered into the other, holds throughout. In "Constantly risking absurdity" (No. 15) not the least of the poem's virtuosity of image lies in the notion of the poet as "acrobat" of "rime"—poised on "a high wire of his own making" and ready for "high theatrics" (30). This is to be faced with the challenge of "taut truth" and "beauty," in all the "little charleychaplin man/ who may or may not" (30) manage to speak for quite the best sightings of the world. The fantastical litany in other *Coney Island*'s poems could not more add to the point—"elephants in bathtubs/floated past us in the sea" ("Sailing thru the straits of Demos" No.2 [11]), "a couple of papish cats/ is doing an Aztec two-step" ("See/it was like this . . ." No. 9 [22]), "the Bosch-like world" ("I have not lain with beauty all my life" No. 10 [23]) or "we ogle the unobtainable/imagined mystery" through "a wide vent in the battlements /where even elephants/waltz through" ("Kafka's Castle stands above the world . . ." No. 16 [31]). Each contributes to Ferlinghetti's open-verse pictorialism, reality given word—wittily, indeed often surreally—and in both wide-angle and keyhole version.

Having so often called up the canvases of other artists and their styles of seeing, notably Goya, Chagall and Picasso, Ferlinghetti takes it upon himself to add his own poet-painter's autobiographical note. He recalls the "pennycandystore beyond the El" where "I first/ fell in love/with unreality" (No. 20 [35]). This cherished childhood locale is to be recalled as a place of magic where the real has spun into the unreal. It remembers a departure-point not only for the other unreal-out-of-real "sightings" in *A Coney Island of the Mind* but for Ferlinghetti's poetry far beyond and, to justified right purpose or not, thereafter long incorporated into Beat convention.

*   *   *

Go is, in every way, a young man's book . . . The reader will have little trouble identifying characters based on Jack Kerouac, Allen Ginsberg, Neal Cassady, Herbert Huncke and other writers and personalities of the Beat Generation.

—John Clellon Holmes,
Foreword to re-issue of *Go* (1976)[36]

John Clellon Holmes's *Go* gives every reason to be thought a first of the shadow-canon texts—1952 as date of publication, his dedicated but one-remove relationship with Ginsberg, Kerouac, Huncke and the rest, and yet at the same time "*my* vision of the times."[37] Determined *romans à clé*, however, tend not to have long shelf lives. Identifications become well-known, the history involved passes and, even if the whiff of scandal once added seasoning, impatience can arise at the thin veil of fiction over fact. Holmes's *Go*, as he acknowledges, lays itself open to pretty well all these risks, not to mention his sometime clinical exactness. Yet despite such the novel continues to hold its place as the first-ever Beat novel, the movement, its prime figures and as the novel terms it the "new season" (162) recreated from source. Subsequent Beat chronicles, notably by Kerouac, di Prima and Huncke, have tended to eclipse *Go*. But Holmes deserves plaudits, the resolve upon capturing the era's change of cultural temperature, America's alternative order. The mapping of this America is given early, "a world of dingy backstairs 'pads,' Times Square cafeterias, be-bop joints, night-long wanderings . . ." (36), and in which people "suddenly disappear into jail" or go "on the road only to turn up again" (36).

As notation these notes from near-underground read wholly to the point. Hobbes, Pasternak, Stofsky, Kennedy, Ancke, Agatson, Verger, and Ketchum, and the women Kathryn, Christine, May, Estelle, Bianca, Liza, make their entrances as though indeed the changing guard. Their affairs, drink, jazz, sex and will-to-art express the impetus of what Hobbes terms "ceaseless movement" (10), "a sort of revolution of the soul" (36), "discontent" (211). This is life-theater edging into myth, the 1940s-50s as emergent Beat choreography.

Times Square acts as the magnet with its "unruly bars, teeming cafeterias . . . petty thieves, dope-passers and 'characters'" (7). Those drawn there, and for whom it serves as vortex, the novel designates "new strange people" given to "disorderly nightlong parties, and fresh ideas" (9). David Stofski ("a huge copy of Spengler under his arm" [5]) and Gene Pasternak ("You know, everyone I know is kind of furtive, kind of beat" [36]) preside. If the one is transposed Ginsbergian poet, and the other Kerouac roadster, their companions in spirit equally pose no difficulty in being recognized—Huncke re-written as the subterranean Albert Ancke ("the flesh seemed to have shrunk in upon his brittle bones" [236]), Cassady as the "bop" westerner Hart Kennedy ("He drove the new Cadillac with reckless precision" [117]), and the gargoyle artist-alcoholic Bill Cannastra as Bill Agatson ("plainly alone in his universe of shuddering misery" [73]). Their slightly querulous Boswell is to be met with in Holmes himself as Paul Hobbes, at once caught out by his own writerly ennui yet not willing to plunge unreservedly into the Beat headwaters. His troubled intimacy with Kathryn, working wife as he stays home to write his own novel, adds perspective, a mirror to the world at hand—to include her affair with Pasternak and his with Estelle.

The novel yields much now familiar track from Stofsky/Ginsberg's Blakean epiphany to the impact of Wilhelm Reich and Alfred Kinsey, from the title's borrowing of a one-word chorus to jazz to Kennedy's broken thumb in his fight with Dinah. Burroughs, as Will Dennison, make his appearance in the "on the road" visit paid him by Kennedy and Hobbes.

Ginsberg's role in the actual Huncke-led theft, and arrest and institution-alization, is retold with near documentary accuracy. Likewise the death of Bill Cannastra makes persuasive good use of the actual gothic death of Bill Agatson, killed after a night's drinking when he leaned out of a subway train window and hit a station pillar. In turn, the closing acceptance for publication of Holmes's novel ahead of Kennedy's replays that of *Go* before *On The Road*.

Throughout Hobbes/Holmes opts for no euphoria of the road, rather, as the third section "Hell" makes clear, and especially the ending where Hobbes and Kathryn look across the river to New York's darkened sky-line from Hoboken, his wary, resigned sense of America as un-home. The novel's people are indeed "children of the night" (311), those whom Hobbes can tell Estelle about as "the beat generation" filled with creativ-ity within "the labyrinths of the underground" (259). *Go* has its flaws as narrative, the set-piece speechifying, the programmatic run of events, a narrator all too readily drawn to Spenglerian notions of decline. But it deserves every recognition as Beat pathway, the terrain, the pathologies of alienation, of an American art-and-life generation put to negotiate its role in postwar history.

*   *   *

I'd come into the Village *looking*, trying to "check," being open to all flags. Allen Ginsberg's *Howl* was the first thing to open my nose . . .
LeRoi Jones/Amiri Baraka, *The Autobiography of LeRoi Jones/Amiri*
—*Baraka* (1984, 1991)[38]

Jones/Baraka has several times added to this remembrance of his bow into Beat life. In the "Statements on Poetics" section of Donald Allen's *The New American Poetry* (1960) he was early to echo Olson and Ginsberg in repu-diating New Critical academicism—" 'HOW DO YOU SOUND??' is what we recent fellows are up to . . . MY POETRY is anything I think I am . . . There cannot be closet poetry. Unless the closet is as wide as God's eye."[39] A 1980s interview speaks of Beat "[coming] out of the whole dead Eisen-hower period, the whole of the McCarthy Era . . . the whole reactionary period of the 50s. The Beat Generation was a distinct reaction to that."[40] In the *LeRoi Jones/Amiri Baraka Reader* (1991) he, or his editor William Harris, gives precise dates for his Beat phase, namely 1957–1962. These, in the *Reader's* words, constituted his bohemian years, Beat as "hip," an affiliation he would dramatically repudiate in his well-known transition from "ethnic consciousness" into "political consciousness," from Black Nationalism to his avowed neo-Marxism.[41]

No text more identifies Jones/Baraka with the Beats than his *Preface to a Twenty Volume Suicide Note* (1961).[42] Yet he writes always guardedly, Beat as essentially white business, middle-class cultural business, as against his up-from-Newark black background. "One Night Stand," for Allen Gins-berg, has about it the air of Beat as resolute yet genial, larky ("We entered the city at noon! High bells. The radio on . . . [21]"). New Bohemia it may be but Beat's vanguard fervor, even so, can also leave itself open to being teased, its bards and storytellers roisterers in motley in search of "cool":

> We *are* foreign seeming persons. Hats flopped so the sun can't scald our beards; odd shoes, bags of books & chicken. (21)

In "Way Out West," for Gary Snyder, the Beat note is more zen, oceanic, spanning the America of Sheridan Square and the Greece of Tiresias. This is the poet drawn towards transcendent processes from "As simple an act /as opening the eyes" to "Closing the eyes. As simple an act. You float . . . [24–5]" yet at the same time aware of his own closing youth-time.

A similar ambivalence, the interaction of two cultural regimes, holds for "Look For You Yesterday, Here You Come Today." On the one hand, as its title from a well-known blues implies, this is a black-inflected poem, ease-ful, jazz-like. On the other it calls up self-aware Beat posture, the speaker alienated and duly bearded and literary—"I have to trim my beard in solitude./I try to hum lines from "The Poet in New York' (15)." Life lacks fulcrum, boundary—"It's so diffuse/being alive" (15). Words grow sinister ("terrible poems come in the mail" [15]). Frank O'Hara for one, the poem reports, prefers the importance of his own silence to "Jack's incessant yat-ter" (15). The speaker's self-consciousness invites a Baudelairean put-down as his thoughts become "Flowers of Evil/cold & lifeless/as subway rails" (16). Only "dopey mythic worlds" (16) hold, whether Tom Mix ("dead in a Boston Nightclub [16]"), Dickie Dare, Captain Midnight, Superman, or The Lone Ranger. These childhood radio and screen icons, all cultural-whiteness figures, however, begin to give way to an arising cultural black-ness (". . . Tonto way off in the hills/moaning like Bessie Smith" [18]).

One just about hears a Jones ready to move on from Beat self-absorption into politicization, the black heritage of Bessie Smith and the blues as against Kerouac and "yatter," Harlem as against the Village. For the LeRoi Jones soon to Islamize himself into Imamu Amiri Baraka there beckons Black nationalism over Beat counter-culture, a quite different existential route, and personal necessity, and in the name of quite differ-ent ends and purposes.

*   *   *

Though at the time it was connected to the Beat Generation, my novel, in fact, was anti-beat . . .

—Barbara Probst Solomon,
"Forward "(sic), *The Beat of Life*
(1960, re-issued 1999)[43]

Sited in a postwar Manhattan of The Village and Columbia University *The Beat of Life* (1960) never explicitly invokes the Beat movement. But Solomon's "Forward," as she calls it, has grounds to make the connection in terms of the 1950s bohemian fringe, jazz, and the sexual new order. For the love affair of Natasha Thompson and Tim Lanahan, both graduate-aged, she Philadelphia-Jewish and he Village New York with Irish-American roots in Green Bay, Wisconsin, portrays a relationship at once drawn into yet in due course disastrously caught short by the alternative culture.

Tim's sense of the world is one of disaffiliation, the feeling that his own times have lost the spirit of World War II America, a sell-out to the consumer ethos ("Every so often I get the feeling I ought to start over from the early 'fifties" [73]). For Natasha the turning point is her Jewishness. What does it signify given her family's assimilation from its German roots into the mainstream and typified in a name like Thompson? Can she hold to the spirit of Passover with which the novel opens? Is she or not to become a New York version of the Nastasha of *War and Peace* for whom she has been named ("Sometimes I feel that my soul has a mystic twist" [61])? The immediacies of their relationship, whether the moving-in together and love-making, the Spanish Harlem or Village settings, Solomon nicely plays against larger history—the holocaust, America's emergence from World War II, Eastern Europe (personified in Tim's Russian studies and his dying Czech stepfather Václav Hlava). Tim's notion of his kind of generation as pariah and Natasha's questioning of "why do we call ourselves Jews?" (110) bespeaks a sense of generational ennui, a condition their shared destiny will abruptly undermine and challenge.

For as much as their lives bid to be "experiments in living," (102), flags against the mainstream, they also veer into the downward curve. That involves abortion, suicide, guilt. Each circling around love and its discontents, belief and unbelief, authenticity and fakery, points to an American 1950s bound for a new but not necessarily redemptive cultural orientation. The two family dynasties, Tim's through his mother Gloria, her three successive husbands and half-sister Sootie, Natasha's through her parents and siblings, Solomon tells as family locale. But Tim and Nastasha seek to make their own kind of family, with un-winning results. If Václav dies and Natasha bears the promise of new life, the pregnancy is aborted with Gilbert Hospital as terminus.

The route through the mescaline-taking artist Donatella (for Tim "a phony and a sell-out" [108]), the two medical students who help set in motion Natasha's fake mental instability in order to "qualify" for the abortion, the malignly named Dr. Gorwitch and then Gilbert Hospital with its recriminatory Dr. Laut and nurses, in fact becomes hell's pathway. Her abortion ("You're good as new now" [187], Nurse Michaels tells her), the break with Tim, and her suicide by gassing—what more chill Jewish script?—the novel foregrounds against a billboard with the logo "NEW YORK IS THE PLACE FOR A SUMMER VACATION"

(192). Tim, early Beat-style disaffiliate yet headed for his Ph.D, carries a "terrible tunneled wail" (222) into "that last great American frontier, that Coca-Cola-plush . . . hopping-with-jazz place known as Western Europe" (220). "The beat of life" (211), in the face of Nastasha's death, has turned bitterly about-face, in Solomon's fashioning less an affirmation than a ghost sonata.

*   *   *

> *The Beard* is a play between Billy the Kid and Jean Harlow as they confront each other in a blue velvet eternity.
>
> —Michael McClure, "Writing *The Beard,*
> Lighting *The Corners*" (1993)[44]

From its first staging on December 18 1965 at the San Francisco Actor's Workshop, and the police action that led to charges of obscenity and ACLU legal defense, Michael McClure's *The Beard* has been a landmark.[45] Censorship threatened, a curtailing of theatre's freedom of imagination in the name of local probity. The court action, eventually dismissed, also threatened to eclipse the play's larger implications. For in its metafictive colloquium of Billy the Kid and Jean Harlow it both calls up other notable stage colloquia—Sartre's *Huis Clos* or Beckett's *En Attendant Godot* in European tradition and Jones/Baraka's *Dutchman* in American—and gives exploration to gender or beauty myths at the very center of American popular culture.

In his brief Introduction Norman Mailer might well speak of the play's "magnetic field," its "mysterious trip." Certainly there has been no shortage of vying interpretation. But of the prime issues at work one, assuredly, has to do with sexual celebrity, indeed celebrity sexuality, Hollywood or media constructions of the masculine and feminine. From the opening lines the exchanges center on "secrets," "the beautiful," "illusion," the body as "BAG OF MEAT," and the iconographies of Harlow's blond hair and of Billy's boots. Both wear *"small beards of torn white tissue paper,"* a suggestion, perhaps, of puppetry, or of some odd version of ritual or sexual mask. Their ensuing flare-ups and four-letter insults, the ready crossfire and irreverence, certainly act out a war of emblematic sexual power. Who rules, beauteous screen goddess or legendary boy-gunman outlaw, or both? Who has the truer or more enviable secrets?

As Harlow's closing outburst of "STAR, STAR. STAR . . . etc" makes emphatic, both have come to belong in the "velvet eternity" of popular-culture myth, competitors yet utterly conjoined in love-hate. A later McClure account speaks of "a play about the nature of human mammals," "a graphic representation of sex," "in a way our answer to the Vietnam war."[46] This, within a one-act play, is American sexuality in majuscule, two historic personages inflated into stereotype, near impossible gender-legends. McClure's feat in *The Beard* lies in using them to highlight, as though from some American mythic other-world, both seduction and surrender, dichotomy and union, the culture's perennials of man-woman flux.

* * *

> I had met Maurice Girodias in New York, and had written the sex scenes for a couple of dull and innocuous novels he had purchased as skeleton plots to which the prurient interest had to be added, like oregano to tomato sauce. Before I left town he had asked me to write one myself . . . Gobs of words would go off to New York whenever the rent was due, come back with "MORE SEX" scrawled across the top page . . .
>
> —Diane di Prima, "Afterword—Writing Memoirs,"
> *Memoirs of a Beatnik*, (1969, reprinted 1998)[47]

Looking back in *Memoirs of a Beatnik* (1969) on her 1950s Manhattan early womanhood Diane di Prima pays handsome tribute to Allen Ginsberg. The text speaks of "Howl" as having "broken ground for all of us," "the vanguard of a much larger thing" (176). It could justifiably be said that di Prima had managed almost as much herself. Given her New York and Village commune life, free sexuality, the poetry shortly to find first-book publication in *This Kind of Bird Flies Backwards* (1958), and her *Floating Bear* and other journal editorship, there is an exemplary generosity to her appreciation of Ginsberg as the energy at Beat's cutting-edge. Certainly if "Howl" had faced the mantra of "couldn't be published" (176) so *Memoirs of a Beatnik* risked, more likely quite consciously invited, the same proscription: Beat Generation sex-and drugs narrative, erotica, outlaw writing.

Sex, indeed "MORE SEX" as requested by Girodias, there is in plenty. But not the least of di Prima's creative virtuosity lies in her command of pastiche. For as much as *Memoirs* draws from actual life, readily to be confirmed in *Recollections of My Life as a Woman* (2001), it also makes for virtuoso send-up of "the Beatnik" as assumed sigla for America's bohemian margin. Publication by Girodias's best-known "underground" Olympia Press duly added status. Whatever the dirty-book frisson, or di Prima's acknowledgment of having written partly for quick cash, the upshot is a work savvier, altogether more nuanced, ever actually to be mistaken for under-the-counter pornography. Amid the plentiful sexual heaves and penetrations, straight, gay, cross-gender and whether one-on-one or group, or the drug-taking, or the transient population involved in the different pads, lofts and flits, or even the babies and child-raising, *Memoirs of a Beatnik* gives its more important insistence to dramatizing the narrator's autonomy of choice—life, body, erotica, writing. The upshot is a Beat text which subverts even as it exploits formula versions of the beatnik, di Prima's canny palimpsest.

This double-seam is worked throughout. From the opening scene with Ivan, its sexually ample "shiver of pleasure" (4) and anatomy of the kiss, through to his brief return at the book's conclusion ("we fucked all afternoon in the patch of sunlight on the double bed" [187]), di Prima pitches for erotica with attitude. Is there not a painterly touch to that "patch of sunlight"? There can be no doubt she knows how to tease the lexicon of borderline fact and fantasy ("mounting tide of ecstasy" [9], "I would lie moist and open" [101], "his incredible male desire" [103], "A feeling of utter surrender swept over me"[124]). Here, as elsewhere, *Memoirs* manages a fine touch in ironic self-monitoring. Having at one point become a nude photographic model she observes "I felt like the heroine in an S-and-M novel" (77). In "The Pad," two mid-chapters that feature a tableau of busy group sex, she displays little short of a postmodern relish in juxtaposing "A Night by The Fire: What You Would Like To Hear" (148) with "A Night By The Fire: What Actually Happened" (150).

Time and again, from her early girl-loves at Swarthmore and subsequent lesbian encounters to the Big Bill/Little Billy/Little John menagerie at the Hudson River farm, di Prima situates the trysts and sex gymnastics within a near-library of cultural allusion. Bach and Brahms, or Bird, Miles and Mingus, supply a musical line of reference. Literary touchstones enter like route-signs, Henry James and Fizgerald, Cocteau and Sartre, Brecht and Hesse, Kropotkin and Ayn Rand, Baudelaire and Lorca, Pound and Mailer, Corso and Kerouac. Time-off from her lovers, a selective gallery of whom she annotates as "six mythologies, six different worlds" (159), allows visits to Brancusi or Monet exhibits at MOMA, Village jazz, the stacks (and when homeless the overnight steps) of the New York Public Library, or screenings of Stan Brakhage and Kenneth Anger. Manhattan is given street and café mapping, especially Village hang-outs like David's, where she first encounters meet Ivan, or Swing Rendezvous, "a meeting place for outlaws" (14).

The story-line also has its disquisitions, controversially the un-need for diaphragm, pill or condom (with a later caveat in the later versions in the face of AIDS), all in the name of spontaneity and sex as reproductive promise. The Diane of the text can exhibit ambivalence toward her own girlhood rape by an older male relative, the sly, and as often oddly unprogressive suggestion that she may even have somehow half-enjoyed it. She is wholly un-ambivalent, however, about Italian American racism towards blacks, her own Brooklyn Sicilian upbringing a relevant credential. During her brief tenure running the Quixote Bookstore manager she ponders its role as literary gathering-place as much as outlet for first editions, journals, prohibited texts. In the figure of her drug-thin bookstore co-worker, Luke, she offers thoughts on junk, its highs and lows, even, as she sees it, its sallow beauty. She also gives an in-close account of the workings of small-magazine literary editorship as cottage labor, the by-hand typing, the routines of setting and distribution.

Di Prima's feat in *Memoirs of a Beatnik* is to make her Beat life the portrait of body, and yet always word, the simulacrum of pornography yet within the encasing sexual fact-fantasy her poet's creative odyssey. Each she purposively has over-lay the other, a species of subtly crafted double-narrative. Put another way it invites being thought its own kind of counter-writing at near perfect pitch.

* * *

I feel a great pride in that I was actually responsible for getting *Sheeper* published. I had published early selections of it in *Gnaoua* . . .

—Ira Cohen, "Interview," Romy Ashby,
Goodie Magazine (1999)[48]

So Ira Cohen, editor of GNAOUA and himself a Beat literary sibling of longstanding, recalls his role in ushering Irving Rosenthal's *Sheeper* (1968) to press.[49] Sumptuously reflexive, homoerotic, it is told as carni-val-requiem to Mohammed ben Abdullah, poet and Rosenthal's mur-dered Moroccan lover. This is redemption as *vita sexualis*, a diary of pain-pleasure, desire, ejaculation, caress, coupling, devotion, and always the role of imagination be it genital or scriptural. But if taken up with priapism it is also taken up with the phallus as pen, narrative as also a sexuality of imagination. For whatever its reputation as Grove Press underground text, the body as its own epic, *Sheeper* equally earns plau-dits for its inventive play, its eight sections however much they inscribe the narrator's journeys into auto-sensation also, almost literally, the *jou-issance* of created story. Rosenthal deserves recognition for virtuosity of a kind Burroughs is right to have thought a "brilliant and specialized performance."[50]

Beat? More than a little likely. Certainly in-house Beat references abound, whether to Ginsberg, Burroughs, Huncke, Trocchi, Elise Cowen, Leo Skir, Alan Ansen, or a Beat circuit to embrace Village and other New York and North Africa as outposts. But *Sheeper* also plays off other intertexts—metamorphosis à la Ovid and Kafka (the latter especially in the novel's insect and rodent imagery), confession of a kind to be met in James Hogg and Thomas De Quincey, and styling which owes indebted-ness to Burroughs and *The Naked Lunch*. Yet Rosenthal writes as ever his own man, the self within the text as serially embodied consciousness.

"The Poet! The Crooked! The Extra-Fingered" reads *Sheeper*'s sub-title, a borrowing from Thomas Nash's *The Unfortunate Traveller*. "Chloral hydrate I am yours" (3) reads the opening chapter. Elizabethan picaresque meets latter-day hypnotic drug: *Sheeper*'s disjunctive coordinates could not more invite even as they startle. The episodes to follow work to shared effect. A tapestry of loving Jewish sado-mother opens proceedings, to be followed by homocentric Manhattan life and bars, the early lover David, repeated scenes of tumescence and relief, and drug life. Rosenthal equally inserts markers as to the book's format—"the style of this memoir is the style of my life as I lived it" [69]). *The Naked Lunch* inspires by its "voltage" (179). The effect is of a self conceived, and monitored, for its endlessly creative experimentation and construction. Rosenthal puts this self-awareness to a variety of purposes, a Beat identity aware of its own fashioning in styling to match.

*   *   *

> I felt like I learned how to write when I was doing *Mexican Memoirs* . . .
>
> —Bonnie Bremser (Brenda Frazer), "Artista,"
> *Breaking The Rule of Cool* (2004)[51]

Part-way into *Troia: Mexican Memoirs* (1969, 1971) Bonnie Bremser offers a hesitant-seeming summary, that of a writer at the time still implicated in the robbery, flight and jail history of her poet-husband Ray Bremser: "I can't figure where to start," she acknowledges, "on the make to get [my] husband out of jail" and in "a country I had hoped never to see again. (76).[52] Bremser, in fact, does scant justice to the life-story she chronicles in *Troia*. The DC rebel daughter who takes up with Bremser, no angel whatever his eventual Beat-and-jazz-poetry legend, writes from a body literally but always complicatedly bought and sold "for love of Ray" as the two seek escape from US law in room-for-the-night Mexico. Whoredom, tricks, johns, dollars, hotel rooms and brothels, streetwalking and pesos for rent or bail: Bonnie Bremser positions herself as nothing if not the young courtesan for love.

"My hours are full of fear and loneliness without you" (57) she writes to Ray even as he mandates her prostitution, demands porn-scripts of her sexual activities, occasionally beats and abandons her, and shows scant regard for their newborn daughter Rachel. Having once typed his poems she agrees to play fallen muse, banker to his continued on-the-run and jailhouse writing. She concedes the degree of her own complicity, the celebrant if often desperate seller of her own flesh ("I am somewhat ashamed at enjoying what I am paid for . . ." [48] or "500 pesos, oboy, I am a success" [50]). Their itineraries give off quite literal geography, whether the Mexico of Mexcity and Veracruz, Huatla, Xochimilco, Mocambo and a run of coastal and hill towns, or the Texas of edge-city Laredo and Fort Worth. But they also frame two lives sado-masochistically joined, he the fugitive, laureate and sexual stage-manager, she the proud sacrifice, and with drugs, sex and writing as mutual currency.

Predictably *Troia* has engendered controversy. Is it Beat-era Abelard and Eloise or misogyny writ large, a version of True Love or cruelest gender politics? Is Bonnie author of a self-selected destiny or self-deluding exploitee? How to reconcile her own "disjointed dreams" (97) as she vaunts playing breadwinner, family mainstay, personal banker? Does her abortion, or her being passed-around as sexual property (typically by the two Mexican brothers), or a lesbian fling, or her relationships with Pedrito and Ernesto Z, or even the closing word that Ray is "making the poetry-drug scene in New York" (198) and whom she re-meets, appropriately, near the new Five Spot in Manhattan and then shares a needle of amphetamine in his 12 Street "all equipped writing room" (208), vindicate or mock her Beat-rebellion status? The questions hover and persist.

It can also little surprise that one of the reading-texts to travel with them is De Sade's *Juliette* or that Bonnie at times writes as though she sexually exists outside her own body—"It's hard to figure out why I do well as a whore in Mexico City" (136). As encounter follows encounter, the prostitution and the panhandling, and from the early Mexican flight to the letter wrongly suggesting that Ray's indictment in New Jersey was flawed to the return to New York, it becomes a mute point as to how much Bonnie gains or loses by living in defiance of what she terms "smelly rules" (125). Whichever best applies there can be little doubt of *Troia* as unique chronicling, a first-person Beat graph of the different freights of love as both exultation and abyss, loyalty and betrayal. As told in *Troia* no easy resolution holds.

＊ ＊ ＊

Things were happening in every room. People were writing, painting, talking, and planning, and Madame Rachou presided in her little bar with the zinc counter.

—William S. Burroughs, Foreword,
Harold Norse, *Beat Hotel* (1983)[53]

Harold Norse's own "Postscript 1963" adds a working template for the Paris world of *Beat Hotel* (1983) as at once fleapit and art-center scriptorium.[54] "In that hotel levels of consciousness and horror (and humor) were reached that few men even dream could exist," he recalls, adding "Dream Hotel . . . in the Latin Quarter . . . a dream that has changed hands" (59–60). His volume amounts less to any guidebook description of 9, rue Gît-le-Coeur, the "No Name Hotel" as Brion Gysin called it, than a Book of Cut-Ups in homage to the Burroughs-Gysin-Sommerville ethos. Two other Norse terms invite use. *Beat Hotel*, to adapt his own term for his 1961 *Librairie Anglaise* exhibition of ink drawings, might well be thought a Book of Cosmographies. Equally it could be designated a Book of Parapoems, as he called his 1960s writings, his free-form literary compositions that draw on Dada and Surrealism and aspire to give liberation, and so revolution, to "the word."

Each of the dozen or so chapters of *Beat Hotel* delivers a fantasy as if it were a chamber, a Gît-le-Coeur room, of imagination. The panorama

turns upon Paris as netherworld of street, bar, *boîte*, métro, gay cruis-
ing, hustle, drug traffic, *les flics*, and at the same time supremely a city
of art both at gallery and museum level and as refracted into the hotel's
cubicle rooms. In Norse's rendering this workshop of writing and painting becomes a form of dream, as fantastical as it is sexual. The language
owes much to Burroughs, richly, and often comically scabrous, and full
of cut-up phrasing, none more so than "Sniffing Keyholes."

Originally published as a separate piece in *GNAOUA*, "and then as the
fifth installment of *Beat Hotel*, " Keyholes" has long served as vintage Norse.
Its portrait of "Queen Z.Z." ("a lush and a nympho") and "Chief Melo"
("Chocolate silk") as respectively white painter-queen and African love-
warrior, and their every-which-way couplings, borders on deliberate cartoon.
The sex becomes acrobatic, every vent and membrane in play, and in which
"all words were made flesh" (26), or as Norse also expresses it, "roulette
orgasm," "vegetable consciousness with Swift Strokes," and true to cut-up
protocol, "Nothing but flow change lust desire flame" (27). The upshot could
not be more like Z.Z's own "weird paintings" (22), a "movie montage floor-
show" (24). The Beat Hotel's no doubt once actual guests thus transpose into
creatures of gothic sexuality, their turnings a mockery of all normative rules
of behavior. This dissasociative imagery, and the cut-up inventions, give *Beat
Hotel* in miniature.

The other installments work similarly, however discrete their particular story-vision. "Strength & Health Circuit" pursues Bob's junk fantasy
("He felt enclosed in a soundproof room" [1]) within the Beat Hotel as
the "hotel nirvana" (5). His mind traverses citied Europe and Tangier,
drug fixes, gender-bends, life as black comedy lived at the sexual and
allied margins ("Rigid heterosexuality is a perversion of nature" [7]).
"Half-Clad Apparition Kids" maps gay life as endlessly embattled,
whether *Pédés* in Paris or *Pájaros* in Havana or "*Homos* of the world"
(16). The call becomes one of resistance to "WIPE OUT THE FAGS"
campaigns from Buenos Aires to Gaullist France. Norse's verve lies in
splicing a mock outfit like the Committee for Pederastic Revolutionary
Action with "respectable" opinion about homosexuality as "a CANCER
in the national bloodstream" (17) and "We want a nation of *real* men
and *real* women . . . under God . . . the Flag . . . the Leader who OBE-
YOBEYOBEYOBEY . . ." (17–18). "Garbage Green Sandwiches" takes
scatological aim at a Europe still locked into illusions of the national
state with its "colonizing blind minds" and "Moneytheism" (52). "Take
A Chance in the Void," with which *Beat Hotel* closes, offers a blend
of postscript, manifesto and cut-up—"Current language so impotent-
thinking-habit-fixated on abuse—cut words shatter groove-think" (54).

These sequences each invite being read with, or against, the hotel
remembered in Norse's *Memoirs of a Bastard Angel* (1989).[55] There, in
un-cut-up narrative, he cites *High Times* for 1978 as giving credit to
Mme. Richou's wonderfully seedy establishment for its role of expatriate

salon and for housing "the vanguard of the Beat generation." Not quite disinterestedly he also adds the further citation—"Allen Ginsberg, Peter Orlovsky, Jack Kerouac, William Burroughs, Brion Gysin and Harold Norse were the seminal hipsters at the funky hotel."[56] The Norse of *Beat Hotel*, however, with an appropriately more flamboyant stroke of the pen, signs off in the telegraphese of his own Beat nom-de-guerre, "HAR-OLD HAROLD NORSE PARIS ORACLE" (54).

*   *   *

> He was a character, a rarity, a real picaresque antihero in the classical
> tradition. Huncke was a great storyteller, usually about his misfor-
> tunes . . . He had all the habits you could possible get.
>
> —William Burroughs, Foreword,
> *The Herbert Huncke Reader* (1997)[57]

Herbert Huncke's *Guilty of Everything* makes a double-bow, first the diminutive Hanuman Books edition of 1987 (3″x 4″) published in Madras, New York, and then the Paragon House edition of 1990.[58] The former's installment of youthful life in Chicago ("the way it started" [71]) spans his early pot use to existence on the heavy-drugs circuit of heroin and opium. Rush Street and North State enter as Beat-like city recesses. Elsie, the giant freak-show hermaphrodite, features for his/her wondrous foul-mouth cascades. His dealer sidekick Johnny meets a Treasury cops shooting death. His relationship with his mother, to whom he gives sex instruction and introduces to pot, gives a frame to his early Gay sex-encounters. New York follows ("the tempo was what I loved. I was full of energy and, boom, the next thing I knew things were happening so fast I couldn't keep pace with myself" [71]), Manhattan as sub-world mecca. The effect is of a one-take diary, Huncke's chosen life of margins.

The subsequent version of *Guilty of Everything* (1990) fills out the contour, story-upon-story told with the same fluency as *Huncke's Journal* (1965) and *The Evening Sun Turned Crimson* (1980).[59] Huncke opens with perfect cognizance of the waywardness eventually to shape his entire history ("I began acting up, going my own way . . . I ended up a drug addict, a junkie on the streets." [18]). His Massachusetts birth, Chicago boyhood, ventures into New Orleans and Texas, shippings-out to the Caribbean, Honolulu and Wales, and above all New York as "my ultimate destination" (21)—in the event mainly the Lower East Side, Times Square and the Village—give the one kind of topography. But the truer life-route lies in drugs ("I was a natural for it" [26]), in hobo vagrancy ("I didn't do anything but float around the country" is his memory of the 1930s [37]), and always in thieving ("the burglary scene" [113]). Both Chicago and New York become dark carnival, whether his sidekick Johnny ("whatever he got into, I got into" [29]), the Alsace-Lorraine born and hermaphroditic Elsie ("so mammoth most people were terrified of her" [30]), 42nd Street hustle ("I was quick to catch on" [43]), and the stretches of jail time that begin with Riker's Island where he is sent for stealing from a car when drunk. Sing Sing ("My first extended bit" [109]), The Tombs, Greenhaven and Dannemara will be among others to follow. For Huncke this truly amounts to parallel tracks, the one of aspirant artist ("I had three dreams as a kid: acting, dancing, and writing" [67]), the one of ground-zero indigency and burglary ("I continued to live on the streets and steal" [68]).

Huncke's life-as-drama has become vintage Beat lore. His rogue's gallery of petty-criminals opens a portal on alternative America, from Ed Leary ("there was certain amount of evilness about him" [49]) to the prostitute-thief Vickie Russell and her sidekick Little Jack Melody. The different thefts, to include that with Russell and Melody which led to Ginsberg's stay in the Columbia Psychiatric Institute and Huncke's five-year prison sentence, have about them a mix of criminality and farce. The encounter with Alfred Kinsey, and Huncke's interviews about his sexual history ("a very delightful experience" [79]) plays perfectly to his story-telling inclination ("I think I pretty much made his Times Square study" [81]). The eventual radio appearance on WBAI and then on the Susskind show, his writing (for which he acknowledges di Prima's Poets Press) and college readings, add aura to Huncke as begetter of his own version of Thief's Journal. He attains his mark as both Beat protégé and avatar.

New York, down-and-out, street-level, gives further setting to the legend. Burroughs, looking to fence guns and find drugs ("I gave Burroughs his first shot" [70]), serves as ambassadorial contact. The names amount to a Beat roll-call: Joan Adams, Allen Ginsberg, Peter and Lafcadio Orlovsky (and their formidable mother), Jack Kerouac, Hal Chase, Lucien Carr, Carl Solomon, Edie Parker, Elise Cowen, Gregory Corso, LeRoi Jones, Alexander Trocchi, Ray and Bonnie Bremser, Diane di Prima, John Wieners, and a major love of his life, Janine Pommy Vega ("absolutely beautiful" [127]) whom he seeks to protect against the painter "warlock" Bill Heine. Huncke's annotations give live etching, whether of Burroughs (he credits *Naked Lunch* with "an incredible style" but "there is that coldness—he's forgotten the human element somehow" [170]) or of Ginsberg ("While I was away Allen had become 'Allen Ginsberg,' "[124]). Lesser names, however, win his interest, among them Peter Orlovsky ("His whole life is poetic in a way" [128]) and Elise Cowen, smitten with Ginsberg and a suicide ("It was just a shame, because she wrote extremely well" [154]).

"We were a strange group . . . we were the people who formed the inner circle" (146) runs Huncke's recollection of the Beat ambit in *The Evening Sun Turned Crimson*. His own several fictional appearances, be it in Burroughs's *Junkie*, Clellon Holmes's *Go*, or Irving Rosenthal's *Sheeper*, does reciprocal service. Few from within this Beat inner circle in fact did not claim lease on Huncke's "gone" myth-status, the Artful (and sometimes not so Artful) Dodger, street-dealer, thief, jailee, sexual hustler, and not least, Beat storyteller from America's world-below.

* * *

> Surely this Beat Generation was the one we really belonged in, not the gray, bottled-up Silent one.
>
> —Joyce Johnson, "Beat Queens: Women in Flux,"
> *The Rolling Stone Book of The Beats* (1999)[60]

Joyce Johnson's interaction with the Beats would not only take her from Upper West Side Jewish girlhood and Barnard into the relationship with Jack Kerouac but into a writing life itself bright with distinction. How else to construe the autobiographer of *Minor Characters: A Beat Memoir* (1983), with its vivid, circumstantial portrait of the relationship with Jack Kerouac and yet of her own rise to womanhood and literary life, and her filling-in of the lives of other Beat women—the earlier tier of Edie Parker and Joan Vollmer, together with Hettie Jones, the sculptor Mary Frank, and above all, her closest friend, the talented but ill-fated Elise Cowen?[61] How not to recognize the author in her own right behind the lover and eloquent correspondent of *Door Wide Open: A Beat Love Affair in Letters, 1956–1958* (2000), a work at once all epistolary present-tense yet made subject to vibrant remembering commentary?[62]

Both operate as though the double-tier, the young, devoted, generously abetting Joyce Glassman of the affair and correspondence with Kerouac yet also the Joyce Johnson as nuanced commentator of four decades later. The upshot is at once twice-over personal, their close-encounter within 1950s Beat-and-jazz Village and Manhattan, and her own retrospect on Beat as time and pageant. As she says in *Minor Characters* "Allen Ginsberg and Jack Kerouac seemed to come from nowhere [and] . . . gave voice to the restlessness and spiritual discontent so many felt but had been unable to articulate" (xxxiv). The letters act as live idiom, personal, full of love for Kerouac and their on-off life together, yet also circumspect in the light of his inability to fully yield himself to her, hence, in part, the emphasis on publishing, their respective writings. Not the least of Johnson's skill lies in having the later authorial voice subtly patrol but not alter its forerunner.

The genteel 116th Street life of a thirteen-year old in 1949 as against Kerouac's on-the-road departure from Ozone Park, Queens, in 1947, the clandestine forays with her friend Maria into Greenwich Village and then reading John Clellon Holmes's "This is the Beat Generation" in 1952: the equations which would lead to her relationship with Kerouac are given with dispatch. Allen Ginsberg sets up a first date. Lucien Carr gives the parties. Elise Cowen becomes her key friend and intermediary. The Orlovsky family becomes a network ("disconcerted people") and the writer-painter

Fielding Dawson becomes one of many lovers. The city geography against which the affair with Kerouac is played out becomes as heraldic as literal, a span of Barnard, Columbia, the Eighth Street Bookshop, cheap Manhattan apartments, the Cedar Bar, the Five Spot, and the offices of the different author agencies and publishers where she gets work. Each as time and place, and in both *Minor Characters* and *Door Wide Open*, situate what indeed was her life in its precocity and challenge with Kerouac but also her own evolving creative identity.

"FLY NOW PAY LATER" she invokes as a commercial airline tag in both books. Well she might. It speaks perfectly to her Beat-era experience. In *Minor Characters* she remembers Kerouac's holding-back and yet liberating effect on her, his "awful success" (190) and yet self-mocking "I'm only an old zen lunatic" (225). She writes with clear-eyed perspective on the 1950s for women, her affair with the Columbia instructor "Alex" (Donald Allen), her abortion, the waits for and re-meetings with Kerouac, and the poignant thread of Elise Cowen's life in her fated love for Ginsberg. Johnson's local powers of style work to great effect as each Beat-connected figure bows in and out, whether Jackson Pollock with his "dizzying webs of paint squeezed raw from the tube" (160), or Herbert Huncke as "hipster-angel" (187), or LeRoi Jones and Hettie Cohen as "young Bohemian couple" (219), or Mary Frank with her personal grace ("She reminded me of the Greek women of Picasso's white period" [242]).

Door Wide Open reminds that for Beat-era America New York could be "the most exciting place in the world" (14). For Johnson in her young womanhood that had to mean Kerouac as human center in all his ambiguity—"as much as Kerouac ever revealed, there would always be a whole subcontinent held back" (xvii). Her letters to Kerouac bristle with information, Joyce not just the lover but confidante and secretary (the updates, the cuttings and reviews she sends him). She writes generously, encouragingly, aware of his drinking, scrapes and other women ("these new sexual opportunities were like money—part of the spoils of fame" [74]) yet from a deep fund of devotion. Her letters especially call back to mind the reception of *On the Road*, both the Millstein review and "the instant media blitz" (65). Typically she writes to him in July 1957 "it's a great, beautiful book. I think you write with the same power and freedom that Dean Moriarty drives a car" (41–2). Kerouac's own letter-manner is to be met with when, in October 1957, he writes to her of his play *Beat Generation*, full of annotation as to compositional process and who should play whom.

She shows a remarkable facility to keep her own balance in the face of his fame, his distance, and amid the turbulence as when in February 1958 she reports "Seems to me that every time I open a newspaper or magazine, there's mention of you, Allen and the Beat generation . . ." (134). For all her "door wide open" stance, her self-possession is the more remarkable given Kerouac's distance and the headiness of Beat as public reference. Time and again she shows a novelist's eye alertness, be it for the "public" Ginsberg,

Corso or Burroughs or the "private" Elise Cowen, and not least for the cavalcade of club and phonograph jazz, the parties and the galleries. She captures the magazine wars, *Partisan Review* and *Village Voice*, along with the ongoing arts-and-letters circuit busy in the accompanying likes of di Prima ("with her baby daughter and writing fiercely funny poems as sexually frank as the ones written by men" [68]), John Clellon Holmes ("Jack always knew that he could count on Holmes's support and good sense" [66]) and Robert Frank ("one of [Kerouac's] closest friends" [79]). In their exchanges of letters Johnson quite as much as Kerouac bespeaks her concern with craft (not least her dissent at his "first thought best thought" ethos), a voice uniquely Beat but never at the expense of a voice uniquely her own.

* * *

Canon and shadow-canon. Beat, in its plurality of expressive ways and manner, operates across texts both better and lesser known. No one template holds but that is far from to suggest that there are not at hand recognizably linking life-views, recognizably shared leanings towards "open" idiom. Ginsberg and Kerouac, however wholly distinct, will for ever likely be assigned the roles of standard-bearers for the movement. But they, no less than their compeers both best and lesser known, require being seen within a complex and greatly wide-ranging context. For whatever its selective prominence Beat has also been the literary broad-band, an always wider body of constituent authorship. In this respect Beat voice, its diversity of imaginative compass and counter-compass, has only just begun to come into better view.

2 Beat Speaking Women
Diane di Prima, Joanne Kyger, Anne Waldman

I just kind of grew up with a tough back to the wall, ready-to-fight-anybody attitude . . .

—Diane di Prima, "Anne Waldman Talks
with Diane di Prima" (1978)[1]

Here I am reading about your trip to India again, with Gary Snyder
and Peter Orlovsky . . .

—Joanne Kyger, "Poison Oak for Allen,"
September 2 1996, *About Now* (2007)[2]

It is necessary to bring the female persona, the feminine principle . . .
into the whole macrocosm that is the beat literary movement.

—Anne Waldman "Fast Speaking Woman,"
*Breaking The Rule of Cool: Interviewing and
Reading Women Beat Writers* (2004)[3]

How to parse Beat authorship by women? Has recent critique, despite amends, yet sufficiently changed perceptions of Beat as essentially the male literary praesidium headed by Kerouac and Ginsberg? These, and like issues, attach to the ridiculously belated fuller recognition of original writing by Beat and Beat-related women. Enough revision has come into play to know that the usual versions—muse, lover, sexual companion, girl in black, wife, often enough just plain extra—do less than justice. In Diane di Prima, Joanne Kyger and Anne Waldman Beat authorship vaults three consequential voices from the wider ambit, contemporaries and successors, yet each the begetter of her own wholly discrete and ongoing body of text. Along with other women given to Beat-connected writing their contributions have been extensive and longstanding.[4]

One necessary measure as to gender in Beat tradition lies in actually recovering women-authored voice. A number of anthologies have been timely. Brenda Knight's *Women of the Beat Generation: the Writers, Artists and Muses at the Heart of a Revolution* (1996) did pioneer labor, thirty-plus main and ancillary voices from Helen Adam and Jane Bowles through to Anne Waldman and Jan Kerouac, with conscientious biographical and literary annotation.[5] Richard Peabody's *A Different Beat: Writings by Women of the Beat Generation* (1997) represents further excavation, both better known and less met-with authorship like that of Edie Kerouac or the poets Sandra Hochman, Brigid Murnaghan and Laura Ulewicz.[6] Nancy M. Grace and Ronna C. Johnson make a double-contribution, *Girls Who Wore Black: Women Writing The Beat Generation* (2002) as creative anthology and *Breaking The Rule of Cool: Interviewing and Reading Beat Women Writers* (2004) as nine first-person conversations with accompanying critical readings (Johnson's introductory "Mapping Women Writers of the Beat Generation" deserves every acclaim).[7] The creativity displayed and mapped in these several compilations, even if it still does not complete the whole span, supplies a pre-requisite frame, the women players and their texts as no longer erasable from Beat's fuller cultural history.

This underlining of women's authorial presence takes on further definition in the also still-gathering round of life-writings, memoirs and autobiographical essays. One immediate round-table, each fiercely independent of accent and fashioning, is to be met with in Diane di Prima's *Recollections of My Life As A Woman: The New York Years, A Memoir* (2001), Joanne Kyger's *The Japan and India Journals 1960–1964* (1981) and Anne Waldman's *Vow To Poetry: Essays, Interviews and Manifestos* (2001).[8] But if they provide route-ways into their respective author's oeuvre they at the same time play into, and alongside, Beat as a women's yet wider domain. Who in this respect more beckons than Carolyn Cassady, the poised and interlinking accounts of a triangle of love, marriage and road in *Heart Beat: My Life With Jack and Neal* (1976) and *Off The Road, My Years With Cassady, Kerouac, and Ginsberg* (1990)?[9] Which accounts better capture the frisson, the sense of an era, than Bonnie Bremser's *Troia: Mexican Memoirs* (1969) in all its gender-complexity liberation and surrender, Joyce Johnson's *Minor Characters: A Beat Memoir* (1983), with its Kerouac love story and self-rise as novelist, or Hettie Jones's *How I Became Hettie Jones* (1988), with its wholly un-recriminatory remembrance of her controversial 1960s Jewish-black marriage and family and Village and small-journal life?[10]

The archive has continued to fill. The Kerouac lineage, love, marriage, turbulence, looks to Joan Haverty Kerouac's *Nobody's Wife: The Smart Aleck and The King of the Beats* (2000) and Edie Parker Kerouac's *You'll Be OK: My Life with Jack Kerouac* (2007).[11] Eileen Kaufman gives a warmhearted, funny account of her first encounter with Bob Kaufman in "Laughter Sounds Orange at Night" (1987).[12] Joanna McClure, Arizona born and raised, briefly married to Michael McClure as a major force in Robert Duncan's San Francisco circle, tells her early life in *Wolf Eyes* (1974), a literary career that has continued in her haiku, eco-writing, other verse and her chapbooks.[13] The vital custodianship of Ann Charters invites matching recognition, a host of contributing scholarship—*Beats and Company: A Portrait of a Literary Generation* (1986), *The Portable Beat Reader* (1992) or *Beat Down To Your Soul: What Was The Beat Generation?* (2001).[14]

The lives of different further Beat-connected women remain to be fully charted. They include those of Mary Caney, the model for Kerouac's Maggie Cassidy in his 1959 novel of the same name, and his wife Stella Stampas Kerouac; Lu-Anne Henderson, Neal Cassady's teenage bride, Diana Hansen to whom he was briefly and bigamously also married, and Ann Murphy, his girlfriend in the late years; Sally November Corso and Belle Carpenter Corso; Joan Vollmer Adams, room-mate with Edie Parker, housemother in Manhattan to the Ginsberg circle, and Burroughs's common-law wife and mother to his son; along with Huncke's associate Vickie Russell and the activist Helen Hinckle. The more discriminating interpretation of powerful maternal-oedipal presences like Naomi Ginsberg or Mémère Gabrielle Kerouac, both palpably determinative in the lives and sexuality of their writer sons, still awaits. How, not least, to estimate the several advertences to Allen Ginsberg in the Camille Paglia of *Vamps and Tramps: New Essays* (1994) and various public speeches, those of a maverick feminist who speaks of him admiringly as a pioneer yet also an inveterate ham?[15]

*　*　*

To address di Prima, Kyger and Waldman specifically as poets (given their life-writing and discursive work) is in equal part to invoke other Beat-connected women's poetry. Helen Adam, Scots-born, feisty, an early San Francisco performance figure and balladeer with a keen edge of language, supplies one immediate precursor lineage. Denise Levertov, born of mixed Jewish and Welsh-Christian origins and also trans-Atlantic, supplies another. Her *Here and Now* (City Lights Pocket Poets, 6, 1957) offers a major touchstone, purposely so titled to emphasize a resolve upon breaking free of all fixed or hierarchic poetic forms.[16] Much as Levertov's later work moves on to other interests and forms, this early affiliation with the open Beat poetics of Ginsberg and Ferlinghetti, as well as with line and spoken measure in William Carlos Williams, Charles Olson and Robert Creeley, remains greatly influential.

For her part Elise Cowen, briefly the girlfriend of Allen Ginsberg, unpublished as a poet in her own lifetime, a onetime Bellevue patient where she met Carl Solomon, and the recurrent figure in the texts of Diane di Prima, Joyce Johnson, Herbert Huncke and Irving Rosenthal, takes on the mantle of heroine-suicide. The recovery of her few poems confirms her always considerable if vulnerably brittle sensibility, whether "Emily" ("the shy white witch of Amherst") or her un-titled last poem with its final couplet "Let me out please—Please let me in."[17] In Ruth Weiss, daughter of holocaust survivors, pioneer and continuing practitioner of jazz and poetry, haiku writer, North Beach regular and one-time resident at the Wentley Hotel, Beat has a poet of no less than eight volumes. That includes her *Desert Journal* (1977) as a first-person verse chronicle of interior life and growth through the years 1961–68, the dozen plays, and the film *The Brink*, originally written in 1961.[18]

For Janine Pommy Vega City Lights has especially featured, from *Poems to Fernando* (Pocket Poets 22, 1966), her memorial pieces written on the early overdose death of her Peruvian painter-husband, to *Tracking The Serpent: Journeys to Four Continents* (City Lights, 1997), her keen, expansive travel observations.[19] Joanna McClure has long worked a Beat-connected creative track, not only the early verse of *Wolf Eyes* but pamphlet compositions like *Extended Love Poem* (1978) and *Hard Edge* (1987).[20] Lenore Kandel's *The Love Book* (1966), the memoir-fiction of a North Beach veteran, would become an object of City Lights police charges and prosecution in the line of Ginsberg's poetry, *The Naked Lunch* and Michael McClure's play, *The Beard*.[21] The female hetero-erotica of *Love Book* masks a quest narrative for women's own indomitability of spirit within, paradoxically as it first might appear, biker and road sex. Kandel, at the time of writing, was married to Hell's Angel William Fritsch. It attempts a genuinely challenging alternative, or at the very least complementary, woman-centered Beat vision to the homocentric textures of "Howl."

Mary Norbert Körte and Mary Fabilli supply two further names to be associated both with Beat and the so-called Berkeley Renaissance. Körte, ex-nun, community worker and teacher, looks to a repertoire of poetry whose Beat affiliations and inspiration from Kenneth Patchen can be recognized in early work like *Beginnings of Lines: Response to Albion Moonlight* (1968), *The Generation of Love* (1969) and *Midnight Bridge* (1970).[22] Fabilli, whose verse and print drawings span *Aurora Bligh and Early Poems* (1968), *The Animal Kingdom: Poems 1964–1974*, (1975) and the twenty-four page *Poems 1976–1981* (1981), has been a mainstay of Oyez Press, long a Beat outlet, and not least through her partner-poet William Everson (Brother Antoninus).[23]

Patti Smith requires her own kind of recognition. *Seventh Heaven* (1972) launched her as a poet as did the song-poem "Piss Factory/Hey Joe" (1974) and the album *Horses* (1974) her musical recording career.[24] One-time Chelsea Hotel lover-companion of Robert Mapplethorpe, whose photography includes brilliant Smith portraits as well as his homocentric male bodies, punk singer-laureate (not least her "Because The Night" with Bruce Springsteen), and rock journalist, she read with nearly all the Beat poets. Her literary claims extend to her work on Rimbaud and *symbolisme* and her Introduction to *An Accidental Autobiography: The Selected Letters of Gregory Corso* (2003).[25] Women's presence, life and word, and paradoxically as often their absence, cannot but be thought intrinsic to Beat.

* * *

Where there was a strong writer who could hold her own, like Diane di Prima, we would certainly work with her and recognize her.

—Allen Ginsberg, *Daily Camera Magazine* (1989)[26]

Thinking back on her student-era "flags of defiance" (90) in *Recollections of My Life as a Woman* Diane di Prima cites a Latin motto passed her way by one of her women professors—"I am human, therefore nothing is foreign to me" (90). It might well supply the working credo for her lifetime as counter-cultural doyenne. Who better to have won credential as established poet, vintage editor-organizer of new work, theater and publishing house veteran, and eventual California resident and publisher in the wake of her vintage Manhattan and Village years. "One of the enduring poets of the Beat Generation"—the composer David Amram's encomium does every justice.[27]

The history di Prima herself invokes in *Recollections*, from the childhood of "Brooklyn Brownstones" (19) to the 1990s west coast where "now I mostly meditate and paint and write" (424), could hardly more have taken on the all-comer fare of "nothing foreign." If, too, her "first years in Manhattan were full of bravado and playfulness" (109), they are also to be remembered as the seedtime of her vocation when "looking at the sky, I know I will be a poet" (78). The account moves easily between personal and cultural context, a work of life-writing variously chronicle, diary and, as she terms them, "memory shards." Each phase has about it the sense of propulsion, life and counter-life met head-on, embraced, and voiced within a plurality of art forms.

She rebels, mainly in sexual terms, against her dynastic Italian upbringing, its rules and probity. At Hunter High School, schoolmate with Audre Lorde, she is entranced with Keats, not least as he calls up her early sense of "seeing the liquid structure language is" (77). At Swarthmore she embarks on dorm and woodland same-sex adventuring even as she studies classical literature. The 1950s see her as writer-bohemian, Manhattanite bad girl, renter, and a center of commune living ("My house was abuzz with all forms of humanity"[113]). She patrols the Lower East Side and The Village, takes a job as a nude model, corresponds with and visits Ezra Pound in St. Elizabeth's, and immerses herself in jazz, theatre and dance. Dexedrine, amphetamines, peyote, eventually LSD ("Acid for me has been totally beneficent" [396]) become an intermittent drug regime. Her sexual politics, as credibly contrary and un-pc as they are progressive, pledge themselves to plentiful free choice of partner and practice yet against contraception and abortion—her own abortion famously memorialized in "Brass Furnace Going Out." She has her first child, Jeanne, and sees the publication of her first book, *This Kind of Bird Flies Backwards*, two kinds of creativity, a momentous double-birth.

Her literary life, "endlessly interweaving" (186), embraces Rexroth and Oppenheimer, A.B. Spellman and Hubert Selby. She corresponds with Ferlinghetti over "Howl," embarks on her liaison with LeRoi Jones both editorially at *The Floating Bear* and sexually, becomes close with John Wieners and in California with Michael and Joanne McClure, Philip Whalen, and Wallace and Shirley Berman. Back in New York her network has her visiting

Burroughs and Huncke in Cooper Square, frequently meeting up with Ginsberg, trying to keep to a friendship with Hettie Jones, and engaging in a "curious marriage of convenience" (317) with the bisexual Alan Marlowe in whose company, and that of the "out" gay dancer Freddie Herko and others, she helps establish against financial odds The Poets Theatre (several times closed on police orders for alleged stage obscenity) and Poets Press.

Life and writing, di Prima has good reason to observe of "this *vie de bohème*" (355)—"For me most of the 1960s, and on to about 1976, was a time bathed in the mythic" (368). Early to respond to Pound's modernism, historic woman Beat with boldest claim to its sexual privileges, a proponent of hallucinogenic and pot use, a Zen follower, she as much has helped create as found herself created by that period myth.[28] Her different writings, certainly, reflect the spirit of counter-culture as style, base, metaphor, but always with her individual stamp. In this respect the poetry has been key, from *This Kind of Bird Flies Backward* to the momentous wolf-myth *Loba* poems launched in 1973 ("she grinned/baring her wolf's teeth"), and to include *The New Handbook of Heaven* (1962), *New Mexico Poems* (1967), *Earthsong: Poems 1957–1959* (1968), *L.A. Odyssey* (1969) and, from City Lights, *The Calculus of Variation* (1972).[29] She displays a ready ingenuity with modernist story-collage in *Dinners & Nightmares* (1961), her food-and-dream recollection of economic hard times, and to include "Memories of Childhood," "Conversations" and the thirty-plus "More or Less love Poems."[30] Her theatre bow is made with *Murder Cafe* (1960).[31]

If these, and *Memoirs of a Beatnik* (1969), all give their signature to di Prima's Beat years, albeit upon terms and conditions of her own, their representative plenty lies to hand in her *Selected Poems 1956–1975* (1975).[32] "Rant, From a Cool Place" especially does service, 1960s-dissident in tone and as its title implies with seams drawn from Beat and Zen. Prefaced with Erasmus's call for *"the turning/upside down of the entire world"* (168) it bespeaks her sense of the age's distemper, an America, a western order, wracked by consumer glut, the Dallas assassination, Vietnam, neo-colonialism in Africa, the CIA, brute dollar power, and the threat and pall of global nuclear radiation. Antidote is to be found in Buddhist-karmic restoration and cleansing, the Beat-inflected rebirth of the spirit.

Given this degree of ambition the poem nonetheless uses a wholly local, even domestic, schema to contrast American capitalist-military ego with "the second childhood of man" (168). The "western man" of "refrigerator and car" she sets against "that blessed definable state known as buddhahood." (168). The roster of injury and death extends through Adlai Stevenson, Jack Kennedy, Marilyn Monroe, Jack Ruby and others, in all a veritable necrology. Threat, more establishment plots and persecution, lie pending, and not least against di Prima's own Beat consortium. "They" are so said to be waiting for Tim Leary, Bob Dylan, Allen Ginsberg and LeRoi Jones, not to mention being behind the killing of Malcolm X.

TV becomes the forum for "LBJ's Reich" (168). Genocide holds in Southeast Asia. Red Guards destroy "great stone Buddhas" (169). What, in the face of this "leveling mad mechanism" (169) best avails? For the poem it has to be the iconographic, generous calm of "homemade flute," "old tales," "shells" (169), each a spiritual marker, an aid to balance and restoration. Through them, and in the face of "glowing and dying radiation and plague" (169), is to be learned that "all beings are from the beginning Buddhas" (169) Di Prima turns, finally, to more Buddhist maxim, to "that final great/love illumination/'FROM THE VERY FIRST NOTHING IS'" (169). This belief, in due argot, arises in all senses "from a cool place," wholly and aptly Beat-transcendent.

Two poems, 1950s and 1970s written, give an indicative Beat parabola to di Prima's poetry. In "The Passionate Hipster to His Chick" she rewrites Marlowe's "The Passionate Shepherd to His Love," Elizabethan pastoral transposed into a homily of Beat road, city, jazz-set, and Friday-to-Sunday kicks. The in-house Beat lingo, "hipster," "chick," "cool" or "gonest notes" (22) risks datedness, fatigue. But it could well be deliberate irony, hip as latest love-idiom. The poem has other teases, whether the promise of shared pad, hot-rod car, "tea," or even suitable Kerouac clothing ("leather cap," "jeans with straight-cut legs," "flannel shirt," and "lots of horse"). The closing transition, shrewdly, and lyrically, blends the two idioms, Elizabethan and Beat, one into another—"If all these kicks thy minde may move/ Then live with mee, and be my love" (22).

"No Problem Party Poem," alive with Beat allusion, delivers itself as though also in Beat voice, expansive, querying, but seemingly as laid-back as is requisite. It evolves as a list-poem, each incremental "no problem" building into the gathering whole. The opening list sets not only pattern but rhythm, selectively "first glass broken on patio no problem . . . interviewer with Berkeley Barb no problem . . . leering Naropans no problem . . . lost Satie tape no problem" (336). Beat literary players enter as of right, almost of necessity. This "no problem" paradigm is pursued with a nice touch of ease and wit—Corso, Ginsberg, Waldman, Dick Gallup, even "Joanne Kyger's peyote" (336). Wine, rum, coca-cola or sex join the "no problem" litany as does "growing up on Brooklyn Streets," life "in Tibet" and "Chicano Texas." "Figuring it all out," together with "giving it all up" and "giving it all away" add to the process, a ply of Tantrism, Buddhism and Beat (337). In a last spin of wit "no problem" itself becomes "NO PROBLEM" (337).

Beat threads, however various the directions of di Prima's oeuvre, are never far from view. Her love poetry, hipsterishly, speaks time and again to the disjunctive play of flesh and spirit, whether the early "More or Less Love Poems" and typical lines like "you are not quite/the air I breathe/thank god./ so go" (12), or the wry, miniature "Book of Days" in which love becomes "all the umbrellas people leave in your house" (112) or "New Handbook of Heaven" with its keen sense of contrariety like "I DO NOT LOVE YOU

LESS BECAUSE my love poem dont rhyme" (63). "The Practice of Magical Evocation" uninhibitedly addresses "awakened sex," womanhood as a Beat-like round of consciousness, pleasure, rhythm, even maternity (39). "I'll Always Remember The Maltese Falcon," Frank O'Hara-style, calls up both remembrance of things past, Sinatra to Bessie Smith, and of things future in the form of a possible farm-based marital and family Zen move ("planning to grow buckwheat and make miso"[161]). The 63-part "Revolutionary Letters" might be a Beat-Digger verse manifesto for the counterculture, not least the culminating summons to liberation of "Free them/ Free yourself/Help to free me/Free us/DANCE" (219).

Place as iconographic geography is embodied in "New Mexico Poem," with its Taos and Rio Grande landscapes and Natives to be compared with Buffalo city life and verse. But place, too, can be query, a one site in competition with another. Thus in "Traveling, Again," set in Tacoma, Washington, the poet-in-residence there dismisses "my poet friends in Denver" and "speaks w/disdain of the beat jargon they write in" (307). The yet more explicit affiliation is to be heard in "Wings-of-Speech", dedicated to Anne Waldman, and "Elephant Power," for Allen Ginsberg. The former invokes the Hindu and Buddhist opposition of Garuda and the Nagas as deity bird and serpents, and the latter Shiva-Matanga as the three-eyed god who conquers evil. Asia's "mantric utterance" (284) as "Wings-of-Speech" calls it, thereby summons India's ancient religio-mythic cosmos while acting to reflect a form of shared Beat communion.

In poems that themselves reflexively take on poetry as creative theatre, vision and prosody, Beat implications would be hard to miss. "Poetics," another early work, gives teasing expression to poetry's taking over from its author's grasp—"I have deserted my post . . . let the language fend for itself" (53).This same language, albeit poet-born but now free to make its own way, keeps open the expressive possibilities from both "fascists & socialists" (53). It is poet's language, aptly, that resembles ocean or other water and in which the poet "like a fat brat catfish" can "move" and "breathe" unless cornered, and extinguished, by "the fishpolice" (53). The call is for open life, open poetry. It will readily serve as one of many verse plaques, a pathway, for all of di Prima's credentials, Beat and otherwise.

*   *   *

She's one of our hidden treasures—the poet who really links the Beats, the Spicer circle, the Bolinas poets, the NY School and the language poets . . .

—Ron Silliman to Linda Russo, April 28 1998[33]

Joanne Kyger's relationship with the Beat movement, as with other postwar poetry movements, has always been intelligently oblique, the insider to a fault and yet scrupulous as to her own independence of stance. A poem like

"October 29, Wednesday," published in *All This Every Day* (1975) and reprinted in *Going On: Selected Poems 1958–1980* (1983),[34] calls up this wary sense of intimacy and yet distance. Witness to a crowd milling around Ginsberg and Snyder, the speaker proclaims "I am suddenly elevated" and "I AM ELEVATING" (*Going On*, 187). Kyger writes as though slightly askant, her poem's wry observations both a tease of the Beat guru-celebrity of Ginsberg and Snyder and of her own imperfect striving for Zen transcendence. She, or her persona, sits cross-legged again the stone wall, clad in Tibetan bathrobe, and in the mind's imagining having once levitated above the noise of youth discipleship, now further aspires to ascended lotus or cloud—albeit, mock-heroically, to a height of no more than the one or two feet. If Ginsberg as Beat's laureate and Snyder as Zen luminary (and her former husband) drink in the world's publicity for their self-appointed masculine duty of leadership, her call, almost in mock-whisper, is to attempt a discrete transcendental lift-off. Can she, can she not, rise above the fray? This is Kyger in balletic good form. The lay-out of the poem is carefully spaced for access, the tone light but determined, the effect one of easeful send-up. If the poem speaks to Beat writ, and how women can be drawn or not into its life-ambit, it assuredly even more speaks from, and to, Kyger's wholly un-marginal sense of self-assurance.

The more than dozen collections between *The Tapestry and The Web* (1965) and *About Now: Collected Poems* (2006), together with her landmark *Japan and India Journals, 1960–1964* (1981)—re-issued as *Strange Moon: Japan and India Journals, 1960–1964* (2000)—confirm this profound commitment to writing as her idiom of presence.[35] Time and again it is hard not to become aware of Buddhist or Buddhist-like immersion in moment, perception, Kyger's interest in the phenomenology of being. Just as she famously reverses the waiting-wife Penelope myth in favor of a sexually autonomous woman in *The Tapesty and the Web* ("Refresh my thoughts on Penelope again/Just HOW solitary was her wait?" [*About Now*, 66]), so in poem after poem she teases all would-be fixed areas of subject or voice. This spans the iconography of the hunt for the unicorn as always centered in the huntsman in an early poem like "Tapestry" ("the maid . . . Searching/for bigger & better things" [*About Now*, 77]) through to the would-be efficacy of the male Beat-hip regime in a poem like "July '92 at Naropa" ("Allen Ginsberg has been busy/taking pictures for the last 30 minutes/of Amiri Baraka with the lens cap on his camera" [*About Now*, 569]). In both she undercuts exclusive presiding male rights to word.

It may well be that this insistent, if un-combative, and often greatly witty self-positioning, paradoxically owes much to the very eclecticism that has fed into her poetry, whether the line of Dickinson, Stein, H.D., Moore and Levertov, the Black Mountain legacy of Olson and Creeley ("Projective Verse" was an acknowledged landmark for her), the Jack Spicer-Robert Duncan circuit of 1960s San Francisco where she honed her skills of image, the Basho-Issa-Buson tradition of haiku, or to be sure, Beat regimen in the persons and texts of Snyder, Ginsberg and Orlovsky. Other presences fill her poetry, not least the Mme. Blavasky of *Some Sketches from the Life of Helena Petrovna Blavasky* (1996).[36] The figures in her male circle she can again tease even as she honors their friendship, notably Philip Whalen ("Philip Whalen's Hat"), Lew Welch ("Snapshot for Lew Welch 25 Years Later"), Ted Berrigan ("The Life of Naropa") and Anselm Hollo ("Trying To Write").

But if each gives a footfall to her verse, a reference, it is never without a clear insistence on her own style of register, cryptic, often given to half-phrase, and disjunctive in a manner at times to recall Gwendolyn Brooks. This insistence is early to be met with in "At The Purple Gate Tent Bolinas, My Memoirs" (1969), with its ironic self-avowals of lack of talent and poor memory ("experiences which I have/ held back because I am too stupid and also I can't remember"), tendency to literary quirk ("being a nonbeliever in /the sequitur flow of the English sentence"), and fake-starlet aspiration ("my face would cover a/ magazine" [*About Now*, 178]). The closing couplet acts out the poem's I as ranking San Francisco poet in scholarship yet cuckoo-by-gender in the nest:

> The pride of my learning was a weapon and to make me contemporary with men. I sweep the floor.
>
> *About Now* (79)

Kyger's emphasis on terrain against any or all gender expectations resonates throughout the oeuvre. "12.29 & 30 (Pan as the son of Penelope)" in *The Tapestry and The Web*, or "The Pigs for Circe in May" and "The Odyssey Poems" in *Places To Go* (1970), show her dexterity in wryly re-stitching the gender focus of Homeric lore. Both Penelope and Circe develop destinies at once subtler, and more independent, than that of Ulysses himself in his wanderings and Ithaca homecoming. In this she allies herself with other long-poem female authorship, whether H.D.'s three-part *Helen in Egypt* (1961) or the ongoing woman-epics of di Prima's *Loba* sequence (1978–) and Anne Waldman's *Iovis* (1993–).[37]

She also, and like H.D. and Waldman, lays claim to making shared imaginative space her own. "Is this the Buddha?," in *All This Every Day* (1975), no doubt mindful of her Zen practice from Kyoto to Bolinas, speaks of seeking the "secret one . . . from the wings" only to conclude "Thank you. It's me" (*About Now*, 321). The Dharma sequence of prose-poems in *The Wonderful Focus of You* (1979) guys not only Kerouac's *The Dharma Bums* but the often pretentious "Zen" California with edicts like "All members of the Dharma committee are Cool" (*About Now*, 383) and nominations for the "Bodhissattva of the Week" (*About Now*, 385). The same volume offers "I'm going to be a poet. I can put it together too," a Dickinson-like verse miniature which inscribes the poet's own sense of her "chance" vocation even as it gives homage to inherited poetic treasury (*About Now*,

326). "Just Space", the opening title poem of *Just Space: Poems 1979–1989* (1991), nicely envisions her distance from "scholarly" duty in the name of "that deer in the backyard eating down the as yet/unborn apples" with its "heart-stopping glimpse of nature's larger grazer."

Two poems give specific terms of Kyger's Beat connection, each again as shrewdly articulated from a working distance as from being up-close. "Town Hall Reading with Beat Poets" (1994) teases not only more high-visibility male Beat celebrity ("Ed Sanders onstage telephones William Burroughs/in Lawrence, Kansas, who stayed at home 'because my cats need me' " but also the *New York Times* notice of her *Going On!*—from which she is to read—with its reviewer-speak of "understated Buddhist influenced miniatures." Having picked up "some trash clogging the exit door" she mock-ruefully turns about all required Buddhist erasure of ego and ends on a note of seeming triumphal yet half-apologetic flourish—"And it's *my* big dusty footprint on the cover" (*About Now*, 593).

"A Brisk Wind is Blowing Thoughts to Philip on the Phone," styled as a fantasy exchange with Philip Whalen, steers again towards the poet's claim to self-space amid the closure of poetry-school labels and taxonomies. *The New York Times* categorizes the poet as a Language Poet, other asks if she is Beat. The response is succinct—"No, I'm my own poet" (*About Now*, 673). Kyger has good reason to reflect upon her own frequent categorization, whether Beat or Black Mountain, San Francisco or *L-A-N-G-U-A-G-E,* Zen or Confessional, Feminist or Eco-feminist. In reality she has always written eclectically, "Beat poet" in particular only to the extent of its suiting her individual imaginative interests. Taking her poetry in the round, the span early to late of *About Now,* could it be doubted that in idiom as vision she has ever not laid claim to her own "own poet" status?

No text links Kyger to the Beats more explicitly than *The Japan and India Journals: 1960–1964,* "a working/writing book" as she describes it in interview, "all autobiographical narrative" and "idiosyncratic in form."[38] At once writer's diary, Asian travel-journal, book of dreams, photography collection, and meditation on "the craft of poetry" (269) with any number of poems to hand, it offers a compendium, her own writer's four-year life episode. Within the lavish observation, Japan and India as linked circuit of place, self, mood, creativity and travel, people both host and *gaijin*, it also, first hand in the cases of Ginsberg and Orlovsky along with Snyder, gives her take on Beat as a pendulum of centerpiece and periphery.

Centered in Kyoto with Snyder at the Zen Institute, she gives Japan in terms both spiritual ("Contemplation & awareness" [34]) and domestic (her annotation of shrine, noh and pachinko or of foodways from rice to tofu, soba to gyoza). The geography becomes iconographic, island Kyushu and temple Nara, Fukui-ken and Ryoan-ji, small islands like Ama or Nishima, even Kyoto-eki and Osaka Castle. The round is both Rinzei Zen yet also laced in "LSD and Sake" (263). Buddhism arouses both meditation and poetry ("From the beginning we are Buddha/—this is gateless gate" [78]).

India, likewise, where she and Snyder meet Ginsberg and Orlovsky, can be Hindu, Buddhist and Jain but also street-excremental and travel-wearying ("I feel constantly on the brink" [157], "India has exhausted me" [198]). As the itinerary builds, Colombo, Madras, Nepal, Delhi, she finds herself drawn out of herself yet given to self-aware mockery of her California pilgrim-status ("I have crows feet at the corners of my lovely beatnik eyes"[195]). Rarely does Kyger yield to the one fixed sense of self or to where she finds herself.

As to Beat allusion it comes across suitably full of ambiguity, query, fondness and un-fondness. Reading Kerouac's *The Subterraneans* she comments "I keep putting him down until I start reading him then I can't" (71). In India she overhears Ginsberg and Orlovsky having sex ("Weird squishy sounds and later much thrashing about" [186]). Ginsberg especially elicits mixed reactions. She can admire his nerve, the tough audacity, and feel sympathy at a "Vicious, unnecessarily vicious article in 'Time' about Ginsberg, Beats & poetry" (192). But she rounds on him for the way he gobbles food, hogs the limelight with the Dalai Lama, and seeks instant enlightenment. Her judgments in fact turn sharper when she speaks of "Something about Ginsberg that's stubborn, unyielding & unattractive, a giant inflated ego part . . ." (190). Beat's network takes the various forms of Snyder's poetry and readings, Cid Corman's presence in Kyoto, Ferlinghetti and Welch letters sent to her from San Francisco, Donald Allen as fellow Japan-dweller, and Philip Whalen as loyal correspondent and the one person who meets her on her return to the States.

The Japan and India Journals: 1960–1964, even so, remains charged in seeing and idiom distinctively her own. Early on she gives a typically oblique, idiosyncratic measure of seeking word for world—"Why write. I want to write the world upside down" (30). Her encounter with Olson's "Projective Verse," she reports, "hits me like a wallop" (60). Ever inquisitory she reflects "I am aware of myself: *who* of *who*" (62). Reading Pound leads her to ask "Could a woman ever be a *great* poet, write an epic in the way he says a great poet must . . . ?" (225). Preparing to leave Japan she sets herself as resolve "*Aim for* a whole new way of using language" (242). On the return journey from Yokohama she compares herself ruefully with better-dressed fellow passengers in the words "I have my beatnik clothes" (278). Beat may indeed persist as a factor, be it lived out in America, Japan or India, but however important it belongs as only the one energy within the assorted creative quantity that has been, and continues, as Joanne Kyger.

*   *   *

In terms of the so-called Beat connection, there's a lot of resonance: I grew up in Greenwich Village, I grew up on jazz. I hitchhiked. I was a spiritual seeker . . .

—Anne Waldman, "Grasping The Broom
More Tightly Now" (June 1998)[39]

A career as inveterate as that of Anne Waldman, and whose span has latterly been reflected in the collections *Helping The Dreamer: New and Selected Poems, 1966–1990* (1987) and *In The Room of Never Grieve: New and Selected Poems 1985–2003* (2003), throws up a wealth of entry-points but none more momentous than her professed "vow to poetry."[40] Other dimensions, however, crowd close: the second-generation Beat presence and poetic comrade-in-arms of Allen Ginsberg, the celebrated performance poet, the editorial nourisher of a vast swathe of contemporary verse authorship, the Buddhist, the activist, and the teacher and anthologist. Her poetry-group and festival performance activity, readings, American and international, has also extended into music-and-verse CDs, a role in the Bob Dylan movie *Renaldo and Clara* (1976), and the visual work with Ed Bowes and others. She might almost literally have been born to an arts-calling through her creative-bohemian parents and Greenwich Village upbringing and her early exposure to jazz, writing, painting and the young Gregory Corso. The Bennington College that followed included a professor-poet as full of craft and pith as Howard Nemerov whom she describes as at once "mentor" and "quirky teacher."[41]

Waldman's role with the St. Mark's Poetry Project in The Bowery, 131 East 10th Street and 2nd Avenue, bequeaths a virtual city-salon of avant-guard literary achievement. With Lewis Warsh she began *Angel Hair* in 1966, a major outlet for the "new" poetry and eventually the anthology of 2001. Few have played a more conscientious role as editor-organizer of the time's poetry. The co-founding with Allen Ginsberg of the Jack Kerouac School of Disembodied Poetics in Boulder, Colorado in 1974 has equally become legend, at once Beat heartland and Creative Writing forum and archive. In *My Education* (1995) William Burroughs for good reason calls her "the Naropa Mother."[42] There has been the plethora of international travel and festivals, the unyielding anti-war and eco-activism, and always the memorable dynamism of performance-readings to include *Iovis* (1993–), her ongoing female epic with (in a nice paradox) its exploration of "male energy." The lifetime's commitment to Buddhist practice has a recent refraction in *Structure of The World Compared to a Bubble* (2004),[43] verse thematically centered in Java's holy stupa of Borobudur.

Within so productive a vitality, and its open poetics, if any one text has become her signature work of the well over fifty collections and recordings it has to be *Fast Speaking Woman*, City Light's Pocket Poets, 33 (1975), and expanded in the 20th Anniversary Edition to *Fast Speaking Woman: Chants and Essays* (1996).[44] Even so, and for all its Beat patina and acknowledged debt to "Howl," it necessarily takes its place in the context of her extensive other writings. The anniversary edition also points to her raft of Beat connections. "Lines to a Celebrated Friend" offers fond-sisterly admonitions to Ginsberg ("Give up idiot compassion," "No one's smarter or more enlightened or more famous/For heaven's sake Allen, pick up those baggy pants"). "Musical Garden" guys her own volubility with its "Can't give you up, speech, can't stop clamoring" and "Can't give up . . . talking about Kerouac." "Billy Work Peyote" calls up William Burroughs Jr., a one-time Naropa visitor doomed by drug-use ("demon hypodermic Billy").

In response to a question about whether *Fast Speaking Woman* is a Beat poem, Waldman speaks of it as "a performance piece. . . . a female proclamation, reclaiming the body, and also being Everywoman."[45] As title-poem, along with the collection's accompanying Buddhist and other verse, "Fast Speaking Woman" could not more invite being thought Beat keystone or centrifuge. Yet despite the Smart-Whitman-Ginsberg affiliation there can equally be no doubt of its own woman-centered liberationist purposes. Waldman's own terms infinitely apply—"female proclamation," "reclaiming the body," "being Everywoman." To this end the 20th Anniversary Edition includes the essay "'Fast Speaking Woman' and The Dakini Principle," a gloss both as to the poem's shamanistic vision and its incantatory chant-form. She speaks there of herself as a "skywalker" (42) inspired both by the Mazatac poet-shaman Maria Sabina and the dakini or female ego-subduing principle in Vajrayana Buddhist spatial cosmology. The poem itself, she underlines, is conceived to be a "list-chant telling all the kinds of women there are to be" (35), an "elemental modal structure" (36), a "litany" (37).

"Let me try you with my magic power" (3). This early line speaks directly to "Fast Speaking Woman" as 30-page pattern-poem, its aimed-for combination of purpose and genre, measure and performance. The poem's opening incantations in turn set up an enumerative gallery, woman as the paradox of serial variation: "I'm a shouting woman/I'm a speech woman/I'm an atmosphere woman/I'm an airtight woman/I'm a flesh woman . . ." (3). Waldman's ongoing conjugation of "I" transforms the pronoun into a species of gendered verb, woman as transitive, embryonic, reproductive, hemispheric, earthly, avian, oneiric, multiple, and from whom flows writing as "water that cleans as I go" (5). The cumulative effect is at once auditory and visual, a gallery of female life-action whose close at the end of Part I's listings reflexively takes up this very process of self-articulation: "I'm a fast-speaking woman/ I'm a fast rolling woman/ I'm a rolling-speech woman" (24–5).

In Part II the mythic implications of woman in the first-person become yet more emphatic—Kali, Dakini, the woman of ten tongues, book woman, Buddha woman, Amoghasiddhi woman, dream-woman. Each bespeaks women's actual and fabular incarnation, or as the poem terms it, "multiple universes woman." This is "Fast Speaking Woman" as both shamanistic text and Beat-feminist Ode to Imagination), a fusion of Mazatac and Buddhist-Hindu vision. The ending captures the stance, and the ongoing line incantation to perfection: "I'm the woman who dreams/ I'M THE ARTIST INSIDE HER MAGIC HOUSE" (34). Waldman's poetry, in common with that of di Prima and Kyger, has long extended Beat's imaginative reach, three voices, three women's trajectories: magic houses indeed.

3 Black Beat
Performing Ted Joans

I cannot deny that the Beat Generation played an important role in my life. I too have known some of the best Beat minds of that generation.
  —Ted Joans, "Je Me Vois (I See Myself)" (1996)[1]

I am the early Black Beat . . .
  —Ted Joans, "I, Too, At the Beginning" (1996)[2]

Were a working synopsis, even, however unlikely, an academic-style *curriculum vitae*, to be sought for Ted Joans as Black Beat, then a number of touchstones immediately enter the reckoning. Foremost has to be his track-record as long published troubadour or strolling player. That embraces the over thirty books, pamphlets and broadsheets which began with now largely unavailable small-press publications like *Beat Poems* (1957) and *Beat Funky Jazz Poems* (1959), which had a follow-up in *All of Ted Joans And No More: Poems and Collages* (1960), *Black Pow-Wow: Jazz Poems* (1969), *Afrodisia: Old and New Poems* (1970, 1976), and which now look to a most recent collection in *Teducation: Selected Poems 1949–1999* (1999).[3] Beat, to one or another extent, they all are—the open itinerary sense of life, the open poetic measure and wordplay to match, along with each invocation of the hip, the cool, the counter-cultural. Yet, and at the same time, can it be doubted that they also carry their own black particularity and sting, the work of a writer both Beat and, more specifically, Black Beat, Afro-Beat?[4]

In this, and of necessity, the published work also links to Joans as performance poet. For whether during the classic Beat-era 1950s and 1960s, or the years since, perhaps only Allen Ginsberg, whom he credits with getting him into performance reading mode at a Village coffee shop in 1958, could more be said to have pursued poetry as live interaction of poet and audience. Anyone who attended a Joans reading would readily give witness. The notion of performance, moreover, has long held a wider ambit for him. Whether a lifetime surrealist in writing and painter or as a trumpeter, installation artist, collagist, veteran inter-Continental European and African traveler, and conference panelist, each likewise gives context to, and interacts in, the making of Joans as Beat literary figure.

Few contexts have mattered more to him than surrealism, a hallmark borne out in his profound, enduring devotion to André Breton, along with names to include David Gasgoyne, Max Ernst, Marcel Duchamp, Man Ray, Réné Magritte, Joan Miró, Roland Penrose, and the black Martinique writer Etienne Lero. One of his own best known surrealist icons, the rhinoceros, to which he gives celebration in the poem "Sanctified Rhino," even became the subject of an early correspondence with Salvador Dalí.[5] In 1984, true to the call, he became the editor of the playfully named *Dies Und Das*, Germany's first ever, if short lived, surrealist magazine.

His outpouring of surrealist verse amounts to a whole genre, whether, typically, a vignette to recall Magritte's canvases like "Jazz Anatomy" or "The Statue of 1713" as an homage written in 1967 to André Breton and classic Joans surrealism in its own right.[6] Among yet other visual art favorites he often mentions the action painter Franz Kline, de Kooning, the street graphic artist Basquiat—calling him a "Black Positive Power" in "The Ladder of Basquiat," and the great African American presence of Romare Bearden for whose canvases he has offered frequent unstinting praise.[7] Appropriately, and throughout his Beat phase and subsequently, his keen use of visual image, and various kinds of collage, have been identifying features.

Not everything, however, has been unabashed reverence as a piece like "Harlem to Picasso" confirms. In Afro-Beat argot, to include "Hey Picasso" or "dig man" or "Huh," he gives a wry salute to European surrealism's most acclaimed name for his inspired incorporation of "my black ancestors scriptural bebop" and Africa's "black thing" into his work. "HEY PICASSO," the poem raps, "how did you know/the black thing would make the modern art world . . . swing?" ("Harlem to Picasso")[8]

Jazz, equally, has been a key, abiding force. Given a lifetime steeped in the dazzling virtuosity of Louis Armstrong, Duke Ellington, Dizzie Gillepsie, Miles Davis, Thelonius Monk, John Coltrane, Sonny Rollins, Dexter Gordon, Archie Shepp and Coleman Hawkins, whose saxophone, in "The Sax Bit," becomes "a modern gri-gri,"[9] can it surprise that it was Joans who on learning of his beloved Charlie Parker's death created a canvas with the historic legend—BIRD LIVES?[10] His "They Forget too Fast" and "Ice Freezes Red"—two of many Joans poems in which Parker, his onetime roommate and friend, features—bear eloquent, not to say angry and sad, celebration of the life and music.[11]

The more general poems which invoke jazz have been just as plentiful, each the ongoing evidence of the music's absolute and necessary priority in his own history. "Jazz Must be a Woman" provides a run-on lexicon of jazz immortals, at once praise-poem and imagist reverie. Each hornman, percussionist, piano maestro or bassist becomes the embodied bearer of an art, an Afro-America, quite transcendent in spirit.[12] "Jazz is. . . ." similarly seeks to go beyond mere almanac or musicology. Joans writes as though to reenact the music's riffs, its contrasting reaches as "joy's highest pitch" and "devil phrases."[13] Given this singularity of "black sound," as he calls it, the closing refrain of "like water and air/Jazz is . . . good for the soul" comes over as perfectly earned, the poet's own overlap of word and music, Blackness and Beat. Blues, Afro-Beat blues as it were, have also become a near-category, whether "Long Gone Lover Blues," with its "WHERE WAS

YOUR LOVER WHEN THE SAD SAD SUN/ WENT DOWN??"), or the poem Joans dedicates to Ntozake Shange as "Commonplace Bulues"— "Bulues" a deliberate imitation of right sound over right spelling.[14]

In this respect Joans's two most vaunted credos have become virtually a mantra or calling-card: "Surrealism is my point of view" and "Jazz is my religion." Often, moreover, he has fused the two. "Jazz Me Surreally Do" offers a case in point, a poem which uses a compendium of disjunctive flight and food imagery ("The propeller is oxtail stew for aardvarks") to convey the "jazz wisdom" he finds typically, and authoritatively, embodied in the "sparse piano touch" of Count Basie.[15]

Afro-America's literary tradition, inescapably, also has weighed. No one name, however, more supplies inspiration than Langston Hughes, and especially the Hughes of classic pieces like "The Negro Speaks of Rivers" (1921), "The Weary Blues" (1923) or "Harlem" (1951) with its "What happens to a dream deferred?" Joans's own "Happy 78 Hughes Blues," for instance, written from Timbuktu, speaks with characteristic affection of his friend and oftentimes mentor. The poem acts as a blend of Africa memory, posthumous birthday elegy, the continuity from one poet to another—suitably styled under its own variety of Afro-Beat inflection ("I SHADOW DANCE NEAR DAWN/ HERE IN UPPER AFRICA ... SAYING HAPPY BIRTHDAY TO YOU LOVELY LANGSTON" ("Happy 78 Hughes Blues").[16]

"Another Dream Deferred?," echoing Hughes's line, links American ghetto privation to poverty, hunger and death in Mexico City.[17] "Promised Land" honors the "LANGSTON HUGHES" he sees having "PAID HIS DUES/IN THE HARLEMS/OF THE USA."[18] "Passed on Blues: Homage to a Poet," written on Hughes's death in 1967, looks to a Harlem whose nightlife and music gave Hughes his own ambit, "The sad soft low moan of jazz ROUND ABOUT MIDNIGHT" and "the glad heavy fat screaming song of happy blues." ("Passed on Blues: Homage to a Poet").[19] Both a 1985 interview Joans gave to *The Langston Hughes Review* makes the affiliation quite explicit ("[he] touched a lot of people because he was natural") as does an accompanying poem building from Hughes's "The Negro Speaks of Rivers" ("Yes sir, Dear Langston, I, too, have known rivers).[20]

Breton and surrealism, Jazz, Hughes, and a warm admiration of African American verse from Paul Dunbar to Robert Hayden and Sterling Brown, along with blues, scat and jive talk, and his Africa and other travel, all play into his "poem life surreality" as he calls it in "Je Me Vois."[21] So, too, does Beat, or again, black Beat, Afro-Beat, and whether in his own lived history, in his art, and or in his very manner of writing "Je Me Vois."

* * *

Joans has spoken often, and readily, of drawing from both Beat and Afro-Beat tradition. If a fellow spirit and one-time Manhattan companion to

Jack Kerouac, a more than passing friend of Allen Ginsberg, Peter Orlo- vsky, Gregory Corso and Lawrence Ferlinghetti, he always emphasized his association with his black Beat compeers. LeRoi Jones/Amiri Baraka and Bob Kaufman inevitably rank, the latter the dedicatee of Joans's magic real- ist blues poem "Laughter you've gone and . . .,"[22] along with A. B. Spell- man and Archie Shepp, the latter his longtime friend and frequent jazz and poetry co-performer.[23]

Two poems especially serve to identify Joans's Beat interests. "The Sermon," written in the Village in 1955 and pitched as playful, ironic advice to white, would-be Beat or hipster women, might almost be a working manifesto. In setting out a list of Beat desiderata, again replete in a slightly dated argot of "dig" and "squares," Joans also writes with typical good spirited tease. The relevant section reads "If you wish to be a sweet child of godlike intelligence, DIG JAZZ."[24] Each constituent Beat, and to be sure Afro-Beat, ingredient could not be better marked. The roll-call is symptomatic: jazz, blues, bop, Jelly Roll, *Howl*, Kerouac, *The White Negro*, lineages back into Dada and Surrealism, Whitman and Poe, *Mad Magazine* and *Village Voice*, and the warning to avoid at all costs being "SQUARE." Each, however, is released as though classic signifying with inflections derived from black sermonry and rap. This is Beat drawn from live black source ("SIT DOWN and LISTEN to Jazz!") as much as white source ("Read *Howl*," "you must have a copy of Jack (on the road) Kerouac"), at once a black poetics of call and response and Whitman-Ginsberg breath line. The effect, in an old African Ameri- can locution, is Beat poetry, more precisely Afro-Beat poetry, as it were "talking to you."

"I know a man who's neither white nor black/And his name is Jack Ker- ouac." So, in a "funny little bit of doggerel" from his 1979 interview with Gerald Nicosia[25] Joans invokes the closest of his friendships within the standard Beat pantheon.[26] The contours of Joans's early Beat involvement, Kerouac among others, is usefully set out to which he gives a brief adden- dum in "The Beat Generation and Afro-American Culture" in *Beat Scene Magazine*.[27] Beat for Joans, as he maps it out, begins in his friendship with Gregory Corso, and first encounter, in 1951 in New York City, with Gins- berg and Orlovsky.

His initial reaction to *On The Road*, however, he acknowledges was not especially warm. How, as a black Mississippi river-rat, to enthuse over white "road" hipsterism? Later he would come to have a better regard for Kerouac's verve and narrative power. He does, however, speak with greatest affection of the poetry and jazz interests which, from the outset, brought the two of them into a close, valued friendship. Kerouac, according to the Nicosia interview, even features as the nice paradox of "the white hipster showing the black one around Harlem."[28] If, there- after, they went separate ways, that was anything but to close Beat as a working energy in Joans's writing.

Few poems, certainly, better confirm the connection, or its impact and meaning for Joans, than "The Wild Spirit of Kicks," written in commemoration of Jack Kerouac's death in October 1969. Seamed in both on the road and jazz allusion, it offers a fond, appropriately exhilarated Afro-Beat tribute to a Beat friendship. Kerouac is summoned as the begetter of *Mexico City Blues*, jeans-and-sweater speedster, a blend of white, black and Native identity, and above all Beat's "PALE FACED CHIEFTAIN," its "RAZOR BLADE GONE MAD" and "FUEL OF A GENERATION." The fund of affection, and Joans's strong, abiding sense of their beyond-race companionship of spirit, is unmistakable, not least in his affiliation of Kerouac with Coltrane—"JK SAYS HELLO TO JC" ("The Wild Spirit of Kicks").[29] This closing link to Coltrane—who better than Joans himself to make the conjunction?—brings all the working elements into best relation: Kerouac's inspirational spontaneity, America as odyssey, life lived on the pulse and for kicks, the jazz, the street, and ultimately, the transcendence.

A yet fuller location of Joans as Beat would point to his auspicious July 4 1928 birth on a Mississippi riverboat in Cairo, Illinois to parents both of whom were entertainers; the brute, white-racist murder of his father in Detroit's 1943 riot (which he recalls in "Dead Serious," a poem written as he says "behind the cotton curtain in the USA while riding in the back seats of a Greyhound Bus");[30] a BFA degree from Indiana University in 1951; and, shortly thereafter, arrival in "the greatest mixed magic institution on earth: New York City's Manhattan" and within it the "Bohemia of Greenwich Village, U.S.A." ("Je Me Vois"),[31] where his talent and ease of personality made him a well-known favorite and Beat had recently become vogue, resistance, a new American culture-wave. It cannot be thought other than symptomatic that Joans was among the first to take part in Fred McDarrah's Rent-a-Beatnik circuit whose playful advertisments first appeared in *The Village Voice* in 1959 and which led to house visits and readings for a monied tier of white upper class Manhattan and East Coast society. Beat playing Beat, Joans playing himself, offers a simulation, its own kind of performance loop, worth some pondering. His birthday parties, never without their rhinoceros motif, were also features of the Village performance calendar.[32]

As to Manhattan-at-large he names Bob Reisner and Babs Gonzalez as "my street teachers"[33] and gives the both of them warmest remembrance in "Him The Bird"[34] (Joans 1999 [167]), another major eulogy to Charlie Parker. Few could have taken more readily to the city than Joans, whether the Harlem round midnight jazz lofts and clubs, or the Bleeker Street and other Village cafe and poetry locations (his own first apartment was in MacDougal Street with a later studio in Astor Place), or the MOMA, Metropolitan, Guggenheim and other NYC galleries many of whose curators like Frank O'Hara or visual artists like Jackson Pollock he came to know first-hand. He was also quick to show the keenest appetite for reading the literature of Afro-America, indeed of the wider Afro-globe, as housed at the Schomburg Library on 135ᵗʰ Street with its indispensable book collections, manuscripts and other holdings.

* * *

As America moved into the 1960s of Civil Rights and Black Power, however, both a vengeful white-supremacist Dixie and a citied north of shoot-outs and burnings, not to mention the loss of each well known life (Medgar Evers and JFK in 1963, Malcolm X in 1965—"My Ace of Spades,"[35] as he names him in the title of a tributary poem, and Martin Luther King in 1968), he found himself from 1961 onwards embarking on self-imposed exile, a cycle of forays and respite both to Europe and Africa. Color-line America, the bullying and racist ill-practice, he has often remarked, had simply become too wearing. A poem like "No mo' Kneegrow," written while flying over Dixie ("I'M FLYING OVER ALABAMA. . . . WITH BLACK POWER IN MY LAP"), and to be sung, as he says laconically, to the tune of "Oh! Susannah," was one typical Joans response.[36] This, as other like verse, also carried forward his Beat style—performative, easeful, countercultural.

By the end of the decade, with more explicit Beat life and activity behind him, he had embarked on sojourns which would take him to virtually every European capital, whether street and bohemia Amsterdam, Berlin, London, the Scandinavian north, or, and above all, Paris. A reminder of the importance of the French capital to him was again underlined in his readiness to contribute to *Fire Readings* (1991) as part of a fundraiser for George Whitman's historic Seine riverside bookstore, *Shakespeare & Company*, after it burned down to a near shell.[37]

In keeping with the spirit of Lawrence Ferlinghetti's "Fireword" Joans's two poems display a typical Afro-Beat flavor. "Good Morning," recalling an African night's sexual encounter, invokes poet and the continent's best-known peak in a state of undress ("Kilimanjaro/without her clouded underwear" ("Good Morning").[38] "To—*bâiller* or not to *éternuer*"— "To—yawn or not to sneeze"—offers a touch of surrealist whimsy (one of its two dedicatees is Marcel Duchamp) but ends with a line from black vaudeville—"So open the damn door Richard!"[39] The Beat performer in him can anything but be said to have diminished.

Beat also enters Joans's continuing, and for him hugely important, itinerary personal close encounters with Africa. Mali's Timbuktu has especially drawn him, but also Africa's wider reach, its plurality of language whether indigenous or English and French, its religions whether Christian, Islamic or animist-ceremonial. Arab Africa, for him, has meant Tangiers as the literary outpost of Paul and Jane Bowles, Burroughs and Brion Gysin and their Beat visitors; revolution shadowed Algiers; and always the haunting, expansive Sahara. As to sub-Saharan Africa, Mali has indeed been a frequent base, but also an Africa extending from Senegal to Sierra Leone, Upper Volta to Nigeria. To each he has brought his own Afro-Beat measure.

Surveying its myriad styles of *négritude*, peoples, language, music, art and terrain in his 1960s poem "Africa" he speaks of a world beyond coloniality and as "my Africa, your Africa, a free continent to be." The nuance can be thought one of blues or rap. But like all the poetry of his inveterate African journeying it carries a Beat insignia. For Joans's on-the-road Africa, a mosaic, and told in due riffs and crescendos, can also be said to possess its own kind of on-the-road voice.

"My Trip," in *Afrodisia*, for instance, written as a species of ongoing and unfinished verse-prose, conjures up desert stays among the Tuaregs, fetish rituals and sex-encounters in Dahomey and Cameroon, cities from Marrakesh to Bamako, Baga girls in Conakry and Highlife dances in Accra. These he calls "zig-zag directions," a Beat cum Black self-insertion into Africa's time and place. Place-names become active energies, verbs as in "I've Moroccod/Algeried/Tunised/Libyad/Egypted/Mauritanied/Malied etc ("My Trip").[40] His own "Harlemese" joins "Africa big Africa wide Africa." He invokes, among others, Ginsberg, Rimbaud, Bebop, Malcolm, Sweet Potato Pie, even himself in third person as "His Hipness." This is confessional rhapsody of a sort, written overlappingly in genial Bad Boy pose in "National Nigger Nuisance" and as Beat blackness ("I have blown St. Louis Blues in Mali").

A similar style of Afro-Beat panorama operates in "Afrique Accidentale,"[41] a poem dedicated to Hoyt Fuller and which he recalls as "a long rhyming poem of mine, of me coming to Timbuktu, in *City Lights Journal*, No.1."[42] Africa, *Afrique*: whether named in English or French the continent becomes for him a hub, a magnet, a place of origins, and in which Timbuktu both real ("I finally made you") and surreal ("for a peaceful night of sleep/I count African rhinos not American sheep") does duty for the Africa-at-large. But he also links himself ("You know I'm a jiving AfroAmerican") back to Greenwich Village ("the Beat bread I made"). Beat in America so becomes Beat in Africa, himself the bridging voice, Greenwich Village to "I finally made you Timbuctoo/Yeah!" ("Afrique Accidentale").[43]

One further refraction lies in how he makes "Afrodisia" not only a poem in its own right, and the title of the 1970 poetry collection in which "My Trip" and his other early Africa-poetry appears, but his own term for a "black," if always resolutely male, view of heterosexual encounter. In this respect, life can be said to have imitated art in the form of an early marriage, resulting in four "natural beautiful zebras" ("Je Me Vois") as he calls his children, not to mention the liaisons which have led to ten offspring overall.[44] "Afrodisia," its dedicatee Aimé Césaire, for sure carries a black celebration of the senses ("IT'S OUR AFRODISIA").[45] Yet however Africa, or Afro-America, centered, cannot also a Beat implication be heard, Blake as Beat precursor perhaps, or Ginsberg and Kerouac in beatificatory mode?

Latin America has also given its beckoning to Joans, notably the Mexico of Diego Rivera, of Frida Kahlo's Casa Azul which he made the subject of a documentary film, and of the country's great *muralista* tradition. He was early to meet, and admire, Octavio Paz, whom he continues to read despite the professed aversion to novels. Cuba has also drawn him, especially on account of the surrealist sculptures of Augustin Cardenas and the startling dream vision canvases of Wilfredo Lam. A poem like "Eternal Lamp of Lam" offers celebratory incantation, a run of word variation, sound and typeset based on the poet's name and the words AFRO, CHINO, CUBANO.[46] But the effect is not without its own kind of Beat echo or cadence.

Trans-national or cross-border as a lexicon might almost have been invented for Joans, "travel" in all its deeper, existential implication as a kind of personal life-art. A poem like "Do Not Walk Outside This Area," based on a visit to Mexico and written up in 1997 in Seattle, uses an airport warning-sign to take off on a celebration of *mestizaje*, whether peoples, art, foodways, or English and Spanish.[47] The point is to challenge, to out-write, boundaries, to bridge the Americas. So, typically, he invokes "*Sor Juana con Bessie Smith*," two legendary women from America south and north of the border, figures of *latinidad* and Afro-America, authorship and blues.[48] Joans's Beat poetry, and different uses of Beat motif, distinctive as they are, at the same time have both drawn from, and filtered into, this synchronicity and span.

Other banners, even so, rank alongside. Vegetarianism has been a well-known Joans preference even as the exotica of the rhinoceros (along with the okapi, tapir, aardvark, pangolin, echidna and platypus) serve him as "mammal totem animals." His birthday parties, never without their own rhinoceros motif, were features of his Village Beat-performance calendar. He has long campaigned to have Lake Victoria renamed Lake Louis Armstrong, or Lake Satchmo, a suitably "hip" or Beat farewell to white-colonial royal matriarchy, along with Azania for South Africa. In these different, and symptomatic gestures, Beat plays its part as a style, a source.

* * *

"Je Me Vois (I See Myself)," with its documentation of Joans's life and the importance of Beat activity to him, also doubles as a greatly revealing Beat photo-gallery.[49] Joans is to be seen as the seven-year old decked out in bandsman's peaked cap, bow-tied arrivee before the Statue of Liberty in 1951, duffel coated jazz action trumpeter in 1955, Paris sidekick to Langston Hughes in 1969, and traveler in seeming hunter garb at the Tropic of Cancer line en route to Timbuktu in the 1970s. Each can be thought a kind of panel in an unfolding visual performance.

Other shots show him with an otherwise white group from the Phoenix Gallery which he helped found and where he had the first exhibition of his own paintings (he has described his own canvases as evolving from "realist surreality" to "abstract-surreal" and "jazz painting"), reciting at a jazz and poetry session alongside Archie Shepp on sax during a Pan African Cultural Festival, and amid a Beat-style happening given over to "food sculpture"—a fruit covered woman—at the Cafe-theatre Vintergaarten in Copenhagen.

He is to be seen with Stokely Carmichael in London at whose death as Kwame Turé, and longtime resident of Guinea, he wrote a poem full of affection like "A Powerful Black Starmichael."[50] He also appears alongside Aimé Césaire at a 1968 Black Power rally in Paris, Jean Paul Sartre again on a Paris panel, a young looking Ishmael Reed, and Romare Bearden before a Senofu votive sculpture at the Metropolitan Museum. In a clearly fond invocation he is to be seen in filial embrace of his mother in Fort Wayne, Indiana.

It would be hard, however, to imagine him in more rapt colloquy than that where he is photographed with André Breton in the latter's Paris studio in Rue Fontaine. Joans's body language speaks volumes, the utter attention, the outstretched arms, the concentrated brow. It offers a perfect companion to a poem like "Nadja Rendezvous,"[51] one surrealist's uninhibitedly admiring salute to another. A 1992 image shows him with his longtime companion and "femmoiselle," Laura Corsiglia, before a window in which, bearded and in checkered muffler, and giving off a characteristically full, warm smile, he and the letters teasingly add up to TEDUCATION, the very titling of his *Selected Poems 1949–1999*.[52]

These all stand well enough in their own right, Joans in his ongoing diversity of presence. They take their place, however, alongside an almost classic Beat portrait: Joans with Allen Ginsberg in London in 1967. Clad in familiar headgear he has his left arm around Beat's best known poet-avatar, himself in full beard mode, jacketed, and with a charm hanging from his neck. The two meet directly, and fondly, each other's gaze. The image's "love-in" configuration, against a background shelf of books, has superimposed the words "BLACK!" coming from Joans's mouth and "Flower!" from Ginsberg's ("Je Me Vois").[53] It offers a near perfect cameo, Ginsberg as Beat, Joans as Afro-Beat.

*   *   *

A roster of yet other Joans poems invite due recognition and annotation as either Beat or, at least, Beat shadowed. One grouping lies in the love verse of *Teducation*. These writings, which run from verse dictionaries like "Alphabetical Love You" or "Collected & Selected Groupings" to a species of self-portraiture like "I Am The Lover," with its slightly antic Beat footfalls like "I howled in prose" or "I snore in code," to "And None Other," written as a Beat-surreal homage to Laura Corsiglia for "Our on-the-road-reality," "Mariachi marriage" and "vegetal entanglement."[54]

Another offers flytings or exorcisms, often of a kind in impetus with Ginsberg's "America." These can always run the risk of polemic, message over poetry as in "How Do You Want Yours?"[55] But they can also show a keenest satiric swerve as in "God Blame America!!,"[56] and a line like "America/your mask has slipped," or "Dear Miss America," written at the time of the Vietnam War and pitched as though mock-apologetic Beat pacificism—"I don't mean to be funny/but you gotta give up/ being square and selfish."[57] To these should be added an early sound poem like "Uh Huh," written in 1949, an assault as much by phonetics as actual speech on the Dixie segregation which has created, as he calls it, "THE COLORED WAITING ROOM!!!!!"[58] Few Joans poems, however, more startle than "The Nice Colored Man," first its iteration of "Eeny Meeny Miney Mo" as a kind of nursery rhyme cladding for the smack of the ending— "Catch Whitey by his Throat/If He says—Nigger CUT IT!" ("The Nice Colored Man")[59]

Three other styles of poem also serve, each of which, duly, carries an accent both Beat and yet Beat plus. In "Why Try" something of his Beat whimsy is on offer, replete in reference to bohemia and the Beat Café, given to Joans's easeful sense of sexuality—liberating or full of male gaze chauvinism according to interpreting readership, and deceptively simple in its rhythm and wordplay.[60] A beauteous brown woman ("she had two beautiful brown eyes/and she would sit in the Beat Café") is teasingly contrasted with a young white girl carrying suntan lotion in hand. "WHY TRY" runs the voice. But more than tease is involved, white skin for brown. At issue, rather, has to be the complex styling of Afro-female pulchritude, posture, dress, thought, bodily show, music, nothing short of a whole way of being. Suntan lotion, indeed, cannot work the change.

Joans's fusion of Beat with surrealism has few better verse expressions than "Sanctified Rhino," written in 1956.[61] His signature icon again comes into play but as part of a wry "hipster" parable of sexual encounter and remembrance. Its use of surreal image—the poem's opening line of "The rhinos roam in the bedroom/where the lovely virgin waits" is typical— plays into an intertextual Beat reference like "the owl howls the Ginsberg address/that only the hipster would know." This Beat-Surreal ply works throughout, a love affair won, lost, and then looked back upon, and told in both Dali-esque exaggeration ("she ran away with a dish and a bat") and Beat patois ("chicklet," "cat," "hipster").

"Him The Bird," a 1958 poem, blends Jazz and Beat, Charlie Parker as ultimate sax genius and hipster, Afro-America's own, yet also, and in life or silhouette, America's own ("his earth name was CHARLES PARKER").[62] All the placing references add their own resonance—the Village, "Bob Reisner's Open Door," Barrow Street, the young James Dean soon to become Hollywood's screen icon of alienation and cool, Weegee as Manhattan's photographer royal and, above all, Bird himself as highwire if fated hornman. This is Bird as not only Kerouac's but Joans's own Beat god. The very spacing in the poem, each indicated pause and run-on cadence, suggests a jazz-Beat fugue of both lament and celebration. The wordplay, as always, give supporting force, whether Parker as "café-au-lait colored bird" or horn-man who "wailed for the world." Is there not, too, a beatifying in that final acclamation of life over death—"Bird lives Bird Lives Bird Lives Bird Lives!!"? Ted Joans truly performing Ted Joans, at once Afro-Beat surrealist and surrealist Afro-Beat, and in a poem given to his best loved jazz *alter ego*, could not be thought to have spoken, or written, in better form.

*   *   *

Why, then, has Joans often seemed to go missing in the Beat pantheon, his too frequent omission from many of the ranking accounts and anthologies? Gerald Nicosia, who contributes a stirring Introduction to *Teducation*, has not been the only admirer to note Joans's absence in key collections from Abraham Chapman's *Black Voices* (1969) and its successor *New Black Voices* (1972) through to David S. Wirshup's *The Beat Generation & Other Avant-Guarde (sic) Writers* (1977) and Ann Charters's otherwise exemplary *The Portable Beat Reader* (1992) and, of late, even the *Norton Anthology of African American Literature* (1997). For Joans as both a Beat contributor, and well beyond, redress has long been overdue.

In part the cause could well lie in his itinerary history, the seeming gaps or absences. Murmurings have been heard about the risk of mannerism in his punning, rhymes and slogans, not least to include the quirk of not caring to read novels on grounds of length and despite a promised one of his own with the exuberantly mock un-pc title *Niggers From Outer Space*. Joans has not been immune from the charge, made against the *fellahin* ethos of the Beat Movement at large whatever its pan-sexual styles, of phallo-centrism, the too ready reduction, and with it a certain boastfulness, of women to sexual play-object.

Yet other factors enter the reckoning. Joans's poetry, whatever its self-evident sources in black life, has never easily been corralled into the Black Power stable: his interests in surrealism, jazz, erotica, painting, even travel as its own kind of performance, have put him ideologically at some distance from the voices of clenched fist black nationalism. Gerald Nicosia nicely underlines something of Joans's reluctance to be straight-jacketed either by subject or genre when, in his Introduction to *Teducation: Selected Poems 1949–1999*, he mentions a conversation they had about the Kennedy-Johnson era of Malcolm and Black Power. Never himself a slouch in tackling racist abuse, Joans, he witnesses, at the same time always asked for the most plural expression of black, and of at-large human, experience. Nicosia recalls Joans's asking for love poems or poems about bears or potatoes or the senses as against riffs on only "white racism and white villains."[63]

There is also the issue of Joans as Beat performance poet, the more so given his ease of wit, the accessibility of his style. Does not poetry like his, more than usually open to improvisation—and spoken performance—as against the silent, self-enclosed reading, almost always tend to be assigned to the lesser margin? Joans himself offers about the right measure of his Beat affiliations and writing when he speaks of its "important role in my life" in "Je Me Vois"[64] It has not been everything. Surrealism, Jazz, the visual arts, Europe, and Africa and his other journeyings, clearly have all given shaping force to his creativity. But Beat, Black or Afro-Beat, remains a hallmark of his vision and, as importantly, of his idiom, that of a career, a life in performance as it were, owed not only recognition but its own kind of garland.

4 Beat International
Michael Horovitz, Andrei Voznesensky, Kazuko Shiraishi

There appears to be a Beat Generation all over the world. . . .
    —Jack Kerouac, "Lamb, No Lion" (1958)[1]

The spirit of Beat maverick writers lives on.
    —Anne Waldman, "Lineages & Legacies" (2001)[2]

As an international phenomenon, and virtually from the start, Beat was quick to possess its overseas outposts and encampments: Europe, North Africa, Mexico City, Japan, India. Few Beat gathering-places more have become legend in this respect than the Paris of the Beat Hotel, 9, rue Git-le-Coeur, discovered by Chester Himes in 1956 as open to black clientele, run by the *sympatique* but not a little garrulous patronne-concierge, Mme. Rachou, and destined to become an art-colony at the heart of the Latin Quarter. Not only did Ginsberg, Orlovsky, Corso, Norse, Burroughs and Brion Gysin live in its seedy, cramped rooms at different times in the 1950s–60s, but it also served as the base for an extraordinary international line-up of other writers, painters, models, artists and photographers. Walls became canvases, marijuana gave off a ubiquitous reek, the so-called Turkish toilet facilities tested even the most hardened of traveler spirits, and loves and affairs happened as if upon a roundabout.

But The Beat Hotel was also where Ginsberg wrote *Kaddish* (1961), Corso his poem "Bomb," and Burroughs and Gysin experimented with cut-ups and "word virus" along with Ian Sommerville, Burroughs's co-creator of the would-be cyber-hallucinogenic apparatus they called the Dream-Machine.[3] It has also been a source of writing and art in its own right. This includes Harold Norse's *Beat Hotel* (1975 in a German edition, 1983 in English)—Norse rented a room from 1960–63 and predicted that this "fleabag shrine will be documented by art historians," Brion Gysin's *The Last Museum* (1986) with its filigree of comedy and sex-talk, the British photographer Harold Chapman's sumptuous black-and-white album based on his own residency, and Barry Miles's *The Beat Hotel: Ginsberg, Burroughs and Corso in Paris, 1957–1963* (2000), his meticulous history of the hotel's prime Beat years and residents.[4]

Those who were drawn to the hotel, often enough given to paying their rent in art-work, prints, and a variety of creative IOUs, include the painters

Guy Horloff from the Netherlands, Robin Page from Canada, Patrick Shelley and Mike Blake from England, and William Guthrie and William Morris from America. Harold Chapman had a fellow photographer in Bill Cheney, not to mention Ginsberg, Corso and Orlovsky each with an interest in visual portraiture. Writers like the Caribbean-born Dixie Nimmo, the Americans Ken Tindall, Kay Johnson, Thelma Shumsky (who married Chapman), Verta Kali Smart, and the poet-painter Kaja from New Orleans, all feature as residents. Not a little glamorously other clientele included art-fashion models like Mirja, Lee Forrest and Diane Barker.

That The Beat Hotel has now been refurbished as the Relais-Hôtel du Vieux Paris, and given its name both to a London pop-club and a Beat-themed motel in Desert Hot Springs, California, does not eclipse its not so long-ago role as a virtual living theater of Beat and related arts. Brion Gysin, looking back also to the musicians and film-makers, offers a relevant summary. Mme Rachou, he witnesses, might have earned serious money "if she had laid away just a few of the manuscripts of what was written under her roof or collected some of the pictures painted in her hotel."[5] Kay Johnson, long passed into anonymity, gives another style of fond remembrance in her ". . . in Heaven at 9 Git-le-Coeur."[6] She invokes the rooms as though "Heaven," an art-residence where "Nobody ever dies."

Amsterdam likewise served as a key European base during the same decade where Ginsberg and Corso, as other Beats, were drawn to a Dutch literary circle highly receptive to Beat writing, a liberal drugs regime, the cheap housing and, for its sumptuous holdings, the Rijksmuseum. To move into other Europe, who but Ginsberg in 1965 could have been crowned Kral Majales, May King, in Prague, summarily deported by the Soviet-controlled Czechoslovak authorities as an American hooligan and imperialist, and then, a quarter-century later, find himself re-crowned by President Vaclav Havel? Vienna's *Schule für Dictung*, founded in 1991 and whose poetics and poetry teaching derive their inspiration from Naropa, has become Austria's Beat academy. Latterly, Lvov in the Ukraine has provided another Beat outpost, notably throughout the 1990s in the activities of the poet-dissident Alik Olisevich.

Mexico City features as frequent Beat stopover, where, in 1951, Burroughs accidentally-or-otherwise shot his wife Joan Vollmer in a drink and William Tell game mishap. Ginsberg, in 1953–4, made a six months Mexican sojourn, exploring the rainforest, the Mayan ruins of Chiapas and Yucatán. In 1955 Kerouac, based mainly in the capital city, wrote his *Mexico City Blues*.[7] The Amazon became another Burroughs working base in his search for yage as ultimate fix and for which his correspondence with Ginsberg, *The Yage Letters* (1963), provides a record. In due course, and with Ginsberg's judicious editorial help, they would transform into *Naked Lunch*.[8] Cuba, in 1963, gives rise to Ginsberg's once again being expelled on the grounds, this time, of importing US decadence, a truly ironic outcome for a half-ideologically, and half sexually, interested admirer of Castro.

Tangiers takes on its own matching force, the colony headed by Paul and Jane Bowles, at once expatriate literary center, Sahara-fringed drug garden and Gay outpost. This same Sahara as cartography, a human echo-chamber, lies behind typical Paul Bowles fiction like *A Sheltering Sky* (1949), with its half-surreal Tangiers city labyrinth and desert expanse as locating the inner lives of Port and Kit Moseby, and *A Hundred Camels in the Courtyard* (1962), with its quartet of hallucinatory kif stories given over to the civilization-primitivism axis.[9] Jane Bowles's fine-edged stories, "Everything is Nice" and "East Side: North Africa" prime among them, similarly use their Moroccan settings to explore the tilt and passion of same-sex love across ethnic culture-lines.[10] Burroughs supplies his own unique lugubrious presence but he had company in Brion Gysin, art-experimentalist and partner to Hamri Mohamed, the painter of Morocco as he was known for his canvases and designs and with whom, from 1954–58, he ran the restaurant *The 1001 Nights* converted from the old Tangiers Palace. It was Hamri who introduced Gysin, Brian Jones of The Rolling Stones, Ornette Coleman, and various Beat visitors to the Sufi trance music played by the Master Musicians of Joujouka (the music, according to Burroughs, of a "four thousand-year old rock 'n' roll band").

Kyoto, Japan's ancient capital, enters Beat iconography for its massive temple and zen culture and where, not inappropriately, Ginsberg experienced a further Blakean revelation on a train in 1963 and Gary Snyder and Joanne Kyger began their marriage (1960–65). Japanese scales of time-space, haiku, the still dynamism of *wa* or harmony, and the treasury of visual art and musicianship all help shape Beat sensibility. It was to Kyoto, too, that Cid Corman, brought *Origin*, the poetry and arts magazine he began in 1951 and that published vital, for many landmark writings by Olson, Creeley, Snyder and the Beats. Since Corman's death in 2004 it has managed to continue, a tribute to his exemplary energies as long-time editor. India, likewise, plays into Beat traveling, whether Benares or Mumbai, or ashrams from the Punjab to Jaipur, especially for Ginsberg, Orlovsky, Snyder and Kyger. The attractions were many, variously the elevation of spiritual over material values, Hinduism and Buddhism as non-western belief-systems and their embodiment in the Vedas and Suttas, the music of the sitar as brought into the west by a musician like Ravi Shankar, and the regard for the calling of the poet as saddhu or holy avatar.

*   *   *

No doubt, in part because of the shared language, Beat was early to find more than an echo in Britain—however deceptive the analogies often made with actually deeply conservative Angry Young Man figures like the playwright John Osborne or the novelist Alan Sillitoe. In 1963 Penguin Moderns Poets 5 issued their slim, but greatly influential, selection of Corso, Ferlinghetti and Ginsberg.[11] Few British poets more took up the Beat call to poetry as live voice, live counter-voice, than Michael Horovitz, self-professed heir to the trans-Atlantic poetic legacy not only of William Blake but Allen Ginsberg.

Anyone present at the momentous Albert Hall reading in London on June 11 1965, the auditorium heavy in pot haze, would have been in little doubt of Beat's outreach. Ginsberg played the harmonium and finger cymbals and chanted. Corso, evidently high, offered a run of short poems, and Ferlinghetti read "The Situation in the West Followed by a Holy Proposal" (later published in *Starting From San Francisco*).[12] A recording was played of the almost spectral voice of William Burroughs reading *Naked Lunch*. The Viennese sound poetry of Ernst Jandl offered its acoustic drama, not least in calling up the work of Kurt Switters. A Finnish voice in the poet and translator Anselm Hollo, equally at home in English and German and later to become a Naropa teacher, brought more multilingual literary weight to bear. A mescaline-fueled Simon Vinkenoog at one point made an intervention repeating the word love over and over. Given an estimated 7000 in the audience and the four-hour duration *The Guardian* would subsequently describe the event as the "biggest poetry-reading meeting in the English-speaking world."

British poets included Adrian Mitchell reading his anti-Vietnam poem "To Whom It May Concern" and Harry Fainlight his drug-visionary poem "The Spider." Christopher Logue offered classical translation. Other readings came from Michael Horovitz, Pete Brown, Brian Patten, Spike Hawkins, Johnny Byrne and Tom McGrath. As compère Alexander Trocchi at one point was heckled for trying to shorten Fainlight's unduly long recitation. The occasion was to have another outcome in Peter Whitehead's prize-winning documentary film which shares its name of with the eventual anthology, namely *Wholly Communion*.[13] English Victorian setting, American Beat auspices ("American poets capture Royal Albert Hall" runs a line in Ferlinghetti's prophecy-poem "After the Cries of Birds" in his *The Secret Meaning of Things*), and an international line-up of like-minded though overwhelmingly male authorship: the occasion still resonates in British cultural memory.[14] Michael Horowitz would offer the following commentary:

> The Albert Hall brought together a lot of things that were happening together and reduced the uptightness and competitiveness and intellectual distancings and narcissism and vanity.[15]

Jeff Nuttall, poet, chronicler, teacher, maker of performance scripts, readily acknowledged the Beat component in his challenges to British class division and etiquette in so ground-clearing a work as *Bomb Culture* (1968).[16] Right through to his death in 2004 he was very much the live, dramatic reminder of Beat's inspiration and residue. Adrian Mitchell, in an accusation-poem akin to the anti-military verse of Ferlinghetti or Corso like "To Whom It May Concern," with its refrain of "Tell me lies about Vietnam," took on the obfuscations of British establishment power and its nuclear unilateral deterrent. Writing in *The New Statesman* on Ginsberg's death, Mitchell recalled with greatest affection "the man who set me on fire . . . his words, his warmth, and sometimes his blood."[17]

Other Beat-linked voicing is to be heard in the Scottish-born Alexander Trocchi's fiction, whether *Cain's Book* (1960) as drug chronicle ("the mind under heroin") or *Young Adam* (1961) as obsessive love portrait ("It is the word 'I' which is arbitrary and which contains within itself its own inadequacy and its own contradiction").[18] Beat also exerts its considerable trace in The Liverpool Poets, Brian Patten as keenly observant versifier of the everyday and who occasionally has read alongside Ginsberg, the more oral-populist Roger McGough (the energy behind the group *The Scaffold*), and the intelligently whimsical Adrian Henri. On offer was Anglo-Beat in a Merseyside accent, the interest also carried in The Beatles whose John Lennon now appears in the columns of Beat reference-volumes.[19]

The London circuit has looked to the sound poetry of Bob Cobbing who for over forty years helped direct the Writers Forum Workshop, and established himself as a doyen of Beat-like events and readings; the contributions of Barry Miles of Better Books and his longtime Beat scholarship; dom silvester houédard (always the lower-case form), Benedictine monk, concrete poet, and whose ecumenical interests are reflected in his use of Beat-Buddhist and Arab mystic allusion; readings throughout the 1960s and beyond at the Institute of Contemporary Arts on the Mall; and Michael Horovitz and Peter Brown as performance poets with a keen self-affiliation to Ginsberg, Ferlinghetti and Corso. Others have written as Londoners-by-adoption, notably the Welsh-born Iain Sinclair, novelist and film-maker of the capital and the poet of the greatly Ginsberg-influenced *Kodak Mantra Diaries, October 1966 to June 1971* (1971), and far later, Brian Docherty, "Glasgow-Irish post-Beat poet for the 90's" as once described in connection with the verse of his *Armchair Theatre* (1999).[20] More obliquely, Beat influence and allusion can be seen to thread into the poetry of Lee Harwood, Tom Raworth and Tom Pickard, each a distinctive English voice yet with a shared American pitch for open sensibility, open form.

Even a wholly un-Beat poet like George MacBeth, who ran the BBC's Radio 3 poetry studio readings and broadcasts from 1955–76 and who took aim at the Beats in his tepid satire "Owl," together with the London-centered circuit of Edward Lucie-Smith, Peter Redgrave, and Alan Brownjohn who became known as The Group, however hard they tried, found it difficult to ignore Beat ease and expansiveness. A major acknowledgement, by contrast, has to be paid to Eric Mottram, critic, poet, and London University teacher, whose longtime championing of the Beats in the *Times Literary Supplement* and as editor of *Poetry Review* in the 1970s with its openness to US contemporaries was both seminal and controversial. His early studies of Burroughs (1971) and Ginsberg (1972), and closely informed Introduction to Kerouac's *The Scripture of The Golden Eternity* (1960), reprinted alongside that of Anne Waldman in the City Lights edition (1994), remain landmarks.[21]

Two names connect the early and late Beat circuits in Britain. Royston Ellis, London born and long a resident first of Dominica and then Sri Lanka, in the late 1950s billed himself the laureate of the beatnik generation and his writing that of the UK's first Beat poet. His credentials would be several: two slim verse collections, *Jiving To Gyp* (1959) and *Rave* (1961), which carry the impress of Ginsberg especially; *Big Beat Scene* (1961) as his account of the creative linkage between verse and rock; and his novel *Myself To Face* (1964) with its portrait of Beat-beatnik-pop celebrity.[22] He long has claimed responsibility for the naming of The Beatles who repaid him in the songs "Paperback Writer" and, according to John Lennon with whom he travelled and brought into a three-in-a-bed sex encounter, "Polythene Pam." Later Beat has an incarnation in Toby Litt, whose *Beatniks: An English Road Movie* (1997) as the story of the British trio of Mary, Jack and Neil journeying from Bedford to Brighton offers a witty, postmodern homage to Kerouac tradition, yet at the same time a chastening exposure of hipster nostalgia.[23]

For the 1960s Beat interests were to be met with in *International Times* and *Oz Magazine*, readings, concerts, reviews and features from alternative press sources. In *Beat Scene*, under the editorship of Kevin Ring, and in 2004 having reached its 45th issue, and in the journal *Transit*, the UK has busy successor publications. These both continue the archive and give tribute to Beat as at once past creative record and, trans-Atlantically and beyond, energetically engaged-in and live continuance.

* * *

Europe adds to the diversity. Germany sees the emergence of the 1960s-and-after literary generation of Wolf Wondratschek, Dieter Brinkmann and Jörg Fauser, writers at once heirs to Nazi pariahdom and then US and allied occupation, and yet freed by the America of Beat imaginative openness. Looking back in 1987 Wondratschek summarized the impact in the form of a list "Jack Kerouac. Ken Kesey. Ginsberg. Burroughs. Later Dylan. Figureheads. Father figures who acted like adolescents, like madmen, wicked, addicted, free."[24] In Jan Cremer's *I Jan Cremer* (1965) The Netherlands offered its own Beat literary bad boy though not without its own self-mimicry ("I'm the kind on the corner, the boy who's always hanging around"), the self-appointed drugs, sex and jazz roué of the modern city be it Europe or the States.[25] Simon Vinkenoog, Dutch poet and author of the novel *Hoogseizoen/High Season* (1962), centers on Amsterdam as European Beat city, underlined also by his translation of Ginsberg's "Howl."[26] A far different voice, yet still with its Beat affiliations, belongs to Andrei Voznesensky, harbinger of a Russia reborn from Sovietism and whose massively popular reading tour of the United States in 1966 (Ginsberg read a translation of his poetry at the Albert Hall occasion), signaled a beginning challenge to received Cold War conventions.

In Australia a Beat succession was to be met with in Michael Dransfield's *Streets of The Long Voyage* (1971), *The Inspector of Tides* (1972) and *Drug Poems* (1972), with their frequent echoes of Rimbaud's *Le Bateau Ivre* (1871) and *Une Saison en Enfer* (1873).[27] Early to Beat-bohemian life, middle-class born, Dransfield remained within his own shores, took against the Vietnam war, and died young at twenty-four of a heroin overdose. Followers saw in him a Chatterton, one whose turn to the needle seemed to complement the dark obsessive-destructive themes of his verse. "Notes for an Inquest," from his posthumous *Collected Poems* (1987), bequeaths a credo like "I am the hand pushing a pen along in random patterns."[28] Robert Adamson made for a fellow Sydney-based spirit of sorts, early drop-out, reformatory boy and jailee, whose bow with *Canticles on The Skin* (1970) has led on to the long life-and-verse career remembered in the autobiography *Inside Out* (2004).[29] His mainly city landscapes bespeak margins—sexual, criminal, countercultural. In another early collection, *The Rumour* (1971), he explicitly acknowledges Allen Ginsberg and Robert Duncan, along with Verlaine and other *symboliste* luminaries, as influences.[30] Andrew Burke, Perth-based, has been another poet to invoke the Ginsberg-Corso-Ferlinghetti circuit as the inspiration for his early poetry and the career launched with *Let's Face The Music and Dance* (1975).[31] The Beat-hippie line found its avatars in Germaine Greer, then London-based, a TV presence and often psychedelically clad, and Richard Neville, founder of *Oz* magazine, a 1960s pop presence and a frequent figure in the law-courts on grounds of supposed obscenity. His Sydney to Swinging London odyssey, conglomerately titled *Hippie, hippie shake: the dreams, the trips, the trials, the love-ins, the screw-ups . . . the sixties* (1995), fondly calls up an era in which youth, rock, sex as spontaneity, and the different drug regimes, all served as calling-cards.[32]

In Japan a Beat counter-note would also sound, not least in the form of an alternative fiction of drop-out. Kaoru Shoji's novel *Akazukin-chan Ki Wo Tsukete/Be Careful Little Red Riding Hood* (1969) situates its love saga under a Beat patina.[33] Ryu Murakami's *Kagirinaku Tomei ni Chikai Buru/ Almost Transparent Blue* (1977), within its GI-Japanese friendship, unravels a whole youth underground.[34] Haruki Murakami's *Noruwei No Mori/ Norwegian Wood* (1987), the title taken from the Beatles song, explores the drift of Japanese postwar urban affluence.[35] No account of Japanese counter-culture voices, however, would be complete without mention of Nanao Sakaki, poet, environmentalist, journeyer, dissident, author of a span of work from *Bellyfulls* (1966) to *Break The Mirror* (1996), and whose East Village video, *Allen Ginsberg Meets Nanao Sakaki* (1988), confirms a Beat connection to last until his death in 2009.[36] Nor, too, could Kazuko Shiraishi go missing from the lists, from the 1950s forward one of Tokyo's vintage jazz-and-poetry performance artists, the supposed bad girl, and the poet behind the collection which led to her association with Beat tradition, *Seinaru Inja No Kisetsu/Seasons of Sacred Lust* (1970).[37]

* * *

The publication of Michael Horovitz's edited Penguin Books anthology, *Children of Albion: Poetry of The Underground in Britain* (1969), did landmark service.[38] For many it offered the would-be alternative rebirth of UK poetic voice with manifesto in tow in the form of Horovitz's own "Afterwords." Here, if nowhere else, and beyond both the Eliot-Auden line and the endlessly vaunted Angry Young Men, was to be met a consciously pitched, affirmatory and kinetic Brit-populist verse.

Horovitz himself, as befits a poet who with the jazzman Stan Tracey has long held sway as an acclaimed performance artist, offered the anthology as a reaction against the staidness of the BBC and British Council literary establishment and against the inert syllabi, as he perceived it, of school and university. That included the Oxford where, in the late 1950s, he took his degree in English and began, and then abandoned, literary research on Blake. *Children of Albion* aimed for accessible poetry, though not at any intended expense of craft, and given to an aesthetic among whose primary inspirations was indeed the glad day visionary boldness of William Blake.

It was, perhaps, inevitable that Beat would seem for Horovitz as for others of his literary generation a ready congruence, be it the shared love of Blake or the insistence on open encounter with experience and accompanying open poetic measure. Among Horovitz's many BBC radio-broadcasts, symptomatically, has to be one under the heading "A New Sound—British Beat Poetry." As usual, too, no one group etiquette or rulebook held. How could it in a gathering of over sixty poets? But there can be no doubt of an engagement with what one anthologee, Piero Heliczer, calls "explicit England" (England doing service for Britain) in a poem which alludes to an imagined London meeting with "Gregory" and "Allen." Horovitz's own included poems, whether "Soho Awakening" ("mind's eye opens afresh") or "Spring Welcomes You To London" (with its shrewdly more-than-it-seems "it's good to be up and about"), the note throughout lies in *disponibilité*, an Englishness, a Britishness, freed of institutional gentility and the controlling power maneuvers of born-to-rule class and privilege.

For all his own UK origins and early activity—the German-Jewish roots, south-of-England boyhood, role in establishing the review *New Departures*, friendship with fellow CND veteran and poet Pete Brown, organization (for many mis-organization) of the New Moon poetry festival in 1966, linkage to the Liverpool poets and art, his collages and paintings and drawings and affiliations with jazz, and a span of culture and politics to run from his love of the Goon Show through to Thatcherism and Blairism—Horovitz has not been slow to acknowledge a Beat influence. But if his Englishness is born out in the "Homages & Updates" sequence of *Wordsounds and Sightlines* (1994), with its encomia to the line of Thomas Gray, Wordsworth, Matthew Arnold, Edward Thomas and Rupert Brooke, he has also been the European translator of, among others, Andrei Voznesensky.[39] Admiringly, moreover, his "Afterwords" speaks of "the unfetter'd insurrection of Ginsberg and Corso" and Beat's healthful marriage of "jazz to art." Ginsberg, reciprocally, would designate Horovitz "Cockney, Albionic, New Jerusalem, Jazz Generation, Sensitive, Bard."

It is this Horovitz who saw himself as belonging to a rising new circuit of British poetry. Chris Challis, in his brief but helpful survey "The Rhythms of My Own Voice: a Brit on the Beats" (1985), invokes the litany of the Scots-Beat Iain Sinclair, the Liverpudlian Brian Patten and the poet-songsters of "The Scaffold"—Roger McGough or Adrian Henri, Adrian Mitchell whose Vietnam indictment poem, "To Whom It May Concern" still weighs, the Jeff Nuttall of *Bomb Culture*, and Horovitz himself as speaking poet and author of verses explicitly dedicated to both Ginsberg and Corso.[40] A yet fuller map of Anglo-Beatdom would say more about the Albert Hall "Wholly Communion" readings in 1965 and indeed its 7000 person attendance. That it brought together a gallery of names like Alexander Trocchi, Lee Harwood, Tom Pickard, Christopher Logue, Adrian Mitchell, Frances as well as Michael Horowitz, and the Liverpool poets, says much about the sense of break-through occasion, a changing British poetic order.

Beat Horovitz can be summoned in any number of ways, few better than his "Jazz Poems" as given their own section in his *Growing Up: Selected Poems and Pictures, 1951-'79* (1979).[41] "Thelonius," for instance, seeks in its performative spatial tactics the very re-enactment of Monk's piano virtuosity ("& we hang/ in there/—sus pended, joyously/ ston'd/ in mid-air/on your telegraphic/ harpstrung twang"). This Beat-jazz fusion is ongoingly to be met with in poems from *Wordsounds and Sightlines* like "For Leon Bismarck Beiderbeck (1903–1931)", with its allusion to "those quicksilver/ jeweled rounds," and "Flying Home," with its near dictionary-riff on Lionel Hampton and fellow jazz luminaries and their "flailing flying/chips and sparks" and "hailstorms of mosaic."

A poem like "Glad Day," necessarily, invokes Blake ("unplanned/ realizations/of being alive"). But there, also, can be little mistaking an affinity with a Ginsberg-Whitman liberative stance and wording (". . . let all my safety catches be blown—undone"). "Poetry for the People," issued as a single pamphlet in Spring 1966 and full of trans-Atlantic references to "Plantagenet stockbrokers" and "Goldwater depths," looks to a world retrieved from locked politics and Cold War surrealism ("our syllabus is spent").

In *Bank Holiday* (1967), however, his Beat-jazz sequence in 40 parts, Horovitz writes his own would-be version of *Howl*, replete in both Blakean "Jerusalem" and Ginsbergian "Sun-Flower" echoes.[42] Its canvas is nothing less than "*this* universe," quotidian life in Britain, the JFK killing, "the sexless dead in Vietnam," Holy Loch nuclear submarines, Big Car and other consumerism and, always, the anti-life of the H-Bomb. The poem's counter-values lie in "elemental earth," an "opened bank" of experience, beatitudes born of un-nuclear human love and sky. The effect is pitched to be one of intimacy, a poet's witness, the epic working-through of life over death as jazz soliloquy or Beat-like blues in verse form.

*   *   *

Translation, it is rightly observed, can rarely amount to other than second-order text, especially in so image-determined a form as poetry. Robert Lowell's term "imitations" wholly applies. In the case of Andrei Voznesensky, together with Yevgeni Yevtuschenko and Semyon Kirsanov, a perhaps special dispensation applies. When City Lights published *Red Cats* (Pocket Books 16, 1962) in translations by the then Beat-connected poet, Anselm Hollo, editor of the influential collection *Jazz Poems* (1962), it seemed that Beat, somehow, had surfaced from deep beneath the political cartilage of Khrushchev-era Sovietism.[43] Years later, as his *"Red Cats Revisited"* bears witness, Hollo would strongly break with the poems—speaking of them as "simplistic, sentimental, and not a little hypocritical in their post- and sub-Mayakovksian rhetoric."[44] The welcome, even so, extended at the time by Allen Ginsberg and Lawrence Ferlinghetti to both poets, and the American readings given by the two Russians during the 1960s, seemed the promise of a small thaw in the Cold War stasis, a recognition, across gaps of language or national fixities of ideology, of shared trans-cultural affinities.

Voznesensky's claims as a poet have always been genuinely as consequential as they have been full of encompassing width. One has only to think of best-known work like "I Am Goya," "Antiworlds," or "Story Under Full Sail". Who, accordingly, could doubt his heirship to Boris Pasternak as spiritual and poetic mentor, not to mention Mayakovski or Pushkin? His brave, and canny, resistance with Yevtuschenko against the 1960s would-be purge of art and writing written outside the lackeydom of the Soviet Writers Union, has become a deserved legend. The command of live Russian idiom, his ingenuities of image and assonance and which native speaker-readers continue to confirm, found testimony in the massive early stadium recitations and print-runs of his work. But there remains, also, his undeniable, and greatly longstanding, affair with America, ancillary as may be in one sense yet not so in another, and within such, his connection into any number of Beat's dwelling-places and circuits.

With *Dogalypse: San Francisco Poetry Reading* (City Lights Pocket Poets, 29, 1972), its photography to include stage-shots with Ferlinghetti as they both participated in a reading at Project Artaud on October 22 1971, Voznesensky can be thought to offer his Beat passport.[45] "Dogalypse" as positioning first poem, does immediate good service, a kind of serious whimsy. The good-faith dog audience ("Here I am, reading half-legally/to you, wolfhounds and hound-dogs"), his own persona as "earless Moscow mutt/who has no medals", and invocation of Ferlinghetti as "a red wolf, in grey sheep's skin,/A lamb in wolf's clothing," fuse into the call for a poetry "without translation" and "No English-Russian dictionary." "Bureaucrats, drop dead!" reads a mid-way line. "Fangs bared" understanding, as the canine metaphor continues, is summoned at the close. It makes for Russo-Beat voice at best pitch, Voznesensky's typically keen, intriguing trope for freedom of, and for, the creative spirit.

Other poems in *Dogalypse* work to shared imaginative ends. "American Buttons," as a portrait of slogans "shouting at the top of their lungs" and "sarcastic" as in "Make Love Not War" and "Ronald Reagan is a lesbian," and with its imagined sighting of "Allen, Allen, Allen," invokes Greenwich Village as Beat center of gravity, a counter to "*booboisie*" America. "Strip-tease on Strike" moves on from an actual New York labor dispute ("Strip-pers are striking/the cancan loose in the streets") to the ways "Coverers-up of the world" have so often sought to hide Art's necessarily artful own truths. Examples include Venus de Milo "done . . . up /in a short-sleeve, polka-dot house-dress" and Holy Fathers "cover[ing] up crotches/ in the Sistine Chapel." "The world longs to be naked" ends the poem, yet one more voicing of the Beat-like desideradum in the stripping of all ideological or political obfuscation ("The Iron Curtain has come down!").

Antiworlds, Voznesensky's 1967 collection, offers perhaps as key Beat an instance as any in the repertoire: "A Beatnik's Lament, The Revolt of The Machines."[46] The allusions again give off a startling unexpectedness as the poem imagines a world given over to the ungentle mercies of its own cyber-technology ("Machines as barbarous as Baru Khan/have enslaved us men"). A Ginsbergian note sounds unmistakably at the outset—"Howling, caterwauling, hordes of fuming machines repeat/ Their cry: "Meat! Human meat!" Luddites are summoned in memory. Cyber-underlings drink gas-oline in court. Machines demand sexual access to their creators' wives. Women birth radioactive Rolls-Royces. The soul appears like a hanged vic-tim in "the city's back alleys." Time "whistles by" always "enigmatic as a griffin/with a Duraluminum chassis." This vision of discord, machine over maker, affords yet another basis to credit Voznesensky with his own unique degree of Beat status.

*   *   *

"The Allen Ginsberg of Japan" pronounced Kenneth Rexroth, early to rec-ognize, and promote, the poetry of Kazuko Shiraishi. "We may as well be husband and wife" witnessed Ginsberg himself, however unlikely the pros-pect for him of heterosexual marriage. "Exclamations of fierce energy and playfulness" would add an admiring Anne Waldman. For Donald Keene, dean of Japanologists, she has ranked as "the outstanding poetic voice of her generation of disengagement in Japan." As far away as England, and as long ago as 1986, the arts critic and journalist, Waldemar Januszczak, speaks in *The Guardian* of her having "for forty years . . . buzzed around the vanguard of Japanese poetry."

Now in her late seventies (she was born in Vancouver in 1931 moving back to Japan with her father, a leading journalist, and mother, in 1937), the Waseda University-educated Shiraishi continues to hold sway as jazz and poetry avant-garde, translator of Beat texts, and a cross-media performance phenomenon quite unlike any previously known in Japan. Since she made her bow in 1951 with *Tamago No Furu Machi*, differently translated as *Falling Egg City* and *The Town That Rains Eggs*, an oblique and Dalí-influenced poetic vista on the drab, fallen Tokyo of the immediate postwar, her more than twenty volumes of poetry, stories and essay-work have gone on to win her a unique place in Japanese annals and prize-giving (not least the prestigious Yomiuri Literature Award and Emperor's *shijuhosho* or Purple Ribbon Medal).[47]

A 1982 collection like *Little Planet and Other Poems* bears witness to her sustained inventive power, especially "Little Planet" itself as translated by Allen Ginsberg.[48] Its nuanced outcry against the arms race and eco-pollution ("green blood dries") takes on a moving severity in lines like "The Whale gets harpooned before/he sends singing Telepathy of love." As important a collection as any has been *Let Those Who Appear* (2002), which gathers much of her post-1980s writing, and in which the footfalls of her Beat and Tokyo alienation years can still be discerned even amid quite new vistas and interrogations (notably the visionary summoning of landscape, time and language in "Little Planet" as title-poem, or a witty, querying self-colloquy like "I and I").[49]

To staider Japan she has served as, and remains, a shock-horror figure with her ready sexual reference. Notoriety quickly settled about her. On the basis of Eros poems like "The Man Root," "Spring," "Once Again, The Season of The Sacred Lecher," "Phallus," and "Phallic Root"—all of them at once playful, and actually concerned with human generative energy, she became known as "the penis poet." Further controversy gathered about her for her un-Japanese affinity with individual over group style, her various white-suit, harlequin and multi-color dress styles, celebrated birthday parties, and relish of the movies and Shibuya or Ropongi nightlife with their menus of jazz, dance-till-dawn nightclubs, transvestite and strip joints and neon liveliness and multimedia. Her 1940s early membership of the Tokyo-based VOU modernist group with Katsue Kitazono, Pound ally and correspondent at its helm, supplies yet earlier evidence, along with an always wry lack of deference to Japan's patriarchal cultural, and certainly political, establishment.

To admirers, in all these respects, she has long incarnated a welcome "other" Japan. Nor has she ever thought herself bound by heritage to write yet more haiku and tanka, or recycle *ukiyo* (floating world) cultural formulae. Rather she has worked to create her own unique Japanese blend of surrealism and the erotic, with debts to Miró, Gaudí, Dalí and to the Dada movement. Her internationalism has been much aided by ongoing participation and feed-back at UNESCO, European, Australian, Mexican, African and different East-West Asian festivals, and by her frequent stays and visits to the USA, among them the year she spent in 1976 and her participation in the Iowa International Writing Program in 1978. The upshot has been a poetry at once eclectic in scope and yet individually marked by her daring of image.

In every kind of stage and club venue, and in various film documentaries, the sight and sound of her reading from unfurling poetry-scrolls in counterpoint to jazz names like Sam Rivers, Leo Smith, Itaru Oki, John Handy, Abby Lincoln, David McKay, Frank Morgan, Nobuyoshi Ino and Kazutoki Umezu, has become the very essence of her public persona. So, at least, she has been heard, and seen, not the least in the company of Ginsberg and Voznesensky, at poetry gatherings from Tokyo to Rotterdam, San Francisco to Milan, along with all the multifarious Asian venues whether in Japan itself or South Korea or Bangla Desh. A translator, especially, of Ginsberg, and arranger of his 1988 "Allen Ginsberg in Tokyo" visit, as in turn several times "translated" by him, and by Rexroth, who would get her published as a New Directions author, and by names like John Solt, Ikuko Atsumi, Samuel Grolmes and Yumiko Tsumura, it would be impossible to designate Kazuko Shiraishi anything short of a literary force of nature. She continues to feature as a doyenne of poetry and jazz performance.

A usual term has been *furyo shojo* or bad girl/black sheep, a poet of *yoki*, meaning life-mystery or atmosphere of magic, together with a flair for *fukyowaon* or engagingly discordant (and to be sure Japanese) sound. Each of these, inevitably, defies full translation into English. But it cannot surprise that among other western influences, apart from the Beats themselves, she early found herself drawn to Dylan Thomas as 1950s-60s poet-miscreant, to Kafka, and to different lines of magic realist as much as surrealist art and writing.

These all find their reflection in *Seinaru Inja No Kisetsu* (1970), or *Seasons of Sacred Lust*, the volume most generally taken to locate Shiraishi as Japanese Beat poet.[50] In "Once Again, The Season of The Sacred Lecher," the closing poem, she sees the world as though from Outer Space, islands of Manila-like death and pain to be eased only by the creative spirit, "eros and beauty", and more particularly still, a 1976 last-of-the-night blues-and-jazz composition in Tokyo's Shinjuku. It can be reasonably taken for her own cosmic state-of-the-union, the "lechery" of the changing seasons as against the sexlessness of bombs and war. A Beat threesome of poems do connecting further service.

In "My America" and "My Tokyo" Shiraishi writes a kind of Beat diptych, two fond-unfond visions of West and East, two visions of modernity, and each pitched in a voice intimate yet estranged and full of vernacular turn. The former's opening verses give the flavor. In the form of a love letter to an American lover, it could not be more self-affectingly talky, flirtatious—"You've got me on the line . . . My darling darling America." If the poem bespeaks personal intimacy ("my private, custom-made America") there is also an implied critique—invocations of America's "egotism" and "money lust," and a social order of race lines and divisions the poem calls "your infernal barbecue." But for the speaker the America that most counts is that which connects her lover to Lou Rawls or Muddy Waters, a relationship of "eating, fighting, making love, traveling." It is to summon, from across-the-Pacific Japan, and from Tokyo's Harajuku as specifically named counter-culture quarter, Shiraishi's own Beat or, to be more precise, Afro-Beat America.

"My Tokyo" exudes a connecting charge. The Japanese capital, however, is one in which "October's knocked me up/With boredom" and which has been weighed down, and corruptly regularized, with "sullen concrete." Only in "poetry and art," or Sandra "a "stunning lesbian" dancer, or "My first meeting with Henry Miller," or hearing Max Roach's drumming, lies redemption. This is Tokyo as the city "that's almost a womb," grey and still figuratively if not actually ash-covered from wartime bombs, and against which "new melody," be it jazz or visions of exuberant sex ("Let's dive beneath the sheets!" and "my tail thrashing as furiously as a crocodile of hatred") need to be counter-posed. The poem speaks for life over stasis, a newborn, and flamboyant as need be, realm of the senses.

"Dedicated to John Coltrane" with its opening of "Suddenly/ He went to heaven," could not more offer a Beat encomium, a celebration of high-risk musical genius ('Full of fleeting eternity," "So full of romanticism and power"). Coltrane, for Shiraishi, personifies solar majesty, soul. She invokes him as "Orange sun, African sun, American sun/ The taste of human sun." As if, too, to write her own beatifying riff, she closes with a run-on of "Your music, your voice/Your glory and rage/Your love and conviction." Coltrane, thereby, serves as inspiration, exemplary human spirit, Shiraishi's own Beat-American jazz avatar against un-Beat Japanese conformity.

* * *

Three voices, three realms: The UK, Russia, Japan. Writing, assuredly to their own measure, Horovitz, Voznesensky and Shiraishi confirm the international ripple-effect of Beat as a poetry, a historic current of voice. This is not to imply that they have not also pursued directions of interest or line quite of their own fashioning, however willing the acknowledgements to Ginsberg or Kerouac, Corso or Ferlinghetti as inspiration. For whether seen as Beat, or Beat-related, they have each been at once symptomatic yet wholly particular, in adding a transnational circuit, perhaps more aptly a transnational counter-circuit, to the legacy.

Part II
Outriders

5 Gonzo Scripts
Hunter S. Thompson

Gonzo journalism . . . is a style of "reporting" based on William
Faulkner's idea that the best fiction is far more *true* than any kind of
journalism . . .

> —Hunter Thompson, Jacket Copy (unused) for
> *Fear and Loathing in Las Vegas:*
> *A Savage Journey to the Heart of*
> *the American Dream* (1971)[1]

So much for Objective Journalism. Don't bother to look for it here—
not under any byline of mine . . .

> —Hunter Thompson, *Fear and Loathing:*
> *The Campaign Trail '72* (1973)[2]

The real power in America is held by a fast-emerging new Oligarchy
of pimps and preachers who see no need for Democracy or fairness
or even trees . . .

> —Hunter Thompson, *Kingdom of Fear:*
> *Loathsome Secrets of a Star-Crossed Child in the*
> *Final Days of the American Century* (2003)[3]

The gun suicide at his Owl Farm home, Woody Creek, Colorado, in February 2005, then the cannon and fireworks scattering of his ashes organized by the actor Johnny Depp who had played him in Terry Gilliam's
film of *Fear and Loathing* (1998), gave a due reminder of Hunter Thompson. Shakespeare's "Nothing in his life/Became him like the leaving it"
could hardly less have applied.[4] Customary versions of Thompson continue
to see in him the manic true-life figure behind the Uncle Duke of Gary
Trudeau's Doonesbury's strip (a cartoon for which he initially threatened
"to set Trudeau on fire"). Was he not American journalism's best-known
roustabout, the reporter as event, vauntingly taken up with drink, drugs,
motorbikes and gun ownership, and for whom, at the time, the typewriter
seemed almost a military armament?

This was the Thompson ever to be thought the eye of the storm, even if
in his later years he came to rue expectations that he would invariably act
out in person the Gonzo persona figured in his writing. It began early—the
Kentucky-raised 1950s High School youth who did a month's jail time as

accessory to a robbery, the airman honorably discharged in Florida but whose commanding officer thought him possessed of a "rebel and superior attitude," and the one-time Night Manager of the O'Farrell Theatre in San Francisco with its 24-hour strip shows. Thereafter the route into fame would see him a copyboy at *Time*, a sportswriter in Puerto Rico, a stringer in the Caribbean, a *National Observer* correspondent in South America and Brazil and for whose columns he would continue writing well into the 1960s, and a columnist for the Berkeley-based radical *Spider Magazine*. Each, together with the biker piece Carey McWilliams commissioned for *The Nation*, led to *Hell's Angels: The Strange and Terrible Saga of the Outlaw Motorcycle Gangs* (1966), the stunning, amply deserved bestseller with which he made his bow.[5]

It seemed but a further sliver of time before Thompson was everywhere, a name from counter-culture house journals like *Rolling Stone* (for whom he wrote from 1970 to 1984) and the short-lived *Scanlan's Monthly*, and besides *The Nation*, a contributor to established outlets like *Esquire*, *The New York Times Magazine*, *Playboy* and the *San Francisco Examiner*. Even his signature couture took on its own familiarity, the trademark sun-glasses, cigarette holder, sneakers, baseball and other hats, rumpled Hawaiian shirts, and ever thinning pate. But Thompson as rowdie, leftie-conservative, drinker and pill-popper, at once NRA member and supporter of the National Organization for the Reform of Marijuana Laws, and the eventually holed-up Rocky Mountain sentinel, at quite the same time always laid claim to something altogether more consequential: author-virtuoso, a stylist of real daring.

New Journalism does only part justice. The label falls short on the exhilarating thread and pace of his writing, his winning miscreant instinct for political and other venality backed, as it seemed, by funds of coruscating invective wit. As the one conscientiously scripted firestorm follows another—politics, religion, Congress, Vietnam, Nixon, Haight-Ashbury, the Beats, pet hates like the city of Phoenix, TV, even journalism itself, it became increasingly evident that not only was he about his own Notes from Underground but a hard-won idiom to match. His more memorable *obiter dicta* continue to bear witness, be it LSD and marijuana ("I wouldn't recommend sex, drugs or insanity for everyone, but they've always worked for me") or gothic sense of vocation ("When the going gets weird, the weird turns pro").[6]

The America of this envisioning, above all politics as a tainted but irresistible carousel from Johnson, through Nixon, Ford, Carter, Reagan, Bush Sr., and Clinton, to Bush Jr., albeit in different degrees, gave him a trove of targets for the skewering of betrayal, double-standard, and sanctimoniousness. Accordingly, and across a huge and still to be completely published roster of writing, Thompson's voice comes across as suffused in well-taken grievance, near Swiftian distemper. It would be impossible not to take account of the "aggressively subjective" stance as it has been called.[7]

Thompson, or his working persona, becomes the teller accorded more than equal part with the tale, and certainly more than supposed New Journalist club-members like the Norman Mailer of *Advertisements for Myself* (1959), the Truman Capote of *In Cold Blood* (1966) or the Tom Wolfe of *The Kandy-Kolored Tangerine-Flake Streamline Baby* (1965) and *Electric Kool-Aid Acid Test* (1968).[8]

Yet for all the counter-strikes and riffs, not to say the often wickedly funny taste for aphorism, swine allusions, and bar-room scatology, it is a voice kept rigorously in harness, genuinely sure of step. That would extend to *The Curse of Lomo* (1983), the roistering text and image portrait of Hawai'i he did with Ralph Steadman (especially in the sumptuous art-house reprint of 2005), *Screwjack* (1991), his collection of short-story metafictions, and *The Rum Diary* (1998), his early novel of journalist adventuring in Puerto Rico.[9] Further confirmation lies to hand in his compelling and hugely energetic two volumes of correspondence, *The Proud Highway: The Saga of a Desperate Southern Gentleman 1955–1967* (1997) and *Fear and Loathing in America: The Brutal Odyssey of an Outlaw Journalist 1968–1976* (2000), late autobiography like *The Kingdom of Fear: Loathsome Secrets of a Star-Crossed Child in the Final Days of the American Century* (2002), his savaging of the Bush Jr. presidency in *Hey Rube: Blood Sport, The Bush Doctrine, and the Downward Spiral of Dumbness: Modern History from the Sports Desk* (2004), and his lifetime of talented photography.[10] Gonzo self-theatre there may have been in most that he wrote, a taste for hyperbole or shock metaphor, but from start to finish and across a prodigious output Thompson showed himself formidably in command of his own dark laughter.

*   *   *

"My dealings with the Angels lasted about a year, and never really ended" runs an observation a few chapters into *Hell's Angels: A Strange and Terrible Saga*.[11] It sounds almost mild. But Thompson's insignia were quick to show themselves, the reporter in his own words as indeed the "participant in the scene," along with the ply of editorial into reportorial voice.[12] If, against the grain, the California Hell's Angels biker phenomenon was to be thought as much authentic America as Main Street, then Thompson showed himself the readiest chronicler in spirit. His purview takes in the biker outlaw myth as existential theatre, the freeway death-risks, the den pugilism and other rules, the colors and chains, the begrimed Levis and leather jacketing, the worship of the Harley-Davidson, and the freeway rumbles, stomping, drinking, gang-bangs and mamas and ol' ladies. It made for a rare debut, subject-matter not for the faint of spirit, writing beyond the expected norms of documentary reportage.

Vintage Thompson, moreover, was on offer from the outset. "The Menace is loose again," he begins, "the Hell's Angels, the hundred-carat headline, running fast and loud on the early morning freeway, low in the saddle . . . like Genghis Kahn on an iron horse, a monster steed with a fiery anus . . . " (3). Even so, and for all that Thompson anything but holds back on his relish of the bikers as edge culture, to include the rides with them and drink sessions in his apartment, he keeps his portrait at a certain arm's length. *Hell's Angels* has all his characteristic shots across the bow ("To see a lone Angel screaming through traffic—is to understand the motorcycle as an instrument of anarchy, a tool of defiance and even a weapon" [85]), but it can also exhibit a meticulous sociology. He is typically shrewd as to the California working-class origins of the bikers and their place in America's overall social strata. The Angel-cop nexus (and the various official State and Federal enquiries and court sentences) likewise gets scrutiny as do the shifting contours of press reaction—in the case of the Hearst newspapers the initial hoodlum demonization and then, in order to create a contrast with leftist Vietnam protesters, a kind of grudging patriot recognition.

Thompson's eye narrows impressively on several fronts. He delves into the accuracy or otherwise of a screen landmark like Brando's *The Wild One* (1954), the pathology of a key Biker chieftain like Freewheelin Frank, the contrast of 1960s Beat-hippiedom with the Angels and the Ken Kesey-Owsley-Ginsberg LSD partying, and with a nod towards the ready columns of groupies, the brute, mean ritual of Biker gang rape ("the most painful and degrading kind of sex assault" [181]). The brief account he gives of his own near-fatal stomping on Labor Day 1966 for venturing too close serves as an apt epilogue ("It had been a bad trip . . . fast and wild in some moments, slow and dirty in others" [265]). *Hell's Angels*, from the initial article for *The Nation* to the book, is not quite Thompson in full-out Gonzo style. But the route-markers, style and groundwork, the acuity of ear and eye, are there to be recognized.

*   *   *

Fear and Loathing in Las Vegas: A Savage Journey to the Heart of the American Dream (1971) rightly is said to have delivered Thompson in yet more classic stride, his personal death-knell to who-what-when press objectivity. If, ostensibly, a trip to Las Vegas first to report the Mint 400 bike race some thirteen miles out in the desert, then the meeting on "Narcotics and Dangerous Drugs" of the National District Attorneys' Association, the upshot in Thompson's fashioning becomes black comedy in the tradition of Ambrose Bierce or Nathanael West. The casino capital he renders as a loop of instant gratification, the twenty-four hour gaming, booze, drugs, sex and show-time. Under one or another of his several sobriquets, moreover, notably Raoul Duke or Doctor of Gonzo Journalism, Thompson quite acknowledges how he himself has been drawn into the glut. Nor does he offer himself as flying solo. Not the least of the text's features has to be the wild companion presence of the Chicano activist-lawyer Oscar Zeta Acosta, whom in mock-proprietorship he calls "my attorney" and "the Samoan," together with Ralph Steadman, whose fierce human reptile line-drawings offer perfect visuals to the text at hand.[13] They both serve as imaginative fellow-voyagers into California and Nevada as America through a glass darkly, often enough indeed, as phantasmagoria.

"We're on our way to Las Vegas to find the American Dream" he tells the for good reason increasingly fearsome student-age hitchhiker they pick up when, drug-addled, they speed out of Los Angeles and past Barstow.[14] Their destination, appropriately, is Las Vegas as "Freak Kingdom" (83), and for which they have provisioned themselves with stashes of cocaine, mescaline, pot, whiskey and rum. They also bring their own LSD—"No, this is not a good town for psychedelic drugs. Reality itself is too twisted" (47). The Stones' "Sympathy for the Devil" supplies the sound-wrap just as Dylan's "Memphis Blues Again" will do so later. Their driving takes the form of hire-car zigzag bursts of speed, whether aboard the Chevy Convertible ("The Great Red Shark") or the Cadillac Convertible ("The Whale"). Bar tabs and room-orders become extravaganza, first at the Mint Hotel, whose reservation suite they are quick to trash, and then at the Flamingo, not a little ironically the gaudy convention center for the law-and-order shindig. Oddball encounters recur, whether Thomson with hotel reception staff, rental car people, and lawyers, or Acosta, typically, with clerks, bellhops, and the plaintive runaway girl Lucy. The effect is one of picaresque, a narrative inventory of casino, gaming table, roulette, slots, strip-joints, cops, lawyers, and punters and conventioneers in clothes-styles he judges left over from the 1950s. If indeed this is a snapshot of the American Dream, Las Vegas-style, then it is the Dream betrayed into Sleaze.

Early into the account he even concedes that he is not entirely clear what exactly is the assignment to hand, albeit that the commissioning Sports Magazine has arranged for $300 in cash to be handed over, the rental of the "fire-apple red" car (28) and the unlicensed use of an expense account. Reflexively he professes himself ready to invent as need be—"The only way to prepare for a big trip like this, I felt, was to dress up like human peacocks and get crazy" (12). The rule becomes "Do it now: pure Gonzo journalism" (12). But if spontaneity is all it can also flatter to deceive. Thompson's writing, page for page, and the more especially when it turns comic-grotesque, exhibits seasoned virtuosity, a practiced pen. The wry version of himself and Acosta as "good old boys . . . stoned, ripped, twisted . . . Good People" (29), hallucinatory drug visions like those of the warning giant bats as they drive into Las Vegas, or observations of the kind which holds that "If Charlie Manson actually checked into the Sahara tomorrow morning, nobody would hassle him as long as he tipped big" (106), hardly come about by random or easy of-the-moment wit.

The account of the DA conference yields Thompson at special strength, alert to the paradox of the gathering ("a crowd that was convened for the stated purpose of putting people like us in jail" [109]) and of a handed-around report on "Drug Fiends" which he wastes no time in pinning down as "dangerous gibberish" (139). In his annotation of this boondoggle realm of wonders, he takes special pleasure in wearing the tag "Private Investigator," a Burroughs-like incognito yet "which was true, in a sense" (141). His observations will include a "344-pound police chief from Waco, Texas necking openly with his 290-pound wife" (143), a conversation with one of the cops in which Acosta seeks to persuade him that in Malibu "goddamn Satan-worshippers kill six or eight people *every day*" (146), and runs of conspiratorial law-speak amid the reactionary heartiness and taste for copious drink. In shared spirit Thompson speaks of the times as "the doomstruck era of Nixon" (178) and "this foul year of our Lord 1971" (201), his version of the End of Days rather than any conventional calendar. Nothing, he further insists, is actually to be learned from the drugs conference, as borne out in the fine trade he does guying each shock-horror and law-and-order cliché. As road trip, and Las Vegas close-encounter, *Fear and Loathing in Las Vegas* offers a kind of personal war-diary, reporting from the trenches. For good reason it has become a landmark, Thompson's star performance.

*   *   *

Fear and Loathing on the Campaign Trail '72 (1973), the Nixon-McGovern presidential contest and its run-up, was conceived according to the Author's Note as "a kind of cinematic reel-record of what the campaign was like *at the time*."[15] The diorama could not be busier, or more exact, a year's playlist of candidates, deals done, cover-ups, backrooms, agendas out-front and hidden. *Rolling Stone*'s observer-eye he may be, but Thompson typically makes no secret of his own partisanship as a McGovern man, with plaudits for Gene McCarthy and a young Gary Hart. The rest, even at times Teddy Kennedy who otherwise wins his favor, become a rogue's gallery of runners and horses, each marvelously and unsparingly snared within his patrolling skepticism, his self-acknowledged Gonzo thunders of irreverence. "More a jangled campaign diary than a record or reasoned analysis of the '72 presidential campaign" (6) is his own verdict. But "jangled" falls some way short on the evident orchestration to his telling of events and displays of working savvy.

From arrival in Washington DC, an account he prefaces with a photograph of a "DO NOT ENTER" road-sign against the Capitol as background, through to Nixon's landslide victory ("Nixon Uber Alles" as he calls it), the election cycle is imaged as fever, a corrupt modern betrayal of the Republic's founding probity. Interviews, judicious excerpts from other journals and position-papers, photography and more Steadman drawings, so build into rolling documentary. Thompson leave no doubt of the presiding themes—Vietnam, drug controversy, the Nixon-Agnew mantra of law and order (with Goldwater and Reagan as hovering guardians of the

Right), and McGovern's unexpected emergence from the Democratic pack together with Tom Eagleton, revealed to have had longstanding drink and mental problems, as Vice-Presidential catastrophe.

Almost all the frontline names provoke his dismay. None more embodies the fall from grace than Nixon, nominated in Miami to the cry of "Four More Years," who combines the roles of Evil Spirit ("the werewolf in us") and homegrown Artful Dodger.[16] Thompson pitches into him at every turn, Nixon the sweatily devious but shrewd Mephistopheles, Nixon the burglar in the White House. Yet he becomes oddly deserving, for Thompson, of his devil's due. "He has been a professional pol all his life . . . He understands that politics is a rotten, frequently degrading business that corrupts everybody who steps in it, but this knowledge no longer bothers him" (325). Humphrey is to be seen as "doomed and useless" (42) and "the most disgusting example of a political Animal in America today" (186). George Wallace features as "one of the worst charlatans in politics" (255). Ed Muskie, who many Democrats hope will save them from McGovern, is said to resemble "a three-toed sloth" (142). Behind-the-scenes operators like Chicago's Richard Daley and the AFL-CIO's George Meany he thinks "senile leeches" (109). As political theatre it could not more be plot and counterplot, each self-advantaging candidature, each shortfall between shadow and reality. Whether, in truth, all amounts to the unashamed double-dealing Thompson alleges may be beside the point. His take on the reach for power, honed, full of characteristic flair, accusatory, sees in a politics which in 1972 re-enthrones Richard Milhous Nixon nothing less than the betrayal of the Republic.

*   *   *

The availability of Thompson's journalism in the form of his four volumes of Gonzo Papers has been of immense service, a key thesaurus.[17] Taken together they represent foremost his "guilty addiction" to the power-politics of which he speaks with deliciously well-chosen allusions to William Burroughs, the Marquis de Sade, H.L. Mencken, and films like *Caligula* and *All The King's Men*.[18] That is not to overlook his other points of focus, from the Kentucky Derby to Muhammad Ali, from an obituary for Oscar Zeta Acosta to extracts from his novels *Prince Jellyfish* and *The Rum Diary*. Whatever else the collections signify, they amount to stunning quantity, sheer reportorial plenty. Given Thompson's readiness for booze and chemicals, and how he managed to sustain so formidable a productivity, has long been a matter worthy of note. None of it, furthermore, dimmed his ability to capture the Zeitgeist in his own marauder's prose, the urgent flair, the razor wit.

The Great Shark Hunt offers a characteristic table of contents. The span runs from the opening Kentucky Derby piece, with Thompson telling a Texas good old boy that Churchill Downs is about to be invaded by the

Black Panthers and a posse of poor-white Appalachians and then lurching into drunken revels with Ralph Steadman, through to the 1978 Ali-Spinks title fights in Las Vegas and then New Orleans. Both pieces show him in phrase-making sharp form. "Pink faces with a stylish Southern sag" (34) is how he pinpoints local Kentucky race-goers. Of Ali he waxes positively contemplative as possessing "a sense of himself so firmly entrenched that it seems to hover, at times, in that nervous limbo between Egomania and genuine Invulnerability" (563). These and other sports pieces, whether the 1973 NFL Super Bowl in a riotous Houston whose Lombardi winner's trophy he thinks "has all the style and grace of an ice floe in the North Atlantic" (76) or the ski-craft Jean-Claude Killy whose "whole secret is his feverish concentration" (88), indicate a Thompson as much capable of articulating the grace of first-tier athletics as of the roiling stew of politics.

Nonetheless it is politics that gives the collection its fulcrum and nowhere more bracingly than in sequences on Nixon and Watergate, from the Woodward and Bernstein *Washington Post* scoop of the cover-up, through the Ervin hearings, and on to the resignation and Ford pardon. "The Strange and Terrible Saga of Richard Nixon" (289), as always, magnetizes Thompson's creative hatred—"He is a monument to the old Army rule that says: 'The only *real* crime is getting caught' " (281). Observations become a headwater, among them "Nixon and his personal Gestapo" (311), "the Nixon Deathwatch" (315), "The man was born *guilty*" (321), "Nixon's awesome tape-recording system" (337) and, a kind of 1973 provisional epilogue, "He will rest for a while now, then come back to haunt us again" (339). Nixon, for Thompson, resides at the very center of the malignity, ever more so as the saga unravels from the burglary itself, then the denials, the Enemies List, the presidential broadcasts, the tapes, the gathering threat of impeachment, and the eventual helicopter flight out from the White House lawn with a grimly smiling and waving death's head Nixon. Thompson manages a nice touch of journalist faux-confession, not out of keeping, when he concedes his own eager membership "in the ranks of all the Watergate junkies" (320).

Throughout "Fear and Loathing at the Watergate," to invoke another of his choices of heading, Thompson follows the chronology of events faithfully enough. But he suffuses each turn of the wheel with his own Washington adventuring, at once the *Rolling Stone* "Gonzo journalist" (250) and precisely the non-"nine-to-five" adventurer.[19] The whole affair becomes "this stinking Watergate summer" (253). As he contemplates the role of Tex Colson, Nixon apparatchik and (quoting Pat Buchanan) "the meanest man in politics" (259), he entertains the fantasy of "dragging (Colson) down Pennsylvania tied behind a huge gold "Oldsmobile Cutlass" (254). John Dean at the hearing exudes what he calls "nasal blank-hearted authority" (263). He summons "an ugly parallel" (289) of a beleaguered Nixon with Hitler in his bunker (289), adding the comment "The trial of Richard Nixon, if it happens, will be the *de facto* trial of the American Dream"

(299). Once Nixon is gone, and having raked over most of the henchmen, notably Mitchell ("an arrogant, triple-chinned Roman" [334]), Ehrlichman, Haldeman, Ziegler, Hunt, and Liddy (dismissed as "some yo-yo," [334]), he orders a smoking-section seat in the flight-out to Denver under the name "R. Nader" (308). His verdict on Watergate, and the pardon in particular, is as terse as it is damning—"Richard Nixon is free now. He bargained wisely and well" (339).The barb carries Thompson to perfection from life into word.

Generation of Swine, in its different political and cultural maps of the 1980s, gives no let-up to folly. Thompson's taste for signs of the times stays as keen as ever, from Reagan confused and wrong-footed abroad with Gorbachev in Reykjavik in 1986 to the evangelist fraternity of Oral Roberts, Jimmy Swaggart, the Bakkers and Pat Robertson spouting sin and redemption on TV. Reagan, "dumber than three mules" (58), he portrays as at the brink of dotage itself ("He is a 77-year old man who was once the best salesman of his time. But now he is like Willie Loman" [186]). Of the evangelists he asks "Are these TV preachers *all* degenerates?" with a special swipe reserved for Swaggart as "a 52-year-old howler from Baton Rouge" (21) when he, Bakker, and others, are hauled into court for their respective financial scams. Their flesh-mongering, equally shabby to a fault, he even compares unfavorably with England's Regency practitioners of vice. For him it is dumbness in the White House, dumbness in the church-house. Put another way he designates American politics a "profoundly atavistic sport" (260), and the preacher born-agains a "phalanx of righteousness" fighting "desperately with the forces of Satan and the shame of their own kind" (227). Little wonder both continued to attract his antennae, his deflationary skills.

Much of the rest of the 1980s gallery comes in for like measure. The spectacle runs through the brute Duvalier-inherited rule of the Ton-Tons in Haiti, Key West as "the last stop in the weird chain of islands that run south of Miami like a national coccyx bone on the swollen spine of Florida (91), and Ferdinand Marcos as "a man who ran the whole Philippine islands for 26 years like it was some kind of personal dog kennel" (109). He does a full hatchet job on Oliver North, "apparently beserk" (196) as he operates the Iran-Contra scam, with Reagan, Ed Meese and the CIA's William Casey as cynical aiders and abetters. Jimmy Carter is skewered as "an awesome bungler who gave once-proud political values like 'decency' and 'honesty' a bad name" (258). These, and other derelictions of the era, he prefaces with a wonderful expression of debt to the Book of Revelation—"the wild power of the language and the purity of the madness that governs and makes it music" (9). He could well have been speaking of his own idiom and, at its best, his unique encapturing of the many declines and falls to hand.

Songs of The Doomed, in offering selective coverage of four decades from the 1950s forward, yields not only a recapitulation of past work but another manifesto-in-small. Sent to report in Vietnam for *Rolling Stone*,

Thompson unsuccessfully attempts an interview with Colonel Vo Don Giang of the PRG (Provisional Revolutionary Government). In part his letter reads "I'm not an especially good typist, but I'm one of the best writers currently using the English language as both a musical instrument and a political weapon . . ."[20] Language as music and politics, in its combined Orwellian footfall, could not provide a better fit. The revels begin with Thompson assuming his Raoul Duke persona as if to win him out of hiding in Beverly Hills in 1990 after the Colorado police investigate his Woody Creek home for suspected drugs, and assaulting Gail Palmer, a one-time porn queen. For him, even after the 99-day trial in which all charges were dropped, it was actual enough life but also a case of fact imitating fiction.

Each decade is given its identifying marker. The 1950s he recalls through his early job as a Sports editor in up-state Pennsylvania ("I had to join the goddamn Elks Club to get a drink there on the weekends" [29]) and his early novel-writing. The 1960s has him remembering his Puerto Rico sojourn and his reaction to the John Kennedy assassination ("all of a sudden that day the country looked different to me, and I felt very bad about it" [101]). That, in its turn, may have linked into his forays into the 1960s' more radical reaches, an America of the edges, or at least of the litany he says beckoned—"Berkeley, Hell's Angels, Kesey, blacks, hippies . . . I had these connections. Rock and roll" (112). *Hell's Angels* indeed would be the upshot, as would his memory of the 1968 Chicago Democratic convention in all its noise and heat and of his run (at a time when he first took mescaline) for Sheriff in Aspen.

The 1970s have him organizing a seminar of like minds in Elko to create a new political direction for the Republic (" '68 had politicized me" [163]). Its point, as he formulates it with a nice smack of vernacular, is to ask "Was Thomas Jefferson a dingbat?" (169). Put more soberly the issue was betrayal, the bloodying of the nation's Enlightenment promissory ethos of liberty. Journalist trips to Vientiane and Saigon follow, Vietnam—"the war"—as chancre, bloodletting. America he sees in the role of neo-colonial occupier, hence the letter to Colonel Giang. He bows out from *Rolling Stone*, no longer for him the "Outlaw magazine" (175), while re-affirming in a 1977 letter to Jim Silberman that "the only real difference between 'journalism' and 'fiction' in my mind is *legalistic*" (203). The 1980s he summons under the logo "How Much Money Do You Have?", pieces to do with the Hawai'i marathon in all its island tourist chic and the cannibalistic Herbert "Pete" and Roxanne Pulitzer millionaire divorce case on Florida's Gold Coast. "What is it," he asks, "about being born free and beyond worry that drives people crazy?" (222). Letters to Ralph Steadman (about Hawai'i) and Ken Kesey (about the art of sports writing) add flavor, as do his thoughts on the Dukakis candidacy. For the 1990s he uses press cuttings and a fake third-person voice to detail his own bust on the drugs, dynamite and sex charges and, for him, their breakage of Fourth Amendment rights. Well may the case have been eventually dismissed by the Pitkin

County Court, but the account is written up in terms of out of control drug hysteria. It hardly needs saying that it carries Thompson's symptomatic flair, the astuteness, the coruscating runs of style.

Better Than Sex rounds out the quartet, the Clinton defeat of Bush Sr. ("a dangerously failed president" [106]) in 1992 through to the event which for Thompson was seminal, maybe epochal, the death of Richard Nixon in April 1994. A usual panel of political rocky-horrors has his pen racing. Clinton himself, with whom he exchanges fond correspondence, calls Bubba, and after a bumpy starts gets on with, at the same time becomes a serial of mishaps. They include Gennifer Flowers, the marijuana "didn't inhale" debacle, and always the waistline and what it signifies about still larger Clinton appetite. "My one real fear about Bill Clinton," he summarizes not a little prophetically, "is that he might fail utterly like Jimmy Carter, and bring another 12 years of greedy Republican looting" (198). There is a bevy of shots at the likes of Ross Perot ("the nightmare" [71]).

But, finally, no doubt inevitably, it is Nixon, this time in the form of his absolutely last bow-out, that concentrates his attention. "Richard Nixon is gone now, and I am the poorer for it. He was the real thing—a political monster straight out of Grendel and a very dangerous enemy" (239–41). Thompson never saw himself other than as a patriot, the fists-up guardian of a heritage he believed ever under threat by political malfeasance and in no more dangerous a personification than Nixon. Unforgiving, wrathful, parodic, and assuredly memorable, this faux-obituary confirms him once more speaking his own kind of truth to power.

*   *   *

Late published compilations like *Hey Rube* and *Kingdom of Fear* bequeath a fitting round-up of Thompson's lifetime's coverage, more aptly counter-coverage, of the American political-cultural waterfront. The former, taken from his ESPN network sports and commentary columns, the latter a recapitulation of scenes from his Kentucky boyhood through to the O.J. Simpson affair, give their reminders of how Thompson's journalism has stayed vital, distinctive. "It never got weird enough for me" runs one of his often cited lines.[21] Whether the reality was the 1960s in all its period contradiction, each Democratic and Republican convention and then campaign, Nixon as blighted spirit of the age, an America as he saw it sinking into political senescence under Reagan, the Clinton years of sex and yet political virtuosity, or Bush Jr. as more betrayal of the American Dream, he kept to the belief that this was reality made unreal, a pageant of true lies. It was a writer's view, a view filtered through his (dare one say) inveterately literary imagination.

Yet though he had no hesitation in speaking of himself as a writer, or invoking admired names from Melville to Faulkner, he never played less than true to his calling as a journalist. Which, in turn, is not to underplay his sense of the kind of outlaw literary writer company to which he thought he belonged. As he told George Plimpton in a *Paris Review* interview in 2000—"we were all outside the law: Kerouac, Miller, Burroughs, Ginsberg, Kesey; I didn't have a gauge as to who was the worst outlaw. I just recognized allies: my people."[22] The point could not be more pertinent. Writing *in propria persona*, or under one or another of his Gonzo hats, his histories of the present have justly earned their "outside the law" status. But that is far from regarding them as mere flourish. To the contrary: American journalism has rarely witnessed a savvier reportorial pen and at the same time more politically intelligent fun, Thompson's counter-scripts as nothing less than counter-art.

6   A View of One's Own
Joan Didion

> But our notebooks give us away, for however dutifully we record what
> we see around us, the common denominator of all we see is always,
> transparently, shamelessly, the implacable "I."
>
> —Joan Didion, "On Keeping a Notebook" (1966)[1]

> I write entirely to find out what I'm thinking, what I'm looking at,
> what I see and what it means.
>
> —Joan Didion, "Why I Write" (1976)[2]

> We interpret what we see, select the most workable of the multiple
> choices.
>
> —Joan Didion, "The White Album" (1979)[3]

Didion the outrider? The label might at first jar given the fierce acclaim
she has garnered. Collections like *Slouching Towards Bethlehem* (1968)
and *The White Album* (1979) long have invited estimation of her as a
doyenne of the discursive form, routinely—if by no means accurately—to
be thought one of New Journalism's leading spirits.[4] This forte, and the
America it draws upon, extends to *Salvador* (1983), *Miami* (1987), *After
Henry* (1992) and *Political Fictions* (2001), each more a meditation upon
American civilization and its discontents than conventional reportage.[5]
Autobiography, life-writing, assumes place in *Where I Was From* (2003),
her winningly turned California dynastic history, and *The Year of Magical
Thinking* (2005), the intimacy and self-exploratory mourning of the heart
attack loss of her writer-husband John Gregory Dunne with whom she also
won plaudits as a Hollywood screenplay-writer.[6]

How, too, not to take account of the fiction inaugurated with her Cal-
ifornia-dynastic novel *Run River* (1963), given a centerpiece in *Play It As
It Lays* (1968) for its dark, astringent portrait of Marie Wyeth as the personification of Hollywood *anomie*, and which embraces both the shorter
work of *Telling Stories* (1978) and the US and Central American political
trilogy of *A Book of Common Prayer* (1977), *Democracy* (1984) and *The
Last Thing He Wanted* (1996)?[7] Add to the literary career the Didion of
a several-generations Sacramento Valley family lineage, Berkeley education, the success in journals from *Vogue* and *Saturday Evening Post* to
the *New York Review of Books,* and the National Book Award and other

prizes, and there might indeed be wonderment at thinking her on some outrider track.

Yet Didion remains oddly at an angle in American writing, out of the liberal-cultural loop—the early two-time voter for Barry Goldwater, the California-raised Episcopalian by conviction, and the un-celebrant of 1960s liberation. The latter took notably controversial form in "The Women's Movement," her celebrated *New York Review of Books* essay of 1972 ("To those of us who remain committed mainly to the exploration of moral distinctions and ambiguities, the feminist analysis. . . . seemed a particularly narrow and cracked determinism").[8] At the same time she was not about to give hallelujahs to the presiding political or cultural Right: witness her barbs at the Reagan and both the Bush presidencies, or at Born Again religiosity, or at the Iraq war and neo-con ideology and figures like Newt Gingrich. In each case there could be no doubt of her doing other than standing her own ground. A view of her own would seem almost the least of it.

Admirers speak up for the almost five decades of commissioned and free-choice essay-work as not only the busiest shelf but major commentary. If cast in the first-person, this is reportage always tactically circumspect, never intrusive in editorial ideology yet full of viewpoint. The less enamored see in the detachment, the ellipsis, and especially the often lacerating specimen detail, not only a conservative temperament but infinite condescension, by intent or otherwise a cold or at best cool heart. It can hardly surprise that Didion wins both serious discipleship and serious reservation. Either way, and be it the voluminous essay-columns or the storytelling, her soundings have made her one of America's key—and for sure provocative—cultural seismographers. In no more decisive respect does that apply than in her essay and other non-fiction writings.

The coordinates of place and time in her work have become familiar. The geographies look foremost to her native California, its European and Anglo dynasties, its architectures and personalities, its coastlines and sierras, and inerasably, its 1960s-and-after social culture. Whether "old" Sacramento, or Hollywood, or Haight-Ashbury, or a California of drugs and violence, beach and freeway car-culture, or endlessly available hedonism and sexuality, these clearly serve for Didion as the index of an America she has often seemed to believe teetering into cultural dysfunction. New York she summons as at once the magnet of a metropolitan love-affair and yet finally a marathon, a toll on the nerves. Hawai'i features as the intriguing ply of *kanaka* indigenous population, *haoles* and Asians, Pearl Harbor and yet hotels like the Royal Hawaiian and Kahala Hilton as her own Pacific viewing-platforms. Miami she comes at as DC-connected Cuban exile fiefdom, recruitment ground for the Watergate burglars, cocaine economy, and a newly evolving mainland *latinidad*. El Salvador and other Latin America, both actual and invented, she holds in view as the uneasy but compelling overlap of hemispheric tropics and power-play. In each there is again little mistaking the will to view, viewpoint, but also to measure, a necessary sufficiency of judgment.

As to history she has from the outset shown an insistence on the sway of antecedent cause-and-effect in a culture notorious for its impatience with reminders of historical current. "The future always looks good in the golden land, because no one remembers the past" she writes of local, small-town California in "Some Dreamers of the Golden Dream."[9] She goes on emphasizing how America as modernity—its culture and tastes, its politics at home and in the Latin Americas to the south—has even so always been caught in its own formative shadow. For all that *Slouching Towards Bethlehem* and its successor collections offer contemporary panorama, each could not more give emphasis to how the past engrains the present, an America, and especially an American west, whose call to the future has ironically been a veritable past of things-to-come, a tradition in its own right. As to the 1960s especially she makes no secret of how it inscribed a time slipping free of any frame of reference with which she was familiar. As she says in "The White Album," having cited the Robert Kennedy funeral, My Lai, and the case of Betty Lansdown Fouquet who abandoned her five-year old daughter at the divider of Interstate 5 near the Bakersfield Exit—"Certain of these images did not fit into any narrative I knew."[10]

Didion's insistence that writing carry a view, however carefully discreet, lies precisely and unmistakably in phrasings like "the implacable 'I'," "what I'm thinking, what I'm looking at, what I see and what it means," and "we interpret what we see, select the most workable of choices." This attention to the issue of view, or again viewpoint, would not do injustice to, say, Henry James, Joseph Conrad or George Orwell, all names she invokes several times to precisely this end and with great admiration. Not only does it bespeak the resolve to get beyond the consensually managed version it suggests a radical awareness of what for her is the key desideratum of the "reportorial" essay: the constituent perspective, the authorial stance.

For those in her camp this willingness to have gone in close yet to have stood back, wins every favor. Here is the eye lowered brilliantly, acuity managed with exactly the right ironic distance. The less persuaded, however, go on insisting that Didion's writing is disingenuously weighted only in its own favor, arch, a kind of literary spectatorship tainted with disdain. Given these cross-spars, how best to judge the fashioning of viewpoint essay-for-essay? What style of witness does she actually bring to bear to the American insignia of her time, and not a little reflexively in the process, to the implications of her own author's life as Joan Didion?

*   *   *

"Fixed Opinion, Or the Hinge of History" (2002), her reflections on 9/11, offers a symptomatic point of departure.[11] Written in the wake of the World Trade Center calamity it typically pitches, against the grain, for analysis and memory, a necessary awareness of causation and America's role in that causation rather than flags and vengeful patriotism. In this respect she has faced the familiar charge of distance, too great or intellectual a gap between herself and the human pain of the events. Starting, even so, from "my numbed condition" (174), and her then in-process book tour to publicize (of all titles) *Political Fictions*, she opens to scrutiny the way "the war on terror" (176), and assuredly Osama Bin Laden, were being made over into simple diagram, a cartoon of what led to 9/11 and what remedy might best apply. Under the banner of national unity, she argues, politics-as-usual has been all too quick to take hold. With the hints of military payback against Iraq gathering force, with Saddam Hussein responsible or not for 9/11, she sees in the pressure to rally behind the government a tactic to approve the rest of the Bush-Cheney program. This means a yea-saying to corporate tax cuts, to the missile shield and an ever swelling Pentagon budget, and to yet greater state surveillance of the citizenry. The one selective White House politics, on this reckoning, slips into sought-after approval for a whole further political program. As Didion cryptically reminds her reader in a phrase taken from George Bush Sr., this amounts to giving license, even endorsement, to the Bush-Cheney "vision thing."

As to 9/11 itself, an "impenetrably flattening celebration of [the] victims" (177), she suggests, has taken hold. The event has become "manageable, reduced to the sentimental, to protective talismans, tokens, garlands, repeated pieties," with due "loved ones," "families" and "heroes." (176–7). In other words, axially, there has come into play "a troublingly belligerent idealization of historical ignorance" (177). Root causes and processes—Islam, Palestine, Israel, diaspora, the very word *jihad*—become shorn of historical complexity by the ease of simple binary or set-phrase. She cites, as a key instance, the vilification of Susan Sontag in her call for "historical awareness" and the charge that the national leadership all too knowingly infantilized its citizenry ("Inquiry into the nature of the enemy we faced was to be interpreted as sympathy for the enemy"[179]). The only permitted currency all too readily invokes "evildoers" and "wrongdoers" (179)—"axis of evil" would remain in the wings—easy, not to say off-the-shelf, manichaeism.

History, on this reckoning, gets put in abeyance. Little wonder Didion herself, no less than Sontag, would be held up as suspect, some fifth column even, whose very suggestion of complexity, and especially the complex historical irony of the attack, was best to be excoriated as academic, some trivial venture into the postmodern as against the all too beckoning, not to say exploitable, them-and-us narrative. The essay, in fact, links 9/11 to a quite more encompassing lineage of eviscerated public discussion. Why no serious American dissection of "the problems of securing Palestine as a Jewish state" (183)? Why no dissection of arming both the Saudis (oil for arms) *and* the Israelis (an overseas military appropriation second to none)? Why has stem cell and related biological research been caught short by right-to-lifers, the one or another evangelical anti-cloning group? What mock-politics is to be read in both the flag-burners and anti-flag-burners? The list, for her, runs on: the Pledge of Allegiance bracketed to pro-life slogans, secular democracy as un-American with school prayer the truer, better American way, the false localizing and personifying of al-Qaeda in Saddam Hussein, and the neo-con ascendancy of "The New American Uni-lateralism" (192).

She so berates a White House politics, and its rhetoric, whether effort-lessly (and so culpably) or calculatedly un-tethered from history and given to hedged phraseology and sound-bite certitude. Like Orwell before her she indicts the ground-zero leveling of language. "We have come in this coun-try to tolerate many such fixed opinions, or national pieties, each with its own battles of invective and counterinvective, of euphemism and downright misstatement, its own screen that slides into place whenever actual discus-sion threatens to surface" (185). This is "reportage" that carries Didion's own species of health-warning as to the dangers of history skewed by both conservative and liberal wings of partisanship, history as cause-and-effect, a complexity, dispatched to the margins. The upshot is greatly vintage Did-ion, by no means above the fray but unwilling to surrender either way to the easy shot. She again does more than enough to provoke all sides and rarely without a flare of expression to match.

*   *   *

This style of contemplative observation has been evident from the outset. In no respect does Didion give better indicative longitudes and latitudes than in the title-essay of her first collection *Slouching Towards Bethlehem*. In going about the tabulation of Haight-Ashbury as the "alternative" San Francisco of the mid-1960s, at once drop-out youth and drug zone, a near classic moment occurs in an exchange with Norris, resident hippie *com-munard* and her Virgilian companion-guide: "One day Norris asks me how old I am. I tell him I am thirty-two. It takes a few minutes, but Norris rises to it. 'Don't worry,' he says at last, 'There's old hippies too' " (94). This wry use of commentary continues as Arthur Lisch, anarch-radical, associ-ates her with the "media poisoners" (114) and she herself inserts an echo of Spengler in suggesting she has been writing her account "as the West declined in the spring of 1967" (108).

"Slouching Towards Bethlehem" has Norris serve as link to the further Haight-Ashbury tableau, whether the streetwise ex-Hell's Angel Deadeye and his poetry-writing "old lady" Gerry, the acid-user Max, the missing-juvenile Debbie, Lisch and his gimcrack Digger co-radicals Chester Ander-son and Peter Berg, or Officer Arthur Gerrans who has busted nearly all of them. LSD trips are de rigueur. Pot abounds. The sexual go-rounds alleg-edly confirm the flight from middle-class family norms and ego. Busts, dealers and cops make for a near inevitable syndrome. The mood music also includes Hare Krishna chanting, Ginsberg, Vietnam-protest, guitars, and flower-power poetry. The Warehouse, as it is known, where all this is refracted, even becomes half-attractive to her as a species of total or living theater. The upshot, however, goes well beyond logging the spectacle, an observer's gallery. What dynamic, runs the implicit larger question, has produced Haight Ashbury? What America does it annunciate?

"Slouching Towards Bethlehem" everywhere implies a California heading into infantile drift. But this is not mere jeremiad; there is also sympathy, the urge to enter and understand—"We were seeing the desperate attempt of a handful of pathetically unequipped children to create a community in a social vacuum" (122). The sympathy may be barbed ("At some point between 1945 and 1967 we had somehow neglected to tell these children the rules of the game we happened to be playing" [123]), yet at the same time it expresses authentic regret ("an army of children waiting to be given the words" [123]). These she powerfully encapsulates in her essay's closing reference to a Haight Ashbury five-year-old given acid by her mother for over a year. The Yeatsian implication of a center losing hold clearly underpins the California, the America, she is recording, one seen and felt firsthand and yet refracted through her scrupulously clinical prism. The effect, whether one thinks it winning or not, is considerable, the virtuosity indeed of the "imposition of a narrative line on disparate images" as she calls it in "The White Album."[12]

Each of the accompanying essays in *Slouching Towards Bethlehem* equally carries a 1960s keened through her own ordering eye and image. In "Some Dreamers of the Golden Dream," her account of Lucille Miller's murder-trial for the killing and car-burning of her dentist husband, Gordon Miller, symptomatically portrays the San Bernadino Valley where it takes place as a kind of degree-zero attenuation ("devastated by the hot Santa Ana wind," "every voice seems a scream," "prickly dread" [3]). Without overdoing the effect she creates her own version of the Valley of Ashes ("Easy to Dial-A-Devotion, but hard to buy a book" [4]). The small-town Banyan Street where the Millers live serves as existential cul-de-sac, be it Gordon Miller's bankrupt dental practice, the tepid motels and roadside eateries where Lucille Miller conducts her clandestine affair with Arthwell Hayton, the Adventist churchgoing, and even Hayton's would-be flighty ownership of a red Cadillac convertible. These, Didion suggests, along with the local tabloid-sensationalist account of the court-case and penitentiary sentence, might have come straight from a James M. Cain novel.

As she renders it, thus, this is California as no golden sunset but small-town 1930s *film noir*, unadorned human sepia and which she tells in matching "flat" viewpoint. The murder done, the distant inexpressive killer sentenced, the oddly hands-off affair recalled, the text primly observes the "For Sale" notice on the Miller house. It reads PRIVATE ROAD/BELLA VISTA/DEAD END (26). For Didion, clearly, this makes the perfect coda, as does Arthwell Hayton's re-marriage to his children's Norwegian governess, Wenche Berg, whose "illusion veil" at the wedding is held with a "coronet of seed pearls" (28). In her orchestration of all this self-indicating irony of detail viewpoint remains all.

It is an ethos—an aesthetic—Didion usefully identifies in "On Keeping a Notebook" in the middle-sequence "Personals." "*Remember what it was to be me*: that is always the point" (136), she writes. The emphasis is far from egotistical vainglory. It points up her insistence on stance, the exigency of a response through which to negotiate the contrariety of the life before her. If she makes no secret of her neurasthenic headaches, diminutive size, and the frequent shyness and public inarticulacy, she also insists, as if by contrast, on a strong, coherent force of viewpoint. This runs through essay upon essay, whether the screen's masculinity-myth of John Wayne ("Nothing very bad could happen in the dream" [32]); Joan Baez as both substance and silhouette ("a personality before she was entirely a person" [47]); the one-size-fits-all "pure" Marxism of Comrade Michael Laski, C.P.U.S. (M.-L.)—"Actually I was interested not in the revolution but the revolutionary" (62); or the California-to-Las Vegas chapel "wedding business" ("Sincere and Dignified" as she glacially cites one of the chapel signs in a Las Vegas itself "bizarre and beautiful in its veniality and devotion to immediate gratification" ([80]).

"Seven Places of the Mind," the final sequence, begins with "Notes from a Native Daughter"—the Sacramento Valley as family legacy and a terrain not exactly lost but under threat of "modern" development, and closes with "Goodbye to All That," a portrait of New York in all its city-culture first-time exhilaration yet eventual excess of demand. They act as bookends, bi-coastal frames for America as cultural knit and un-knit, with herself put to discerning the balance of forces in play. Hawai'i she so remembers as Pearl Harbor icon and "big rock candy mountain" vacation-land (189). Alcatraz can be "rock of ages" yet paradoxically yellow-flowered memorial prison-house. Rhode Island's Newport summons the literal dwelling-place of Edith Wharton and a visiting Henry James but also "a "fantastically elaborate stage setting . . . in which money and happiness are presented as antithetical" (212). Mexico's Guaymas can be Hispanic yet also America-abroad Pacific Ocean. Los Angeles is both Santa Ana actual weather yet a beguiling species of fluid cultural weather, be it Ralph's Market, Beverley Hills, or the city's piano bars. Each is portrayed as necessary American iconography in which, reflexively, she acknowledges herself to be embedded even as she equally acknowledges her need to keep perspective, her writer's space. This bid for a sense of personal equilibrium amid the un-equilibrium about her is her mark, the view in-close but kept always at the right working distance.

*   *   *

Few essays better typify Didion's quest for the usable viewpoint than "On The Morning After The Sixties" in *The White Album*. Her concern is to take measure of an era just after her own 1950s Berkeley years, and within a California to which she is tied by geography of birth and upbringing. She finds herself drawn back to her prior "silent" generation in the following terms—"We were silent because the exhilaration of social action seemed to many of us just one more way of escaping the personal . . ." (206–7). And by "personal" she means, clearly, not some head-in-the-sand egoism, but the self she specifies in "The Women's Movement" as "committed mainly to the exploration of moral distinctions and ambiguities" (113). If in this respect she finds herself unwilling to espouse the liberation politics (if such they are to be considered) of campus or barricade she equally eschews any easy retreat into niche or comfort-zone. "What I have made for myself is personal," she acknowledges, "but it is not exactly peace" (298). The point is scrupulous, the reminder that for all the aggregate call to "revolution USA," or its affiliation to the era's international revolt, "the implacable 'I' " invoked in "On Keeping a Notebook" persists—remains ever its own kind of refusenik ("If I could believe that going to the barricade would affect man's fate in the slightest I would go to that barricade . . ." [208]).

The twenty or so other contributions to *The White Album* give further emphasis to this unyielding sense of self, the call as of necessity to stance, an achieved take on the world to hand. The title essay does especial service: the self which is Didion that can be named an *L.A. Times* woman of the year yet generate a psychiatric report on its "vertigo and nausea" (15) and a 1960s spanning the Ferguson-brothers' murder of Ramon Novarro in Laurel Canyon through to the Charles Manson murders of Sharon Tate and her companions at the Polanski home in Cielo Drive, Los Angeles. "We tell ourselves stories in order to live" (11) begins "The White Album," a nostrum then used to ask what story indeed, what interpretative version, might best hold given each apparent dislocation or fissure. To this end she reprints the Santa Monica psychiatric report on her "attack of vertigo and nausea" (15), as though it were bodily manifestation of her reaction to the malaise about her.

There follow the portraits of key *dramatis personae*, each a situating player in the 1960s roster. The Fergusons, one unaware of Novarro's silent movie career, the other a self-identified hustler, cause her to ponder how best try to "bring the picture into some focus" (17). Jim Morrison and the Doors strike her as "the Norman Mailers of the Top Forty" (21). Janis Joplin yields her observation that "Music people never want ordinary drinks" (25). Huey Newton, Black Panther chieftain, she interprets as some aspirant world-historical personage—"almost everything Huey Newton said has the ring of being a 'quotation,' a 'pronouncement' " (31). The Eldridge Cleaver of *Soul on Ice* might launch a rage against the racial-capitalist order yet she meets him as his wife Kathleen is cooking sausages and he is "listening to a John Coltrane record" (33). The San Francisco State student militants, for her, work under "industrious self-delusion" (39) and to a remit in which "Disorder was its own point" (37). This 1960s mosaic is offered as memorial, at once near-phantasmagoric yet insistently actual.

Finally there is Linda Kasabian as Manson follower, LSD groupie, and trial witness: she serves to embody the "senseless chain of correspondences," "the jingle-jangle morning of that summer" (45), even though she and Didion will share a trip with their children on the Staten Island Ferry. The Tate-La Bianca murders, graphic, drug-fueled, and which Kasabian will describe in detail in court before sentencing, are invoked as epilogue to the 1960s, their quite literal death-throe. How, the Didion of the essay asks, to make these different cross-lights yield some kind of coherence, a story to live by, or to make her own writing "see what it means" (47)? The ambition, she acknowledges, may ever prove elusive. But what does not is her command of an operative viewpoint, eye and voice given to framing the issues in all their serial contrariety yet with a coherence quite her own.

In each of the essays that follow in *The White Album* the same resolve upon focus holds. Whether tackling the media "spiritual" phenomenon of Bishop James Pike in the contexts of a 1960s ("when no one at all seemed to have any memory of moorings" [58]) in "James Pike, American," or The Getty Museum as the "odd monument" of wealth and easy-viewing ("The place might have been commissioned by the Magic Christian" [74]), or Doris Lessing with her "arrogantly bad ear for dialogue" (119) yet sheer resolute endurance as writer ("Doris Lessing"), Didion always avoids the merely querulous. The tone remains calm, the assumption of viewpoint scrupulous—and quite the more so when Didion builds her own "sure" admission of un-sureness as to overall signification or semiotics into that viewpoint.

* * *

Lowered of eye, laconic, self-distancing: this kind of critical register for Didion goes on repeating itself in reactions to the discursive writing that has followed *Slouching Towards Bethlehem* and *The White Album* as signature collections. The terms in play have worked both ways, to her favor and otherwise. Whichever the case they give notice of Didion's ongoing resolve to assume a view, a stance, yet without giving in to the merely editorial. In no way does this become more evident than in *Salvador* and *Miami*, both indicative of Didion's weight of interest in the Americas as hemispheric realms caught up in each other's political entrails. Both, as ever, also offer a keenest show of viewpoint, but only as buttressed with detail, confirmation that she has done her groundwork in the form of interviews, consultation, source-material, documents, and all relevant scholarship. The upshot is wholly engaging, a rare taking of political temperature in the Salvador of the Reagan 1980s and the exile Miami steeped in the counter-memory of *fidelismo* and the Bay of Pigs.

Salvador opens on a note near sardonically magic-realist as "a state in which no ground is solid, no depth of field reliable, no perception so definite that it might not dissolve into its reverse."[13] From arrival through to her press visits to each *desaparecido* site and killing-field, Didion summons a country under not just political but existential siege ("Terror is the given of the place" [14]). This is a Salvador of death-squads, a killer-warlord like Roberto d'Aubuisson, the Mozote massacre of 1981, the grotesquely mis-named Human Rights Commission with its inexact lists of the dead ("the dead or pieces of the dead turn up in El Salvador everywhere" [19]), and the murder of Archbishop Romero. For all the tough well-meaning of Deane Hinton as US ambassador the murk of CIA operations and arms-supply exert their shadow. Didion perfectly well identifies the political groupings, Communism and the Right, The Reagan White House and the Magaña Salvadoran Presidency, but her forte lies in her seizure of metaphor to cap-ture time and place. It offers itself early in the sight of literal vultures that "go first for the soft tissue, for the eyes, the exposed genitalia, the open mouth" (17).

The edge to this observation barely wavers. 1980s Salvador resembles nothing if not Márquez-like tropic nightmare. The Salvadoran mind-set "turns on plot" (30). Public speech becomes mouth-eats-tail, in which respect Didion lists phrases like "progress," "turning the corner," and "*la solución*" as a kind of binomial parody. The Metropolitan Cathedral insults the country's poverty, a "vast brutalist space" (79). US military policy might have come from Joseph Heller's *Catch-22*, to be designated "delusion" (85), a "kind of dreamwork" (92) in which the catch-all American banner of anti-communism has led to an addled aid-and-arms menu. The "local vocation for terror" (104), vulturousness itself, feeds not only on its own citizenry (not least indigenous Nahuatl-speakers), but the four US nuns, the occasional journalist, children. A down-the-street stroll becomes laden in threat. An actual earthquake strikes Didion as pathetic fallacy, Nature's refraction of Salvador's own violent discord. Intellectual life comes over as cowed, furtive, café-talk. Didion finally boards her plane "without looking back" (106). She thinks it has been a glimpse into Conradian darkness, a "sentence" (105). Her own best effects, however, lie precisely in deploying a right language of viewpoint for that condition.

Miami works on a shared wavelength—"Nothing about Miami was exactly fixed, or hard."[14] Didion makes her departure-point *el exilio*, local-ized in Miami's Woodlawn Cemetery where many of Cuba's pre-Fidel lead-ers are buried, having fled to Florida with family and treasure. It is an image the text expands upon throughout. She draws attention to Cuba "as birthright lost" (17) and "*patria, machismo, la lucha*" (20) as operative terms of rally. The politico Raul Masvidal is cited on JFK in the aftermath of the 1961 Bay of Pigs as "the number two most hated man in Miami" (84) with due adulation of *Brigada Asalto* as martyr freedom fighters. The *Grupo Areíto* (117) she re-iterates as "Cubans outside Cuba" (117). Dade County, with Calle Ocho as iconic thoroughfare, suggests ideological as physical geography, a Miami over 50% Hispanic and networked with more than 300 CIA case officers. Organizations as anti-Fidel as the Cuban American National Foundation or the secretive Omega are tracked for their obscure funding and personnel. The portrait is one of arms and the man, plot and counter-plot, activism and nostalgia, in all a political witch's brew. The gaze across the waters, and ever voluble street and talk culture, feature as ongoing reference-points, those of an exile Cuban Latinity dynamically everyday (if ever more "American") and yet still gun-and-coterie clandestine, even paranoid.

As usual, however, Didion's eye is keen, un-blinkered in its own view. She speaks of internal splits—members of the Miami exile community in endless "ideological confrontation" one with another (129–30). Likewise she sees generational shifts from exile to the process whereby the sons and daughters of the first anti-*fidelistas* edge towards Cuban American status. Her comments are typically diagnostic—"the scars *el exilio* inflicts upon its own do not entirely heal, nor are they meant to" (114–15). The DC Cuban lobby, Reagan's "freedom fighter" talk, the machinations of Oliver North, almost inevitably come into the conspiratorial reckoning. Didion's abiding trope is that of Miami as whole ganglia of competing "story," any one "hard to follow" (202), all "low and lurid" (202). In this vista Cuban America in the aftermath of Fidel's assumption of power in 1959 is to be seen as machination, heat, a querulous roster of players drawn into a mythology of return nothing if not of a kind with the volatile tropical ecology to hand.

After Henry and *Political Fictions* continue the plenty, twenty or so meticulously angled further weights and measures. The former, cast in a three-part sequence of "Washington," "California" and "New York," develops a linking panorama: Reaganism, Pattie Hearst, Honolulu, the Los Angeles of Mayor Tom Bradley, and a New York of Central Park "wilding," rape and graft which somehow never dislodges the sentimentality of its mythus as the Big Apple "because it matches our energy level" (319). The latter rounds back on Reagan as "scripted" President, the 1992 presidential campaign, the Newt Gingrich of "Taking Back Our Streets," and the DC of the Gore-Lieberman run for the presidency against George Bush Jr. At every turn Didion's excavates with un-exhausting skepticism, antennae raised, scopes narrowed.

As symptomatic a piece as any has to be "Clinton Agonistes," a tour-de-force in its take on how the 1998 would-be impeachment of Bill Clinton offered a configuration of politics, alpha-male sexual behavior, and public image. For Didion's focus is less the detail of the case, be it the C-SPAN telecasts, the Kenneth Starr prosecution, the sexual close encounters with Monica Lewinsky right through to her semen-stained blue dress, or even Clinton from Little Rock to the White House as serial womanizer, than with how the whole business featured as an American public narrative.

Who owned the story, Clinton himself with his lawyerly parsing of "sexual relationship," Lewinsky's belief that Clinton was in love with her, Starr with the charge of Oval Office miscreancy and the added issue of Whitewater, or Linda Tripp with her phone recordings and court witness? What was the good or bad faith of the punditry like that of *Time*'s George Will and *Newsweek*'s Joe Klein, PBS's Cokie Roberts ("speaking as a mother") and CNN's Wolf Blitzer? In other words, and like its cognate Watergate, how was "Monica-gate" to be told—presidential mendacity, Starr's Christian-values zealotry, the ambiguous vulnerability of a twenty-year old intern, a private family matter best left to resolution with Hilary and Chelsea? For all that she tracks the evolving turns of the story, Didion also tunnels, quite inexorably, into the assumptions of those given political and media custody of the matter, the pro-impeachers and the defenders, the outraged at moral lapse and the tut-tutters about an escapade inflated out of all proportion. The account thereby not only offers close-burrowed enquiry, it evinces the would-be tellers of the tale as much as those who were themselves the tale, along with the frequent overlaps of both. Vintage Didion, it might be said, in subtlety of compass.

"The way I write is who I am, or have become" writes Didion in *The Year of Magical Thinking*.[15] It offers a working perspective, recognition of her own scrupulously pitched and managed presence in any given account. It would be hard to miss the circumstantial observation, the un-spelled out irony, the readiness to eschew "ideas" in the interest of seeking out the reality behind the official or managed version, and in its considerable subtlety, the recording self in play. Each of her discursive texts carries this singular interaction of fact and lens, narrative and critique. "Interpreting what we see," to invoke "On Keeping A Notebook," has so led to reportage, whether to be agreed with or not, that leaves no doubt of the times made subject to a weight, a styling, of view always nothing if not her own.

7   Pirated Words
Kathy Acker

I could never be a pirate because I was a girl. I couldn't even run away
to sea like Herman Melville . . .
> —Kathy Acker, "Seeing Gender" (1995),
> *Bodies of Work: Essays* (1997)[1]

This book is dedicated to my tattooist.
> —Kathy Acker, *Empire of the Senseless* (1988)[2]

Kathy Acker got attention for her arresting image, relentless outsider
status, and provocative reading style . . .
> —Amy Scholder, "Preface," *Lust for Life:*
> *On The Writings of Kathy Acker* (2005)[3]

In legacy, as in life, Kathy Acker continues to raise hackles. A decade on
from her death of cancer in a Mexican alternative-medicine clinic in 1997
the courts of opinion differ almost totally, praise for her soaring icono-
clasm in the one quarter, wariness, even dismissal, in the other. Is she to be
thought a kind of meta-feminist, a brilliant writer-diagnostician answering
back misogyny and the circumscription of women's lives through her own
recriminatory sexual figurations and mythologies? Is she, on the opposite
tack, to be thought simply the opportunist dispensing cartoon erotica or
violence dressed up in postmodern games and circles?

One line of estimation sees a serious New York-bred scion from William
Burroughs's literary stable out to bravely subvert all gender and related
hierarchical power structures, with de Sade, Rimbaud, Artaud, Genet,
Bataille, Duras, Robbe-Grillet, Foucault and Deleuze in a French line of
influence, not to mention an inwardness with deconstruction theory in Der-
rida and Baudrillard. Another sees only the attention-seeking Bad Girl, the
infinitely knowing shock-horror author whose avid sex-scenes and recur-
rence of anatomical four-letter words—for all their reflective intent—could
be as dismaying to feminists as to guardians of literary respectability. Not
a few have seen her as actually, not to say ingeniously, the hybrid of both.
Whichever the version the issue persists of how to read her fiction, the
world it envisions, the styling in play.

Acker in life hardly held back from presenting herself as an evolving
multi-text. She made no secret of her bisexuality, her "bares all" career

as punk and stripper, or her body-building, tattoos and piercings. The body, she said often, itself offers a text to be worked on and remade. Other aspects of her biography run from bike-freak to file clerk and secretary, 1960s New Yorker to 1980s Londoner with stays in France and Germany in the mix. Born Karen Alexander, she had grown up the daughter of an affluent, Sutton Place, New York City Jewish mother who committed suicide in 1978 and a father who absconded before her birth. There were the two marriages, the multiple affairs, the abortions, and the eventual double-mastectomy and the pain and complications that followed. Her education was wide, and suitably eclectic, to include undergraduate study in classics and the humanities at Brandeis and the University of California at San Diego, enrollment for a PhD at CCNY, then visiting university appointments at Santa Barbara, San Diego, Idaho and Roanoke, and from 1991, an adjunct professorship at the San Francisco Institute of Art.

These academic affiliations, however, always ran alongside her creative track, to include the early taste for Black Mountain writers and painters, connection to the Dada-ist Fluxus Movement and the creative work of George Maciunas, Joseph Bueys, John Cage or Yoko Ono as performative, playful, often child-like, and mentorship by figures as otherwise disparate as Herbert Marcuse, philosopher of Eros fused with Marxism, and David Antin, poet-practitioner of "talk" verse. These also sat well with her interests in edge popular-culture, whether Manhattan and Village alternative art-circle activity, Warhol cinema and the East 47th Street "factory" silk-screen and other paintings, or biker gangs, the S&M scene, and punk music and life-style. Arising, throughout, was the insistent turn, the hallucinatory playfields and narrativity, of her novels, along with ventures into libretto for the opera *The Birth of The Poet* (1985) and screenplay for the film *Variety* (1985). Jeannette Winterson, the British novelist of *Oranges Are Not The Only Fruit* (1985), gives a nice recollection of these various double aspects to Acker. She suggest that "Acker positioned herself on the outside—on the side of exile" less out of anti-American impulse than "because her cultural and literary interests were wider than any single tradition could offer."[4]

As to her fiction it positively revels in brazen pastiche of all fixed narrative, her adaptive plagiarism if, in truth, that is what it signifies. From the start Acker used a whole repertoire of non-linearity, cut-up and bricolage, different scripts and fonts, writing which often resembles the jumps and transformations of dream or trance. Narrators shift to match, the dislodging and, in a now familiar phrase, even the death, of any single authorial/authoritative or "patriarchal" narrative voice. One charge, odd in the face of Acker's obvious exuberance of invention, has been that her writing edges towards nihilism, the postmodern text taken to the point where it reduces to depthless mosaic. Those in her corner respond that this is precisely the way needed to confront not just the hierarchy of all "master" or "authorized" literary narrative, but the capitalism of market and corporation, law and religion, media and schooling, and always historic male sexuality and domination. In this way her texts indeed become counter-texts, each story a counter-story.

To this end, too, Acker persistently asks what identity, and female identity in particular, can now mean, its very making as a gender, a sexual practice, a condition of desire, a body, a consciousness. The impetus was to be seen at the outset in *The Childlike Life of the Black Tarantula* (1973, expanded 1975, and reprinted in *Portrait of an Eye* [1992]). It continues through best-known landmarks like *Kathy Goes to Haiti* (1978), *Blood and Guts in High School* (1984), *Empire of the Senseless* (1988) and *In Memory of Identity* (1990), and into posthumous compilations like *Eurydice in the Underworld* (1997).[5] If these texts use whole threads of gymnastically displayed sado-masochism or terrorism, they do so, for Acker, as ways of reflecting and undermining the remit of entrenched power. She has been insistent that this makes her not so much anti-male as anti-control—she is well known, for instance, to have taken off after Andrea Dworkin for suggesting that the act of sexual penetration is itself quasi-fascist.[6]

At the same time almost every Acker text asks how to construe, let alone conduct, love or some redemptive humanism in a world, and an America in particular, under rule by capitalism's lords of the universe, media controllers, God-preachers, sex authorities, military and legal bosses, as all the one or another kind of patriarch. Writing as though from the margins of power she sees the implications for women as wholly evident and pervasive. How to defy objectivization and disambiguate self from role—daughter, wife, mother, fashion model, beauty-myth trophy, spoil of war, rape or porn object? How, she persists in asking, to recognize the body as likely the only true site of desire and to envisage not just the equality but the life-and-art promise of gender difference, gay, bi-, androgynous, transvestite and the like? Acker's riposte across the board was to take up her favorite trope and position herself as pirate, the guerilla-user of images that transgressively reflect the very conditions in which women have come to be situated.

Nowhere does this become more emphatic as both theme and narrative strategy than in her rewriting, and appropriation for her own purposes, of classic past (and male) authorship. The span embraces Dickens in *Great Expectations* (1982), Hawthorne in *Blood and Guts in High School*, Cervantes in *Don Quixote, which was a dream* (1986), Rimbaud and Faulkner in *In Memoriam to Identity*, and Robert Louis Stevenson in *Pussy, King of The Pirates* (1995).[7] Amid the brouhaha about plagiarism, interestingly, the question rarely gets raised of whether these works in fact not so much plagiarize as act as palimpsests. The subsequent text, un-reverentially as may be, writes over the earlier text, new from old fare, the one story now the different story. In this respect Acker would be far from alone. One can think not only of related authorly tactics by Burroughs, but by Borges, or other fellow Americans like John Barth and Donald Barthelme.

One notable difference, however, is how Acker's novels opt for what can be called their own anarcho-gender agenda. Whether it is the authorial self, or that of one of the text's characters, piracy is indeed the name of the game in which any or all are to be imagined as outlaw, shape-shifter, masochist, killer, gang-member, sexual obsessive, prostitute, precociously sexualized child, or borrowed artist (the list includes the Bronte sisters, Toulouse Lautrec, Bataille, Pasolini, even Agatha Christie). This is modernity, or more aptly postmodernity, in which the self (women, or in the case of Rimbaud in *In Memoriam to Identity*, men) act out the terms of how that self believes itself created by society—narcissistically hurtful or self-hurting, obsessive, sexually both vulnerable and revengeful, and given to whatever countering extravagance of action or imagination best applies. That has a prime focus in America and its sex-and-consumer systems whose remit she parodies, synoptically, in the faux-autobiographical opening chapter of *My Mother: Demonology* (1993)—"Into that Belly of Hell Whose Name is the United States."[8]

Little wonder, perhaps, that towards the end of her life Acker drew attention to how her work had always pitched for a new myth of "biological" as much as social being, not least given latest bio-medical experiments and even cloning. The greatly useful *Bodies of Work: Essays* (1997), as she titled her collected essays on language, authorship, cities, film, textual politics, and sexuality, might thereby be said to carry its own reverse mirror. Acker, who always believed herself a revolutionary-philosophical writer, invites being seen as having given herself to the "work," which by her own lights was to mean the comprehensive un-imprisoning by whatever daring of language or obscenity, of the modern body. In this sense she more than readily gives herself given to counter writing, counter in format as in imaginative vision, and always in the interests of a counter politics.

*   *   *

Almost any selection of the early, middle and late writing gives confirmation of Acker's resolve to play pirate, to deconstruct and assault all bastions of fixed class and gender roles, and to keep faith with the Fluxus credo of open text, free imaginative flow. In this regard her first full-length fiction, *The Childlike Life of the Black Tarantula*, showed that most of the Acker hallmarks were already there to be recognized.[9] *"Intention: I became a murderess by repeating in words the lives of other murderesses"* reads a prefatory first page, a forewarning of the reflexive imaginative menu to follow. Under the pen of a sixteen-year old, and then an older, sexually self-compelled, daughter of hated middle-class parentage, the novel operates as the imagined voices of a prior-time Mississippi murderess, then a prostitute, using re-written quotation from different porno texts, and among others, Leduc, De Sade, Alexander Trocchi, and Yeats. Each, as the narrator enters it, is angled to escape the society of her raising, its mores, institutions, its very language ("I love lonely criminals and thieves" [40]).

The strategy is utterly, fantastically, textual ("I am thrown into prison for trying to figure out my desires" [79]). Desire, gender-bending, projections of the self as eighteenth-century cutpurse, French Revolutionary witness, sex-show artiste, and New Yorker ("I move to New York because I write and want to meet writers" [81]), assume their role in the text in no cause-and-effect sequence. For the aim is truly text itself, as onanistic as the narrator herself, even, if amid sex scene and fantasy, she says "I'm scared to always follow my desires in this sick society" (90). No such scare actually inhibits Acker herself, an early counter-narrative as lavish in its imaginings of desire as turns of composition.

Kathy Goes to Haiti offers another early and especially symptomatic touchstone, its very title a parody of some might-be adventure series format. "This is what Kathy sees" reads an opening line.[10] Her seeing is a Haiti of ferocious actual poverty under the heel of its governing rich elite, with CIA and American corporate interests involved, and a Haiti where women serve only as possessions, playthings, cosseted wives, dependents, or sex-consumables. To be sure, in the latter respect, Kathy gives as good as she gets in terms of sexual currency. The novel almost brims in sexual heat and thrust. But if a pilgrim's progress through one of the world's most conspicuous examples of the ruins of capitalism and colonialism, the novel also implies in Kathy the search for love amid the ruins of gender role. It does so on both counts, moreover, as pastiche, the white single-woman's Caribbean holiday novel turned upside down.

Albeit twenty-nine years of age, a New York sexual veteran, Kathy plays a female version of Candide to perfection. From the moment she is collected in Port-au-Prince by the taxi-driver Sammy to her every-opportunity sexual infatuation with Roger Mystere, pampered son of the local mining magnate, she is hit upon, taunted, calumnied as a whore, by each of the men (and boys) she encounters. Her only currency, for them and so for herself, is sex, to which she gives herself as though to achieve autonomy, however temporary, through copious and repeated orgasm. "I want to be free" (12) she alleges even as Sammy seeks to take possession of her as girlfriend and Roger as his sex-partner. In a Haiti the degree-zero image of all male gender regimes, with the Ton-Tons Macoute as ultimate sexual gendarmerie, how to find love, freedom, escape from the writs of female fidelity and male prerogative to philander, in all any real escape from her own imposed status of being?

Scene upon scene in the novel works to expose this unequal quest for equal love. In a chapter called "Passions" Kathy, or an authorial voice reporting her thoughts, speaks to a transformation in gender: "Someday there'll have to be a new world. A new kind of woman. Or a new world for women because the world we perceive, what we perceive, causes our characteristics." (77–78). Not only does this carry the underlying impetus of the novel, it does so in Acker's typical sentence run-ons, her un-etiquetted appropriation of sexual vocabulary. The upshot is one in which Kathy experiences Haiti as though herself lost in translation as white woman in black culture, New Yorker in the Caribbean, English-speaker amid Creole-speakers, and above all woman inside male hegemony. When Roger complains of women that, "when you think you have them, they simply disappear," she retorts "That's the only way they can act. They don't have any power" (150).

Each encounter refracts Kathy's sense of existing in a parallel universe of un-freedom, whether Roger and the men in his circle, his sequestered white wife Betty, or the island "wives" and "girlfriends" all under male custodial possession. Sex, every which way, urgent, ecstatic, frequent, is hers more or less to dispense. But she finds herself bounded as a woman in almost every other respect—no "new world" here, no "new kind of woman." Her encounter with a supposed Voodoo healer, accordingly, turns out fake, and is said to leave her "more dazed than before" (170). As she becomes aware of the Haiti of Baby Doc Duvalier ("You know you don't go to jail in Haiti for political crimes. You just disappear" [114]), and of the island's poverty and massive divides of wealth, so, whatever her sexual readiness or savvy, Acker uses Kathy to signify a world hyper-reflective of wider coercive gender rules and behavior. The mock-ingenuousness underlines the point throughout. *Kathy Goes to Haiti* deploys a shrewd fund of irony, the one story, the one politics, folded into the other, a vintage Acker pirate text vintagely told.

*   *   *

With *Blood and Guts in High School* Acker moves into yet more emphatic self-referential mode, "story" as collage, panels of non-procedural or inter-changeable fantasy. The life it tells, that of Janey Smith, envisions a female destiny *in extremis*, a sexual-gothic universe of skewed love, language-as-control, and the issue of whether identity is mere subjective fabrication (Acker is notorious for her assertion that there is nothing left that can be called identity). On publication there were cries of pornography, court cases and censor-ship in Germany and South Africa. The serious reviews had questions of their own. Was Acker's text, albeit told as dream-like speculation, a good-faith narrative of women's destiny within the gender matrix of self and society? Or did it give sure and certain proof of dalliance, a fake avant-gardism not much more consequential than how-far-dare-you-go sex talk? Admirers were unhesitating. Here was *Jayne Eyre* or *Little Women*, and certainly Hester Prynne's story in *The Scarlet Letter*, again given hall-of-mirrors magnifica-tion, a three-part "woman's novel" made subject to sublime travesty.

Set first in Yucatan ('Inside High School") it begins as active incest-love, twelve-year old Janey's for her father, Johnny, and her jealousy as he begins a relationship with a young starlet. It might almost be Freud's Electra-complex fleshed into literal form, willingly engaged in if prohibited first love, first adoration. It also works both ways—"Johnny said he thought I was his mother and all the resentment he felt against her he now felt against me."[11] Janey draws diagrams of genitalia, male and female, as though to iconize, if not mock, fixed sexual anatomy as fixed social destiny.

"Outside High School," the second section and set in the New York to which Janey has relocated, becomes an overlap of classroom-taught and street culture. Fact vies with fantasy: Janey joins a marauding street gang, the Scorpions ("We hurt each other sexually as much as we could" [32]), undergoes a macabre factory-line abortion, works in an East Village hippie bakery, and concocts page-size fairytale and dream maps of her life. A Mr. Linker acts as her teacher and white slaver. In her High School "book report" (65) she parodies, and graphically sexualizes, *The Scarlet Letter*. Dimmesdale becomes the Reverend Dimwit, Chillingworth a "top cop" (68), Hester "a freak . . . because she wouldn't be quiet and hide her freakishness" (65), and New England a realm where "sex has become S&M" (99). Janey, in other words, and under no inhibition, writes her own experience of patriarchy and sexual control through Hawthorne's novel. Sold into prostitution by thieves and imprisoned by a Persian slave trader as a whore-in-training, she steals a pencil and endeavors to "free" herself into a new language adventure. This, in turn, produces a Persian-English verse sequence, the "punk" translation of the elegiac love poetry of Sextus Propertius, graffiti, and complaints about, and to, President Jimmy Carter.

"A journey to the end of the night," the third oneiric section as named from Céline, has her become the co-voyager and colloquist through Egypt and North Africa with Jean Genet who hates her when she most aspires to be what he wants. Alive only in her writing, she even composes a posthumous memoir. For, in shared animus with Burroughs, Acker has her narrator rally imaginatively against all command-and-control regimes, against logocentrism. In her case that means the agencies of patriarchy, social gendering, and indeed language itself where, expressly or subliminally, it mimics control systems (as in "mastering a language"). To contest all of these Acker so has Janey use language against itself, taboo words, explicit drawings and compositions, plagiarism, translations, parody-conversation, pictographs, dream-maps and phone-sex.

But Acker's challenge is by no means only that of compositional form. It is whether her novel's fantasy-fact investigation rings true, modernity/postmodernity as unremitting sell and be sold, gender as ongoing domination-submission and violence. It is also her asking, as the novel explicitly asks at its conclusion, whether real or imagined "other Janeys" (165) can be sources of counter and redress. Acker proponents, on each of these counts, could not be less in doubt.

*   *   *

In both *Great Expectations* and *Don Quixote, which was a dream* the issue necessarily arises of plagiarism, or to perhaps greater interpretative advantage, of appropriation (not to mention palimpsest). Both work as dream narratives, a species of projection in which Acker's own texts— discontinuous, assemblage-like, full of forays into the 1980s as social condition—stalk those of their illustrious predecessors. Each, too, relies upon multi-vocal storying, no single narrator to control the line, the zig-zag, of imagined event. Nonetheless it is not hard to discern that however compound, or fused, the narratological agencies of disclosure, they derive from a single overall imagination, one that can dip into Dickens or Cervantes even as they make their departure-point a contemporaneity of fraught mother-daughter relationship in New York (*Great Expectations*) or abortion (*Don Quixote*). Acker leaves no doubt that all the Aristotelian unities have been ditched: this is text as transformative consciousness, the bid as much to write present-day texts of power and gender into prior literary texts, anything but simple emulation of the originals. It can again be called piracy with a purpose.

In *Great Expectations* the voices, the textual ventriloquies, begin from Dickens's Pirrip and quickly become those of the bisexual Peter, Sarah Ashington, the prostitute Rosa, Anwar Sadat, the Pauline Réage of *L'Histoire d'O*, and even a shadow authorial self called Kathy. Scenarios, true to dream, shift from New York's 42nd Street and its strip-and-peep shows to Egypt's Alexandria and its brothels. Timelines transpose from 1978 New York back to the era of Sextus Aurelius Propertius, whose Elegies to his muse-lover Cynthia bequeath traditions of Romantic Love as against the predatory sex-and-power control the novel envisions as shaping contemporary relationship. Indeed Propertius and Cynthia metamorphose into modern lovers, he the insouciant city Romeo, she the self-razoring dependent on his male powers of decision and control. Acker even places an author-speaks-to-the-reader sequence mid-way into the text, a kind of manifesto in miniature as to the kind of narrative in play.

Each filament in the text aligns with the other, as usual not in the form of cause and effect but rather as pageant, co-equal episode, a conscious dissonance. The opening sequence on "my mother," with its minute physical detail of body, sets up a vision of daughterhood—at one and the same time devoted, resentful, driven, full of sexual escape-fantasy, above all called to the act of writing. The text summarizes the relationship in fake Dickensian style as follows—"Thus ends the first segment of my life. I am a person of GREAT EXPECTATIONS"[12] These expectations take realization in the various fantasies that ensue. In Alexandria, and various brothel scenes, she imagines seeking her family inheritance. In a New York she thinks hateful, oppressive, she plays witness to husband-and-wife colloquy shot through with violence. In her reflexive role of woman-author of the text she says reiteratively "I feel I feel I feel I have no language, any emotion for me is a prison" (24).

Her search for writer-recognition, even so, leads to a letter to Susan Sontag that begins parodically "Would you please read my books and make me famous" (27). As "O" she subverts even as she re-enacts Réage's austere sexually domination-submission paradigm in the celebrated erotic classic. As Sarah she fantasizes herself as plaintive daughter and abused love object. As woman artist she veers into incarnations as photographer's sex-model, commentator on America and the arts ("American culture allows only the material to be real (actually, only money)" [77]), putative feminist, and finally Cynthia given to sexually unbounded desire. In each Acker leaves little doubt that these are imagined, and imaginary, incarnations, her text and its vision of women's "great expectations" as much a work of self-plagiarism as plagiarism (or defacement) of Dickens's original novel.

Don Quixote operates to similar tactics and coordinates. Cervantes's epic is transformed from patriarchal epic-journey into a search which represents "the most insane idea that any woman can think of. Which is love."[13] To which end Acker creates an upside-down, about-face *Quixote*: the knight as a woman whose abortion and its pain releases her visionary senses—she will now become the journeyer who "sees," and seeks to empty, the world's controlling misogynist myths and screens, not to say various myths of feminism. Sancho Panza is her friend St Simeon transposed into talking dog, La Mancha a contemporary New York and London and an older St. Petersburg, and modernity a death-culture to be mocked in the rituals of courtly quest. An early chapter, "History and Women," cites Cid Hamete Benengeli, Cervantes's own fantasy Moorish author whose work he purports to be translating, as having said "the history of women is that of degradation and suffering ... Nevertheless ... a woman has the power to choose to be a king and a tyrant." (29).

Acker's *Don Quixote*, in other words, will also be liberationist theatre, a no-holds-barred assault on the windmills of sexism, the incarcerations of female self inside prescribed gender role. And it will also deploy whatever degree of fantasied graphic sex or violence or brutality requisite to do the job—love travestied as marriage-contract, nuclear power as male-engendered plague, a Nazified male world played by transvestites, the constraints put upon desire mocked in graphic scenes of orgasmic abandonment, war as penis, women as the amputees of Oedipal myth, and the female body chronicled for multiple sexual penetrations. The novel ends in a chorus of pirate songs given over to seizure of the prime myths of male ascendancy and a posthumous message from the female narrator as Quixote—"Even a woman who has the soul of a pirate, at least pirate morals ... even such a woman who is a freak in our society needs a home ..." (202)

That home, for the Quixote of the text, lies in private as public art, symptomatically a Spanish Republic of 1931 with its anarcho-syndicalist imput allowed to thrive, a language pried free of all authoritarianism. The narrator, writing as it were from the vantage-point of her own death, declares that she has awoken to "the world which lay before me" (207), one whose political and cultural control-mechanisms over the should-be autonomous body she deplores and indicts. Acker's endlessly ingenious and overall flailings of this world, and the compositional sleights and epi-sodicity with which it is told, for ironic good reason has been called noth-ing less than "radical realism."[14]

* * *

Empire of the Senseless, another text which has elicited fierce division of opinion, makes its bead a near-future society, Paris as jailor and jailee ter-rorist city-world in which nausea is all. Revolutionary Algerians have taken over and subjected the French to a mirror of their own colonialism—arbi-trary, mean, violent, oppressive. Acker's two terrorist-figures, Abhor and Thivai, themselves act true to the spirit of this post-revolution new order, the one part-robot of white and black parentage, the other a conscienceless bother-boy and would-be killer pirate. Disgust indeed prevails, a dystopian writ somewhere close to Anthony Burgess's *Clockwork Orange* or William Burroughs's *Naked Lunch*, though without the former's explicit Pavlovian seams of brute human conditioning or the latter's capacity to endow his user-supplier-junk narratives with wicked black humor.

As the novel fills out this next Acker mirror-world, all her usual narrative levers come into play, a human order hoist by its addiction to patriarchal ideologies, practices of control, history as pain, the Sadean reels of sex and abuse. Abhor and Thivai serve as tutelary spirits, figures at one with the skulls, daggers and rose tattoos which literally decorate the narrative. Nag-isa Oshima's stirring film classic, *In the Empire of the Senses* (1975), with its spirals of obsession and sexual climax in strangulation, may or not have been an influence. But the novel is similar in spirit. Violent narcissism, the body's resort to pleasure in destruction and torture, become the very integer of the body politic. Abhor speaks of "post-apocalyptic mess" (109), of the "fathers," family or social-political, of this world as monsters—symptomat-ically Acker's collection of 1970s pieces would be published under the title *Hannibal Lecter, My Father* (1991).[15] Paris features as entropic condition, one of "racist, sexist, classist mores" (154), and in which the waters have been poisoned, mutants are commonplace, and the rest of the population is drugged. The upshot for Abhor and Thivai is rogue existence, pirate life as itself a-moral, terroristic. Even so, Abhor closes the text on a revelatory note of hope: "And then I thought that, one day, maybe, there'd be a human soci-ety in a world which is beautiful, a society which wasn't just disgust" (227).

* * *

In Memoriam to Identity, four texts-in-one centered on the interacting life, art, and love-misery over Verlaine of Arthur Rimbaud, French Decadence's archetypal literary *enfant terrible*, the figure of Airplane, sex-dancer at Fun City, the equally fictional figure of Capitol in her incestuous brother relationship with Quentin as taken from the pages of Faulkner's *Absalom,*

Absalom!, and the return of Airplane as situated in a fiction that shadows *The Wild Palms*. It takes no undue effort to see that the novel carries most of Acker's trademarks—identity as illusion, obsessive love, sex as the conscienceless index of that same love mocked by convention and its controls, anachronism, plagiarism, crossed timelines and geographies.

In "re-telling" the life of Rimbaud, and in a voice that overlays his, Acker gives pointers to the compass-points of her own art. "Why," the text asks, "do people most hate those artists or image-makers who mirror, or present, their actions and most love those image-makers who lie, lull, and soothe?"[16] The novel, in these and related respects, stands as symptomatic late Acker oeuvre. It pursues several ends at once—the persistence of patriarchal authority as snare and violence to the human spirit, the narrativization of love in relation to violence in modernity, the world seen from the obsessional margins of art and sexuality. Acker's text asks always, and in a variety of ways, how to free life, art, of commodification, and with it, as throughout her writing, for women to live lives un-imprisoned of mind, body, and not least, language. Each of the four sequences anatomizes the decay of love under patriarchy, capitalism, war, religion, marriage, and not least to include the male "magistracy" of a Margaret Thatcher.

"Rimbaud" so re-enacts his poet's season in hell, the miserable childhood and scorn of his mother for his sexuality, the furious madness of his relationship with Verlaine, the failure of the communes, the German invasion of France, the shared indigency of their flight to England. The antidote lies in creativity, or as the text italicizes it *"The only nation is the nation of the imagination"* (77). "Airplane" explores the social sexualization of the female body, fear, touch, submission, rape, strip-tease, object of male gaze, little-girl memory, identity as breasts and genitals. "Capitol," told as though the diary of Quentin Compson's lover-sister, pursues incest as but the reflection of far wider sexual distortion and during which transgression she experiences the only sensations which make her feel alive—Rimbaud, moreover, can re-enter the text and rape her. "The Wild Palms," two parallel stories like Faulkner's original, invokes both Capitol and Airplane, love hexed by dependency, father-memory, the female body as social barter.

In Memoriam to Identity bids to exorcize the ghosts, literally to write out the worst, above all to find a way back to love, to include self-love, as un-coopted ontology. It makes for one of Acker's most challenging narrative performances, a mirror or intertext, of the self bound and unbound from within history's patriarchal boundaries. In its as always graphic picturings, as in its virtuoso "plagiarizing," it offers a late example of what most identifies her, veteran counter-writing.

* * *

Acker's texts pose any amount of challenge. Her scenarios use whole lenses or circuses of looped sexual pain and pleasure, of abuse and willful violence, to give envisaged magnification of how women have been made to operate under regimens of phallocentric/logocentric and capitalist power. Her narrative forms, in kind, deliberately undercut the comfortable read, the appeal to some residual "dear reader." Rather, almost everything she writes proposes textuality, story un-storied, language un-languaged, voice un-voiced, as though in these disruptions, the world of the fathers can indeed meet come-uppance, wholly and irrevocably be countermanded.

Part III
Ethnics

8 Ethnics Behaving Badly
Texts and Contexts

> I am not tragically colored. There is no great sorrow damned up in my soul, not lurking behind my eyes. I do not mind at all. I do not belong to the sobbing school of Negrohood who feel that nature somehow has given them a lowdown dirty deal and whose feelings are all hurt about it . . . No, I do not weep at the world—I am too busy sharpening my oyster knife.
>
> —Zora Neale Hurston, "How It Feels To Be Colored Me" (1928)[1]

Hurston's celebrated refusal of ethnic victimry casts a forward light of immense significance. It does so, too, with all her typical bodaciousness, wonderfully engaging in idiom and bold in the point being made. No "sobbing school of Negrohood" indeed, no suffering minority status whether by race, class or gender but rather wit, savvy, singularity, a true oyster knife celebration of appetite for self and world.

Given her upbringing in the all-black town of Eatonville, Florida, her subsequent time at colleges like Morgan State, Howard and Barnard, and the triumphs (however insufficiently acknowledged at the time) of a best novel like *Their Eyes Were Watching God* (1937) or a virtuoso self-chronicle like *Dust Tracks on a Road* (1942), it could hardly be open to doubt that Hurston did not understand, or experience, any amount of vintage racism.[2] But her characteristically sassy refusal to indulge the piety of what she terms the "tragically colored" syndrome adds its own twist. Self-pity of all kinds, but black self-pity in particular, invites not merely being decried but the loftiest smack of dismissal.

Bad behavior? For sure, yet as with so much of her work, it could not have been more intrinsic to her general style or quite more inviting. Nor do matters rest only with her own example. Among other implications, few weigh more than how she anticipates later "ethnic" writers who also complicate, not to say outmaneuver and subvert, stereotypic expectations about the whole issue of belonging to an assumed minority niche. Nor, in this respect, would it be accurate to advance Hurston as somehow the only begetter of Bad Behavior within modern African American tradition. Companion voices have been several and emphatic.

George Schuyler's *Black No More* (1931), with its plotline of a rogue geneticist able to change skin color, takes a zany, Menckenite tilt at America's supposed "chromatic democracy," and within it, at black-bourgeois fantasies of becoming ever whiter.[3] Wallace Thurman's *Infants of The Spring* (1932) turns an unflattering spotlight on the black literary-cultural efflorescence once trumpeted by Alain Locke's anthology *The New Negro: An Interpretation* (1925), an insider's satire of the grandstanding, spats, gender-bends, and frequent illicit liaisons of Harlem's 1920s literati.[4] Chester Himes's *Pinktoes* (1961), if at first thought little more than a sexually off-color Olympia Press confection, uses its comedy of uptown Manhattan partying to probe not only the fleshly but the larger cultural implications of inter-racial close encounter.[5]

Few contemporaries have better carried forward this genealogy of constructive irreverence than Ishmael Reed. The bow he made with *The Free-Lance Pallbearers: An Irreverent Novel* (1967), as originally and aptly subtitled, and *Yellow Back Radio Broke-Down* (1969), inaugurates a career of satiric metafiction as controversially keen-eyed, and agile, as quite anything in the supposed mainstream. Does not a version of the Nixon years as Science Fiction dream-novel, or a western well ahead of Mel Brooks's screen comedy *Blazing Saddles* (1974) with its trickster black sheriff and a rancher-cum-villain in the person of Drag Gibson, challenge if not all the rules, then at least the usual expectations, of the two genres in play? Reed's subsequent fiction, to include *Mumbo Jumbo* (1972), his circling pastiche of 1920s race manners with "Jes Grew" as a trope for the spread of black style and jazz, and *Flight To Canada* (1976), his spoof slave metafiction with helicopters over the quarters and TV broadcasts, gives witness to no dip in virtuosity or ironic fashioning.[6]

Carlene Hatcher Polite's *Sister X and The Victims of Foul Play* (1975), "jazz narrative" in her own words, and a text which shows nothing it not another kind of postmodern willingness to patrol its own telling, likewise does an about-face in terms of literary genre.[7] It turns a conventional murder plot back on itself, for the death of Arista Polo, dancer-artist, points to far larger stakes, the plot whereby back art, and with it black grace of music and movement, can be reduced to show-time, an updated commercial sale of flesh. Which foul play most applies, that of the murder in question or that of history?

A shared against-the-grain spirit animates Trey Ellis's *Platitudes* (1988), a novel like its follow-up *Home Repairs* (1993) and the tongue-in-cheek short story "Guess Who's Coming to Seder" (1989), not only full of self-referencing but written under the rubric of what its author calls Cultural Mulatto or New Back Aesthetic auspices.[8] Ellis so makes a conscious pitch to move on from historic themes of protest, slavery or color-line and ghetto, into contemporary Manhattan black young-writer life. This is Manhattan un-ghettoed, a cyber-savvy world of mixed schooling, pop culture, foodways, sex talk and dress. In the computer linkage of Dewayne Wellington and Ishee Ayam, writers both, he a would-be experimentalist and she an Alice Walker style womanist, Ellis, however, goes a great deal further than the portrait of access to the mainstream. It asks what narrative best tells contemporary Afro-America and its context. The novel's montage of snippets and computer letters, photographs, fact-fiction teases, even fake SAT tests, the one fictional story (that being shared by Deewayne and Ishee) mirrors their own actual and mutual story. Amid pc and gender ideology, black sisterhood and new black manhood, how is contemporary man-woman love to work or find its right working language and measure? Has one set of platitudes simply been replaced by another? Ellis's novel steps boldly, inventively, and with its own armory of provocation, on to battle-strewn ground.

In Darryl Pinckney's *High Cotton* (1992) W.E.B. DuBois's notion of The Talented Tenth, in yet another irreverence, is put under ironic auspices, as The Also Chosen.[9] This is 1960s black Middle America drawn to Black Power as a kind of suburban chic, Africanization as gesture—hair, dashikis, argot. The funny, rueful shies come fast and many, from the narrator's "No one sat me down and told me I was a Negro" (3) to riffs on the one hand about "the paradise of integration" (82) and on the other "Negrofirstism" (131). In keeping with, say, James Weldon Johnson's *The Autobiography of an Ex-Colored Man* (1912), a story of black-for-white impersonation matched in the fiction of fact genre of the novel, Pinckney rings his own changes on the novel-as-autobiography.[10] The alter ego voice, reflexive, adroitly mock-heroic, gives an ironic gloss to its own call to radicalism: "Then came the Revolution, that loss of meridian, brought to the suburbs by elder siblings in Easter break" (108–9).

Hurston, throughout, acts as an antecedent, a working marker. Her imaginative making-over of the black Florida of Eatonville, of the Hoodoo she calls "a sympathetic magic," and of the turns of vernacular black etiquette and speech as she garnered it from her own upbringing, the Caribbean, the Gullah and other islands off the Carolinas and the folklore she began under "Papa" Franz Boas, has belatedly won its better recognition. That, nonetheless, and since her rehabilitation in the 1970s, is far from ignoring the other kinds of controversy she has aroused. Is there, or not, still an insufficiency, to her takes on the politics of segregation, and behind it, the historic shadow of slavery? Did she, most notably in *Dust Tracks on a Road*, too readily trim her sails, edit, appease, even self-censor, for a white readership?

The paradoxes extend in a number of directions. Her relish, and affirmation, of Afro-America's cultural vitality can hardly be doubted. It expresses itself in the stories, folklore and the novels begun with *Jonah's Gourd Vine* (1934) and whose high point, in most opinion, is to be found *Their Eyes Were Watching God* (1937) as the tough but warmly fond, even lyric, life of Janie Crawford.[11] Yet Hurston, symptomatically, would also oppose the Brown v. Board of Education decision of 1954 outlawing "separate but equal" schooling on the not a little unusual grounds that its effect, as she believed, would demean black teachers and schooling.

Alice Walker, to whom much of Hurston's recovery is owed, offers a greatly relevant perspective in the Dedication of her *I Love Myself When I Am Laughing . . . And Then Again When I Am Being Mean and Impressive:*

A Zora Neale Hurston Reader (1979): "Zora Neale Hurston was outrageous—it appears by nature. She was quite capable of saying, writing, or doing things *different* from what one might have wished."[12] It may well be an irony in keeping that if Walker could write fervently in praise of Hurston as womanist founder, even while alleging "oddly false-sounding" notes in *Dust Tracks On A Road*, Ralph Ellison, whose *Invisible Man* (1952) exhibits its own contrarieties of voice, speaks of the "blight of burlesque" in Hurston's writings.[13] Either way, in her every swerve and counter-flow, bad behavior comes into play, the unwillingness on Hurston's part to settle for the received wisdom, the comfort of stock formula. Henry Louis Gates, in his Afterword to the Library of Congress edition of *Dust Tracks On A Road*, gives a furtherance to this by arguing for a necessary complexity to Hurston's writings that "refuses to lend itself to the glib categories of 'radical' or 'conservative,' 'black' or 'Negro,' 'revolutionary' or 'Uncle Tom'— categories of little use in literary criticism" (288).[14]

Reminders of Hurston's resistance to easy categorization virtually jump out from *Dust Tracks on a Road*.[15] On the one hand the text offers an abundance of down-home nuance ("I have been in Sorrow's kitchen and licked out all the pots" [280] or "I was a Southerner and had the map of Dixie on my tongue" [280]). On the other hand a kind of fighting talk is always in evidence, not merely her sideswipes, muted or not, at white Dixie, but at being held to any one-note "Negro" category ("There is no *The Negro* here" [230]) or "Why should Negroes be united? Nobody else in the United States is" [237]).

The willingness, in other words, to fire more than one shot across the bow at any one time, or to take few prisoners be they white or black, is unmistakable. In telling her life in *Dust Tracks on a Road*, whether Eatonville as "the first attempt at organized self-government on the part of Negroes in America" (3) or her girlhood will to creativity and set-to physical fight with her stepmother ("This was the very corn I wanted to grind" [101]), or her friendship with the great blues queen Ethel Waters pitched as a French kiss ("I am her friend, and her tongue is in my mouth" [245]), or the memory of early publication like *Mules & Men* (1935) ("You know the feeling when you found your first pubic hair" [211–12]), the cumulative effect is of a kind.[16] These, and like sayings, amount to un-piety given its own Hurston style, a force of voice at once guardedly intimate yet full of public daring. They offer a perfect departure-point for the "bad behavior," the play of contrary self-register, within US multicultural fiction.

*   *   *

The use of the word "Indian" is postmodern, a navigational conception, a colonial invention, a simulation in sound and transcription.

—Gerald Vizenor, *Crossbloods: Bone Courts,*
Bingo, and Other Reports (1990)[17]

Postindian mixedblood. Gerald Vizenor's self-description in his *Interior Landscapes: Autobiographical Myths and Metaphors* (1990) carries his typical style, a touch baroque, neologistic, challenging.[18] Born of White Earth Anishinaabe (Chippewa-Ojibway) and white fur trader origins, his fractured Minneapolis upbringing would lead on to army service in Japan, social work at the city's American Indian Employment and Guidance Center, a considerable stint as reporter for the *Minneapolis Tribune*, and an eventual professorial career spanning Bemidji State to Berkeley to the University of New Mexico. As one of the most published authors in Native American history, and across novels, stories, drama, poetry, and a huge body of discursive work, he has been both genial and fierce in exploring how Native peoples have been figured, or rather disfigured, in the standard versions.

"I believe we are all invented as Indians" he says in a 1981 interview.[19] "Indian is a nominal invention of racialism and colonialism, an invented name, unheard in native oral languages" he writes in a 1995 autobiographical essay.[20] Few have more teased even as they have been serious in their nay-saying to the triumphalist Euro-American narrative of hemispheric discovery and conquest. In this he has sought to counter through an array of trickster irony the almost casual travesties of name or typecasting, derogation or stereotype, that have enclosed Native America. That, as much as anything, embraces the notorious binary of Noble Savage or Devil, the Vanishing American ethos, victim figurations of reservation and city, and each and every turn of savagist mystique to do with the tribes. Against each of these, and without the slightest overlooking of cavalry and other war defeat, or the removals, or the Dawes and other allotments, or the trails of tears, or the set-backs of disease and poverty, he has posited his notions of *postindian* and *survivance*. These bespeak Native life as more than mere survival, but rather a vast and wholly ongoing enactive human reservoir of creativity, whether belief-systems or story both spoken and written, and managed against historical odds and both on the reservations and in the cities.

Rarely has his trickster irony been more energetic, even irreal, than in his novels. *Bearheart* (1978, revised 1990) gave early notice with its pilgrim vision of a regressive and consumerist America as much out of spiritual balance as oil. Thereafter the span has included *Griever: An American Monkey King in China* (1987, 1990), with its parallel trickster turns of the Anishinaabe, Griever de Hocus, and the Chinese monkey-king, Sun Wu k'ung, as well-aimed shies at the politics of American prolificacy and PRC state authoritarianism; *The Trickster of Liberty: Tribal Heirs to a Wild Baronage* (1988), an antic campus detective story as much to do with American history as with anthropology and purloined museum holdings of Native relics and bones; *The Heirs of Columbus* (1991), a quincentennial about-face portrait of the High Admiral as himself a returnee Native mixedblood; *Dead Voices: Natural Agonies in The New World* (1992), his Beckett-like parable of modern bear-transformation and shamanism; *Hotline Healers:*

An Almost Browne Novel (1997), his pastiche of New Age and "psychic Indians" not least through Almost's Blank Book business; and *Chancers* (2000), more trickster fantasy set in the University of California's Phoebe Hearst Museum in which anthropologist skulls exchange with those of Natives.[21] With *Hiroshima Bugi: Atomu 57* (2003), Vizenor sends a latest trickster, the *hafu* Ronin Browne, to Japan's Peace Memorial Museum in a memorialization of both Japanese and American war death. In *Father Meme* (2008) he tackles pedophilia on the reservation, the priestly abuse of Anishinaabe youth with the "Altar Boy War" as narrative at once lyric and fiercely redemptive. [22]

Manifest Manners: Postindian Warriors of Survivance (1994) and *Fugitive Poses: Native American Scenes of Absence and Presence* (1999), Vizenor's two full-length discursive works, demonstrate the same gamester virtuosity, an impatience with set-piece versions of history.[23] Both continue the contradance of earlier essay and polemical writing to include *Word-arrows: Indians and Whites in The New Fur Trade* (1978), *Earthdivers: Tribal Narratives on Mixed Descent* (1981) and *Crossbloods: Bone Courts, Bingo, and Other Reports* (1990).[24] The reckoning further needs to include the panels of memory, White Earth to Minneapolis, Japan to Berkeley, built into *Interior Landscapes: Autobiographical Myths and Metaphors* (1990) and the wide-ranging contrariety of view given in *Postindian Conversations* (1999).[25]

Ceci n'est pas une pipe. Magritte's celebrated jugglery of a title, a painting as text belied by its own accompanying visual image, gives Vizenor his cue for *Manifest Manners.* The cover's Andy Warhol silk-screen acrylic profile of Russell Means, AIM luminary alongside Dennis Banks, he takes as symptomatic of each endlessly reiterated fiction of The Indian. Braided, in a bone choker, apparently silent-wise in demeanor, in warrior regalia and with a pastel brown-red daubed from his forehead to chest, Means looks to be the perfect brave—impassive, and to be seen as silent. In fact he is out of time, posed, painterly, a beguiling and indeed artful travesty from a New York studio. In a repeated phrase throughout *Manifest Manners,* and with an additional nod to Michel Foucault's *This Is Not a Pipe,* Vizenor observes of Warhol's fiction of The Indian, and as though in countering obligation in the face of all other like fictions, "This portrait is not an Indian."[26]

The disclaimer does immediate, and almost literally and appropriate eye-catching good service, a simultaneous yes and no to the ironies of The Indian as endlessly imaged, and multiplied, as shadow, harlequin, hologram, manikin, chimera, other, or rather, in Vizenor's purposive coining, "double others." As title-phrase, too, "manifest manners," another of Vizenor's revamps, contributes its own working gloss: this is manifest destiny de-triumphalized, guyed, for its privileging of the one version, the one language, of American history over another. Each working sequence builds out from these standpoints.

"Postindian Warriors," as opening chapter, typical essay-cum-story, takes a range of ironic soundings at the imaging of Native people, from Lewis and Clark to *Dances With Wolves*, the Indian entries in the *Encyclopedia Britannica* to Michael Mann's *Last of The Mohicans*, and with time called on AIM's Clyde Bellecourt, Banks and Means for playing their part in the collaborationist fakery of The Indian. "Double Others," with a greatly affecting reference to Charles Alexander Eastman, Ohiyesa under his Santee Sioux tribal name, as the only Native doctor at the Wounded Knee massacre, leads on to the question of why no memorial of a kind with the Vietnam Veterans Memorial to honor less "the last major battle of the Indian Wars" than a "massacre of tribal women and children" (50). The same refusal of step-lock versions of history underwrites "Shadow Survivance," an essay that moves several ways at once: a further smack at anthropology (Vizenor calls it "anthropologetics"), a dislike for the narrow reservation cultural nationalism of Elizabeth Cook-Lynn, the teasing of Paula Gunn Allen for her "lesbian spiritualism," and skepticism at literary critique like Charles R. Larson's *American Indian Fiction* (1978) as deploying "wrong categories" (80).

Shorter pieces deal variously in Columbus and Mother Earth as more styles of *figura* than fact ("Eternal Havens"); Ishi, the last Yana survivor, as infinitely more elusive than some turn-of-the-century California stone-age exotic ("Ishi Obscura"); casino culture as at once footfall of when Luther Standing Bear had coins thrown at him and the modernity of "white people throwing money at the tribes" (139) with all its implications for Native gain and loss ("Casino Coups"); and AIM as "more kitsch and tired simulation than menace or moral tribal visions" (154), a view that has put Vizenor much on the firing-line ("Radical Durance"). Controversialism was rarely so adept, a refusal to follow the one or other prescribed viewpoint.

Delivered as the Abraham Lincoln lectures at the University of Nebraska, *Fugitive Poses* tackles, as Vizenor sees it, the fatal, if unintended, discrepancy between Indian and Native. Indians he takes to signify Baudrillardian simulation, the silhouettes or indeed the "double others" perpetuated in the dominant culture. These have found their forms in the demonology of captivity narratives, museum artifacts and bone displays, set-piece Noble Savage canvases like those of Charles King, the static Indian portraits of Edward Curtis's photography (precisely "fugitive poses" [161]), anthropological case-study, and every manner of film, sports, cartoon, and literary imagery. Notably Vizenor will again have nothing of romantic victimry. He refers to it as the "archive of victimry," or its equally romantic noble savage opposite.

Natives, in Vizenor's counter-coining, and as one of his continuing motifs, do and must look to survivance, imaginative sovereignty, the terms of the living not the dead. To this end *Fugitive Poses* advances a number of theaters in which native sovereignty becomes less an issue of land or, for sure, of blood quantum, than of self-imagining, memory, story (be it oral or scriptural), humor, tease, play, a repertoire of living continuity he terms transmotion. For Vizenor Native presence trumps absence, the active over the passive verb. In this, novelist, essayist and poet, he has seen his role as calling time on all the usual historical and social science formulations of indigeneity in the Americas.

In the writings of Leslie Marmon Silko, Laguna storyteller and eco-activist, one meets further contrariety of voice, tribal-political but far from narrow nationalism. In "Listening to the Spirits" (1998), she observes: "I believe that the Pueblo people, the indigenous people of the Americas, we're not only Indian nations and sovereign nations and people, but we are citizens of the world."[27] The novels bear every witness: *Ceremony* (1977) as the play of two war-zones, Pacific World War II and the Laguna-Keres terrain of Los Alamos with the story of the returning Tayo told in the form of a life-history yet reflexively itself a story-ceremony; *Almanac of The Dead* (1991) as a hemispheric parable of the indigenous Americas bent upon restitution of sovereignty and human spirit in the face of colonialism and war; and *Gardens in the Dunes* (1999) as a multi-narrative of American exile centered in its imaginary Sand Lizard People heroine and with the garden as orchestrating metaphor.[28] No stranger to controversy, as born out both in her critique of the capitalist west and her attacks on Gary Snyder and other white shaman figures and on Louise Erdrich as too ready an acolyte of the postmodern turn, she sets out her own interests and styling in *Storyteller* (1981).[29]

Of her recent writings few more exhibit this pugnacity than *Almanac of the Dead*, her resolutely hemispheric text of the Americas. For it envisages nothing less than the restoration of historic landscape—the return to indigenous custody through a risen people's army of a borderless, brown, nature-respecting human order in despite of all European (and Euro-American) cooption. In this respect Tucson, the American Southwest, acts as the novel's geo-historical centre, a place-name originally meaning "plentiful fresh water . . . in Papago" (190) yet where the city has "built its largest sewage treatment plant . . . next to the river" (189). Sewage, corruption, people and territories despoiled, underwrite the novel at every turn. This is the Americas as broken history, dysfunctions of caste and family, modernity as glut. Tucson itself is designated a "city of thieves" (610).

According to the passed-down Mayan Almanac of the Dead, however, actually a Book of Life, there is the prophecy of a reversal, a taking back of the land. This will take form in an eventual south-to-north indigenous alliance ("The prophecies said gradually all traces of Europeans in America would disappear and, at last, the people would retake the land" [631–2]). Silko, even so, offers no reductive white-brown cultural binary, a too ready blame narrative. Her vision remains one of the Americas historically forged of myriad nomenclatures and genealogies, be they tribal, Euro-white, north and south American, military or corporate.

Silko's novel, to this end, sets its narrative register as one of politics, crime and betrayal. Guns and cocaine rule. Oil, uranium mining and like excavation have left the land scarred. The CIA operates unchecked. Regimes run from Cuban revolutionary schools to police and army video torture pornography. Hollywood and TV Hotline Indians appear in the media. Selective imaging of Chiapas-like insurrection implies a controlled media. Real estate is endlessly finagled. The human organ trade lurks. Marxism and Capitalism vie, the one all plots and assassination, the other consumer frenzy. Either way, tribal dispossession continues. Above all the writ is war large and small ("War had been declared the first day the Spaniards set foot on Native American soil, and the same war had been going on ever since: the war was for the continents called the Americas" [133]).

The upshot, its more than seventy characters, ply of plot-lines, and compendium of indigenous sites—whether Arizona, New Mexico, Mexico, Central America, Alaska, New Orleans or Las Vegas, and desert, city or jungle, could not more aspire to be the eco-epic *de nos jours*. Silko unhesitatingly makes use of Yaqui, Navajo, Laguna, Hopi, Cherokee, Seminole, Mayan, and Inca tradition. She invokes the Aztecs as original blood sacrifice sorcerers who caused tribal peoples to flee north. The novel's inventory reworks Native snake creator-gods and paired twin mythology (Lecha and Zeta as heiresses to the almanac, Tacho and El Feo as leaders of the coming insurrection guided by macaw spirits). Shamanism prevails, or as Comrade Angelita, tribal revolutionary, observes "The ancestors's spirits speak in dreams. We wait. We simply wait for the earth's natural forces already set loose, the exploding, fierce energy of all the dead slaves and dead ancestors haunting the Americas" (518). Other gods enter the reckoning, not just Quetzacoatl, but the African and Haiti-to-New Orleans ancestor godheads of Damballah, Ogoun and Eursulie.

Opinion, predictably, has varied. Silko over-reaches, her novel is too crowded, or hectoring, or damagingly under-edited. Admirers speak of rare brilliance, the New World as indeed a very old world, replete in its own wisdom of populations and languages. The novel, even as it fills out its tapestry of fissure and self-loss, its show of multiple sexual desire or damage, so bears the promise of a redemptively better world of the Americas than that preyed on by the modern raptors of both capitalism and communism. Within the novel the almanac supplies the banner of resistance, complex prophecy, a codex. Born down across five hundred years and weathered by time and transport, and annotated by the grandmother Yoeme and others before her, its deciphering remains incomplete. Literally its "horse-gut parchment" (570) has been part eaten by starving fugitives at one point. That it is given by the psychic Lecha to the coke addicted Seese, searching for her kidnapped infant son, to transfer to computer files, implies unfinished history, a text of life still to be fulfilled.

To this end Silko can list past tribal and slave insurrections. Spanish *encomienda* and Dixie plantation labor give departure-points. The role of the Seminoles with Andrew Jackson in his victory at the Battle of New Orleans and unedifying expulsion to the west-of-the-Mississippi Indian

Territory that becomes Oklahoma acts as symptomatic historic irony. Geronimo and Wovoka, Wounded Knee, the Navajo code-speakers in World War II, and the recent indigenous rebellions in Guatemala, El Salvador and Peru, all bespeak a Native trajectory. The novel's proliferating strings of story and cause-and-effect build into the one composite narrative.

Each contributing folder of characters and action is so conceived to work as the narrative subsequent to the original Aztec-Death Dog rule across the Americas. Lecha as psychic and Zeta as smuggler serve as inaugural voices. Seese becomes adoptee amanuensis for the almanac. The Tucson desert ranch with its family of Ferro, Jamey, Paulie and their dogs and companions might be time's outpost, a remnant tribal colony. Seese's connection through her stolen child Monte into the David-Eric-Beaufrey-Serlo gay circuit, the latter with his monied search for *sangre pura* eugenics with body parts supplied by Trigg, throws a morbid light on both death cult photography, the raising of children, and race and gender purity. In the Max, Leah and Sonny Blue imbroglio, New York mafia crime is brought south to the country golf world of Arizona, another layer of corruption. The figure of Menardo, self-denying mestizo and global insurance entrepreneur, his affair with the greatly mis-named Alegria, his half-membership of Arizona's power-elite El Grupo, his willing collusion in the CIA arms operation, and his farcical death on being shot through a supposed bullet-proof vest by his chauffeur-spy Tacho (a not so veiled allusion to the 1890s Ghost Dance and imagined immunity from bullets), supplies both truth to history and pastiche. The Angelita La Escapía-Bartolomeo axis nicely undermines Cuban-style Marxism as solution ("The Indians couldn't care less about international Marxism; all they wanted was to retake their land from the white man" [326]).

In Sterling, initially banned by the Laguna for breaking tribal community protocol and showing their sacred stone snake to a film-crew, the novel has its conciliator and returnee. As he makes his way out of Tucson, the very vortex of historic ill, he encounters the pueblo's new giant snake ("The snake was looking south, in the direction from which the twin brothers and the people would come" [763]). On Silko's part this is *Almanac of The Dead* as hemispheric vision, mythic while would-be actual, ecological while sedimented in the humanity of its indigenous peoples, the Americas in their entirety as first and last landscape.

Other Native authorship has long added to, and complicated, this consortium of voice, various in standpoint yet always the necessary claim to a Native America as its own complex historical self-fashioning. Vine Deloria's *Custer Died For Your Sins: An Indian Manifesto* (1969), and its sequel *We Talk, You Listen: New Tribes, New Turf* (1970), call time on Natives as margin, exotica, the butt of exceptionalist American history.[30] Elizabeth Cook-Lynn (Crow Creek Sioux), founder-editor of *Wicazo sa review*, in *Why I Can't Read Wallace Stegner and Other Essays: A Tribal Voice* (1996) both berates white cultural constructions of the west and argues for a reservation-centered Native authorship.[31] Craig Womack (Muskogee-Creek-Cherokee) in *Red on Red: Native American Separatism* (1999) also posits a "redstick" ethos, Native writing, however more widely accessible, also to be read (and written) from a tribal-specific base.[32] Sherman Alexie delivers satire as fast on the improvisory literary draw as it is given to portraying Coeur d'Alène and other Native lives of the Pacific Northwest, reservation and city, in a story-collection as dexterous as *The Lone Ranger and Tonto Fistfight in Heaven* (1993).[33]

In "The Invention of John Wayne" from his *Mixedblood Messages: Literature, Film, Family, Place* (1998) the late Louis Owens (Choctaw-Cherokee), quite one of Native America's best voices, bracingly tackles the supreme actor-incarnation—the costs and burdens—of Hollywood's version of the white frontier west and its opposing "Indian Country."[34] Vizenor's notion of postindian does not always, or in every respect, extend to each of these writers as the appropriate working gloss. But they all share with him the will to imagine, or as much to the point to counter-imagine, a Native America in word and story unfixed of any and all cliché.

*   *   *

Aztlán, like *la raza*, bears the banner, the call to awareness and rally, of *chicanismo*, especially as embodied in legendary 1960s activism like that of César Chávez's UFW, José Angel Gutiérrez's la Raza Unida and "Corky" Gonzalez's Denver-based Crusade for Justice. Gonzalez himself would supply a panoramic verse anthem in his incantatory *I Am Joaquín/Yo Soy Joaquín* (1972).[35] A new fiction beckoned in novels like Tomás Rivera's bilingual migrant labor story-cycle ". . . y no se lo tragó la tierra/And the Earth Did Not Part* (1971), Rudolfo Anaya's affecting New Mexico child memoir *Bless Me, Ultima* (1972), and Rolando Hinojosa's Río Grande Valley/South Texas sequence begun with *Klail City y sus alrededores/Klail City* (1976, 1987).[36] A Chicana surge of literary voice lay to hand in voices like those of Cherrié Moraga's *Loving in the War Years: lo que nunca pasó por sus labios* (1983) with its challenge to sexual boundary, Ana Castillo in *The Mixquiahuala Letters* (1986) as inter-ethnic sorority and travel, and Sandra Cisneros in *Woman Hollering Creek and Other Stories* (1991) with its vignettes of childhood, family and love relationship.[37]

Luis Valdez and his Teatro Campesino revolutionized Chicano drama, rarely more so than in the stage-performance and film of *Zoot Suit* (1981) with its memories of Sleepy Lagoon and the 1940s *pachuco* riots.[38] Edward James Olmos brought "East Los," the inner-city *hispanidad* of Los Angeles, to the screen in *Stand and Deliver* (1987) just as Cheech Marin became a voice of comedy. Guillermo Gómez-Peña's *Warrior for Gringostroika* (1993), and related texts, supplied quite dazzling performance art.[39] A *Latino/a* renaissance, to draw upon Puerto Rican, Cuban American and each other Latino culture, could not have looked more in prospect. Yet, as ever, no orthodoxy, or one presiding consortium, was to prevail; quite the contrary. The contending voices have been many, few more interestingly against-the-grain or mutually contrastive than Oscar Zeta Acosta and Richard Rodriguez.

The Brown Buffalo. La cucaracha. On his own reckoning The Samoan. Hunter S. Thompson's 300 pound Dr. Gonzo in *Fear and Loathing in Las Vegas* (1971).[40] Under any or all of these sobriquets, Oscar Zeta Acosta (1935–74) supplies a stirring, if often marginalized, name in the making of 1960s counterculture. Something of his flavor as man and writer is to be gauged from the following exchange with Hunter Thompson, his companion-in-arms in their notorious ventures into Las Vegas and Hawai'i:

> I guess you wetback freaks have a special god.
>
> —Hunter S. Thompson, Letter to Oscar Zeta Acosta,
> February 9 1969[41]

> Once upon a time I was a liberal, yesterday I was a militant, today I am a revolutionary, trying like hell not to become uptight.
>
> —Oscar Zeta Acosta, Letter to Hunter S. Thompson,
> April 1968[42]

There is Acosta the anarcho-libertarian Chicano raised in California's Riverbank-Modesto and who makes his name as legal aid lawyer in Oakland and Los Angeles after qualifying in San Francisco in 1966. There is the Airforce enlistee who, on being sent to Panama, becomes a Pentecostal convert and missionary there (1949–52) before opting for apostasy and a return to altogether more secular ways and times in California. There is the jailee in Ciudad Juárez, Mexico in 1968, forced to argue in local court for his own interests in uncertain street Spanish (or *caló*) after a spat with a hotelkeeper. Not least there is the Oscar of the barricades, the battling lawyer of the High Schools and St Basil's Cathedral protests in 1968. This is the "buffalo" who becomes the *La Raza Unida* independent candidate for Sheriff of Los Angeles in 1970, who regularly affirms his first allegiance by signing himself "Oscar Zeta Acosta, Chicano lawyer," and who leaves for Mexico in despair, madness even, at the marring internal divisions of Chicano politics.

To these, always, has to be added the rombustious tequila drinker and druggie ten years in therapy; the hugely overweight ulcer sufferer who spat blood; the twice-over divorcee; and the eventual *desaparecido* in 1974 aged 39, who was last seen in Mazatlán, Mexico, and whose end has long been shrouded in mystery. Was he drug or gun-running, a kind of Chicano Ambrose Bierce who had created his own exit from history, or a victim of kidnap or other foul play? Even in summary Acosta can hardly be said not to invite attention as an American one-off, an original, a counterwriter. Above all, perhaps, there has to be Acosta the legendary first person singular writer of *The Autobiography of a Brown Buffalo* (1972) and *the Revolt of The Cockroach People* (1973).[43]

The "I" persona assumed by Acosta in *The Autobiography of a Brown Buffalo* bows in with a suitably Beat gesture of self-exposure: "I stand naked before the mirror" (11). He sees a body of "brown belly," "extra flesh," "two large hunks of brown tit" (11). Evacuation becomes a bathroom opera of heave, color, the moilings of fast-food leftovers. Hallucinatory colloquies open with "Old Bogey," James Cagney and Edward G. Robinson (or at least their screen personae). In their wake he turns to "my Jewish shrink," Dr. Serbin, the therapist as accuser, and whose voice echoes like some Freudian gargoyle throughout. Glut rules, a build-up of "booze and Mexican food," (12) Chinese pork and chicken, pills for dyspepsia, and his shower room tumescence and betraying fantasy coitus with Alice, the leggy, blond Minnesota partner of his friend Ted Casey back from overseas military duty in Okinawa.

The opening ventriloquy comes over busy and comic in its own right, at once self-serious yet self-mocking. There is even an "on the road" intertextual shy as Acosta plunges "headlong" in his green Plymouth into San Francisco traffic. "I'm splitting" (33) he writes in colloquial idiom to his office mate. Procul Harum sings "A Whiter Shade of Pale" on the car radio. He buys liquor opposite City Lights bookshop, "a hangout for sniveling intellectuals" (36) and throws in a reference to Herb Caen long celebrated for his coining, however facetious, of the term beatnik. Memories of marijuana and his first LSD come to mind. He roars drunkenly into Dr. Serbin's in the guise of "another wild Indian gone amok" (42), another *faux* barbarian. Acosta so monitors "Acosta." The one text engagingly patrols the other.

At Trader JJ's watering hole, he gives vent to the bar-room and wholly un-pc macho patois of "chinks and fags" (43). The Beatles's "Help" spills its harmonies and plaintiveness on to Polk Street. Ted Casey tempts him with mescaline. "Powdered mayonnaise" (67), as he terms heroin, appears at a Mafia restaurant where he stops for food. Women, his ex-lover June MacAdoo, Alice, and her friend Mary, all weave into his sexual fantasies even as he frets, with reason, at his own male prowess. The diaroma is motleyed, a comic-cuts weave of illusion and fact.

So it is, too, on July 1 1967, that Acosta announces himself as "the Samoan," island brown hulk, ethnic transvestite, a figure of guise, mask, harlequinry. "I've been mistaken for American Indian, Spanish, Filipino, Hawaiian, Samoan, and Arabian" he witnesses, adding ruefully, "No one has ever asked me if I'm a spic or greaser" (68). Is this not Acosta as live American multi-text, Latino lawyer yet Latino outlaw? He invokes one John Tibeau as "Easy Rider" bike poet on a Harley Davidson, as his *alter ego*, a latter-day and Beat-styled West Coast fantasy troubadour, a fusion of Lord Byron and the Bob Dylan he listens to with admiration.

These various incarnations compete and yet collude throughout. On the one hand he looks back to his Riverbank boyhood with is gang allegiance and fights against the Okies "I grew up a fat, dark Mexican—a Brown Buffalo—and my enemies called me a nigger" (86), war-games, peach-picking, clarinet playing and early first loves. On the other hand he heads into the Pacific northwest with the hitchhiker Karin Wilmington, a journey busy in allusion to Tim Leary, Jerry Garcia and The Grateful Dead and which takes him into the Hemingway country of Ketchum, Idaho. Both give contour to his Panama years, his onetime bid to serve as a "Mexican Billy Graham" (132).

As he weaves his way through more drugs, characters like Scott ("a full time dope smuggler and a salesman for Scientology" [152]), he thinks back on "Oscar" as would-be author—"The beatniks in the colleges were telling brown buffaloes like me to forget about formal education" (152). For all that he can self-mockingly tell the waitress Bobbi that "My family is the Last of the Aztecs" (140), the call is equally to the free flow of life and pen.

Overdoses, bad trips, successions of women, memories of writer alcoholics like Al Matthews, car crashes and blackouts in Aspen, and odd jobs across Colorado, give the ongoing trajectory. His Chicano self come into focus in the remembrance of being detained in Juarez jail amid "the ugliest pirates I ever saw" (192) and the need to prove, as if playing out the formula migrant script, his "American" identity." A border official tells him "You don't *look* like an American you know?" (195). Almost inevitably, given a journey text as mythic as actual, the pathway back into Los Angeles is the hallowed Route 66.

Acosta next speaks of a time when he will become Zeta, as taken from the last letter of the Spanish alphabet (and, as *The Revolt of the Cockroach People* confirms, also from the name of the hero in the movie *Las Cucarachas*), "Oscar" as *auteur* equally in life as text. For the moment, however, he gives the following as his working certificate of identity: ". . . I am neither a Mexican nor an American. I am neither a Catholic nor a Protestant. I am a Chicano by ancestry and a Brown Buffalo by choice" (199).

Back, finally, in East LA, the *barrio* known vernacularly in *caló* as "East Los" and "the home of the biggest herd of brown buffaloes in the world" (199), he opts for a moment of rest, temporary and recuperative pause. To hand is "Oscar" as both *chicanismo*'s own literary *vato loco* and yet activist warrior, its own would-be Sheriff of Los Angeles, all to be continued over into the "another story" (199) pending in *The Revolt of The Cockroach People*.

"A faded beatnik, a flower vato, an aspiring writer, a thirty- three-year old kid full of buffalo chips is supposed to defend these bastards." (53). In antic pose (his name card reads "Buffalo Z. Brown, Chicano Lawyer, Belmont Hotel, LA" (48), the "Oscar" of *Cockroach People* so positions himself in relation to the Chicano militants involved in the local school strikes of 1968. This authorial "I" again gives off a beguiling equivocation of self and persona, participant and observer.

One the one hand, as novel-cum-autobiography, the text yields an actual Acosta of LA courtroom and barricade, counsel in the St. Basil 21 and

East Los Angeles 13 trials, would-be exposer of the Robert Fernandez and "Roland Zanzibar" murders (the latter the journalist Reuben Salazar of Station KMEX), conferee with César Chávez and "Corky" Gonzalez, and candidate for Sheriff of Los Angeles County. On the other hand, it yields an Acosta always the writer *semblable* who sees his own silhouette in the Aztec warrior founder god Huitzilopochtli (11), speaks of himself as "Vato Número Uno," and "singer of songs" (207), and uses the court to give a parallel history of *chicanismo* with due allusion to Quetzacoatl, Moctezuma, Córtes and La Malinche through to 1848 and the Anglo appropriation of the southwest and its latterday aftermath. He casts himself as first person and yet, alterity itself, third person, the participant in the bombing by Chicano militants of a Safeway Store and Bank of America branch. He equally envisions himself as the *carnal* (brother/dude) edging into madness at the petty conspirators and fifth columnists and their delusions and betrayals within Chicano activism. Throughout, and in an address to the court which as much serves as an appeal to history as to the law, he again emphasizes a Chicano/Hippie nexus—"A hippie is like a cockroach. So are the beatniks. So are the Chicanos. We are all around, Judge." (228)

This parallel of Chicano and Beatnik recurs, the interplay of two counter-types. The LA Cathedral built by the Vietnam War supporting and autocratic Cardinal McIntyre becomes "a personal monstrosity" (11), McIntyre's architectural outward show, to Acosta's eye, of an inner spiritual blight. The Chicano poor who protest against this high tier Catholicism, in the text's hallucinatory telling, transpose into a "gang of cockroaches" (11), replete with Gloria Chavez, golf club swinging heroine.

As a "religious war" (14) erupts, "Oscar" envisions himself as both his own familiar and his own stranger: " 'Come on,' our lawyer exhorts. I, strange fate, am this lawyer' " (14). The whole event then veers into serio-comic opera, a politics of the real and yet surreal, as signaled in each of the rallying placards: "YANKEES OUT OF AZTLAN" (32) or, during the fracas over the schools, "MENUDO EVERY DAY" (41), or, in the author's own rise to fame, "VIVA EL ZETA!" (164). Questing, as he says, for "my Chicano soul" (47), "Oscar" also looks back, and with a mix of reproach and yet nostalgia, to "my beatnik days" (65). To the one side stands his trial work with the St. Basil 21 and East LA 13, his flurry of contempt imprisonments (Prisoner "Zeta-Brown, 4889") and eventual political campaign. To the other he gives himself to heady flights of phantasmagoria. "We are the Viet Cong of America," he proclaims (198) more than a little headily. Sexual euphoria, aided by an ingestion of Quaalude-400s, takes the form of his imagined Sheik of Araby practices with his three girl followers and the love tryst with the black juror Jean Fisher. If not actually, then again in his mind's eye, he finally has the entire Californian judicial bench subpoenaed on grounds of historic racism.

Two sequences give added particularity to this use of text as also meta-text. First Acosta/"Oscar" addresses the arrest, self-hanging and, above all, autopsy of Robert Fernandez, Chicano prisoner. The corpse ("just another expendable Cockroach"[101]), anatomically sliced and jarred under the guidance of Dr. Thomas A. Naguchi, "Coroner to the stars" as he is known, becomes Acosta's textual autopsy, as it were, of the abused larger body of *chicanismo*. The same holds for the police shooting of "Roland Zanzibar." Acosta far from hides his view that an iconographic and more inclusive process has been involved, that of the ritual silencing of an unwanted and demonized *chicanismo*. "Someone still has to answer for Robert Fernandez and Roland Zanzibar" (258) he editorializes, both in the way of a memorial and yet also to prompt future action.

This doubling, or reflexivity, holds throughout. He depicts both the *vatos*, *cholos*, and *pintos*, of barrio and street, and the cops and white authorities who make up *los gabachos*, as belonging to their own time-frame of the 1960s and yet also to far more ancient white-brown historic timelines and clashes. Acosta enters the text on equally shared terms, lawyer yet metalawyer, as he engages in each reeling, often absurdist exchange with Judge Alacran during the "Chicano Militants" and Gonzalez trials. In his role as "Oscar" or "Zeta" he offers himself as located in both a contemporary Los Angeles courtroom and the courtroom of history.

In truth all the text's main figures are pitched to take on their own kind of myth, none more so than César Chávez and "Corky" Gonzalez, legatees as Acosta construes them, of an "Aztec" warriordom of Zapata and Pancho Villa. In another doubling Mayor Sam Yorty plays Janus, smiling sympathizer yet for Acosta *agent provocateur* who in bad faith counsels Chicano insurrection. A crazed Charlie Manson, "acid fascist" (98), hovers as the presiding spirit of a Los Angeles "the most detestable city on earth" (23). Gene McCarthy features as a radical from the mainstream, one politician in two guises. Robert Kennedy enters and exits as both Democratic Party and *campesino* supporting martyr, killed by Sirhan Sirhan as "mysterious Arab" (98). A celebrity, and appropriately on-stage, performance of support of his campaign for sheriff is given by "hidden" Chicanos like Anthony Quinn and Vicki Carr. Acosta's technique is always to emphasize this duality of time, and place, the one timeline, the one location, held inside the other.

Fittingly Hunter S. Thompson makes his appearance as "Stonewall," yet another life figure consciously given textual or virtual alternative identity. He serves as journalist confessor. For Acosta, too, has his own "other" self to add to the parade, his own mediation of reality and word, the two configurations in one. The upshot is autobiography yet not, a Chicano self locked into actual time and place yet also a self always deftly aware of performing its own fictionalization. Oscar, or "Oscar," this is bad behavior with style, life into text never less than under the opposition flag.

In Richard Rodriguez America vaunts quite another kind of opposing voice, one, however, quite as wired from the start to stir the hornet's nest, to spark ire. *A Hunger of Memory: The Education of Richard Rodriguez*

(1982), typically, argues for an end to bilingual education and affirmative action, the re-imposition of the Latin Mass, and a break with piety about ancestral migrant-Catholic family culture.[44] Here was transgression from the Cultural Right, no Chicano nationalist rather a writer of Chicano heritage laying claim to the American mainstream. To detractors, few more vocal than Chicano activists, his refusal to join—in fact to oppose—their camp signaled a *trahison des clercs*, his refusal of any or all minority status a species of self-absorption, too great a pondering of his own face in the mirror. To admirers he offers a vindication of the virtues of assimilation whatever the pains of cutting free from family and ethnic-cultural intimacy. That Rodriguez managed a style of rare, even soaring fluency, seemed almost to add insult to injury.

Little, however, could he, or anyone else, have foreseen how "this intellectual autobiography" as he terms *Hunger of Memory*, together with each *Time, American Scholar* and PBS McNeil-Lehrer *News Hour* essay, would make him the media conservative favorite he has become. For there can be little doubt of his bravura, the willingness to play mainstream cat among the ethnic pigeons and with an eloquence as ready as his stance of end-of-history melancholy. In this his autobiography can be compared to great advantage with, say, Linda Chavez's *Out of The Barrio: Towards a New Politics of Hispanic Assimilation* (1991), like-minded in assimilationist ethos but wholly workaday in style.[45]

As six "essays impersonating an autobiography ... chapters of sad, fugue-like repetition" (7) *Hunger of Memory* thus gives a new imaginative turn to the continuum of *Latino* autobiography—"an intellectual autobiography" (175) he insists. The effect, depending on ideological viewpoint, is to be applauded or decried. Is Rodriguez simply affirming America's promise of the sovereign self, for all the talk of loss, parental and community severance, too indulgent a preoccupation with his own needs? Is he guilty of mainstreaming, as it has been called, an over-ready willingness to cede the importance of his Mexican American origins to what he dubs public America? Whichever holds there can be no doubting Rodriguez's willingness to speak against the grain of ethno-piety and to take his polemical chances.

Each essay proffers both witness and challenge. In "Aria" he insists that "bilingualists simplistically scorn the value and necessity of assimilation" (26), as if to have done once and for all with the special-pleading, the self-ghettoization, he believes perpetuated by a carried-over insistence on *barrio* or family Spanish ("a private language" [5]) in a larger American culture whose prime tongue is English. The opening terms of reference are, in keeping, high-literary, and to his detractors not a little pretentious—"I have taken Caliban's advice. I have stolen their books. I will have some run of this isle" (3). If he seeks to anticipate denigration as "Tom Brown" or "the brown Uncle Tom" (4) he also has his boldness, a self-stance that offers no concession to the easy show of ethnicity. "Aztec ruins," he avers, "hold no special interest for me. I do not search Mexican graveyards for unnameable ancestors . . ." (5). Rather, he celebrates a life of books, study, and which has one culminating expression in his Fulbright year in the British Museum Reading Room as preparation for a Berkeley thesis on Renaissance literature, even as he asserts how greatly he rues leaving behind parents who "have never heard of García Lorca and García Márquez" (5). Is this, again, special pleading, self-indulgence, or a show of fierce honesty?

"The Achievement of Desire" casts him as the "scholarship boy" (46) à la Richard Hoggart, and who, again, "cannot afford to admire his parents" (49) if he is to enter America's public domain. "Credo" has him arguing for a return to Latin for "the high ceremony" of the Mass as a signifier of universalism and necessary bulwark against the "ghetto Catholic" church with its Spanish or other ethnic-language religious services. "Complexion" turns upon the contemplation of his own Aztec features, over which he lingers at, for some, all too narcissistic a length. His dark complexion and skin-tone have caused him to feel "mysteriously marked" (125), a "divorce from my body" (125), but now exorcised by his plunge into a larger (and within it and at the time an unstatedly Gay) world.

In "Profession" he looks back to his time doing graduate work in the English Department at Berkeley when he became, in a term he repeats with some scorn, a celebrity "minority student" (142), believing himself favored, and so demeaned, by a process which has put category above self. Finally, in "Mr. Secrets," and with a dip back into his resoluteness to be a book reader in a home where manual work set the standard, he returns to the need to enter, to exist in, and to turn to his own working advantage, America's public language, namely English as against the provincializing US Spanish of his ancestral migrant-Catholic family culture. Little wonder *Hunger of Memory* was, and remains, a jousting-ground for notions of cultural center and periphery, the canonical as against the ethnic self. Rodriguez, in his own phrase, "languages" himself, the Chicano-who-was articulating the American-who-is and who speaks of ever hoping to "form new versions of myself" (190). Articulacy, and the education which produced it, undoubtedly reigns, a rise to word, consciousness, book, literature, media, the world.

In his follow-up volume, *Days of Obligation: An Argument With My Mexican Father* (1992), and in remembrance of his young life in Sacramento, California, he speaks of his own eclectic pathway into an America beyond any one ethnicity ("Asians rounded the world for me. I was a Mexican teenager in America who had become an Irish Catholic" [166]). He deplores "the simply bipartite" version of America, "the simplicities of black and white America" (166).[46] In *Brown: The Last Discovery of America* (2003), by his own designation the third of a trilogy "on public life and my private life" (Preface, v), he argues for thinking the United State a North as much as a West, ever browner, ever more mixed, and decries race as any kind of usable category.[47] His own California credential becomes that of "a queer Catholic Indian Spaniard at home in a temperate Chinese city in a fading blond state in a post-Protestant nation" (35). Even so, the jury remains out as to any absolute or final balance of gains and losses. Has the public life so sought, and found, and for all his talk of multiple and beyond-ethnicity gain, been at a cost under-recognized even on his own part?

* * *

The contrarian range within Asian American writing has been yet another species of plenty, the very repudiation of the quiescent "ethnic." Frank Chin, notably, has led the charge with his fists-up essay-work, stories and plays, as trenchantly as anywhere in "Come All Ye Asian American Writers of the Real and the Fake," his Preface to the landmark *The Big Aiiieeeee! An Anthology of Chinese American and Japanese American Literature* (1991).[48] There, under his fighting-Cantonese colors, he berates images of passive Chinese, by rote assimilationism. His wrath is especially aroused by Christianized Chinese, false myths of China as he sees them and as perpetuated by Maxine Hong Kingston, Amy Tan and David Hwang, and the sequence of Asian caricature—John Chinaman, Charlie Chan, Fu Manchu and Tokyo Rose. David Mura has taken a controversial bead on "racial" sexuality in *A Male Grief: Notes on Pornography and Addiction* (1987) and *The Colors of Desire* (1995), as well as on Japanese identity in America by contrast with its origins for him in Japan in *Turning Japanese: Memoirs of a Sansei* (1991).[49]

Key contending women's authorship embraces Maxine Hong Kingston's *The Woman Warrior: Memoirs of a Girlhood Among Ghosts* (1977), with its story-telling analysis of Chinese American gender genealogies and power, Theresa Hak Kyung Cha's *Dictée* (1982), with its Korean American collagist-postmodern deciphering of split legacy—nation, gender, mother-daughter, and Jessica Hagedorn's *Dogeaters* (1990), with its fantastical, satiric multi-component vision of the Philippines under the shadow of both Marcos-style legacy and US cultural colonization.[50] Epifanio San Juan's *Racism and Cultural Studies: Critiques of Multiculturalist Ideology and the Politics of Difference* (2002) gives more energy to the frays with its contention that multiculturalism amounts to no more than boutique good feeling and fad in the face of Filipino and other labor migrancy and exploitation.[51] All of these texts have contributed to de-stabilizing, variegating, the one Asian American literary phalanx, necessary reminders of stances pitched against several kinds of canon.

One text carries a particularly historic charge, Monica Sone's *Nisei Daughter* (1953, 1979).[52] It operates at several interfaces: Yellow Peril, Seattle waterfront hotel, Pearl Harbor, and the memory of Executive Order 9066 and the internment of 120,000 Japanese Americans in abrogation of due process and civil rights—a time when we "became prisoners of their own government, without charges, without trials" (Preface). Graphically, in the light of Pearl Harbor, Sone recalls a window sign saying in the Seattle of her upbringing "We kill rats and Japs here" (160). She leaves little doubt of the potential for self-division, the fissure of allegiance: "I didn't see how I could be both a Yankee and Japanese at the same time. It was like being born with two heads. It sounded freakish and a lot of trouble" (19). She lives amid not only two languages but also two calendars, Lincoln's Birthday but also *Tenchosetu*, the Emperor's Birthday. If she listens to big bands on American radio she also hears her parents at Nippon Kan Hall singing *naniwa bushi*, "old Japan . . . a type of ballad singing" (77).

She also gives voice to a reversal of situation in her first youthful visit from America to "old Japan," "a strange land of bicycles" (90) in which "people stared at our foreign clothes and I felt self-conscious" (91). She meets her grandfather with his Japanese dream of America, is struck by the silences of Japanese culture as against the volubility and noise of America, and collects a kind of mini-museum of Japan to take back to America—a toy samurai sword, a kimono, Japanese stockings, her mother's scroll, and a host of exquisite small sculptures and silk and other designs. These all contrast with the War Relocation Authority's order to de-Japanize their home, though Monica's mother will take "a gallon can of soy sauce" (168) on their next journey into the camps. She remains stalwartly upbeat, even so, about her double-identity, a posture which in some quarters has led to her being thought too forgiving of the treatment accorded Japanese Americans. Yet by her own lights Japan remains a cultural resource wholly in kind with America, however directly or indirectly both have led via Pearl Harbor and 9066 to the camp's wire fence. Together she sees them as "a real bargain in life, two for the price of one" (236). That remains a contentious claim.

It would not take any great excavatory effort to add further to the Asias being written as American, each with gains and yet fissures, advances and yet costs. Whether Amy Tan's repertoire from *The Joy Luck Club* (1989), with its mother-daughter play of life and memory across the mah jong table, through to *Saving Fish From Drowning* (2005), with its Myanmar jungle setting and east-west shock of recognition, or Lan Cao's *Monkey Bridge* (1989), with its point-counterpoint of Vietnam and America as two warring homelands both suffused in loyalty and betrayal, Asian American writing has made every claim to be as literary mainstream as any other.[53] Equally versatile, and intriguing, has to be Chang-rae Lee's *Native Speaker* (1995), New York, America, seen through a Korean American lens as spy-ground, identity parade, language-game, race politics, and in which nothing other than ethnicity itself becomes the object of detection.[54]

Max Yeh in his novel, *The Beginning of the East* (1992) adds further to the challenge of the national culture as monolith with "diversity" thrown in as nominal concession.[55] He depicts a "New World" modernity as mapped by Christopher Ng, latter-day Chinese American Columbus, the very cartography of global capital, labor migrancy, media and power-politics ("Like the China watchers . . . [Ng] would be the first Chinese, maybe the second, to pursue an off-shore American watch" [70]). The resulting

narrative amounts to an irreverent tour-de-force, the world seen th
fresh-explorer Chinese American "Columbian" eyes as not just Ame......
economic hegemony but a counter-map of historically co-existent cultures
of place and ethnicity. It is a novel deserving of better recognition, a provocative imagining and querying of all oriental-occidental binaries.

*   *   *

Bad Behavior, on this still too selective account (one would want to extend
its remit to a range of Jewish, Euro-American, Arab American, Pacific
Islander, Indo-Pakistani and other south Asian texts) does service a number of ways. It reminds that multicultural voice, in this case of Afro-
America, Native America, *chicanismo* and Asian America, and exactly on
account of overlaps as much as differences, eclecticisms as much as inno-
vations, yields anything but literary clubmanship. Quite in kind with the
US's assumed mainstream, or white-ethnic writing, or different gender and
class groupings, each has been a gallery of sometimes shared, sometimes
contrary, soundings. How, in a sense, could it have been otherwise? How,
even so, could that not have met with scrupulous better acknowledgement?
Majority-minority divides, stereotyping, indeed all literary and intellectual
ghettoization, have exacted not only serious price but also loss. A number
of further cross-bearings underline the point.

In his "Rebirth of a New Rican" (1994) Ed Morales, journalist, DJ and
the author of *Living in Spanglish* (2002), with its opening observation that
"to be Spanglish is to live in multisubjectivity," suggests that is so "porque
only a multiculture pueblo can understand/ El adentro y the outside of the
dynamic . . ."[56] Carter Revard, Osage poet, Oklahoman, Oxford Rhodes
Scholar, longtime St. Louis academic with a literary speciality in Old and
Middle English and author of the prose-and-poetry autobiography *Winning The Dust Bowl* (2001), offers a shared perspective.[57] In his essay
"Herbs of Healing: American Values in American Indian Literature"
(1987), he writes "There are some Big Guns of American culture who aim
to shoot down "Minority Literature," claiming that it is trash unworthy
of our classrooms . . ."[58] He then proceeds to offer a rich trove of daring literary comparison between Native and white-canonical authorship
(Simon Ortiz with Wallace Stevens, Wendy Rose with John Milton, Louise
Erdrich with Robert Frost). For his part Sherman Alexie, whose fiction
and film-making has shown little deference to any supposed consensual
status quo as to Native and non-Native America, gives explicit voice to his
sense of counter-role. Asked in a 2003 interview if, given his mainstream
success, "you really feel like you have sold out your own people," his reply
was symptomatically combative and yet considered: "You know as an artist, it's not my job to belong. I'm not a social worker; I'm not a therapist.
It's my job to beat the shit out of the world. I'm not here to make people
feel good."[59]

In *The Shock of Arrival: Reflections on Postcolonial Experience* (1996), looking back on a life that bridges Allahabad and Kerala, the Sudan, England and New York City, Meena Alexander speaks of her own Indo-American identity as both a prior and ongoing dynamic of multicultural shapings. She annotates the debts that have helped make her "ethnic identity as an Indian American," namely "I learn from Japanese Americans, Korean Americans, Chinese Americans, African Americans, Native Americans, Hispanic Americans, Jewish Americans, Arab Americans . . . And my artwork refracts these lines of sense, these multiple anchorages."[60] "Multiple anchorages" applies to perfection: the challenge and possibilities of American literary voice.

Ishmael Reed, long one of US literary multiculturalism's banner figures and who speaks of "planet-nation" America as against "the American literary industrial complex,"[61] gives a further and typical counter-perspective in his "America: The Multinational Society" (1983):

> Western civilization . . . becomes another confusing category like Third World, or Judeo-Christian culture, as man attempts to impose his small-screen view of political and cultural reality upon a complex world. Our most publicized novelist recently said that Western civilization was the greatest achievement of mankind, an attitude that flourishes on the street level as scribbles in public restrooms: "White Power," "Niggers and Spics Suck," or "Hitler was a prophet," the latter being the most telling, for wasn't Adolph Hitler the archetypal monoculturalist who, in his pig-headed arrogance, believed that one way and one blood was so pure that it had to be protected from alien strains at all costs? Where did such an attitude, which has caused so much misery and depression in our national life, which has tainted even our noblest achievements, begin?[62]

Discomforting language. Disruptive quipping. Whether Reed does or does not persuade all-comers to this round of argument, quite assuredly he will have no truck with grand clichés about America as the single narrative or the simple-mindedness that imagines "ethnic" or "multicultural," as if by rote, to signify margin, periphery, or the slippage whereby a demographic minority is imagined to write minority literature. Does not Bad Behavior of this kind, and of the kind attended to throughout this account, turn out to be nothing other than multiculturalism's own necessary, not to say contrary, form of good behavior?

9 Home and Away
US Poetries of Immigration and Migrancy

Five Nations: Dutch, French, Englishmen, Indians, and we . . .
—Robert Lowell, "Fourth of July in Maine" (1967)[1]

Indentured to dreams
we imagine America,
the soft green breast of an island
almost a mirage beyond our eyes.
—Russell Leong, "The Country of Dreams and Dust" (1993)[2]

My own words somersault naturally as my name,
joyous among all those meadows: Michoancán,
Vera Cruz, Tenochtitlán, Oaxaca. . .
—Lorna Dee Cervantes, "Visions of Mexico While at a Writing
Symposium in Port Townsend, Washington" (1981)[3]

Standard writ has long held that, from the Anglo-Puritan landfall
through to postmodern California, the United States has been nothing
if not an immigrant nation, an ongoing process of arrivees. Not only
New England, but *Nueva España* and *Nouvelle France*, bequeath their
shaping European passage and geographies. *Gum Sahn*, Gold Mountain in English, reflects the West Coast as America's parallel beckoning, the index of Chinese and other Asian inward population flow. Can
it be doubted that immigration, be it across the Atlantic from Britain
and Europe, or across the Pacific from Asia and the islands, or as the
lure of *el norte* for the Americas to the south, or from the Caribbean
to the mainland, together with every manner of internal migration, lies
other than at the heart of America's making, as multicultural as it has
been ongoing?

Little wonder that this evolution of the American Grain, in William
Carlos Williams's memorable phrase, find refractions throughout American writing, whether fiction, drama, every manner of autobiographical
and discursive work or, wholly in kind, poetry. Robert Lowell, Russell
Leong and Lorna Dee Cervantes, to be sure, supply but a selective literary roster from amid the variously sedimented, and sometimes warring,

American legacies of origin, ethnicity, class, gender, and languages far from English. Yet as the opening extracts from their work confirm, and from across the span of the two coasts, they also can be said to exhibit an unmistakable shared interest: that of America's enduring memory of migrant timelines and routes.

Lowell, upper-tier Massachusetts WASP poet for all his maverick confessionalism and politics, invokes the founding European immigration of "Dutch, French, Englishmen" and their encounter with the "Indians," likely Algonquin, together with the arising "we" of America. The poem's remembrance of a Maine Independence Day parade, full of wry flourish, reflexive, looks to how America, and certainly Anglo-America, has indeed "paraded" its 17th Century and an ensuing, not to say pre-emptive, white-cultural or anglo mainstream. Leong, Chinese American poet raised in San Francisco and longtime editor of *Amerasia*, looks to an exodus from the era of the last Chinese emperor and from the legendary Chinese mainland rebellious regions of Canton and Guandong province. The paradox for these journeyers could not more lie in being indentured to their own kind of Asian-Gatsbyesque dream of America, the hardship of Pacific crossing and survival within the "green breast" of hope. Cervantes, her poetry rooted in the *chicanismo* of a bluecollar mestiza-California upbringing, uses the one America of the Pacific northwest to situate the other of Mexico. Her "own words" she thinks of as having been migrantly compounded of silence and quill, Nahuatl and Spanish, and an English nowhere, ironically, to find apter expression than at a writing symposium.

Other poetries of American migration, not only European, Asian or Mexican but still further beyond, inevitably give their own stylings, the redemption, and sometimes un-redemption, of older regimes in the promise of the new. These bespeak the exhilarations of setting forth yet the pains of uprooting, crossings of sea and land, a chosen path or flight, enforced asylum or exile, each, one way or another, the need, the resolve, to make home of away. America as Brave New World has just cause to celebrate triumphs, be it the forging of a "nation of immigrants," a first generation's journeying, the labor and the benefits for later generations, community upward well-being, or new individual freedom. That, however, is anything but to overlook the caveats.

If America has created a sense of nation what to say of migrant labor, populations often race or color marked and at the bottom of the work-ladder? What sense of migration, and its causes, most appropriately holds for the Afro-America first of Middle Passage slavery, and as post-bellum Dixie re-imposed Jim Crow in its wake, the northwards Great Migration? More than a million black southerners would head for Harlem, Chicago or Canada, a "wave of black people running from want and violence" as Toni Morrison calls it in her novel *Jazz* (1992).[4] Has not *chicanismo*, whatever its own historic claims to the southwest and west, and in common with the Caribbean of Puerto Rico, Cuba and other Latin American populations seeking the dream of *la abundancia*, often enough been thought a "border" culture welcome only as manual labor? Luis Omar Salinas's "Ode to Mexican Experience," with its allusions to the poet's own "Aztec mind" and to "roving gladiators" and "those lost in the wreckage," gives a pointer to the fuller human nuance.[5]

What version of immigrant America would best hold for "bachelor" Chinamen initially denied their families by the 1882 Exclusion Act, or, against the backdrop of the Spanish-American War of 1898, the Filipino diaspora as colonial-Asian workforce, or each Japanese and Korean passage through Hawai'i into the continental USA? In "Minority Poem" the Chinese-Hawaiian poet Wing Tek Lum gives his own cryptic gloss to this history, each immigrant community "just as American/as apple pie" yet with the kicker "That is, if you count/the leftover peelings."[6]

The issue turns especially acute in connection with America's first peoples, Native America, even allowing that many of the tribes, Pequot or Sioux, Anishinaabe or Navaho, and across today's US-Canada and US-Mexico borders, engaged in seasonal moves for food-gathering. A right wording, spoken or written, poetry or otherwise, would be the challenge of any Native writer seeking to capture the "migrant" history consequent upon the homesteader and cavalry wars, imported disease, the massacres, and the deportations into, and out of, "Indian Country" of which the well-named Indian Removal Act of 1830, the Cherokee "Trail of Tears" in 1838, and the surrender and dispatch of Geronimo and his Chiricahua Apaches to Florida in 1886, were typical. The successive Allotment Acts of 1887 and 1906, and the rise of the reservations, add their shared history. Native poets, no less than novelists and fellow writers of tribal descent, have rightly refused Vanishing American victimry. But from New Mexico's Scott Momaday (Kiowa) to Alaska's Mary TallMountain (Athabaskan), or Simon Ortiz (Acoma Pueblo) to Gail Tremblay (Onandaga-Micmac-French), that is not to understate their recognition of migrancies anything but self-chosen.

Lowell, Leong and Cervantes, to re-emphasize, give no more than sightlines. Their extracts, however, help to underline how in all its several and overlapping forms, American migrancy can be said to have been taken up in modern poetry quite as much as elsewhere in American culture. Migrations from Europe or Africa across the Atlantic, or from Asia across the Pacific, indicate the one scheme of reference. Migrations within America, Anglo or Irish, northern or southern European, the border southwest or west, tribal or black, or under religious auspices like the Mormons in their trek from New York to Utah, indicate another. None, in all the human flux of leave-taking and arrival, the mix and match of Americanization, has failed to attract the languages of poetry. Beginning from a contextual map of immigrant and migrant America, the account to hand looks to a spectrum of poetic voice: WASP, Euro-American, Jewish, Arab American, Asian American, Latino/a, African American and, as a reminder of bearings, Native American.

* * *

Pilgrim Massachusetts, with the Bay Company or Plymouth Rock as key memorial insignia, its poets Edward Taylor and Anne Bradstreet and whose lineage leads to Robert Lowell, would quickly be obliged to share their migration. The Irish, Scots and Scots-Irish become key players, more than five million in all, and for whom steerage, indenture, the Great Famine of 1845–7, and even lace-curtain respectability in Boston, Chicago or San Francisco, provide their own migrant *aides-memoire* among which, from another literary domain, can be included the bittersweet "poetry" of Irish American retrospect in Eugene O'Neill's *Long Day's Journey Into Night* (1955).

The same century, and the early years of its successor, witnesses the arrival of an estimated seven million Germans, the Scandinavians headed for the upper Midwest, the Italians, Greeks and other Mediterraneans of the cities, and each Slavic population with its poets like the Belgrade-born Charles Simic in lines like "Touching me, you touch/The country that has exiled you" from "The Wind."[7] Migrancy equally stalks the poetry of the more than two million Poles who sought America, Adam Miskievicz as their nineteenth-century national poet yet whose voice continues through to a current Polish American name like Mark Powlak in the memorial poems of his "The Buffalo Sequence."[8] Russia has its formidable modern émigré presences, few more consequential than Joseph Brodsky. Jewish America's migrations look to 1820–1880s emigration from Germany, the Russo-Polish pogroms, the 1930s flights from the Nazis and, despite marring anti-semitism, the rise out of the Lower East Side or other lowly arrival into successful Americanness.

The Arab and Muslim world, a citizenry likewise currently numbered at six million, adds its own human plies and skeins to the trans-Atlantic pathway, migrancies which time and again underwrite landmark collections like *Grapeleaves: A Century of Arab-American Poetry* (1988) and *Post-Gibran: Anthology of New Arab American Writing* (1999).[9] Naomi Shihab Nye's "Steps" succinctly, and delicately, conjures the inscription of a migrant Middle East, with its Arabic into English, upon America's storefronts: "A man letters the sign for his grocery/Arabic and English . . ./ The thick swoops and curls of Arabic letters/ stay moist and glistening till tomorrow when the children/ show up jingling their dimes . . ."[10]

The Pacific seaboard, and California as prime territory, tells the corresponding story. Inerasably the Native and Latino/a dispensations require full recognition, a massive indigenous and US migrant history. Way stations, direct and indirect, include the western tribes, Cortés and La Malinche,

mestizaje, the missions, Mexican Independence in 1821, the Mexican Revolution (1910–17), the 1940s *bracero* fieldwork program, Delano and the
1960s *huelgas* (or labor strikes) as led by César Chávez against agri-busi-
ness, and barrios and communities from the southwest of New Mexico and
Texas to East L.A. and the Central and Imperial Valleys. The onetime province of Spain, and then Mexico, it quickly also became a territory competed
for by the different currents of Anglo and Euro-American settlement. The
relevant poetries, and the migrancies to which they give witness, deservedly
continue to invite recognition as borne out in collections like Duane Niatum's *Harper's Anthology of 20th Century Native American Poetry* (1987)
and Nicolás Kanellos's *Herencia: The Anthology of Hispanic Literature in
the United States* (2002).[11]

Asia's journeyers represent another of the west's plenty to embrace Chinese track-builders for the Central or Pacific railway, Chinatowns from Los
Angeles to Vancouver, and each Japantown, Manilatown, Little Korea, Little Saigon or Indo-Pakistani community. This, however, is not to overlook
Yellow Peril anti-Asianism, notably the 1882 Exclusion Act or Angel Island
from 1910 onwards as mainly immigrant-Cantonese detention center with its
trove of 125 etched-in wall stories and poems of immediate past transit and
"all kinds of abuse from these barbarians."[12] In *AIIIEEEEE! An Anthology of Asian-American Writers* (1974) and *The Big Aiiieeeee!* (1991), Frank
Chin and his co-editors called time on anti-Asianism, the cartoon images,
the model minority patronage.[13] Both anthologies, if calls to rally, and greatly
controversial for their attacks on Maxine Hong Kingston and Amy Tan, carried the built-in literary tracing of Asian American settlement. Companion
volumes have been plentiful, whether woman-centered like Shirley Geok-Lin
Lim *et al*'s *The Forbidden Stitch* (1989) or given to Indo-Pakistani and connected regional migrant memory like Maira Sunaima and Rajini Srikanth,
eds., *Contours of The Heart: South Asians Map North America* (1996).[14]

East Coast, West Coast: internal migration, in its turn, has been equally
resonant. New Englanders embark upon their celebrated errand into the
wilderness, Boston, Salem or Amherst as cities upon a hill and to be carried
into the mid-west and beyond. New York takes up succession as America's premier metropolis, its ever burgeoning immigrant multiplicity to be
found, typically, in Jewish Brooklyn, Italian Hell's Kitchen, 125th Street
and Spanish Harlem or, latterly, Russian Brighton Beach. Be it Manhattan's YMHA, or Sixth Street's Nuyorican Poets Café, or any of the Irish,
Italian or other ethnic clubs and meeting-places, literary remembrance has
been a prerequisite.

Victor Hernández Cruz, leading Nuyorican poet, in his "Loisaida"—
Spanglish for Lower East Sider—encompassingly, and symptomatically,
invokes a cityscape of those he explicitly names as "immigrants." The spectrum includes Blacks, Poles, Italians, "Broome Street Hasidics," one-time
"Mississippi sharecroppers" and, inevitably given his own roots, "Ricans"
as derived from the migrant cross-overs of Caribbean Tainos, Africa's

Moors and Spain's Andalucians, and from inter-American migration from island Puerto Rico to Manhattan's East Harlem of 116th to 145th Street. Yet at the same time they are to be identified by their wholly contemporary city-American "Pra-Pra" headwear.[15]

The America of the farms and prairies of Illinois, Iowa, Wyoming, Minnesota or Idaho, with Chicago pivotal as trade-route and South Side stockyard, is to be heard as a migrant ethos, if slightly at a remove, in Carl Sandburg's "Chicago," the city as "Hog Butcher," "Stacker of Wheat" and "Freight Handler to the Nation."[16] The South, whatever the magnolia Jeffersonianism of Virginia, looks also to poor-white migrancy, that of sharecropper and hill and backcountry indenture, and brought through the Cumberland Gap into Appalachia and the Dixie of the eventual Confederacy. Its poets, notably, and among other interests, have included Robert Penn Warren in his Kentucky-centred "Audubon: A Vision" and the James Dickey both of the novel *Deliverance* (1970) and a verse-collection seamed in southern reference like *Buckdancer's Choice* (1965).[17] Nor, again, is this to downplay slaveholding's sales and transfers (Dickey's own poem "Slave Quarters" well applies), or Seminole, Cherokee, Chickasaw and all other Native adjustments to white intrusion and land-seizure.

The Mississippi as America's inspirational arterial river, from the Minnesota headwaters to the New Orleans Delta, supplies yet another symbol of migrant change and adaptation. Its human freight, as Herman Melville's *The Confidence-Man* (1857) and Mark Twain's *Huckleberry Finn* (1884) bear witness, runs from homesteaders to steamboat merchants, trapper-hunters to runaway slaves. A poem like Langston Hughes's lyric "The Negro Speaks of Rivers" gives an African American memory, the Mississippi made over into a blues and linking to the Euphrates, Congo and Nile as coeval rivers of migrant blackness.[18] In the southwest the Rio Grande acts as territorial marker, yet also, and from the vexed 1848 Treaty of Guadalupe-Hidalgo to the present-day, the means of every kind of legal and illegal human transit. Much to the point Jimmy Santiago Baca, born in New Mexico of Chicano and Apache background, orphan, jailee, wanderer, and eventual teacher and poet, entitled his first verse collection *Immigrants in Our Own Land* (1979).[19]

The Rockies, the coastline west and Pacific northwest, all give out their call, whether in consequence of the Lewis and Clarke expedition of 1804–6, The Oregon Trail, or the building of the railroads as the iron horse. So inexorable a westering has become the very stuff of legend, the national mythology of frontier, America as endlessly being peopled and re-peopled. It embraces the pioneers and prairie schooners, the Plains Comanche or Dakota's Sioux and all other tribes, the cavalry, the family ranch or smallholding, the cowboys and cattle drives and trails, or panhandlers seeking instant fortune, the mother-lode, in the 1840s-50s Gold Rush of the Sierras. Lawrence Ferlinghetti's "Starting From San Francisco" (1961) invokes this America in a nice reverse-itinerary perspective, a poem as he calls it of "all night Eastward" and "Back and forth, across the Continent" (1961–5).[20]

California, the Golden State, inevitably acts as mecca, at once Pacific Garden and ocean vista, the nation's ever more populous state. But shadow, once again, there has again been, whether Native dispossession under the Spanish and then successor American regimes, or Roosevelt's Executive Order 9066 which, in 1942, and in the aftermath of Pearl Harbor, "relocated" 120,000 Japanese Americans. As to the Pacific, Hawai'i has also long taken on its own migrant transformations of identity: kanaka homeland yet haole America, idyll yet sugarcane and other plantation labor for Chinese, Japanese, Filipinos and Koreans. The poetry reprinted in *The Best of Bamboo Ridge: The Hawaii Writers Quarterly* (1986), from the journal and press established in 1978 by Eric Chock and Darrell H. Y. Lum and whose luminaries include Wing Tek Lum, Cathy Song and Gary Pak, issues a reminder of how Hawai'i has historically been the Pacific's migrant crossroad of Polynesia, Europe and America.[21]

Even amid the settledness of American family, township, and the eventual cities and suburbs, a defining migrancy persists. For whether millennial voyaging in the name of the would-be New Jerusalem or Atlantis, or each ensuing European and Asian wave, or Native and slave transportation, the effect has been shared, a vast, eclectic, multilingual, and often enough abrasive, surge of Americans-in-the-making. There can be little surprise that tropes of pilgrimage recur in American poetry as elsewhere. The use of pilgrim itself, certainly, with its echo of John Bunyan, runs from frontier to western movies. Few icons of America's immigration, in this transfer of peoples, have become better remembered than New York's Ellis Island, a first historic port of entry for so much of Europe, and beyond, during its working life of 1892–1943.

A whole literary iconography arises out of this immigrant and internal migrant America. It can include nineteenth-century steerage, ethnic city enclaves, the western trek and settlement; Nantucket's whale boats and Commodore Matthew Perry's 1853 landing in Japan; the automobile from the Ford Model T onwards; Steinbeck's Joad family and other dustbowl-era flight; the Pullman, the freight train, or latterly, the Greyhound and Trailways bus; south-to-north hispanic and Filipino field workers; Cuban *balseros* or boatpeople (a tenth of all Cubans have left since Castro's 1959 revolution); fleeing Vietnamese or Haitians; and, in all its Beat counterculture and youth loading, the 1960s of "on the road." Even space-travel, under John Kennedy's presidency, becomes a form of internal American migration, a latest frontier.

The composite effect of migrancy, sought and unsought and despite the prejudice and exclusions, gives grounds to being thought the very wellspring, as Randolph Bourne was early to term it, of transnational America. Whether European, Native, African, Asian, Hispanic, Pacific Island or Middle Eastern in origin, or given to the one or another ethnic, regional or class formation, or to the interplay of identity, it has made for an America indeed both home and away. Even literal names give confirmation, William Carlos Williams as of English, Puerto Rican and Jewish stock, or Charles Olson of Swedish and Irish American parentage.

In "Song of Myself," the 15th chant from the landmark poem first published in 1855, Walt Whitman duly lays down an apt visual cameo with "The groups of newly come immigrants cover the wharf or levee."[22] In "Howl," exactly a century later, Allen Ginsberg closes his visionary Beat poem with an allusion to "a sea-journey on the highway across America."[23] Both verse-lines, however different in time or intent, speak linkingly to the America of first arrival, the America of onward journey

Two celebrated poems give a yet further frame. Robert Frost's "The land was ours before we were the land's," written in 1942, read at the Kennedy inaugural in 1961, and later titled "The Gift Outright," suggests a seeming pre-ordained migrant juncture of people and country.[24] Latterday doubts as to its implication of manifest destiny have not been overlooked ("She was our land more than hundred years/Before we were her people"). Hart Crane's *The Bridge*, even as it sacramentalizes Brooklyn Bridge, warns of the dangers of mis-civilizing Whitman's open road—"Macadam, gun-grey as the tunny's belt,/Leaps from Far Rockaway to the Golden Gate."[25]

Whitman, and Ginsberg in his wake, offer voices of testimony and prophecy. Both Frost and Crane imply the necessary attraction of America's expanses of time and space. A myriad of poets, be they so-called mainstream or margin, give every further continuance to America as immigrant or migrant past-into-present. No one would claim, even so, that American poetry, pre-modern or modern, affords a simply ready-made sheaf of immigration or migrancy poems. Rather it has been a matter of image and echo, at times explicit, other times oblique, and worked into the poetry's overall directions of interest. But whatever the fashioning, the memories, literal and visceral, persist of America as ever an ongoing migrant cultural process and creation.

*   *   *

Robert Lowell may well supply a link back into New England's founding, the legacies of Atlantic crossing begun with the *Mayflower*, the Puritanism of election theology, congregation and magistracy, and assuredly his own poetic dynasty of James Russell Lowell and Amy Lowell. But whatever the Brahmin mantle, or longtime assumption of establishment status, New England has in fact been not only the one England for another but, eclectically, an interaction of Native (hence the naming of Massachusetts), Irish, Italian, Jewish, African American and other migrant legacies.

Different migrant footfalls even play into New England's vaunted Anglo-Saxonism, and not least its circuit of confessional poetry. In this a key resonant name has to be that of Sylvia Plath. For if her voice, too, was effortlessly thought to be WASP, it draws powerfully on the German roots of her entomologist professor-father, Otto Plath, given he was actually born in Poland. In "Daddy" she speaks of him as "a man in black with a Meinkampf look."[26] In "Lady Lazarus" he becomes the Aryan patriarch "Herr Doktor."[27] Plath uses German migrancy as extremity, Nazi shadow. This history, in shared graphic reach, is again to be heard in William Heyen's *The Swastika Poems* (1977).[28] But others, and from beyond New England, give a less asseverating bead.

Theodore Roethke, raised in a German American family in Michigan, calls up an older imported heritage of country-German good order, *ordnung*, in typical nursery-greenhouse poems like "Cuttings" or "Root Cellar." In his "Frau Bauman, Frau Schmidt, and Frau Schwartz," three "ancient ladies," employees of the family business, serve as the near virtual migrant continuation of a largely nineteenth-century farm Germany ferried into both the mid-west and, hauntingly, into Roethke's own childhood.[29] Charles Bukowski, German-born, in his "Near Hollywood" and using Los Angeles's "Grand Central Market" as metaphor, explores a migrant perspective well beyond his own. Within a busy overall and multicultural picture to include "the Spaniards all the way from Spain" he invokes the interplay of "old Mexican women . . . arguing with young Japanese clerks," a California shared, however contendingly, by its contributing migrant peoples.[30] Inescapably most of the poetries of Euro-America derives from similar workings of immigrant/migrant memory. Three, Ireland, Italy and Jewish Europe, do service.

The poetry of Irish America draws upon a greatly distinctive body of migrant allusion, whether Susan Howe's "Speeches at the Barriers" in her *The Europe of Trusts* (1990) with its reference-back to "earth of ancient ballad," or John Norton's prose-poem "Com-plaint" in his *The Light at the End of the Bog* (1989) with its "A Difficult people the Irish. Difficult stuck in the past. . . ."[31] This collective memory calls up emigration, blue-collar, poor-white and "respectable" assimilation (or not), churchgoing and politics, song, or festival like St Patrick's Day. It has been a migrancy whose poets have been suitably diverse.

The "mainstream" voices of Galway Kinnell and Robert Kelley, however mutedly, give one source. Tom McGrath, descended of Catholic-Irish stock and a Gaelic speaking mother and the founder of *Crazy Horse* magazine, supplies a vast populist-radical oeuvre. Migrant Irishness surfaces throughout the generation of Terence Winch as in "The Irish Riviera" from his *Irish Musicians American Friends* (1985) with its memory of fiddler, accordionist and song during a Rockaway summer; or Susan Firer in her vivid, often irreverent retellings of an Irish American Catholic childhood in *The Lives of Saints and Everything* (1993)—not least "God Sightings" ("I have never seen all of God/only the red-glow tip of Her cigarette"); or Eamonn Wall in a poem like "Immigrants" with its pluses and minuses of trans-Atlantic journey ("At night we go home to break our bread./Our doors are bolted to America./Our dreams are fastened to no promised land"); or the many collections of Edward Byrne, editor of *Valparaiso Poetry Review*.[32] Seamus Heaney, Irishman-in-America, Nobel prizewinner, shows himself wholly alert to Ireland's not only American but global migration. There has also been interwoven ethnic legacy as articulated, and not without tease, in the poetry of the Irish- as well as black-ancestried Ishmael Reed.

In John Ciardi, born in Boston's Little Italy, America looks not only to a distinguished critic and translator of Dante, but a poet of longstanding whose very titles give an apposite geographic touch whether his *Homeward to America* (1940) or *The Birds of Pompeii* (1985). His poem "Firsts" calls up the two-way nature of Italian migration, the arriving generation in America, the generation which seeks the Italy behind that arrival ("I had been in Italy rinsing my vowels/ She had been in Medford, Massachusetts/ Thickening her tongue on English crusts . . . ")[33]

In "The Old Italians Dying" Lawrence Ferlinghetti thinks back on an early generation "telling the unfinished *Paradiso* story," whereas in "Backyard" Diane di Prima calls up that generation's nostalgia: "O Brooklyn! Brooklyn! where . . . /the phonograph . . . creaked Caruso come down from the skies;/ Tito Gobbi in gondola; Gigli ridiculous in soldier uniform;/Lanza frenetic. . ." Whether "Paradiso" or "Brooklyn" both make for America's immigrant Italy, the coexistence of America as Dantean dream and the Little Italy of New York backyard reality.[34] Other poetic versions of the legacy run from Gregory Corso's Beat-centered serious whimsy to Sandra Mortola's vision of feminism from out of the context of patriarchal *Italianitá*, and into a current generation of Gerry LaFemina, Paula Corso and Daniela Gioseffi. A rueful backward glance, its references both to Dante and TV, is to be heard in Felix Stefanile's well-titled poem "The Americanization of the Immigrant"—"Like Dante/I have pondered and pondered/the speech I was born to/lost now, mother gone."[35]

Denise Levertov, in "Illustrious Ancestors," summons the Jewish Europe of the "Rav/of Northern White Russia," her own actual, historic ancestor. English-raised of Welsh Christian-mystic and Hassidic background, a US resident from 1947, she would act as one of poetry's best-known voices of the Jewish Atlantic. Looking back to her beginnings in "A Map of the Western Part of the County of Essex in England" she speaks of herself as the onetime "child who traced voyages/all indelibly over the atlas, who now in a far country remembers."[36]

Diaspora, and America as the Goldeneh Medina, have long won their poetic measure, whether from the perspective of European high culture, in this case ironic, of Philip Levine's "I Was Born in Lucerne" or the brute ground-zero of the Nazi camps as in Gerald Stern's "Soap." In Samuel Menashe's "The Promised Land," from his *The Niche Narrows: New and Selected Poems* (2000), he speaks of exile, and by implication the migrancy behind it, as "always/green with hope."[37] The American poetry which remembers this diasporic history, Europe to America or Israel, and out of a continuum to include Russia, the Warsaw or other ghetto, Freud's Vienna, or Auschwitz and Belsen, along with its treasury of Yiddish writing, belongs to a startlingly extensive gallery. It would be difficult, not to say negligent, to ignore a listing of Delmore Schwartz, Louis Zukofsky, Muriel Rukeyser, Stanley Kunitz, Karl Shapiro, Howard Nemerov or David Ignatow.

Hilton Obenzinger takes on quite another kind of vantage-point. A poem like "This Passover or the Next I Will Never Be in Jerusalem" plays upon the notion of "lost tribe," questioning Zionism as a one-dispensation politics, and with the poet himself nicely, and ambiguously, positioned in California as "a schoolteacher with the Indians." "The X of 1492" might be a roll-call of migrancy as descended from Columbus into Americas both north and south. 1492 is invoked as the historical weave of Catholic Spain's restoration of monarchy and yet Jewish and Arab expulsion. "The Great Expedition" becomes the lure of Asia's gold, the East "discovered" from the West. Columbus himself transforms into the migrant-serial identity of Colón, Italian and Jew, and both Las Casas's St. Christopher yet "whore" and the "admiral of Hell" responsible for "the devastation of the Indies." European migrancy with Columbus as its pathfinder, for Obenzinger, becomes a species of contraflow, Jewish dispossession at one with Native American and Palestinian dispossession, an America won and yet always reflective of both indigenous and wider human loss.[38]

* * *

"Chinamen in the New World" and "wherever Chinamen mine/minerals or track trains." Russell Leong's further phrasings from "In the Country of Dreams and Dust" deliver a telling overlap of time and place, the nineteenth and early twentieth-century of immigrant Chinese in America's "mother lode" west. They also lead into the poetry of Asia's overall migrancy, China as one prime source but an Asia also, and equally, of originating geographies from Seoul to Manila, Saigon to Calcutta. Marilyn Chin keenly addresses her own second-generation identity within the China embedded in America in "How I Got That Name" with its "The further west we go, we'll hit east;/the deeper down we dig, we'll find China."[39] Wing Tek Lum movingly celebrates a past generation's Chinese-Hawaiian migrant hardship in "At A Chinaman's Grave."[40] The poetry of Li-Young Lee inscribes his Chinese family's itinerary from Indonesia to Hong Kong, Japan to Pittsburgh, rarely to better effect than in "The Cleaving" from *The City in Which I Love You* (1990). Lee's speaker situates his face among those of the neighborhood butcher and the larger migrant Asian America about him ("this immigrant/this man with my own face").[41]

Kimiko Hahn's "Resistance: A Poem on Ikat Cloth" uses the image of traditional fabric to locate her inherited migrant Japanese legacy of womanhood within a multi-America and as a gift of voice to her daughter.[42] Lawson Fusao Inada's "Legends From The Camp" deftly elaborates the lives, the culture, of the Japanese America carried into the "relocation" of "10 camps, 7 states/120,113 residents."[43] Cathy Song, born of Chinese and Korean parents in Honolulu, takes up that joint migrancy in her "Easter: Wahiawa, 1959" with its remembrance of a grandfather's sugar cane labor.[44] Asia-in-America as migrancy finds wholly ongoing poetic articulation, whether Myung Mi Kim's "Into Such Assembly" with its keen Korean immigrant remembrance, or Jessica Hagedorn's "Souvenirs" as a Filipino American poem of transmigration and the ironic interplay of Catholic Manila and California Disneyland, or Thuong Vuong-Riddick's "Seeds" as a roll-call of Vietnam as *patria*, colony and war-zone, and, always, the haunting of America, or S. Shankar's "Passage to North America" with its boldly imagined contour of migration from equatorial south India to a Chicago whose "wintry rest/promises a future beyond history."[45]

*   *   *

If Lorna Dee Cervantes's "Visions of Mexico . . ." calls up the migrancy implicit in her own Chicano/a make-up, then Rodolfo "Corky" González's anthem-poem, "I Am Joaquín/Yo Soy Joaquín," written in parallel English and Spanish, supplies the unfolding larger canvas. Its opening paragraph serves to summarize the transformation from the historico-mythic Aztlán of Mexico into a USA of contested proprietorship. "La Raza!/ Mejicano!/ Español!/Hispano!/Chicano!/ Or whatever I call myself. . . "[46] These keywords the poem fills out in busiest allusion and image, a memorial verse roll-call of transition and the mestizaje it has entailed, across pueblo and barrio and a borderlands America of family, politics, labor, belief and, always, the dialectic of no one but a genuine plurality of language.

Further Chicano/a verse gives abundant confirmation. Carlos Cumpián's "Cuento" wittily offers a reminder of why Aztlán, especially amid the 1960s era of Brown Power, becomes both a call to rally and the reminder of how a people's whole history itself can migrate ("You'll hear more about it soon!")[47] Pat Mora's "Immigrants" speaks cryptically to first-arrival anxiety, whether the need to "wrap their babies in the American flag," "thick English," or the acceptability of the American son or daughter they have newly parented.[48] Few Chicano poems take on a more Whitmanesque itinerary sweep than Jimmy Santiago Baca's *Martín and Meditations on the South Valley* (1987), a retracing of his surrogate persona's migrant progress through the south and southwest with its affecting remembrance of the "broken chain of events" and the "embering stick/I call the past."[49]

Puertorican, Nuyorican. Few poets of Caribbean island to New York origins have had greater impact than Tato Laviera, most of all his collection *AmeRícan* (1985) as the portrait of immigrant Manhattan ("we gave birth to a new generation/AmeRícan"). The eclecticism of "all folklores,/european, indian, black, spanish" finds an enclosing metaphor in the notion of a bridged America ("AmeRícan, across forth and across back . . . our trips are walking bridges!")[50] Cuban America, overwhelmingly Florida-centered, can look to a poem like Pablo Medina's "Madame America" with its sense of immigrant challenge—"'Ven' he said, accented/but impervious, 'dame lo que das'" (English version "'Come' . . . Give me what you give'").[51] In "English Con Salsa" Gina Valdés teasingly offers a species of summary, "ESL" as "English Surely Latinized," America's English as "English refrito" and "thick as Zapotec tongues." Her poem, in effect, speaks to the vast Hispanic inter-migrancy of peoples and languages, a multi-hemispheric America and its ongoing and widely shared poetic en-wordment.[52]

* * *

Migrancy may well be an inadequate term also for the remembrance of Afro-America's passage out of Africa: the rot, and yet the resilience, of slavery as seizure and transport. Few poems more richly take up these implications than Robert Hayden's three-part "Middle Passage," with its opening irony in citing slave ships named *Jesús, Estrella, Esperanza* and *Mercy*, and beginning and closing designation of the middle passage as a "voyage through death to/life upon these shores." Each part acts upon similar paradox: Christian America imprisoning "black gold, black ivory, black seed" on vessels both of slave and sexual cargo; a mariner haunted by past manacled slave-columns from "Gambia, Rio Pongo, Calabar"; and the crossing to "New World littorals" as "unlove," "charnel stench, effluvium of living death," and yet the *Amistad* rebellion led by Cinquez who bequeaths a "deathless" image. Hayden's command could not be more availing, slavery's enshipments from Africa to America as "shuttles in the rocking loom of history."[53]

The silhouette of this coercive migrancy lies everywhere in African American poetry, not, evidently, its only concern, but a begetting point of reference. Countee Cullen's "Heritage" famously asks *"What is Africa to me?"*. He thinks it "copper sun," "scarlet sea," "jungle track," "heathen gods," yet also *"three centuries removed."* This is migration as left-behind time, life lived in an Afro-America of now as against an Africa of then, and in which the poem's speaker acknowledges his own costly "double part."[54] Gwendolyn Brooks's "To The Diaspora," with Africa this time as also Afrika, speaks of a migrancy from, and to, the Africa not so much there as here—"You did not know you were Afrika./ You did not know the Black continent/that had to be reached was you."[55] Rita Dove's *Thomas and Beulah*, her wholly accomplished verse history, chronicles an intimate black family migration from Tennessee to Akron and from pre-Depression to postwar America. In its play of memory it tells yet another kind of black migrancy, lives of domesticity, parenthood and labor southern-style and northern-style.[56]

For Jayne Cortez the migrancy of Africa is as much to be heard in its dynamic of sound worked consciously, and simultaneously, into sense. In "For the Poets (Christopher Okigbo & Henry Dumas),"[57] a dirge and a celebration of two poets racistly killed before their time, she collates, as though in a chant, the Africa of Damballah and "one hundred surging Zanzibars" with the America of Bessie Smith and Harlem. Appropriately she end-lines her verses with "ah"s, "huh"s and "uhuh"s, the Africa-originated call-and response of griot and, as in her own case, of an American jazz bard longtime the verse-and-musical collaborator with her husband Ornette Coleman.

Ted Joans, performance poet, trumpeter and surrealist (typically playful-serious in "I'M FLYING OVER ALABAMA . . . WITH BLACK POWER IN MY LAP" from his "No mo' Kneegrow"), creates a notable run of poems which bear upon a kind of reverse African migrancy.[58] In an Afro-Beat panorama like "Afrique Accidentale," which he describes as "a long rhyming poem of mine of me coming to Timbuktu," the rap asides and improvisations lead into the celebratory "I finally made you/Timbuctoo/Yeah!". The multiple glosses and spellings of Timbuktu convey an obvious affection for this most fabled of cities. Joans's Afro-America, engagingly, and wholly un-mumbo-jumboed of western condescension, so rejoins the Africa of its beginnings.[59]

*   *   *

Native verse, that of America's first peoples, affords a wholly appropriate place to conclude. Which cultures more have known migrations stretching back into the unknown time of Bering Strait to Tierra Del Fuego and the Caribbean to the Pacific, or undertaken tribal journeyings of coast, woodland, prairie or pueblo, or more keenly, and at cost, been witness to conquering Euro-migrancy? In "Columbus Day" Jimmy Durham (Wolf Clan Cherokee) calls for a "holiday for ourselves," a "parade" not a little the opposite of Lowell's in "Fourth of July in Maine." This works to counter the supremacist "bloodline" from Cortez to Eisenhower and to celebrate the "grass" and "every creek" in which Native migrancy has its history.[60] For Gail Tremblay in "Indian Singing in 20th Century America" the America spaced by "patterns of wires invented by strangers" and "highways" is to be set against "remembering what supports our life."[61] Simon Ortiz's "Wind and Glacier Voices" speaks of "continuing voice," the birth of a daughter within a migrant timeline both present-day and yet, anciently, that of a "glacier scraping . . . thirty thousand years ago."[62]

It falls to Joseph Bruchac, of mixed Slovak and Abenaki ancestry, to give in his "Ellis Island" an appropriate version of these differing yet joined American migrancies. On the one hand he thinks back to Slovak grandparents at Ellis Island, yet "Another voice/speaks of native lands . . . when the earth became owned."[63] Bruchac speaks from the plies of his own history, Europe, Ellis Island, Native America. But he has far from wanted company in seeking a poet's voice for the migrations, literal and figural, of the America-at-large always, and quite more than most, to be thought both home and away.

10 Out of the 1990s
Latino/a Un-bordering in US Fiction

The US-Mexican border *es una herida abierta* where the Third World grates against the first and bleeds.

—Gloria Anzaldúa, *Borderlands/La Frontera,
The New Mestiza* (1987)[1]

This interlude between Anglo-North America and Hispano-Criollo Caribbean keeps all issues of identity intensive throughout the island and within all the Puerto Rican diaspora communities on the U.S. mainland.

—Victor Hernández Cruz, *Red Beans* (1991)[2]

Cuban America defines itself . . . not only in novels and plays, but in fashion and food, jewelry and jacuzzis, in advertising slogans and in popular music.

—Gustavo Pérez Firmat, *Life on the Hyphen:
The Cuban-American Way* (1994)[3]

Latino/a. Hispanic. La Raza. The Browning of America. These terms, even if they arouse reservations in some quarters, bespeak a US cultural dispensation at once ancestral and hemispheric. Yet, given recent Mexican border and migration controversies, media reportage frequently designates the population now collectively America's largest minority and however in fact longstanding somehow a "new" demographics. The heading excerpts offer counter-sightlines. For where the 1960s can be said to have put Afro-America and its history to the forefront in the form of Civil Rights and Black Power, Martin Luther King and Malcolm X, the 1990s and after almost more than at anytime previously have pointed to yet another order of North American life and word: *Chicano/a, Nuyorriqueño/a,* Cuban American, alongside cultural geographies originating among others in La República Dominicana (and from the same island Haiti), Chile, Colombia, Perú, El Salvador or Argentina.[4]

Nothing less than a dazzling array of American fiction and other writings in the 1990s confirms this plurality, reflecting histories born of *Nueva España* and the evolving *mestizaje* or mix of Native, Spanish, European, African, and Jewish peoples, the ongoing momentum of Mexican and other Latin American migrancy south-to-north, and the different Caribbean horizons. In a US population of 300 million Hispanics currently number 42.7 million, more than 14% of the whole. Those of Mexican descent account for 66.9%, Puerto Rican descent 8.6%, Cuban descent 3.7%, Central and South American descent 14.3%, and other Hispanic descent 6.5 %. An inevitable upshot has been not only the always evolving patterns of life, with its bi- and multiculturalism, its code-switching and language mix, but also art. Theatre so co-exists as *actos*, poetry as *poesía*, and novels and stories as *ficciones*, *corridos* or *cuentos*. In these, accordingly, is to be met not just America but *Las Américas*, a body of writing wholly implicated in the cultural if not literal un-bordering of the US as white-canonical society.[5]

That embraces, first, the hispano-mestizo/a southwest once historically Mexico and today's California, Texas, Arizona, Colorado, New Mexico and Nevada, whose 2000 mile border has become increasingly iconic (the more so since 9–11), and whose cities include Los Angeles with its "East Los" as *barrio* and *la raza*, San Diego, Albuquerque, Houston, Tucson and Denver. *Ristras*, the chains of multi-colored dried peppers, hang indicatively, whether in pueblo homes, migrant-worker camps, cities, or even the suburbs. The further dynamic is to be found in Manhattan's Spanish Harlem and island origins in El Estado Libre de Puerto Rico, the Miami of Cuban America with its Florida Straits proximity to Havana and central thoroughfare of Calle Ocho, and each other hispanic community. For many in the cities this can mean what Judith Ortiz Cofer's stories call "El Building," a tough, bustling world of tenement or street.

This so-called "browning of America," the legal citizenry and the estimated 12 million illegals, bears all manner of cross-border or island-to-mainland footfall. Chicano memory readily summons the Treaty of Guadalupe-Hidalgo (1848), the César Chávez and the West Coast agricultural worker-activism of the Johnson-Nixon decade, and latterly the impact of the North American Free Trade Agreement (NAFTA) on Mexican small-holding and immigration into the US. *Riqueños/as* think of 1898 and the Spanish-American War in which suzerainty passed to America and always the debate between *independentistas* as against those favoring US citizenship under Autonomous Commonwealth status. Florida's anti-Castroism arises out of the rankling political tapestry of the Batista years (1929–59), the Castro-Guevara revolution (1959), the Mariel Boatlift (1980) with its exportation of 125,000 refugees, the Elián González child-custody affair (1999), and always the speculation and ideologies of "after Fidel."

Generally shared *Latino/a* reference can also look to vernacular Catholicism and Pentecostalism, the different inflections of *barrio* culture, language issues, the controversies as to "documented/undocumented" migration with, in 2006, the nation-wide Hispanic demonstrations as to identity and work-contribution. Whatever, too, the degree of assimilation and access to wealth (New Mexico farmland or Miami business) there persists the class-structure inherent in employment and *la pobreza*. The community calendar can be *fiestas patrias*, Cinco de Mayo or *quinceañeras* (for girls reaching fifteen). Musical heritages include Tito Puente, Los Lobos, the Havana-born Gloria Estefan, and Cuba's re-emerged Buena Vista Social Club. Film-making calls up Edward James Olmos's *Zoot Suit* (1981), with its high-energy musical remembrance of the 1942 hounding of *barrio* youth, or *American Me* (1992) as prison screen epic. Foodways offer their alimentary markers variously of *burritos* and *tamales* and, from Puerto Rico and the islands, *arroz con habichuelas* or root vegetables like *yucca* and *malanga*. TV can be both the English-language networks and *Univision* or *Telemundo*.

Little wonder this hybridity of ancestral past and American present, migration and settlement, has seized the literary imagination, worlds-within-worlds yet also cross-worlds with the rest of the USA. English, however much America's "official" language, co-exists with a community Spanish of home, street, workplace. As to the literary fiction of the 1990s, like any other decade it looks to writers both whose bow belongs earlier and to those who bring new voice to bear. Either way the fictions to hand confirm little short of a treasury.

*   *   *

Rudolfo Anaya's *Bless Me, Ultima* (1972), with its Portrait of the Artist set in postwar New Mexico, along with Tomás Rivera's *". . . . y no se lo tragó la tierra"/And The Earth Did Not Part* (1971) as the story-cycle of a migrant-worker year, rightly are credited with having inaugurated a Chicano literary renaissance.[6] Anaya's career, since, has seen a steady output, not least his 1990s Sony Baca Private Eye trilogy of the American southwest—*Zia Summer* (1995), with its cult murder and witch-criminal (or *brujo*) antagonist Raven, *Rio Grande fall* (1996), with its opening of the Albuquerque International Balloon Fiesta, killing and further *brujería*, and *Shaman Winter* (1999), with its ventures into shamanism, supernatural dream-territory and fusion of Native and Mexican fable.[7]

These each delve not only into the one or another crime but the southwest as itself a "mystery," a hybrid American world-order, Spanish and Anglo in settlement but only in the wake of the diverse, rich seams of Native population—notably Rio Grande pueblo populations like Santo Domingo, San Felipe, Isleta, Cochití or Jémez with their networks of people, belief systems, land cultivation and art and story. Thus he offers a physical New Mexico of the *llanos* (plain-lands), the Sandía and the Sangre de Cristo mountains, the historic Camino Real, adobe architecture, the desert in its sumptuous colors, light, and rock and plant variety, and also Albuquerque with its Central Avenue, Bernalillo County, *barrios* like Barelas, hosting of the annual Gathering of Nations Pow-Wow, and proximity to Roswell of UFO fame and Los Alamos of the atomic Manhattan Project. New Mexico, in Anaya's writing, has ever been the borderland complexity of history and people, a vision that has long situated him at the very forefront of Chicano authorship.

With *Alburquerque* (1992) he characteristically layers New Mexico in symbolic resonance, a labyrinth of ethnic and family borders, in-laid politics, a boxer's quest for his true parentage and a city's hispano-mestizo lineage signaled in the novel's title which restores the original "r" to its place-name (legend holds that it was removed by an Anglo postmaster unable to pronounce it correctly).[8] Its central figure, Abrán González, light-skinned Golden Gloves boxing champion and student at the University of New Mexico, finds himself caught in a quest for his true parentage ("He was a child of this border, a child of the line that separated white and brown. La raza called people like him 'coyote' " [38]). As his story unravels he finds himself not alone, for this is a fable of Albuquerque as endemic *mestizaje*. The local politico Frank Dominic, with his plans to turn the city into a new Venice, a new Las Vegas, and for all that he affects his ducal Spanish lineage, in fact is of migrant Italian stock; his rival, the banker-landowner Walter Johnson, is of lost white-Chicago immigrant stock and his wife Vera of hidden Jewish ancestry; and Abrán, fostered-out son to Sara yet the offspring to the then unmarried Johnson artist-daughter Cynthia and the Hispano writer Ben Chávez, finally arrives at not only his own identity but that of the very culture about him. For as these personal borders elide and fall, so Anaya un-borders Albuquerque Native (notably in the person of Joe Calabasa), Spanish, Mexican, Anglo, Jewish and African. It makes for a rare, engaging perspective.

Rolando Hinojosa has similarly long weighed for the series he began with *Klail City y sus alrededores* (1976), re-issued as *Klail City* (1987), in which the Río Grande Valley of south Texas is made over into the collagist Tex-Mex border kingdom of Belken County.[9] In *Ask A Policeman* (1998) Hinojosa continues his multicultural estate with genuine virtuosity, a detective fiction whose violent drugs-and-murder portraits of warring family is given its unraveling in the figure of Chief Inspector Lieutenant Rafe Buenrostro.[10] As each circle vies, the Lee Gómez-Felipe Segundo Gómez brothers tied into prison escape, cocaine and fratricide, bank fraud, pathological nephew-sons, the killing of the Assistant DA Theo Crixell, the sex-and-partying Laura Castañón de Grayson, and an ancillary cast of informers and miscreants, the whole comes under the auspices not only of Buenrostro but his opposite number, Lu Cetina, Directora of the Mexican Federal Police Office in Barrones. Two jurisdictions hold, the one Napoleonic and the other Anglo in their begetting legal codes, along with two styles of gendered authority. Yet the Río Grande against which each intrigue or revenge is played out bears witness, literally and figuratively, to both Americas as quite inextricable the one from the other, a live, always plural cross-border of people, estate, language and, to be sure, crime.

This same "border" impulse equally threads through Sandra Cisneros's *Woman Hollering Creek and Other Stories* (1991), rarely more appositely than in "Tepeyac," a story-memoir of the hillside borough in Mexico City with its Aztec and San Juan Diego history.[11] Remembrance turns on the narrator's return to Tepeyac and her fond cross-border memory of childhood amid the local world of goods, church, cafés, food and inhabitants inhabited by her storekeeper grandfather/*abuelo* and religious *abuela* ("it is me who will remember when everything else is forgotten"[23]). Other vignettes span childhood to maturity, the US-Mexico borderland as rite-of-passage. "My Lucy Friend Who Smells Like Corn" captures the fidget and word-inversions of childhood. "Mericans," told as the reluctant Mexico-Chicano churchgoing of two grandchildren, takes a slap at Anglo condescension ("But you speak English" says a white woman tourist, "Yeah . . . we're Mericans" replies the brother [20]). "Never Marry a Mexican" tells a woman teacher-artist's love affair with both a father and son which leads her to fantasize a borderland of shifting genders. "Woman Hollering Creek" as the title-story, uses the legend of *la llorona*, the weeping woman, to confront a failed cross-frontier marriage. "*Bien Pretty*," on a lighter note, looks to the narrator's affair with Flavio Michoacán ("I'd never made love in Spanish before"[153]), a story full of winning border idiosyncrasy, love as its own kind of emotional and linguistic *mestizaje* which can cause the world to seem a field of chattering *urracas* or magpies.

Cisneros has been but one voice, albeit a leading one, in a consequential generation of Chicana authorship whose texts echo and expand these perspectives. Roberta Fernández's *Intaglio: A Novel in Six Stories* (1990) offers the lives and rise to consciousness of different southwest border femininities.[12] In sequence these are the album-keeper ("Andrea"), the seamstress ("Amanda"), the religious bird-keeper ("Filomena"), the card-reader ("Leonor"), the local movie-house beauty ("Esmeralda") and the memorial war-narrator ("Zulema"). Each closely fashioned portrait interacts with the other to supply a form of intimate *Latina* sisterhood, border-located women who amid gain and loss arrive at their own kind of life-signature.

Ana Castillo, whose *The Mixquiahuala Letters* (1986) won her immediate recognition with its two-woman epistolary styling of an American journey into Mexico and magic-realist echoes of Julio Cortázar's *Rayuela* (1963), in English *Hopscotch*, continues the blend of real and irreal in *Sapogonia* (1990) and *So Far From God* (1993).[13] The former, in the finally murderous relationship of Máximo Madrigal and Pastora Velásquez Aké, both anatomizes and subverts patriarchy, male sexuality as customary power dominance. *So Far From God*, its title adapted from the celebrated pronouncement of Porfirio Diaz, Mexico's autocratic president from 1876–1911—"Poor Mexico, so far from God. So near the United States," portrays two *Latina* generations both bitterly caught out by history yet in the case of its main figure put to take possession of that history.

Set in the central New Mexico township of Tome *So Far From God* narrates lives bleak in their fate yet lively in their living, whether the mother, Sofi (for Sofia) or her four daughters, in turn, Esperanza, a journalist who is tortured and dies as a Middle East hostage, Fe, the conformist, who dies of cancer brought on by toxic chemicals in a weapons factory, Caridad, mutilated in an attack and eventual suicide, and the youngest, La Loca, whose psychic and *curandera* abilities do not prevent her contracting AIDS. Sofi outlives her offspring, founds Mothers of Martyrs and Saints (M.O.M.A.S), and becomes a political and community activist. Against evident cost she so transcends her mythic status as *la llorona*, the weeping mother. If Castillo tells a Chicana-feminist fable she does so with wit, a willing ply of fact and fantasy, the rejection of hispanic life as American margin in favor of a *latinidad* of hard-won but necessarily sustaining femininity at the very center of things.

"It's a long story"(4) says Soveida Dosamantes, waitress in the New Mexico restaurant El Farol in Denise Chávez's *Face of an Angel* (1994).[14] So it proves as the restaurant ("cockroach-ridden, leaky-assed, chile-splattered, greasy-smelling" [461]) acts as both home and a memory-chamber of voices for the four generations of women in the Dosamantes family. These are women who have spent their lives "in service," whether as wife-mothers (the break-up of Soveida's parents is given in mutual and parallel column narrative), domestics, cleaners, servants like Chata and Orelia, or waitresses like Soveida. The upshot is a female-worker southwest epic, a Book of Service as Soveida calls it (Chávez mines the implications of "service" to rich effect) and a full-length successor to the story-collection *The Last of The Menu Girls* (1986) with its chronicles of Rocío Esquibel's New Mexico young womanhood from hospital orderly to student and teacher.[15] *Face of an Angel*, pledged to female body and spirit within the specific border world of the Dosamantes family history, can be at times antic, roistering, but also tender even as it remembers the toughness of *Latina* women's blue-collar working continuity.

History has always been a necessary dynamic in Chicano/a fiction, not just as literal timeline but as the memory of generational advance and retreat, both the actual and visceral remembering of "border" across two countries. The dynamic can be family networks and origins, or *la lucha*, the struggle, against migrant and *barrio* indigency, or the shifting contour (especially with increased wellbeing) of individual and community identity. In this respect Alejandro Morales's speculative fiction *The Rag Doll Plagues* (1992) invites special esteem: a serial fable which spans Mexico as nineteenth-century autocracy, the America of contemporary Orange County and the AIDS crisis, and a futurist war-zone America called Lamex.[16] Don Gregorio, living in the earlier period, serves as ancestor to Gregory Revueltas MD, a thread of history subject to three distinct waves of pestilence, physiological but also cultural-political and military. The footprint of Camus's *La Peste* is not hard to discern, along with seams of magic realism. Variously the novel has been termed metatrope, trauma narrative, a hall of mirrors: each applies, Mexican into Chicano history, a future shaped by each past, in all a triptych of dark self-reflection.

More linear history-into-fiction has not gone missing. Daniel Cano's *Pepe Rios* (1991) envisages the Mexican Revolution as both epilogue to dictatorship yet prologue to the cultural formation of *chicanismo*.[17] Arturo Islas's *Migrant Souls* (1991), the second in his Moma Chona trilogy, turns on literal border in the form of California and Texas but also the internalization of light and dark skin in the figures of Josie Salazar as against the Aunt Jesús María.[18] Demetria Martinez's *Mother Tongue* (1994) blends the north-south politics behind US-supported Salvadoran military repression and the American sanctuary movement into the Albuquerque love-story, not always sentimentality-free, between Mary, the retrospective narrator, and José Luis, political refugee.[19] "Story medicine" is the apt term given by Mary. Helena María Viramontes's *Under the Feet of Jesus* (1995), dedicated to César Chávez, uses the coming-of age love between Estrella and Alejo to refract California farm-worker migrancy, and with it *la migra*, the toxic effects of fruit-spraying, and worker exploitation.[20] Poised, and greatly delicate in its play of image, the novella's overall portrait explores a mutual humanity well beyond Mexico and the US as fixed counter-sites.

1960s counter-culture yields few names more transgressive than John Rechy in *City of Night* (1963), the near autobiographical novel-diary of America's Gay borders as midnight-cowboy hustle, quick sexual fix, bars and edge cities.[21] It is a career that has continued into *The Miraculous Day of Amalia Gómez* (1991), pitched as its title-heroine's religious vision of a cross in the sky set against the shabbier end of Hollywood, her jealous *copiloto* of a husband, a son edging into gang-life, and a daughter at the verge of sexual adventure.[22] This is America's screen capital as class-oppressed hinterland, a species of Chicano dark cinema.

✻   ✻   ✻

If, like other hispanic writing, Puertorriqueño/a fiction looks to contexts of history and site, it also plays against a rich contour of life-writing. Piri Thomas's *Down These Mean Streets* (1967) was early to offer one departure-point, a contour of tenement *barrio*, gangs, jail and survival. Companion autobiographies have included Edward Rivera's *Family Installments: Memories of Growing Up Hispanic* (1983), with its island village of Bautobarro to Nueva York father-and-son emigrant chronicle, Judith Ortiz Cofer's *Silent Dancing: A Partial Remembrance of a Puerto Rican Childhood* (1990), thirteen *ensayos* or essay-moments in alternating prose and poetry of busy island girlhood and an America of tenement Paterson, New Jersey, and Esmeralda Santiago's *When I Was Puerto Rican* (1993), another island upbringing of *boriquén* family yet one of fractured kinship with to follow migration into a "cooped up" Brooklyn block. Alongside, and of necessity, has to be Nuyorican Poets Café, founded in 1973 by the poet Miguel Algarin, situated first on East 3rd and then East 6th Street known as *Loisaida* (the Village's Lower East Side given Spanish adaptation), and always a vitally important multicultural literary gathering-place and performance venue.[23]

Few writers of fiction, however, have established a better-known name than Nicholasa Mohr, the prolific storyteller who made her bow in acclaimed narratives like *Nilda* (1973), with its portrait of ten-year old Nilda Ramírez in the *barrio* New York of 1941 as "a familiar world of noise, heat and crowds," and *In Nueva York* (1979), Puerto Rico and Manhattan as lived-in memory. Whether the New York of the Bronx or Central Park or "the island" Mohr winningly decants a shaping round of girlhood-into-womanhood, family, school, employment, love and marriage. That also runs through her juvenile fiction like *Growing Up Inside The Sanctuary of My Imagination* (1994) and *The Magic Shell* (1995). Her story-collection *A Matter of Pride* (1997) develops a gallery of *Latinas* encountering different borders of self—becoming a bride, a dip into the seeming supernatural, or femininity to be refracted and measured in a visit to a drag queen show. Mohr cannot be regarded as other than a major literary presence, her tales of rite of passage, individual and community language, each always densely sited in the multi-ethnicity of America's first city.[24]

Puerto Rico takes on virtuoso imagistic form in Judith Ortiz Cofer's *The Latin Deli* (1993), a mural-in-small, and which has its follow-up in the twelve-story collection for young readers of *An Island Like You* (1995).[25] Using stories, often in the form of anecdotes, poems, dream sequences and letters, *The Latin Deli* centers on life in El Building, the Paterson New Jersey tenement block that is the family's successor home to island Puerto Rico. These two worlds span the 1960s to present time but whose borders join in the life of its girlhood-to-college teacher narrator. "American History" offers one story touchstone, El Building and its residents as stigma, unwanted lower depth, in the view of the mother of the narrator's fellow-student Eugene and in the wake of the Kennedy assassination. Another lies in "Twist and Shout" with its portrait of heady but risk-laden teenage love and "Corazón's Café" in which El Building is remembered as "filled with the life energies of generations of other island people" (93). The island itself can be the place of loved, ailing grandparents ("The Witch's Husband") or an old man's near magical death as he is taken out to sea clinging to dolphins ("Letter from a Caribbean Island"). As she interweaves verse and story the narrator builds a one composite narrative, a juncture of seeming disjuncture. The Puerto Rico of New Jersey and of the Caribbean both carry their contrary yet overlapping pasts-into-present. This evolution as child, woman, mother and writer, accordingly becomes a spectrum of viewpoint, involving innocence, threat, query, celebration, memory, time and place, always and coevally the one and the several American life-histories.

Ed Vega, albeit that he bristles at the label of Puerto Rican-American writer, was early to win plaudits with *The Comeback* (1985), his satire of too solemn an emphasis on *hispanidad* as ethnicity with its Eskimo-Puerto Rican hockey-player and Freudian shrinks.[26] *Casualty Report* (1991), by contrast, uses its ten stories to explore a ground-level panorama, lives often held at the margins within the New York of Sixth Street ("Spanish Roulette"), the Port Authority Terminal ("Revenge and Prelude To A Well Deserved Suicide") or the Welfare Department ("The Kite").[27] Few more trenchantly catch the implosion of being treated as the stereotypical poor-stupid Puerto Rican than the title-piece, "Casualty Report." It tracks the planned revenge-terrorism of Sonny Maldonado against an America that has colonized the island ("For as long as Puerto Rico was a colony, not one person could hold his head high" [47]), New York-ghettoized Puerto Ricans, made him participant in the killing fields of Vietnam, and filled his life with scenes of "people with broken dreams" as against the gilded tidings of TV commercials. His own life, even with his wife Carmen, has become fracture, life inside a multi-America as may be but one itself the seeming endless casualty report.

*   *   *

Cuban America achieved an almost flamboyant step into American literary consciousness with Oscar Hijuelos's *The Mambo Kings Play Songs of Love* (1989).[28] This was Havana and island music brought to 1940s-50s New York as a *latinidad* full of life, sexual heat, the fiction of fact figure of Desi Arnaz from CBS's *I Love Lucy* (1951–57), and above all, the mambo as triumphant-sad dance. Hijuelos's subsequent fiction exhibits a shared full-ness, rarely more so than in *The Fourteen Sisters of Emilio Montez O'Brien* (1995).[29] Two family geographies join, Irish and Cuban, in the persons of Nelson O'Brien, photographer, and Mariela Montez, his well-born wife, and in their plenitude of daughters born in the Pennsylvania township of Cobble-ton. ("The house in which the fourteen sisters of Emilio Montez O'Brien lived radiated femininity" [3]). The upshot, a genealogical time-map cen-tered mainly in the eldest girl Margarita and the one son, Emilio, who edges his way into Hollywood, might indeed be a photographic album of the US as Hispano/a destiny. Whether second-generation America with a backdrop running from the Spanish American War through to Castro, or the memory of Ireland and Cuba as snared by two imperialist regimes, the novel rarely loses touch with family as an epic of migrant strands and evolution.

Cristina Garcia's *Deaming in Cuban* (1992) deftly pitches its story as the Havana and Brooklyn lives of a three generation woman dynasty.[30] In Celia del Pino, *fidelista*, wife to the long dead but en-ghosted Jorge del Pino, and memorial letter-writer to a long-ago lover Gustavo, the novel has its matriarch, at once the embodied dream of the revolution and yet its worn, despotically cancerous sick body. Her daughters, Lourdes Puente who is raped by soldiers of the revolution and eventually sets up her Yan-kee Doodle Bakery in Brooklyn to become at once capitalist and fiercely anti-Fidel (she fantasizes becoming his assassin), and Felicia, three times married, mother of twins, and eventually the unhinged acolyte of *santería*, throw a contrasting light on Cuba as heritage. As the novel devolves into the life of Lourdes's daughter, Pilar Puente, runaway, art-punk Brooklyn painter, who journeys to Cuba and there meets her dying *abuela*, the elusive border meaning of this dynasty and its counter-histories is made yet more emphatic. "Cuba is a peculiar exile," she observes, "an island-colony. We can reach it by a thirty-minute charter flight from Miami, yet never reach it at all" (219).

A trio of 1990s Cuban American authorship suggests no drop in imaginative vitality. Virgil Suárez's *Havana Thursdays* (1995), set in Miami but sited also in Cuba, Mexico City and Brazil, depicts the Torres clan—Zacaría, recently dead of a heart-attack, his wife Laura, and their disjunctive clan of son, three daughters, Laura's bibulous sister, and arriving grandchildren.[31] Pitched to the motif of "since they left Cuba" the novel envisages America as dynastic loss as against gain within the paradigm of exile and assimilation. Roberto Fernández's *Holy Radishes!* (1995), on another tack, lowers the liveliest satiric boom on Miami as Cuban exile community, oddball figures like the poet rock-star Lisander, ex-hooker Dina now owner of a radish processing factory, and a cadre of all-talk male weekend warriors against Castro even as women like the dreamer Nelly Pardo and her ally the ex-cheerleader Mrs. James B III actually do the real work behind community life.[32]

Achy Obejas's story-collection *We Have Come All This Way From Cuba So You Could Dress Like This?* (1994) and novel *Memory Mambo* (1996) have been dubbed tropical eroticism, Jewish-lesbian close encounter with an eye to the more encompassing gender hierarchies of dynasty spanning Cuba to Chicago.[33] *Memory Mambo*, focused in the life of Juani as an out gay daughter in a family marked by hidden pasts and splits, gives an especially sensitive portrait, at once a given sexuality as a life in its own cultural right and the reflexive measure of the very shaping of Cuban America. With some justification Obejas speak of "creating a new syntax from the pieces of our displaced times" [13]).

*   *   *

Dominican American fiction has shown an ever strengthening hand throughout the 1990s. In an interview for November 1994 Julia Alvarez offers a working perspective: "I am a Dominican, hyphen, American . . . As a fiction writer, I find the most exciting things happen in the realm of that hyphen"[34] *How The García Girls Lost Their Accents* (1991), and its follow-up *¡Yo!* (1997), both vindicate this standpoint, the former as the telling of the García family's flight from the Dominican Republic and gains and setbacks of Americanization, the latter a cleverly self-circling novel in which the family "answers" the story told about them by Yolanda García ("yo" as abbreviation of her name and the Spanish for "I") as celebrated but again wholly imagined fact-fiction author. With *In the Time* *of Butterflies* (1994) Alvarez ponders Dominican history, the Trujillo dictatorship (1931–65) and the heroic three Marabal sisters ("las mariposas," the butterflies) who played a heroic part in opposition for which they paid with their lives. Told as documentary, fiction and poetry, it makes not only a formidable indictment of US-Dominican political collusion but a working context for Alvarez's other fiction. In this it was *How The García Girls Lost Their Accents* that established her name, and with good imaginative reason: for, however upper-echelon the family genealogy it depicts, the novel speaks with well-honed energy to another hitherto much overlooked US *latinidad*.[35]

Speaking in fractured English Carlos García, MD and Green Card refugee in the wake of a failed CIA plot against Trujillo, mock-bewails his situation—"I am given up Mami! It is no hope for the island. I will become *un dominican-york*" [107]). It is a comment that underwrites the zig-zags of migrancy enacted in the parentage of Carlos and Laura (Papi and Mami) and their Dominican American daughterhood of Carla, Sandra (Sandi), Yolanda (Yoyo, Joe, Joey, Yo) and Sofia (Fifi). Told as a retrospect of successive times (1989–72, 1970–60, 1960–56), the upshot is a consortium although under the narrative direction of Yolanda, schoolteacher, storyteller and whose own break-down ("she spoke in riddles" [79]) further confirms that migrant un-bordering can be set-back or fracture as much as any cliché of always upward and onward American advance. Her journey back to the island in the first chapter, to find, symbolically, the guava she relished in childhood makes for a lived-in landscape as against some postcard Caribbean, just as the last chapter calls up the one-time childhood shadow of Voodoo, a darkened shed, a mysterious cat and a one-eyed Haitian maid. Both present and past time, however, she takes on from the vantage-point of what her cousin calls "Miss America," the now Dominican American woman with gains and losses to match.

This contrast is explored throughout, girlhood and womanhood, Dominican strict Catholic rules as against American secular laxity—dope, contraception, lovers. For Yolanda, as her sisters, it has indeed signified the divided life. Carla, the eldest, becomes a psychologist and argues for out-and-out assimilation, a "fading into walls." Sandi goes in an opposite direction, un-assimilable and psychologically broken by the consequences. Fifi, initially the rebel, has two children by her German lover and, ironically, becomes the good daughter long called for by her father and not least in producing a grandson. As the novel discloses the García family's lower and higher ground, "so many husbands, homes, jobs, wrong turns among them" (11), it shadows Dominican America as at once refuge and hell, always competing memory. Dominican American life as tenement, drugs, casual labor or sexual threat is to be found in Junot Díaz's *Drown* (1996),[36] an eleven-part *barrio* cycle set overlappingly in island Santo Domingo and blue-collar immigrant New Jersey, and Loida Maritz Pérez's *Geographies of Home* (1999),[37] the memory-fiction of a hard-pressed large family barely able to maintain psychological equilibrium in the American journey which has brought them from the Trujillo-era Dominican Republic to Brooklyn.

Junot Díaz's stories in *Drown*, full of *caló*, or *barrio* vernacular, cast a cool, almost clinical eye upon the Dominican immigrant family history of Ramón and Virta de las Casas and their offspring Rafa and Yunior— his baptismal name Ramón, in whom the stories have their center. This is the Dominican Republic and blue-collar New Jersey shorn of heroics, a brilliantly and sparely observed diet of betrayal, cruelties large and small, pinched and furtive sex, and drugs. The father, bigamously married to both Virta and Nilda, often cruel, cheats as though dissembling were intrinsic to survival. His sons can be equally victimizers and victims, respectively in "Ysrael," set in the Dominican hamlet of Ocoa where they stalk and abuse a boy marred by facial defect, and "Fiesta 1980," where the father threatens Rafa for his habitual car sickness and makes both brothers secret witnesses to his philandering with a Puerto Rican woman. Other pieces add to the tenement mosaic—"Aurora" as a portrait of Yunior's drug-dealing and romance amid heroin and theft, "Aguantando" as Yunior's recognition that waiting for his father in the Dominican Republic is all sham, and the title-story "Drown," Yunior's sexual encounter with the gay, college-bound Beto as a glimpse of the vulnerability behind the predatory toughness.

Pérez's *Geographies of Home* likewise eschews any roseate picture of Dominican immigrant life. Told as another family chronicle, that of Papito, Seventh-Day Adventist deacon, his wife Aurelia, also an Adventist but still drawn to island folk belief, and their large sprawl of offspring, the borders are not one but several: migrant, linguistic, sibling, but above all internal and often enough broken. Three daughter-sisters take center-stage, Marina, a rape-victim who becomes increasingly unhinged, Rebecca, obsessively unable to disconnect herself from an abusive husband, and Iliana, whose destiny is to become the voice of this refugee dynasty. All of their borders, as it were, have traveled with them. Each bespeaks the darker reaches of migration, the will-to-sufficiency or efficacy yet also the spiral of set-back, even despair. Iliana, college-educated but a returnee to her family, and who has evolved into a writer ("She would leave no memory behind. . . . All of them were home"[320]) so further defines home as "not a geographical site but . . . a frame of mind able to accommodate any place as home" (320). For her, and for the family, the one American border-crossing can be said to have begotten others each yet to be fully resolved.

* * *

A number of perspectives help situate the borders and un-borders implicit in these different fictions. Lauro Flores's *The Floating Borderlands: Twenty-five Years of U.S. Hispanic Literature* (1998), eighty or so contributions of prose, poetry and artwork—to include cover reproductions from the pioneer journal *Revista Chicano-Riqueña* (founded 1972) and its successor from 1984 *Americas Review*—attests to the ever burgeoning literary *hispanidad* which has continued into 1990s and beyond.[38] An intra-hispanic novel like Alex Abella's *The Killing of The Saints* (1991), Cuban-written with a Little Cuba setting in what normally is thought the Chicano/a urban terrain of Los Angeles, unfolds a fast-moving jewelry heist, murder, and a link into *santería* cults.

Film, likewise, especially those developed from literary fictions, offers a working purchase on an America caught up in its own historic un-bordering. Instances are to be found in *The Milagro Beanfield War* (Dir. Robert Redford, 1988) as the screen version of John Nichols's novel in which the New Mexico earth becomes also the very sediment of Chicano history; *Lone Star* (Dir. John Sayles, 1996), set in the emblematic Frontera, Texas, in which a cross-border of Mexican, Anglo and Tex-Mex lives confirm hybridity as norm; and *Traffic* (Dir. Steven Soderbergh, 2000), the "un-bordered" USA and Mexico of drug supply with due profiles of users, cartels, routes, and police and politicians from both domains.

In Francisco Goldman's *The Long Night of the White Chickens* (1992) the archive again extends in range with its chronicle of Roger Graetz, born of a Jewish father and Guatemalan mother, who leaves his comfortable milieu to plunge into a Guatemala ravaged by thirty years of civil war, Reagan-era CIA machinations against the various Marxist cadres, death squads and the eradication of Mayan and other village communities.[39] In his search for Flor de Mayo and her sacrificial politics of child rescue and sanctuary, and along with the journalist Luis Moya Martínez, Graetz finds himself involved in an awakening to the hemisphere's power-structures and their costly human consequences as to any merely spatial north-south border.

The America written into these texts, one of formal border and yet abrim in cultural un-border, has had few better exponents than the performance artist-writer Guillermo Gómez-Peña. Describing himself in *Warrior for Gringostroika* (1993) as a "deterritorialized Mexican/American living a permanent border experience" with a commitment to "the territory of intercultural dialogue" (46–7) he writes, "Today, if there is a dominant culture, it is border culture. And those who still haven't crossed a border will do so very soon. All Americans (from the vast continent of America) were, are, or will be border-crossers" (46–7).[40] It is a comment full of both history and prophecy, the multiple *Latino/a* Americas within the USA as not only longtime human and cultural cross-border but in the 1990s, as also throughout, the source of any number of its quite most engaging literary fictions.

11 A Western East
America's China Poetry in Marilyn Chin, Russell Leong, John Yau and Wing Tek Lum

Today in hazy San Francisco, I faced seaward towards China . . .
> —Marilyn Chin, "We Are Americans Now,
> We Live in the Tundra" (1987)[1]

In China . . . the world was like a skating rink, a finite place, walled
. . . Here [in the USA] the world was enormous, all endless horizon.
> —Gish Jen, *Typical American* (1991)[2]

Where is my country?
Where does it lie?
> —Nellie Wong, "Where is My Country?" (1991)[3]

Imaging China, in American literary texts, in historic popular culture, and in film and TV, has taken any number of quite startling turns. How, quite, to account for Melville's "China Aster" parable in his Mississippi river-novel, *The Confidence-Man* (1857), with its satire of Emersonian optimism and trust, or Whitman's myth-centered "Down from the gardens of Asia descending" in "Passage to India" (1868, 1871)? How do Pound's webs of China-reference in the *Cantos* (1915–) play as markers both of his interest in the Confucian and Han classics and the Atlantic and European modern movement? What, now, to make of the "China" values of Pearl Buck's *The Good Earth* (1931), her earnest chronicle of North Chinese peasantry which in large part won her the Nobel Prize in 1938?

Alongside have run the figurations of Mark Twain and Bret Harte who contribute the stock figure of the pig-tailed, compliant card-player "John Chinaman" in their melodrama *Ah Sin* (1877). Jack London comes up with his notorious Yellow Peril confections, typically the novel *A Daughter of the Snows* (1902) with its Yukon setting and paean to Anglo-Saxonism and race-hierarchy, and a tale like "The Unparalleled Invasion" (1914) with its not so figurative account of China-defeat and bacteriological infection and warfare. Stereotype, text or screen, has its continuance in Earl Derr Bigger's Charlie Chan and Sax Rohmer's Fu Manchu (albeit British written), the one all Hawaiian-Chinese mandarin ratiocination yet delivered in sing-song, the other all "oriental" fiendish and sexually charged criminality. Both have come under Frank Chin's excoriation as "racist fantasy" and "Christian white racist love," typically in his essay "Confessions of a Chinatown Cowboy," reprinted in *Bulletproof Buddhists* (1998), and *Gunga Din Highway* (1994) with its roll-call of screen versions of Chan, a caricature of a caricature.[4]

Other invented American "Chinas" use Chinatown as alien borderland, the ethnically sealed city-within-a-city, a span from, say, Dashiell Hammett's *The Continental Op*, launched initially in *Black Mask* in 1923 and whose hardboiled San Francisco operatives steer their way through San Francisco as shadow and corner, to Roman Polanski's movie *Chinatown* (1974) with its themes of murder, manipulative Los Angeles water politics, and incest emblematized in the very place-name as an image of silent-inscrutable mystery. Other American "Asia" film gives China as silhouette, a politically viral menace, notably and for all its Korean War backdrop, *The Manchurian Candidate* (1962). In the voluminous Vietnam literature and film, Robin Moore's *The Green Berets* (1965, film 1968) to Michael Herr's *Dispatches* (1977), Ron Kovic's *Born on the Fourth of July* (1976, film 1989) to Bobbie Ann Mason's *In Country* (1985, film 1989), there almost always looms a China shadow, the ideological or world-conspiratorial power behind the throne.

But a century on from the Chinese Exclusion Act of 1882, the Angel Island detention in 1910 onwards of mainly Cantonese in meanly crowded barracks, and the follow-up 1924 Immigration Act, together with other inflections of sinophobia, what of the imaging of China and China-in-America by Chinese American writers, and to immediate purpose, by Chinese American poets? Does one China hold or many, especially as the different processes of diaspora—the Chinas of Hong Kong, Singapore and Taiwan, or of Sydney, London and Paris, or of New York, Vancouver and San Francisco—make negotiable at the very least which China is to be assumed center and which margin (or whether either, in fact, fits).[5]

In *The Beginning of the East Beginning of the East* (1992), his novel of a world re-mapped as if by Christopher Ng, Chinese explorer, Max Yeh makes a link of the Chinese character for map and for China itself—"because the ancient Chinese thought the universe four-square, like the Emperor's domain in Beijing."[6] But if China was indeed "the centre of the world," what has it come to signify as a reference-point in history, culture, politics or philosophy for those within America once designated *Gum Sahn* but every more distanced by generation or further internal migrancy—perhaps most notably Hawai'i? In the light of Angel Island, railroading, bachelor societies, laundries, picture-brides, the transition into English from Mandarin or Cantonese, Hakka or Teochew, what are the implications for how a Chinese past, indeed often more than a one Chinese past, has become an American present, an East a West? What, even more specifically, is it for an American writer to make China into an imaginative term of reference?

Four poets, four refractions or bodies of image: the writings of Marilyn Chin, Russell Leong, John Yau and Wong Tek Lum offer different articulations, an American China, a Chinese America, there which has become a here, a self acculturated to the New World but ever mindful or an older regime of origins. These might be thought historic transformations powerful enough in their own right. But as in all literary creation, and poetry perhaps most of all, yet another comes into play—that whereby the solvent of language and image takes hold of history in ways of its own transformative shaping.

*   *   *

Of Marilyn Chin's three collections, *Dwarf Bamboo* (1987), *The Phoenix Gone, The Terrace Empty* (1994) and *Rhapsody in Plain Yellow* (2003), few poems have won wider currency than "We Are Americans Now, We Live in The Tundra"[7] This little surprises: it reads with a witty, agile sense of rumination, a China, an America, brought into uncertain mutual encounter, a play of gain and loss, finding and letting-go.

To the one side there is China as "giant begonia," at once pink and fragrant and yet subject to its own afflictions, at once a place to arouse fond blues and yet an infected bloom. "Pink, fragrant, bitten/by verdigris and insects" is how Chin images this *patria*, even as she alleges "We are Americans now, we live in the tundra/Of the logical, a sea of cities, a wood of cars."[8] She bids farewell to "my ancestors," all "Hirsute Taoists" as she embraces her American life of speed, efficiency, the access to a New World modernity which plays against an Old World ancient wisdom. This reckoning of pluses and minuses, "Chinese" selves caught neither wholly to advantage nor disadvantage and in America as in China, can be said to shape virtually all of Chin's poetry.

A poem like "The End of a Beginning," for instance, written to "Grandfather," has the speaker seeing him/herself poised teasingly at the turning-point of two histories, two languages.[9] The writer's "paltry lines," moreover, bear back upon both American and Chinese regimens—both cases of hard-won survival in despite of historic family losses. Immigrants to America ("only to die under the wheels of the railroad") succeed the generation that "fell/building yet another annex to the Great Wall." These both she remembers in the process of her own selfhood—"I,/the beginning of the end, end of a beginning" who "scrawl these paltry lines for you."[10]

No poem more acerbically takes up these the threads than "How I Got That Name," at once confessional, full of rueful ambiguity, and pointedly subtitled, "*an essay in assimilation.*" Much as it gives acknowledgement to how China and America have gone into the making of the first-person speaker, the synthesis remains neither simple nor seamless. Chin's persona as may be, and so Hong Kong born, Oregon raised, educated in Massachusetts, and living in California, the recall is of how "Mei Ling" has become "Marilyn," in name at least the Chinese daughter metamorphosed into the American daughter. She speaks as both a species of co-resident of simultaneous realms and of a third: the cultures of her upbringing and also of "her own bamboo grove/minding her poetry."[11]

These and other gaps and overlaps cause the speaker to believe herself a kind of ongoing human helix, a live figuration of dual cultures and inheritances. The voice to be heard, accordingly, is wry, witty, full of double-talk (her father, say, as Chinese "paperperson," or the iconic Marilyn Monroe for whom she has been named "some tragic white woman"). Yet, as each wordplay gathers and resonates, she insists upon her own singularity, no undue partisan of all-one or all-another allegiance. She so begins, ironically, under two lines of nomenclature, as mock-ingenuously, "herself." Her name "Marilyn Mei Ling Chin" carries the mix of legacy, be it Angel Island or Monroe as "bombshell blonde," in sum the transliteration as she particularizes it of Mei Ling into Marilyn.[12]

Patriarchy, in turn, is given its slap, a bittersweet tribute, with a mother loved but eased into compliance with the father's "tomcat" waywardness. She re-imagines herself as "a wayward pink baby/ named after some tragic white woman/ swollen with gin and Nembutal." She conjures up her mother's version of her as "Numba one female offshoot" and her father as "gambler, petty thug." Even "face" is brought into view, double-face, the gambler-thug-father sanitized by upward-bound American offspring, "devoted" daughters and "industrious" sons—"as if filial piety were the standard/ by which all earthly men are measured."

America so succeeds China, but ever ambiguously, a play of two worlds perpetuated as mutual shadow and substance. Nor does this China-America dialectic turn only on Chin's own immediate dynasty. In "Child" she thinks of history as time-and-space, a linkage of San Francisco's Golden Gate, New York's Avenue of the Americas and China itself as "Your relentless wife."[13] In "Repulse Bay" the link is between "Kowloon, in Granny's/ One room apartment" and New England and Oregon, a geography of mind and feeling as much as land and sea.[14] In "Barbarian Suite" she ponders "AmerAsia," as she terms it, as at once "dead ancestors" and "jazz," China bones and American musical riff.[15] These connections, however, whether personal or generic, can again look to "How I Got That Name" for a working summary, a digging-out of ancestry suitably in the image of bamboo ("Oh bamboo shoots, bamboo shoots!"):

The further west we go, we'll hit east;
The deeper down we go, we'll find China.[16]

West as East, down as up, America's China as China's America—dialectic remains all, and if never without its cost then never without its treasury of returns.

*   *   *

Raised in San Francisco's Chinatown, and since 1977 editor of *Amerasia Journal*, Russell Leong's one poetry collection, *The Country of Dreams and Dust* (1993) deservedly became the recipient of an Oakland, California P.E.N. award in Spring 1994—in 2001 he would win the American Book Award for his *Phoenix Eyes and Other Stories* (2000).[17] Among quite the most striking of the assembled poems has to be "Aerogrammes," a five-part sequence developed from Leong's visit from Los Angeles to Sunwui County, Guandong, in 1984.[18] It works very much as a species of colloquy, an interplay of encounter and memory between the speaker's two lived-in worlds, a Chinese America of modernity and a China of ancestry.

A highly interrogatory note of doubt underwrites these different equations. What is the true meaning of this South China voyage. Is it the honoring of lineage or some species of tourist curiosity on the part of the speaker? Is it the welcoming back of a China son or extended begging on the part of his Sunwui relatives? Should he exult in his "roots" or regard China's opening of the door to its American "China sons" as a ruse to bring in dollars? Does ancestor reverence have to be forever perpetuated or does a time come to end, or at least reduce, "filial piety"? As self-narrative, "Aerogrammes" moves with nice agility through these different equations, excitement tinged with suspicion, the resolve to break with a sense of foreboding and loss.

The note of ambivalence is struck in the journey verse-sequence which prefaces the five "Aerogrammes" with its trope of a China borne epistolatorily across the Pacific. This is also a speaker bearing witness as though having been caught by surprise, history as much as geography in pursuit of his own tracks. The key metaphor is "Par Avion/via airmail," the franking upon envelopes "glued and stamped/westward" and which serves to connect Pearl River Delta with Los Angeles, village China with metropolitan America, and all of it "generations later." This is journeying at once immediate and yet born of older history, the speaker's temporary migration to the East "caught up," as the poem says, in earlier permanent migration to the West. He is thus shadowed in time as well as space. Both are embodied in "the five blue- and red-striped/aerogrammes," each a China yet subsequently carried into America.

The prolegomenon, which re-enacts his arrival in Sunwui with a "woman driver," calls up their car-journey conversation as to how China has now become the capitalist-roader—replete with Coca Cola and to which he has brought the gift of Marlboro cigarettes—as against the country of his own youthful American-campus infatuation with "Mao,/ revolution, socialism." The driver offers her own dialectic (". . . a little capitalism today/is a good tonic to cure feudal ideas!"). Arriving at the clan hall ("Forwards and backward/they lead me through alleyways . . .") he meets a family gathering in which his own father is remembered in a wartime portrait and he himself transposes into "Uncle." As though metamorphosis personified he finds himself inspected ("No, no; yes, yes"). It makes for a keenest image-play of contraries, going-away and home-coming, China-kin and America-kin.

The five "aerogramme" sections, responses to each "eight-legged ideogram," chart his own zig-zag of feeling, the China he has visited, the China inside his American self. "Aerogramme One: Los Angeles" summons back the symptomatic exchange of gifts on his visit, Chinese "bags of dried orange peel" for American "wine, cigarettes and money." Has this been a show of unequal wealth? Are the queries as to age, marital state, offspring, meant in good faith or not? In "Aerogramme Two" there is the appeal for funds to open a dry-goods shop yet also a recall of the Japanese invasion, a first ancestor, an uncle, in California and the Cold War. How, again, to hit his own right balance? "Aerogramme Three" brings the request of a nephew for $5000 to buy a condominium. Opinion about him divides. A close friend from China says "Send the money," another from America "Crazy, man." He himself speaks of "split vision" until, after delay, he sends some of the money ("I telexed money from L.A. Chinatown—/to Hong Kong, to Canton, to Sunwui Village"). What, he implies, are his obligations of kin, the more so the less close the family tree? "Aerogramme Four" contains a marriage proposal from the family, a sent-over bride even as he cruises bi-sexual Hollywood Boulevard in his '71 Ford Maverick, dynasty indeed seen from the un-dynastic flesh and modernity of California.

"Aerogramme Five" contains a letter from a twenty-one year old girl alleging their mountainside meeting. The importuning again raises doubts as to the validities of clan, the call of the old upon the new ("I wrote off filial piety/as useless,/ a fallen branch."). But there persist matters not in his gift to revoke. The connecting push and pull of lineage, and with it memory, almost as if by will of its own refuses to be severed. "I wait the arrival/of the next/immutable/aerogramme" confesses the compelled voice of the poem. This last ambiguity does perfect service. Well may Leong's speaker wish China written off, out of his life. But in Los Angeles, as in Guandong, the "immutable" aerogrammes—and the China they write in—continue to holds sway, unwanted and yet wanted, foregone and yet quite as equally awaited, both sealed and opened. This gallery of China-America paradox gives the poem-sequence edge, a presence of voice engagingly in debate with itself.

* * *

With John Yau Chinese America steps, nothing if not daringly, into the postmodern, a poetry of reflexivity not unbefitting a leading art critic with books on Jasper Johns and Andy Warhol as well as versifier who looks to one kind of provenance in the painterly, free-form New York School writings of Frank O'Hara, John Ashbery and Kenneth Koch. Yau was early to establish himself in *Crossing Canal Street* (1976), and extending into *The Sleepless Night of Eugene Delacroix* (1980), *Corpse and Mirror* (1983), and key text-and-image collections like *Notarikon* (1980), *Dragon's Blood*

(1989) and *Postcards from Trakl* (1994). But "China," albeit often tacitly, has all along supplied a key seam in his work.[19]

Symptomatic early instances can look to a spatial calligraphic poem like "Cameo of a Chinese Woman on Mulberry Street" ("Her face// this moon// a house/always nearing the end of its road") through to his meditative lyric on a recently broken love-affair, "A Suite of Imitations Written After Reading Translations of Poems by Li He and Li Shang-yin" ("Tonight, I am all alone in the Palace of Clouds")—both to be found in Yau's *Radiant Silhouette: New and Selected Works, 1974–1988* (1989).[20] This same collection yields the virtuosity of his seven-part poem "Genghis Chan: Private Eye," each soliloquy one in a series of observations and intimacies under a persona which takes its own several forms (Yau first published the series in *Dragon's Blood*, with a reprinting in *Radiant Silhouette*, and has now added further sequences in *Edificio Sayonara* [1992] and *Forbidden Entries* [1996]).[21] It is perhaps less the imagery of the constituent poems that call up "China" than the disclosing persona: the narrator, the "I," as a species of surreal Chinese American, an imaginary private-eye/private I of the senses and of each linking shift or turn of feeling.

In "I" a Magritte-like displacement occurs—gapped increments of voice from "I was floating through a cross section/with my dusty wine glass" to "She laughed/a slashed melody of small shrugs" to "A foul lump started making promises in my voice."[22] In "II" the self as lost inside its own alien patterns of sensation becomes even more marked ("In less than half a pedal of time/I would be entering the hyena zone").[23] "III" has the speaker imagining himself in the role of failed lover as storyteller ("I wanted to tell you/ about how the sun dissolved all of this long ago/leaving us in different rooms/registered under different names").[24] In "IV," "V," and "VI," he sees himself as variously "a tendril adrift," "a lost shrieker," "just another particle cloud," the voice of his own inefficacies of speech, or as he expresses matters, the "owner of a pockmarked tongue."[25]

Finally, in "VII," an accusation is lodged, both against the loved one ("You will grasp someone's tongue with your teeth and pull") and against his own powers of tongue as if even the poem's contrivance of "words" still do not meet his self's will to a commanding articulacy.[26] As the title of the volume overall implies, Yau's penchant is for an understanding of life—his speaker's, his own—as indeed "radiant silhouette," self and relationship transposed into image. That these are all pitched as the investigations of "Genghis Chan: Private Eye" gives precisely a sponsoring "Chinese" sense of perceptual difference, an America of personal intimacy seen up close yet as though from afar.

*   *   *

Chinese Hawaiian, a major in engineering at Brown, an MA in Divinity from Union Theological Seminary, a one-time social worker in both New York's Chinatown and for Hong Kong's Society for the Deaf, and a family businessman in Honolulu—Wing Tek Lum's cv, by locale and career, might well qualify him as model of the multicultural. To which, emphatically, has to be added the poet of his still best-known volume, *Expounding The Doubtful Points* (1987), issued from the illustrious Bamboo Ridge literary collective and press. It is a collection that moves with greatest fluency between poetry sharply specific to "Pacific Island" Chinese American legacy and yet always the play of other cultural lineage in the making of America. Three poems especially show him in strength and with characteristic focus.

"Translations," a three-parter, offers an overall frame—cryptic, bittersweet, in its view of the history and the miniaturization whereby China in all its Asian plenitude has become the stereotypical miniature of American Chinatown.[27] In its first section the poem invokes "ghosts," that most loaded of Chinese figurations, a double reference-back to "childhood scenes . . . in old bedsheets" and "reading comics," but also to "ancient rites" and "*Gwái*," the "Old Demons who wear/white skin/and make believe/they behave like men."[28] In the second section the note turns upon the memory of Chinese shadow-acting for "the demon," but a two-way mockery as it also involves Chinese self-abasement. Lum calls it "a comedy/of errors,/ part fawning, part/deception and contempt." In summary, and accusingly, he writes "There is no word for fortune cookie in Cantonese." In section three the acidity becomes yet more pronounced—as it does in pieces like "Minority Poem," "Local Sensibilities" and "The Return of Charlie Chan" with its "You are still the most famous Chinaman in all America/and you will never let us forget it" (Frank Chin, with his counter-strikes against orientalist caricature has long been an influence).[29] Lum takes aim at Chinatown seen only as exterior, street and sign but absent of human texture, language, community dynamic. "Translations" so parodies its own meaning, the Chinese into English one which has lost the word "people."[30] This is cultural semantics with a sting-in-the-tail, translation as indeed traduction. "*Tòhng Yàhn Gáai* was what/ we once called/where we lived: China-People-Street." The formulation, however, has turned into the mockery of Chinatown with the one difference—"the people disappeared."

"A Moon Festival at Kahala Beach park" strikes the more personal note, a family outing and thoughts of Hong Kong, "overseas Chinese lives" and "new traditions."[31] As in his other poems of reminiscence, notably "A Picture of my Mother's Family" and "It's Something Our Family Has Always Done," Lum's rumination moves adroitly from collective to the inflections of the personal, the single self within the plurality. Prefaced with a couplet from Sun Tung P'o—"*But why is it always full/just when people are parted?*"—"A Moon Festival" starts in seemingly casual voice: two families at the beach "reciting/a Cantonese nursery rhyme." Thoughts in the speaker, however, widen to an August ("eighth") moon, past Hong Kong family gatherings, Chinese foodways, the Star Ferry, the moon itself as on a "flightpath" that has now become "some discarded umbilical cord" or "lifeline unraveling" between China and America, and finally the coastlines of Hong Kong and Hawaii. How, he asks, to manage old and new, "all of China" and "our overseas Chinese lives"?[32]

The response is interrogatory, confessional, and imagined as though in the lives of the children to follow. It asks what new traditions will be passed down to a next generation. What picnics will follow for his young daughter and others at this same beach and under "this same full-flowering moon"? The attractiveness here lies in not just the speaker's intimacy with parent-child families but the confirming hold of imagery—ocean, sky, beach and moon as spatial coordinates for his own tightly-held daughter. This is a China, a Chinese America, at ease with itself.

A more playful Wing Tek Lum is to be encountered in "Chinese Hot Pot" in which Chinese foodways augment from some ethnic enclave into the very trope of America-at-large.[33] "My dream of America," he says, "is like *dá bìn lòuh*," a "common pot" of squid, beef, tofu and watercress "all in one broth . . ." It is a poem that carries its vision with lightness, alimentary, familial, everyday and close-to-hand. But it serves, too, to remind of the far larger "dream" cycles of self and culture which have implicated, each to their own style, almost every Chinese American poet.

American China, in this envisioning, becomes ever more Chinese America, a process shadowed in each other human seam in the national company, and each seated "around a common pot," "at the table," and sharing "fire." Nor, to be at table in this way, is that to lose respective paths of identity. Herein, for Lum, as for Chin and Leong, beckons the poet's prospect of a Chinese East and Chinese West, along with other Easts and Wests, meeting in their own species of equilibrium in despite of all persisting disequilibrium.

12 Insider, Outsider
Japanese America Writing Japan

> An astonishing book might be written about those things in Japanese
> life which no foreigner can understand.
> —Lafcadio Hearn, "Bits of Life and Death" (1895)[1]

The West has hardly been short on interest in *japonisme, japonoiserie*. The literary roll-call, at least, has grown familiar, be it Pound and Yeats as vintage avatars of modernism, Lafcadio Hearn as cultural interpreter and storyteller, Edmund Blunden as *gaijin* poet-teacher, or a latter-day Beat literary pantheon to include names like Gary Snyder, Joanne Kyger and Cid Corman, poet and editor of *Origin* who first established himself in Kyoto in 1958. But what of quite another literary version of Japan, albeit also constructed in English by authorship with its own unique historical linkage into Japan—pre-eminently Japanese American and Japanese Canadian and, almost singly in the person of Kazuo Ishiguro, Japanese British? How has this writing rendered Japan, diasporically as it were, the one cultural geography at whatever remove the screen or mirror through which to refract the other?

This of necessity raises the issue of quite which Japan is being put into view. For Japan itself offers no easy formula, no single paradigm. Despite familiar recitations to do with homogeneity, conformism, the Chrysanthemum Kingdom as bound into itself more tightly than most other national cultures and certainly those of the Asian mainland, a first step would be to ponder Japan's own self-debates. One iconographic port of call would be *nihonjinron*, the long-aborning (and often self-congratulatory) national tradition of discourse as to what has made Japan unique, a world with its own pre-emptive latitudes and longitudes.

The ancestry for this activity is considerable, pre-dating the Edo (1603–1867), Meiji (1868–1912), Taisho (1912–1926), Showa (1926–1989) and Heisei (1989–) eras, and at once scholarly and popular. What have been the implications of Japan's figural descent from the sun? Have its people indeed been wholly distinct from other Asia, the *Ainu* to the Edo and prior shogunate courts, Shinto to emperor-worship, ancient Nara to metropolitan Tokyo, tropical Okinawa to wintry Hokkaido? What of its political family-caste systems like those of the recent premierships of Hashimoto, Obuchi, Koizumi, Abe, Fukuda, Aso and Hatoyama, or its infinite nuances of etiquette, or its time-space configurations?

Its religious practices and arts likewise invite particularization. Each plaits into a longstanding body of reflective self-expression. whether *zen,*

Kyoto temple culture, *noh*, *haiku* and *kabuki*, visual work to span Hiroshige's Edo-era *ukiyo-e* prints and cinema like Akira Kurosawa's *Rashomon* (1950), *manga*, *sumi-e* (wash painting and calligraphy), *hanami* (cherry-blossom viewing), *irezumi* (tattooing), and even erotica like *kinbaku* (rope bondage). To these can be added the *kanji* and two *kana* systems, *tanka* (31-syllable verse), *ocha-kei* (tea ceremony), *shodo* (calligraphy), *teien* (rock garden composition), *kakejiku* (scroll-making), *byōbu* (folding-screen), and even *tatami* (straw floor-mats). How not to take account of the alimentary roster, an art of eating and drinking, whether *sushi*, *sashimi*, *ramen*, *soba*, *sake* or *nama biru* (draft beer)?

Another key term would be *aikokushin*, loosely patriotism, a greatly vexed notion in the light of imperial Japanese history and eugenic doctrines of race. On the one hand it has been associated with pre-war fascism, the Greater East Asian Co-Prosperity Sphere and 1930s Tojo-Hirohito nationalist politics. On the other, as in the current *mombukagakusho* (or Ministry of Science, Education and Technology and Sport) controversies about High School teaching of patriotism and suitable textbooks, it is argued to be more innocuous, a pride in art and culture. In July 2005, in Fukuoka, Taro Aso, senior LDP politician, foreign minister, later to become Prime Minister like his own grandfather, and heir to a mining company that used Korean and other near-slave labor in the 1940s, spoke of Japan as "one nation, one civilization, one language, one culture, and one race."[2] Sparks flew, old sores flared. Beijing cried foul, Seoul protested, Pyongyang took umbrage. Was this not more supremacism, self-glorification? And how did it comport with a Japan infinitely more various, far from some undifferentiated political and cultural order.

In fact both Japan, and Japan-watchers, and especially since the Meiji restoration, have long held greatly conflictive views of the nation, a ply of accusation and defense, admiration and yet resentment. One arena has been the different perceptions of the nation's recent history: Japan in one view as aggressor and in another as victim. In the former column the indictment usually invokes the suzerainty over Korea (1910–1945), the invasion of Manchuria, the rape of Nanking, Pearl Harbor, the Bataan death march, the Pacific devastation wrought from the Philippines to Singapore, Tokyo Rose, "comfort women," and for current times, the issue of August 15 governmental visits to the Yasukuni Shrine (a practice actually ended by Emperor Hirohito in protest at enshrinement of the Class-A war criminals but not Prime Ministers Yasuhiro Nakasone and Junichiro Koizumi and other LDP politicians). This is Japan as insufficiently repentant, unfavorably to be compared with Germany, a culture still un-shriven of its supremacist inclinations. Contrarily there has been the Japan-as-victim syndrome. Hiroshima and Nagasaki serve as prime stigmata. There has been the under-recognized financial contributions to the UN and its peace activities. Latterly the publicity given to North Korea's abductions during the 1960s, most notably through the Yokota family, and Pyongyang's missile and nuclear technology, has entered the lists.

At a slightly different reach there is the Japan that has seized economic triumph out of defeat and risen to the world's number two global-economic status. Consumer standards rank among the highest and wealth has generally and more equitably than in other advanced economies been widespread. But in another respect Japan has become Japan Inc., state and corporate-controlled, and despite the so-called new capitalism of companies like Livedoor in its financial rise and fall and whatever the degree of change in employment for life, still rigid in its decision-making and work-hierarchy. It also invites being thought avidly protectionist, if not as market-conspiratorial along the lines of a bestseller like Michael Crichton's *Rising Sun* (1992) with the film version to follow in 1993.[3]

As to nationalist Japan a home-grown bearing is afforded by Tokyo's Governor Shintaro Ishihara, journalist, novelist, and long a maverick ex-LDP presence ("They say we made a holocaust there," he has said several times in public of Nanking, "but that's not true. It is a lie made up by the Chinese"). In the book he co-authored with Sony's founder, Akio Morita, *The Japan That Can Say No: Why Japan Will Be First among Equals* (1989), he argues for a Japan more internationally assertive as to its own interests, freed of American military presence, and even prepared to consider re-writing its peace constitution.[4] More recently he has condescendingly warned of likely *gaijin* panic in the case of major earthquake as against an assumed orderly Japanese response. But his petty nationalism, and that of Masahiko Fujiwara in the best-selling *Kokka no Hinkaku/The Dignity of a State* (2006), with its harangue against western thought and logic, ill-comports with a Japan facing an increasingly global economic and cultural order.[5] These attitudes take far from due cognizance of Japan's need for migrant labor given the fall in national birthrate and greying population. They also do an injustice to the nation's small but important demographic mix, whether its Korean-Japanese citizenry, the Yokohama of a Chinatown the largest in Asia, a Finnish-born Diet member, the rising number of "mixed" marriages, or even NHK's TV showing of Mongol and East European faces currently at the top of the *sumo* ladder.

Japan's economic image has been equally and busily contradictory. If, on the one hand, it is to be thought a serious market leader through its Mitsubishi and other mega-corporations, is it not also the supplier of a species of perpetual Disneyland of toys, fashion, pop-art, and the youth-tastes of Shibuya or Harajuku? How, quite, to square the Japan of Zen and Shinto with the rampant consumerism—from Sony Walkman to Toshiba computer, DoCoMo phone (*keitai*) to Toyota car? How to explain the endless fascination with *karaoke, tamagotchi, manga, anime, enka, pachinko, sudoku, j-pop,* and even former Prime Minister Koizumi's hairstyle.[6] If a model of relentless profit is not Japan also a culture of supreme consumer service and public manners? How, too, to explain the export of the sushi bar and sake, borrowed Japan as it were?

How, in turn, to get the measure of Japan as source of American and other outside popular culture? Foreign film has supplied one plenty, from Alan Resnais's *Hiroshima Mon Amour* (1959), with its wartime French-Japanese love affair and Proustian memory of a prior wartime relationship, to Sofia Coppola's *Lost in Translation* (2003), with its portrait of American dislocation set against the seeming comic (but actually culture-biased) hyper-courtesies of fashionable hotel Tokyo. Debate turns on whether they capture the one or another truth about Japan or engage in exoticization, more sepia-tinged orient, more Tokyo as some kind of alien planet. Both have been greatly applauded yet also remain open to charges of screen orientalism. Stereotypes proliferate, whether of office salaryman or geisha—the latter in Arthur Golden's novel, *Memoirs of a Geisha* (1997), with its Hollywood follow-up in 2003. A figure like Yoko Ono has been both loved and reviled, either performance artist of talent or off-the-wall fake, either John Lennon's muse-savior or thief of a Beatles icon.

*   *   *

This same contrary nuance as to race, nation and the global holds in especial, yet with necessary greater articulacy, in Japanese literary matters. Two names, by way of example, help locate the cross-hatch of viewpoint, Yukio Mishima and Kenzaburo Oe. When, on November 25, 1970, Mishima committed *seppuku*, ritual *hara-kiri*, having called for opposition to the peace constitution and restoration of absolute emperor-power, cried *banzai* and harangued members of the Japanese Self-Defense Force as weak, not a few observers thought the spectacle a scene from Grand Guignol theatre. For all the talk of *bushido*, the *samurai* ethic, was not this out-of-time suicide by a same-sex martial cultist with a grotesque follow-on in the beheading that took several hacks from one of his acolytes? In calling for a re-born Japanese nationalism Mishima was to be thought some live anachronism, both subject and object of his own narcissistic hero-martyr delusion.

Yet he also spoke to something much germinating in postwar Japan: the sense that mere economic efficacy has tilted the society off-base, a world in which yen consumerism (the 1980s bubble economy Japan itself would call "the lost decade") had replaced moral or cultural better national purpose. If, too, Mishima ended up the intending sacrificial figure out of one of his celebrated Saint Sebastian-style photographic images, was he not also the deservedly acclaimed author not only of the seminal story "Patriotism," with its aesthetic (and phallic ecstasy) of sacrificial death in the face of a 1936 mutiny within the ranks of Imperial troops, but of *Confessions of a Mask* (1949), *The Temple of the Golden Pavilion* (1956) and the 4-volume *The Sea of Fertility* (1965–70) as well as of Noh and Kabuki plays? Which Mishima best deserves to survive?[7]

In Kenzaburo Oe, Nobel prizewinner for 1994, avowed internationalist, lifetime student of French, and a figure who in a culture which has often shunned its disfigured (as in the case of Hansen's Disease patients) continues to exhibit an exemplary fatherhood towards his disabled musician son, Japan looks to a wholly different order of thinking about the national-global axis. In *The Day He Himself Shall Wipe My Tears Away* (1972) he actually took an early swipe at Mishima's dream of a reborn warrior-imperial Japan.[8] Nowhere is Oe's perspective given clearer force than in the Nobel Prize Address he entitled "Japan, the Ambiguous and Myself" (1994) and in which he speaks of Japan's being "split between two poles of ambiguity." His observations invite citation:

> The modernization of Japan has been orientated towards learning from and imitating the West. Yet Japan is situated in Asia and has firmly maintained its traditional culture. The ambiguous orientation of Japan drove the country into the position of an invader in Asia . . .[9]

Oe richly localizes many of the dualities (and multiples) of Japan as national culture, modernization as both historic Meiji and post-Meiji self-advance and yet historic will-to-power over other Asia. A postwar Japan, in turn, is put to negotiate not only its relationship with the West, or new Asia, but also Africa and the other Third World, along with the aggressor-victim dialectic, and the ambiguity of the atom bomb as not just Japanese but Korean-Japanese calamity. His Nobel Address, in its recognition of Japan's historic cultural ambiguities, might with good cause be advanced as the very ground-text in any serious discussion of Japan along the race-nation-globe sightline.

* * *

In moving on to authorship on Japan by writers to one degree or another of Japanese provenance (*issei, nisei, sansei, yonsei*, together with *kibei* as US-born but Japan-educated), yet other cross-lights and tiers of ambiguity enter the reckoning. Each, by very identity, could not but address being "Japanese" in America, Canada or the UK, but always against the silhouette, sometimes the substance, of an ancestral Japan, the memorial force of family, place, language, custom, and past-into-present. To this end Kazuo Ishiguro offers a first bridge, in one sense a wholly one-off presence in contemporary British literature yet, and not the least of it, the refusal (in company with, say, Timothy Mo or Ali Smith) to be held always to the assumption of personal heritage as subject-matter. Even so, and for all that *Remains of The Day* (1989) almost vaunts its interwar regime of English class, a "Japanese" novel like *A Pale View of The Hills* (1982) indeed does draw upon Ishiguro's Japanese childhood, a reference-back into the Nagasaki after the bomb.[10]

A novel of wistful inter-memories, Japanese atomic city and British countryside, parenthood and lost children, it also directly invokes Japan as

contested history. Nowhere is that given clearer expression than in the relationship of the retired former teacher, Ogata-san, and Jiro, his salaryman-
son. Ogata-san's learning that a Japanese wife has voted independently of
her husband extends into his generational lament as to the loss of correct
attitude, the one-time Japan of Confucian hierarchy and tradition. "Dis-
cipline, loyalty, such things held Japan together once," he alleges. "People
were bound by a sense of duty" (65). Yet, to his dismay, "The Americans
decided that our schools would be like American Schools" (66). Jiro, as
he takes up his father's question and even though constrained by the duty
of filial respect, speaks for a more open, individuating Japan, recalling
the aggrandizement of a Japan supposedly descended from the gods and
"divine and supreme" (66).

With characteristic understatement Ishiguro goes to the heart of the
matter. Whose Japan is it, or should be it? Is the father's attitude simply
reactionary nostalgia as against the son's modernity and wish to move on
in history? Has the Japan shaped, and to a degree democratized by the
Douglas MacArthur legacy (1945–51), been to advantage or not? What to
make of the virtually unbroken government tenure of the LDP, the *Todai*
(Tokyo University) and other elites, the dominance of the corporations and
state monopolies? Certainly a Japan with US bases in Okinawa and its
waters patrolled by the Fifth Fleet, or with youth tastes in American fast
food, jeans and pop music, might feel itself in some ambiguity. The suspicion arises that full independence has to co-exist with the footfalls of
military occupation, a Japan of unique ways and tradition yet increasingly
(or at least in the cities) drawn to western idioms of culture.

*   *   *

Much as there has been a tendency to think Japanese American fiction
and autobiography largely postwar, a feature of America's multicultural
literary renaissance, the tradition begins early with Yone Noguchi's
wholly imaginary *The American Diary of a Japanese Girl* (1902).[11] Told
in the gender-crossing first-person voice of Miss Morning Glory it offers
a panoply of comparative views on both Japan and America. Between
this portrait of first encounter, East inside West and recent autofictions
like Garrett Hongo's *Volcano* (1995) and David Mura's *Turning Japanese:
Memoirs of a Sansei* (1991), the span has been considerable, its own genuine efflorescence.[12]

Whether the departure point is Commodore Matthew Perry's "black
ships" arriving in the Edo Bay in 1853 and landing at Uraga, the first Japanese plantation laborers of Hawai'i, the 1882 Exclusion Act (however much
aimed at the Chinese), the subsequent 1924 Japanese Exclusion Act, or the
infamous *Ozawa v. United States* case of 1922 with its bearing on citizenship, the making of Japanese America has been its own kind of vexed
and always contrary fare. In no greater respect could this have been more

so than with Pearl Harbor (Franklin Roosevelt's "date which will live in infamy") and the signing of Executive Order (EO) 9066 which put 120,000 Japanese Americans into internment camps like Manzanar, Topaz, Lake Tule, Amache or Poston. That the all-*nisei* 442 Regimental Combat Team became the most decorated of US army units, or that so ranking an authority as Henry Steele Commager would write "the record does not disclose a single case of [Japanese American] disloyalty or sabotage during the whole war," adds a further irony.

Garrett Hongo's poem "Stepchild" in his collection *Yellow Light* (1982)[13] speaks to the costs, and especially the silences, brought on by the camps and the Yellow Peril phobia redivivus that underwrote them ("Someone pulled out the tongues/of every Nisei/raped by the felons/of Relocation" [56]). In fact, as the considerable camp literature of story, memoir and other poetry bears out, it has much come to be "talked about," and with it the issue of "Japan" as national iconography, a constructed site of culture and race for both Japanese-descended and non-Japanese descended Americans.

* * *

If any one name invites being thought to hold founding sway it has to be that of Toshio Mori (1910–80), California *nisei*, San Leandro nurseryman, detainee and camp historian at the Topaz Relocation Center in Utah, and author of *Yokohama, California* (1949).[14] On the one hand suggestive of Sherwood Anderson's cyclical small-town portraiture in *Winesburg, Ohio* (1919), and on the other of Japanese comic-satiric tradition, this affectionate, and nothing if not wry, collection of twenty-two stories depicts both Japanese America and the memorial Japan behind it with a nuance only possible to an insider.

"Long ago, children, I lived in a country called Japan" (15) says the grandmother-narrator to her grandchildren Annabelle and Johnny in the opening story "Tomorrow is Coming Children," as though the Japan at issue belongs in nursery-story, a once-upon-a-time place. Her memory alights on her Japanese village farewell, the sailing from the port of Kobe, her sea-sickness, the sight of San Francisco's Golden Gate ("the city with enticing food; the city with gold coins" [16]), and her husband's requirement that she replace her best kimono with American clothes. The Japan she once embodied is to be discarded as redundant, un-modern, other. Yet between the two of them they create another Japan: they buy a Japanese-style bathhouse, give rise to a family of appropriately bi-cultural names (Mamoru, Yuri, Willie, Mary Ann, Yoshio and Betty), and see their first-born, Mamoru, fighting abroad in the US infantry in a war between "my mother country and my adopted land" (20). But the true kick of the story lies in the final revelation: "If there were no war we would not be in a relocation center" (21). Even so, and whatever the loss of their Market Street home, Mamoru's war-service, and the internment, the balance favors

America ("My San Francisco is everywhere"[20]). For herself and her family Japan has come to stand as double-sign, fond origins yet stigma, with the America of her aspirations no less double, if desert prison-house then still also sumptuous dream.

The almost title-story, "Lil' Yokohama" gives off a similar resonance, a Japanese Japan made over into an American Japan. Mori's careful accretion of everyday detail, births and deaths, housewives and retirees, business people and artists, subtly connects the township to every other American city. A baseball game takes place between the Alameda Taiiku and the San Jose Asahis. The school day parallels the work day. The death of Komai-san, long-time gardener, occurs at the same time as the birth of Franklin Susumu Amano. Yuko Takaki, a painter living on Seventh Street, like Mori himself, takes inspiration from the street. Sam Suda expands his fruit business. Satoru Ugaki gets married. The sight of a new Oldsmobile Eight stirs neighbourhood gossip. Ray Tatemoto leaves to study journalism in New York. Radios blast out Benny Goodman jazz. If the *Mainichi News* reports a world in, and of, two languages (a community whose "news belongs here as does the weather" [71]), then is not this version of Japan quite equally America? The clock, work, school, meals, gossip all take on quotidian familiarity. "The day is here and it is Lil' Yokohama's Day" (76) runs Mori's perfect low-key gloss, a township at peace with itself and all other America despite coming international war. The American Japan of this portrait is to be relished, or simply recognized, and if distinctive, then just as equally, no more nor less than as the one more America.

Mori, who never visited Japan, keeps this same Japan wonderfully in view throughout. "The Woman Who Makes Swell Doughnuts" offers near zen parable, a Japanese-in-America vignette. The visiting youngster witnesses to the culinary craft of the old woman known as Mama whose perfect doughnuts with their craft and balance emblematize life-art in its very time and history. Her house becomes a retreat, temple-like stillness from which to view the world. In "Say It with Flowers" the refusal of the young Japanese American florist's assistant to pass off old flowers for new, and who offers a free bouquet to the older woman client as compensation, costs him his job at the hands of the owner Mr. Sasaki. But it bespeaks Confucian good faith, Japanese good faith, albeit in present-day America. As poignant and symptomatic as any of the pieces is "Slant-Eyed Americans," its backdrop Pearl Harbor and the transformation of all Japanese Americans into "enemy aliens." When a son, Kazuo, leaves his flower-grower family to fight in an all-*nisei* regiment, his mother wishes him off with the words "Give your best to America." (135). The train taking him to the Pacific, in its turn, leaves with the blinds pulled down: an America, it might well be thought, un-loyal to, and unseeing of, its own loyal Japan.

For John Okada (1923–1971), as landmark in name as Mori yet equally at the beginning overlooked and soon out of print, the scenario in his *No-No Boy* (1957) is wartime Seattle, a Japanese American novel given over to division in America, division as to Japan.¹⁵ Told as the life of Ichiro Yamada who, as both *nisei* camp detainee and then ex-jailee for refusing the draft, he also hears the taunts of "Sneaky Japs," "Go back to Tokyo boy" and "Shinto freaks," each the particularizing of a time when "Everything and everyone Japanese became despicable" (vii). Having said No both to enlistment and the Pledge of Allegiance in the wake of 9066 and the camps, he returns to a family divided also by generations and loyalties.

His mother, who runs the grocery-store with his father, edges into the madness of denial. Japan, for her, is truly the Chrysanthemum Kingdom, a descended-from-the-gods imperium which, according to letters from a Japanese family in Brazil, is about to ferry her home by ship. All else, Japanese starvation, or military defeat, she takes for American conspiracy, a war ruse. Impaired, anorexic, she drowns to be found in the family bath by her returning son. His kindly, if ineffectual, father decays into alcoholism, an *issei* for whom neither Japan nor America can be safe domicile. Taro, his brother, repudiates Ichiro, the citizen-warrior who signs on for the army in compensation for his sibling's refusal. It is a family caught out by Pacific war, by generational gap, and for sure by "relocation" ("It wasn't all right to be American and Japanese. You had to be one or the other" [91]).

Ichiro increasingly loses bearings—the death of his friend Kenji whose leg has been amputated fighting in Asia, his inability to reciprocate the affection of his woman friend Eti (her Japanese American husband ashamed to return from military service in Europe), his turning-down of even reasonable job-offers, and the increasing violence of his life. His life becomes interior trauma, the internalization of the "Japanese in America" being treated always as "security risks and saboteurs" (186). He tells his mother "it was a mistake . . . to think that you could keep us completely Japanese in a country such as America" (186) He has indeed become a No-No Boy, heir to both a "Japan" there and here and an America which has put him at the margins.

* * *

A further sequence of Japanese American (and one Japanese Canadian) fiction amplifies, and greatly deepens, these touchstones of Japan as America's both home and away. Mid-Pacific Hawai'i could hardly not feature, first landfall for many Japanese emigrants, the site of Pearl Harbor. Few texts have more born that history than Milton Murayama's *All I Asking for Is My Body* (1975), a three-part fictional memoir of 1930s sugar-plantation life.¹⁶ Narrated by Kiyoshi Oyama it delineates the world of working-class *nisei*, native Hawai'ian, Filipino and other plantation labor, with frequent resort to the island's creole and kindred vernaculars ("we spoke four languages: good English in school, pidgin English among ourselves, good or pidgin Japanese to our parents and other old folks" [60]). Each sequence, full as it is of Hawai'ian camp detail, shadows that Hawai'i with Japan as legacy. "I'll Crack Your Head *Kotsun*" depicts Kiyo's friendship with the son of a Japanese prostitute who plies her wares in the Filipino camp which for his parents brings up old lines of social caste and pariah-dom. "The Substitute" explores how Kiyoshi's sick, put-upon mother believes her illness to have been brought on by *bachi* or ancestral Shinto-Buddhist cosmic bad spirit. "All I Asking For Is My Body" follows Kiyoshi's rite-of-passage into young manhood as a cane-cutter, driver, boxer, rival sibling to his brother Toshio, and then Japanese-American enlistee in World War II. The novel speaks with genuine authority, Murayama's island chronicle of the inlaid Japanese etiquette of the Oyama parents as against the American pathways of their offspring, the migrancy of a domestic round as against hands-on physical labor.

Joy Kogawa's *Obasan* (1981), her Canadian Japanese *nisei* internment novel as told by Naomi Nakane, grade teacher, takes as its human axis the figure of Aunt Emily, the *obasan* of the title.[17] Kogawa presses hard at what it means to be accepted as full and equal Canadian citizen against historic stigma, resentment, citizenship but with an Asian face and name. Japan may be dynastic past but for Naomi it is no more than that. With often striking eloquence and frequent questioning as to origins the novel has her insist of Canada "This *is* my own, *my* native land" (40). She makes it clear that there is no "back" in the repeated query "Have you ever been back to Japan?" (225). In Emily, her *obasan*, she equally sees the still untold human story of immigrant passage, family, their prairie internment, language both spoken and as articulate unspeaking, and reflexively both asks and answers the question "Where do we come from Obasan?" (226). To which she proffers the answer "We come from our untold tales that wait for their telling" (226). That is—from a Canada haboring hidden histories, as yet unspoken lives. In this perspective Japan and Canada are to be understood as a one first-generation voice re-heard in a second-generation voice, doublings of time as much as place.

For Cynthia Kadohata in *The Floating World* (1989) Japan-in-America finds narrative idiom in Olivia Ann, *sansei* teenager, her family caught up in a species of J.D Salinger-esque serio-comic road drama as they search for seasonal work across the Pacific west and Dixie in the wake of internment.[18] But if travelling itself becomes its own American home this is to reckon without her tough, acerbic, thrice-married *obahsan* (here grandmother not aunt). She it is who unyieldingly carries Japan into America, full of ceremony, elisions of time, tea, memories of her husbands, sayings and story. "My memories are a string of pearls and rocks" (24) she witnesses. Olivia, whom she harries and pinches as her way of loving her, even hears her speaking American dreams in Japanese.

When, albeit in her eighties, she surprises the family by dying (where more appositely than in a California motel?), she has already taught her family to perceive the world of the *hakujin*, the white people of America, through her imported screens of Japaneseness. She hears again her grandmother's sense of this New World—"We were traveling in what she called ukiyo, the floating world." (2). This ukiyo is the gas station, restaurants, motel towns, the family to be thought of as stable yet "traveling through an unstable world" (3). Olivia Ann's opening brush with a quietly crazed ex-professor points the way. Only her grandmother's Japanese guile, her smile, saves Olivia from likely murder. "Hakujin don't know when a smile is an insult" (8) she tells the girl.

Fostered out to Isamu, a lonely Japanese farmer in Nebraska, Olivia helps him write out his entire world of seven names. En route to Gibson, Arkansas, she summons up childhood, in vintage Japanese manner, as always transition ("Pictures of one world fading and another took its place" [55]). In Gibson she translates her grandmother's diaries, each a "revelation" ("I liked the two languages, Japanese and English, how each contained thoughts you couldn't express exactly in the other" [91]). Her life moves on to love with her fellow chicken-sexer, David Tanizaki, the con-man Andy Chin, and career as owner repair-woman in the wake of having seen the "ghost" of her father. On her part, and Kadohata's behind her, this is truly to put America under Japanese auspices, Japanese America as not only tale but telling.

Jessica Saiki's *From the Lanai and Other Hawaii Stories* (1991), seventeen stories based upon *nisei* life in the port township of Lunalilo ranges through a spectrum of island life—everyday Hawai'i Japanese American, *kanaka* or native Hawai'ian, *haole* or local or mainland white, and Filipino.[19] In "Oribu" a young Japanese maid remembers her domestic service with the Finches, an American couple literally enwalled and mutually divided by their affluence. In "The Hermit" Saiki depicts a recluse, Ito-sensei, who retains an exquisite Japaneseness of manner even in his self-chosen American isolation. In "From The Lanai" (*lanai* meaning veranda, sometimes the littoral) Mrs. Hattie Crumb, another wealthy *haole*, is slowly brought to the recognition of her own loneliness as she learns of the birth of a child to the wife of her house-servant, Hamada-san. Japanese consciousness patrols American consciousness, a perfect, exquisite reversal of western employer to eastern-employee status.

Few *nisei* have written with greater exactness or weight of style than Hisaye Yamamoto (1921-), a story-teller since the 1920s, internee at Poston, Arizona, long-time Los Angeles resident, and whose only book publication remains *Seventeen Syllables and Other Stories* (1988).[20] The title-story, set on a Los Angeles tomato farm, tells with great elliptical skill the story of a mother's prize-winning talent for the delicate seventeen-syllable art of haiku, her *issei* husband's brute reaction when word of her prize comes from the *Mainichi Shimbun* (he burns the certificate and smashes the glass case), her daughter Rosie's lack of interest and first kiss with a young Mexican American employee, Jesus Carrascos, and the mother's final, near hysterical insistence that her daughter never marry. The Japan refracted in this history is one of male gender privilege (the mother, Tome Hayashi who writes in a second identity as Ume Hanazone, has been married off to her husband having previously conceived and lost a child out of wedlock). Yamamoto exhibits no illusions about Japan as patriarchy, the *issei* as seeking to perpetuate in American their Japanese assumption to dispense power both public and private as of ancestral right.

Other like triumphs are several. "The Legend of Miss Sasagawara" gives the portrait of an aloof ballet enthusiast sent to Block 38 in internment camp and whose fetch-and-carry servitude to her father, paradoxically a Buddhist minister, leads on to oddities of behavior. Her breakdown, in the face of an imprisoned but still patriarchal Japan, does not preclude her composition of a sublimely spiritual poem. "A Day in Little Tokyo," the California day's outing of the Kushida family explores two keenly ironic, cross-generational Japanese perceptions (and languages) of America: parent and child, Japanese-born and US-born. "A Life Among The Oilfields" develops a meticulous contrast between Jazz Age white America and smallholder Japanese America in the form of a hit-and-run episode which damages the narrator's small brother. The couple responsible, Zelda and Scott as she figuratively calls them, imply a Boom Era mainstream indeed careless if not outright hostile towards its Japanese fellow citizenry. Yamamoto writes always with the shrewdest eye, Japan as importing its own cultural contradictions only to have them meet and contend with America's own.

*   *   *

Of the equally voluminous body of autobiography and memoir two texts do immediate service. To Garrett Hongo, the West Coast *sansei* poet of *Yellow Light* (1982), in his formidable memoir *Volcano* (1995), the ecological formation of Hawai'i ("craters and ancient pit fire and huge black seas of hardened lava, the rain forest lush with all varieties of ferns, orchids, exotic gingers, and wild lilies, the constant rain and sun-showers" [4]) runs parallel with his own self-formation as writer. If he can think of the literary education which leads him to the western canon, the *Iliad* to Shakespeare, Kafka to Naipaul, he also summons the Japanese literary virtuosity of *The Tale of Genji*, Basho's haiku, the theatre of *noh, bunraku* and *kabuki*, and the postwar fiction among others of Mishima and Oe. Mainstream popular culture (*I Love Lucy* to *Star Trek*, Roy Orbison to Janis Joplin) overlaps with both that of Hawai'i (poi and papaya foodways, hula, ukulele, "Portuguese *chang-a*-lang") and a migrant Japan (*"Shina no Yoru"* as 1930s hit song, *manga*, Godzilla, and *yakuza* films).

This extends into other Japan brought across the Pacific ("My grandfather had sold liquor and prepared food (mostly Japanese things like beef *teriyaki*" [10]), his wife Cynthia's *yukata* as a reminder of Japanese dress code, the local *minka* roof designs with their migrancy of architecture, and the Japanese-American heritage of a play like *And the Soul Shall Dance* by the one-time internee Wakako Yamauchi. Pondered-over foodways (*kinako* or soybean flour, *tempura*) give an alimentary imagery to the text. His father Albert is remembered as having attended Tokyo High in Honolulu. Each Hongo family history adds to this sense of dynasty—the paternal grandfather Torao's love affairs, the flight of his first wife Yukiko, the marriage to the one-time stock-girl Eveline. Above all stand the Hongo Store as memorial icon: at once a registry of family, family and culture (Yukiko or Grandmother Katayama performing to *shamisen* at more than eighty years of age and in modern Honolulu the stylized dance of her *geisha* youth).

In the same sweep, and as born out in the portrait of his silent, wistful maternal grandfather, Kubota, who comes under investigation by the FBI, Hongo does not sidestep the rankle of larger Japanese American history. Kubota remains un-reconciled to America yet unwilling to return to Japan, dying of Alzheimer's, of all ironic dates, on "Pearl Harbor Day, December 7, 1983" (277). Hongo imagines his legacy as one of ceremonial lanterns, each lit and strung across the sea with "the silvery names of all our dead" (278). Both grandfathers he locates against a history of *issei* labor and Hawai'i's sugar-cane plantations, 9066, the camps and the ongoing courts cases to gain restitution of rights and property. *Volcano* operates on these and an array of related fronts, self-story, book of days, eco-diary of fern and volcano, a map of ethnicity, a poet's geological and botanical science, but always and throughout, the double-view of America and Japan.

"I am a Sansei, a third-generation Japanese-American. In 1984, through luck and through some skills as a poet, I traveled to Japan" (7). So begins David Mura, poet, essayist, and confessional autobiographer, in *Turning Japanese: Memoirs of a Sansei* (1991).[21] It could not better encapsulate present purposes. For what Mura puts on offer is a mutually refractive series of personal and cultural mirrors: self and history, an American identity bound up in Japanese identity, and perhaps above all, and precisely, Japanese America writing Japan. Raised in a Jewish Chicago suburb and schooled in Grinnell College, Iowa, unlikely credentials as might be thought, he plunges into Japan with a fervor pondering his Japaneseness of face as he travels each train and yet his inability to speak Japanese to his fellow passengers: indeed insider yet outsider.

His diary grows busy with observation. He reports on learning the disciplines of a contemporary Japanese dance-form like *buyoh*, practicing the calligraphic wash painting of *sumie*, and painfully apprenticing himself to zen posture. He visits Ryoanji temple and stone garden, attends the *Kurama* festival, relishes Kurosawa's films and Tanizaki's fiction, thinks the geisha in Kyoto "sexless, almost robotlike" (295), speaks of Gary Snyder as "one of the first white West Coast Buddhists" (299), recognizes the privileged elitism of Tokyo University, and comes to think the Tokyo of Shinjuku, Shibuya and Roppongi "the wacky Japanese *Doppelgänger* of New York" ([294]). He learns the necessary functions of *hone*, honest truth, and *tatemae*, convenient or tactical truth (137), gets involved with an artist-radical cadre and an anti-establishment demonstration ("I wasn't going to a political protest; I was attending a masquerade" [208]), and even, against Japanese local custom, engages an American friend in heated debate over *butoh* ("We were like two Talmudic soldiers. Very un-Japanese" [82]). Each increment of encounter so educates, Japan as a regime of attraction and challenge, his own face-in-the-mirror and yet not. "The Japanese," he suggests, "regard themselves as one huge family" (208) which may or may not explain why they "have trouble understanding the American belief in the primacy of private feeling" (138).

On the one hand he can take a visitor's pleasure in Japan's sense of courtesy, the honed etiquette, the gift relationship, and the refusal to engage in discursive conflict. Linking Japanese culture to its feudal roots, he speaks of qualities of "patience, endurance, obligation, and honor" (264). On the other hand he bridles at Japanese nationalism and its history, "ethnocentrism," and with a reference to mistreatment of the Koreans "the Japanese sense of their own superiority . . ." (201).

Of newspapers reports as to the likely Korean roots of the Imperial succession he remarks "The Japanese wanted none of this connection with the Koreans" (136). Likewise he is severe on the self-failure to recognize Japanese war history—"A greater number of Chinese, almost five million, were killed by the Japanese than the number of dead in Hiroshima and Nagasaki; the average Japanese, though, is much more cognizant of the latter than the former" (202).

In all of these weight and measures, credits and debts, his own American relationship is to Japan as *"the land of lost connections"* (356) and at the same time as enabling him to see "how much I am not reflected in American culture, how much is not my culture" (368). He also knows his own cultural preponderance—"In the end, the society felt to my American psyche too cramped, too well-defined, too rule-oriented, too polite, too circumscribed" (370). Which is not say he does not aim for a balance—"The Japanese place far more value on surface, on beauty and appearance, than the depth-seeking, psychologically and morally conscious Americans . . ."(35)

In all these respects *Turning Japanese* has aroused a fair degree of controversy. Is Mura too self-regarding, too conspicuously given to the drama of his own identity than that of Japan? How deeply does he enter into the synapses, the governing space-time frames of Japanese culture? Does not his account hit some truths but at the expense of others? Mura himself cannot be said not to recognize his own status as a species of cultural transit passenger ("We were just passing through" [338]). Whatever the best judgment, Mura closes with the surmise that "This split I have between America and Japan" will somehow "fuse" in his newborn daughter (372).

For himself, and acknowledging the balance in America's favor, he sees himself as neither wholly inside not wholly outside either culture—conscious, too, of his assumption of a self-positioning authorial voice. *Turning Japanese* undoubtedly offers but the one highly personal cultural measure. Yet at the same time it deservedly takes its place, with considerable distinction, in the compendium that has been Japanese American "writing" Japan.

*   *   *

No easy generalization can or should hold. Japan as constructed in these texts, any more than the Japan in its own Japanese-language texts, inevitably eludes the essentialist or totalizing version. But each helps build if not a composite then an ongoing map. At issue is always the negotiation of two stories in one: the "Japan" of Japanese America, Canada or the UK, and the America, Canada or UK seen through western-Japanese eyes. One country to offer a comparative touchstone would be Brazil through its own pattern of Japanese settlement and which Karen Tei Yamashita treats with magic realist virtuosity in her Amazon-novel *Through the Arc of the Rain Forest* (1990).[22] But as much as these different texts call up the one or the other Japan, the one of another America and western world, so they each invite recognition of an individual power of idiom.

Mori's "Yokohama, California" shadows both Japan and America, a tribute to the portrait's quiet subtlety of voice, its shaping nuance. The storytelling of Hisaye Yamamoto, as it deals with an America of the camps or California, may distantly call to mind the landmark story-cycle of, say, Shikibu Murasaki in her eleventh-century masterpiece, *Genji monogatari* (*The Tale of Genji*), but it remains always its own discrete plait of several stories-in-one. The fictions of Okada, Murayama, Kogawa and Kadohata all refract a Japan brought into an America of Pacific and mainland, but in styles that tread from naturalist-realist to the fantastical. Likewise, and with considerable invention, autobiography as given in Sone, Hongo and Mura folds the Japanese America story into self-story. The upshot overall could not be more beckoning: a textual America, a textual Japan, if written out of shared history then never less than under authorship always of its own individual key.

13 Bad Boy, Godfather, Storyteller
Frank Chin

> It makes no sense to me to be thought of as the first yellow writer of anything, much less plays, in the history of my people.
>
> —Frank Chin, "In Search of John Okada,"
> Afterword, Okada, No-No Boy (1979)[1]

> We were Chinamen in America—and the most suspicious kind of Chinamen.
>
> —Frank Chin, "Confessions of a Chinatown Cowboy,"
> Bulletproof Buddhists and Other Essays (1998)[2]

> This book could not have been written without the help of Michi Weglyn, author of Years of Infamy . . . encouraging me, a Chinese, not Japanese American, to write this book.
>
> —Frank Chin, U.S.A. Ni Umarete, Born in The USA:
> A Story of Japanese America, 1889–1947 (2002)[3]

Shoot-from-the hip Bad Boy. Ideological godfather. Fifth Generation and self-nominated US "Chinaman." Berkeley graduate and veteran. Novelist. Playwright. Story Writer. Essayist. Anthologist. TV documentary maker. Comic book artist. In life, as art, Frank Chin offers nothing if not the liveliest repertoire, and always to include a love-hate reputation as controversial as almost any in contemporary letters. "Writing is fighting," he cites Ishmael Reed (Writin' is Fightin' [1988]), himself in turn citing Muhammad Ali, as the prefatory tag to Bulletproof Buddhists and Other Essays.[4] It could not read more aptly. Chin signed on early as one of American writing's best-known disturbers of the peace, the companion in spirit to a Norman Mailer, bell hooks, Richard Rodriguez, or Gloria Anzaldúa. Certainly he has had few peers within Asian American, and especially Chinese American, domains, embattlement itself at the polemical center of things.

The two landmark collections, AIIIEEEE! An Anthology of Asian American Writers (1974) and The Big Aiiieeeee! An Anthology of Chinese American and Japanese American Literature (1991), the latter with its banner essay, "Come All Ye Asian American Writers of the Real and The Fake" (1–91), left little to doubt that Chin views China and its diasporic legacies as hedged in a dark circuit of pastiche, the perpetuation of what he calls "cultural fraud."[5] For him this amounts to "Christian Americanized Chinese" history, the west's pre-emptive denigration of China as supposedly authoritarian and backward in contrast with America as openly democratic and modern. China-to-America autobiographical texts like Pardee Lowe's *Father and Glorious Descendant* (1943) and Jade Snow Wong's *Fifth Chinese Daughter* (1950), and their literary ilk, he argues, all too incriminatingly have perpetuated the distortion.[6]

From the start, he proposes, this has been selective Chinese American identity, model-assimilationist by rote, passive, Christian, and with little or no history other than that of closed-to-outsiders Chinatowns. Chin's Preface to the anthologies thus famously issues his call to arms against the America he alleges "has kept . . . Asian Americans off the air, off the streets, and praised us for being Asiatically no-show" (*AIIIEEEEE!* [xxxi]). The USA, he elaborates in "Confessions of a Chinatown Cowboy," invites the charge of "Christian white racist love" (75) with its duplicitous model minority talk and not so hidden desideratum of "loyal nonblack Charlie Chan mascot people" (*AIIIEEEEE!* [76]). Nothing short for him, and whether America's Chinatowns or beyond, suffices but an end to racist distortion of "us as a visible Native minority" (93).

Perhaps more than anything else, however, and in arising vein, it has been Chin's attack on best-selling luminaries like Maxine Hong Kingston, Amy Tan and David Hwang that most has provoked heat. Has not each been guilty, runs his charge, of consciously parlaying this travesty China into America, a mix of fortune-cookie exotica and misogynist fiefdom, Shangri-la and dungeon? Given China as Middle Kingdom, or Han, Ming or other dynasty, or its Confucian and Taoist systems of thought, or massive popular culture of gods, humor and story, or welfare as against one-note criminal role for the Tongs, or each Overseas Chinese dispensation and especially those of Cantonese origin, are not these histories sold short by Kingston or Tan? The stylishness of their writing, not to say their sales, often thought a Chin jealousy, almost compounds the offense. Hwang's *M. Butterfly* (1988) does no better. The transvestite reversal of Puccini or not, and with Gallimard as against Cio-Cio-San/Butterfly for the deceived main figure, Chin sees only more figuration of Chinese men as ever passive-effeminate.[7]

The assault has been unrelenting on these "icons of our pride, symbols of our freedom from the icky-gooey evil of . . . Chinese culture" ("Come All Ye . . ." [2]). Kingston's conversion of Fa Mu Lan into feminist forerunner and 1960s woman warrior notably, for Chin, offends. The "White Tiger" sequence in *The Woman Warrior: Memoirs of a Girlhood Among Ghosts* (1977), with Lan as swordwoman "female avenger" (43) and precursor of "Maxine," is to be judged, witheringly, as the very pandering to a credulous western readership.[8] Her related use of monkey and trickster lore fares no better, not only bad-faith, but even worse, ignorant skewings of the originals.

For his own part Chin looks rather to an "authentic" Cantonese mythic fighter like Kwan Kung, "the god of war, plunder, and literature" as he calls him in *Donald Duk* (1991), and in whom the novel's adolescent title-figure will discover utterly un-passive inspiration.[9] Certainly the plays which won him repute as supposedly "first yellow writer," and their Off-Broadway production, gives every evidence of attack mode, whether *The Chicken-coop Chinaman* (1972) with its search for a usable China-past, or *The Year of the Dragon* (1974), with its corruscating send-up of Chinatown tour-guide versions of China in America along with John Chinaman or Suzie Wong stereotype.[10]

The writer-protagonist of *The Chickencoop Chinaman*, Tam Lum, who in his American childhood has sought Chinese hero stories, even imagined the Lone Ranger to be Chinese, and gone through a failed "white" mar-riage, ends up reprimanded for his own loss of culture by the black boxer whose life, ironically, he hopes to make into a documentary film. Lum is last to be heard as the kitchen storyteller to children of his Grandmother's memories of the American railway west's Chinese tracklayers. A far less assuaging fate awaits Fred Eng, Chinatown tour-guide, as the protagonist of *The Year of The Dragon*. The bitter, wearing argument with his father, Wing Weng, himself, symptomatically, a travel agent, and caught out by the re-appearance of a first Chinese wife, ends up in his collapse and death. For Fred, caught between American assimilation and loyalty to his version of Chinese heritage, it gives a final turn to his "shrunken" identity as Charlie Chan sound-alike. But if the play's tone can be accusatory, even darkly funereal, rarely does it lack saving wit.

Behind both works, moreover, lies Chin's will to the recovery of accurate cultural practice within the history begun in China, toughly given over to diaspora migration and sojourn, and against odds, eventually making good on a hard-won American residency. Chin returns time and again to the role of the Chinese in the winning of the west as literal, historic layers of rail and track, live repudiation of any and all images of submissive Chinese manhood. No longer, for him, any more than, say, for a fellow-spirit like Shawn Wong in *Homebase* (1979), whose focus also includes the Central Pacific Railroad and the Sierra Nevada, can there be either erasure from the US national narrative or continuation of the passivity myth.[11]

Caveats, inevitably, arise. Is not Chin given to selective heroization? He oddly fails to acknowledge Maxine Hong Kingston's respect for this very genealogy in *China Men* (1980), from her Great-Grandfather Bak Goong, first generation railworker, to her brother who sees service in Vietnam.[12] Nor has he shown much cognizance of female heroism in a line of woman-authored China fiction which can look to Ruthanne Lum McCunn's Lalu Nathoy, the equally strong, and certainly heroic, protagonist of *Thousand Pieces of Gold* (1981), or Sky Lee's Kae Ying Woo, also the inheritor of railworker Chinese (in her case for the Canadian Pacific Railway) as well as a tough Vancouver Chinatown female lineage, in *Disappearing Moon Café* (1991).[13] Nor can the heroic always be said to come in the one shade as borne out in Gish Jen's *Typical American* (1991) with its engagingly *mock-heroic* US life of Ralph Chang, the Yifeng-as-was from Jiangsu Province, who becomes the New York engineering student, would-be but defeated millionaire restaurateur, and Tarrytown suburbanite and cuckold.

Chin's attacks, to be sure, have elicited answering questions and contestation, above all as to whether there can be no adaptive, and especially diasporic, rights of imagining to Chinese writ. Does not his version of China veer close to some self-appointed new essentialism or too selective an emphasis on Guandong-Cantonese sources? Does not his recurrent railroad image of Chinese masculinity itself shadow, or reiterate, white codes of masculinity, to include a discomforting, and little disguised, homophobia? In his concern with Asian masculinity has not much of the writing under his name relegated women to the margins, Chinese women as one-dimensional or white women to be sexually conquered as revenge and compensation?

Other doubts arise as to whether he has been sufficiently clear, even consistent, about Chinese, Chinese American and what he terms US "Chinaman" identity. But whether in his written work, be it indeed "fighting" or otherwise, or in any number of the community, college and media forums in which he has featured, one constant, at the very least, persists. There can be no gainsaying Chin's ability to continue stirring the passions, the diaspora of China-in-America for him as far from a done deal, some comfortably agreed or assimilated past into present.

*　*　*

All of the discursive pieces which make up *Bulletproof Buddhists* give confirmation. But as much as they take up any one combative polemical or ideological position, they also give off a larger resonance: sharp eyed, vernacular when need be, full of the command and styling of a vintage essayist.

"I Am Talking To The Strategist Sun Tzu About Life When The Subject of War Comes Up," the opening essay, has Chin seeking his own self-reflection in Sun Tzu within a double-track of China as ancient war manoeuvre and America as 1960s Berkeley counter-culture with interposed a near-absurdist stay in Castro's Cuba. The upshot is the diary-narrative of his having been the only Chinese face at a 1960s army induction center in whitest Iowa, driving with two white campus radicals through Texas and witnessing cross-the-border Mexican bars and brothels en route, experiencing, close-up, segregation in New Orleans, and, finally, arriving in Havana where he is recurrently asked if he is from the PRC and detained as a spy. Sun Tzu, as though Chin's own mentoring *alter ego*, his co-voice, supplies the mantra of life is war, a way of negotiating both the Red China phobia of the USA and the Red China heroicized by Cuba. Chin's authorial self-positioning in the essay, always robust and with dips into sometimes foul-mouthed brio, becomes one of seeking to decipher, and bridge, his multiple plays of self. As West Coast "Chinaman" in white America he mirror-like becomes Yankee-Chinese in Cuba. As student short-term adventurer he also recognizes his own longer-term call of writer.

This bid to disarm all false Chinas, and with them all false China personae, especially offers a cue for the collection at large. "Confessions of a China-town Cowboy" sets the labor organizer, Ben Fee, "Chinese swordslinger" (66) and "life is war" (75) activist, a son of San Francisco's Chinatown and adoptee New Yorker, along with each Chinaman railway worker, against "our place as Americanized foreigners ruled by immigrant loyalty" (93) and the "racist fantasy" of Chinese men as "Confucianist, hands-down sissies" given to "backing off, bowing, kowtowing Chinese pride" (109). The essay keeps its balance even if the discontent, the anger at the historic phobias involved, runs close to the surface.

"Bulletproof Buddhists," in New Journalist style, looks to China-warrior tradition, from the Three Kingdoms and the Tongs through to current Los Angeles and Oakland Asia gangs, a trove sharp in comparative historical perspective. "Lowe Hoy and The Three-Legged Toad" begins by suggesting "It's a good time for this Chinaman boy to dive into unknown Chinatowns, find out if I know anything at all, and fill my well" (201). This resolve upon a right pathway into the different Chinas within American culture alights upon border Mexico, Tijuana, Calexico and Mexicali as intersecting sites of China, the US and Mexico and each with its evidentiary survivor voices.

"A Chinaman in Singapore," derived, appropriately, from Chin's atten-dance at an international writer's conference, delivers more than a little irrev-erence towards the island state authoritarianism of "Lee Kuan Yew's miracle kingdom" (353), along with shies at British colonial and Japanese imperial occupation, present-day "Lego-block buildings" (367) and the Maxine Hong Kingston suite (formerly the Ernest Hemingway suite) at the Raffles Hotel (338). Ironically, with the earlier publication of *Tripmaster Monkey: His Fake Book* (1989), Kingston was widely taken to have paid Chin mixed-blessing recognition in her maverick, and always teasingly reflexive, figure of Wittman Ah Sing.[14] The novel's very title, with its allusion to Chinese opera prompt books, more than implied a degree of riposte. But if the portrait of Ah Sing as 1960s San Francisco Chinese American beatnik, the would-be, yet contrary, pacifist dramaturge of *The War of Three Kingdoms*, carries a deflationary edge, that is not to underplay on Kingston's part her one writer's wry, or fond-unfond, salute to another.[15]

Chin, from the 1960s on, and with his own wholly distinctive kind of eye to diasporic China, has been an unavoidable presence. Yet amid all the ideo-logical sound and fury (is life *always*, and irrefutably, war?), and assuredly his self-pitching in *Bulletproof Buddhists* as California's warrior-writer version of Sun Tzu, something of Frank Chin can increasingly be said to have gone missing: namely Chin as storyteller, the nuance of his own powers of story.

*   *   *

"Railroad Standard Time," the first of the eight stories written mainly in the 1970s and which make up Chin's *The Chinaman Pacific & Frisco R.R.*

Co. (1988), exhibits most of his working strengths.[16] For the narrator, himself a writer and one-time brakeman, his grandfather's Elgin railroad watch becomes the perfect mnemonic of Chinese life lived in the time-space of America's western railroads. On his grandmother's death it is passed on to him in kitchen-room intimacy by his mother, the legacy of his rail-worker grandfather, a kind of China-talk "spell" as it is described. The kitchen, in turn, serves as corroborating locus, both a "paradise for conspiracy" and a "sanctuary for us *juk sing* Chinamen." It calls back "old memories," and as if in a language of special sanctification, his mother's resort to Chinese "words I'd never heard before" (1).

Watch, railway, and the ghosts of past family mealtimes and gatherings, in the story's fashioning, blend into a composite seam, the very quiddity, of the narrator's China life in America. However defective on account of its missing two jewels (albeit that the narrator uses it despite breaking the rules of his own brakeman job), the watch has set time for his "day-off courthouse marriage," his copy deadlines as a Seattle newsman reporting the race riots, and his wrenching bow out of his marriage to Barbara and farewell to his son and daughter Sarah. It marks the writing of the narrator's own would-be Chinatown novel to answer "snobby . . . autobiographical saps" (3) as he contemptuously designates Pardee Lowe and Jade Snow Wong. It sets the hour for his insatiable movie-watching along with his up and down West Coast marathon car drives. It is worn for his grandmother's funeral. It even gives a wry-funny timeline back to Mrs. Morales, his ogled over and large breasted High School music teacher, singing "Home on The Range."

The effect is to fold all these acts of remembrance into each other, the railroad timepiece as the connecting tick of historic dynasty and migration, the narrator's icon of remembrance. In prose full of its own poetry, along with the mantra of "Ride with me, Grandmother," nowhere can this be more said to hold than at the story's close. The narrator sees the Oakland of past Chinatown streets strewn in left-over vegetables. They remind him of "the Western Pacific and Southern Pacific railroads" (7). The "tracks" in play, in all their multiple implication, interact to shared purpose, memory, street and railway joined to summon America's China-history as marking or footprint. Chin tells his story as coevally time present and past, the narrator's one self literally, but also figurally, in continuity, however vexed, with all those Chinese who, as it were, can be said to have laid down American track before him.

This pattern of self caught up in the long shadow of dynasty holds throughout the collection, and rarely to closer-worked effect than in the two domestic stories which follow. In "The Eat and Run People," the title a term for the Cantonese and with its recitative of "Ride with me, Grandfather" (9), the narrator's voracious sexual coupling on a Maui beach becomes yet another foray into bittersweet memory. If cast as the sexual conqueror his battleground is that of a white ex-nun, aged forty-three, her body an unsatisfying love-hate whiteness. If the lover, he is equally the divorced father, and suffused with sadness at the loss of his children. TV and movie Asians shadow his consciousness as, tauntingly, do the white heroes of films like *Salerno Beachhead* and *North to Alaska* (10). His Cantonese ancestry is recalled as that of "the badasses of China" and "rebel yellers and hardcore cooks" (11). His American July 4ths, however, are those of American absentee fatherhood.

The sexual exchange and action becomes its own kind of Chinese against white locomotive imagery, the thrusts and pauses, accelerations and shuntings. As the unfolding priapic reverie of a narrator who gives his identity as "an idiot Chinatown brakeman" (22) the play of railway allusion could not in fact more weigh, whether the Seattle yards, the boxcars, the sixty miles an hour engine speed, or his remembered exhilaration at urinating from the footplate. Chin's portrait reflexively monitors its very telling of this life-railroad, the narrator's journeying, if at one remove, as the win-and-lose re-enactment of his own Chinese and Chinese American heritage.

"The Chinatown Kid" turns upon a marrying-out, that of Chinatown's ah-Pete who weds the Mexican girl María but loses her in death at the birth of their daughter Hyacinth. Pete's well-intentioned, if inadequate, parenting of Hyacinth, and the family act of face to buy him out and raise the girl by his sister Rose and her husband Wai-mun, compounds his sense of having been caught out by America. His mind travels back to the "converted grocery store" of their Mexican protestant wedding, María's bible and coffin, and his one-time fantasies of becoming the Chinatown Kid—all martial arts flash and filigree with an added tier, by marriage, of stylish Aztec-Quetzalcoatl warriordom. In fact what he has been left with is sham, the stranded acceptance before his sister and family of his dispossession. The bitter alignment of dream and un-dream is unmistakable, the death not only of his Mexican bride, or his own promises of life, but their like, once again, and by implication, for other Chinese before him.

This use of memory as internal drama continues into the collection's ongoing chronicle of family. "The Only Real Day" creates a busy, affecting father-son elegy, Yuan's death after migration from China and an American life as restaurant-worker in contrast with the indicatively named Dirigible's American boyhood and ever-receding China. "Yes, Young Daddy," an exchange of intimate, sexually loaded correspondence, plays out the fantasy fatherhood for Dirigible visited upon him by Lena, his young girl-cousin from across San Francisco Bay, with its ironic footfalls of an American past of required Chinese bachelordom. "Give The Enemy Sweet Sissies and Women" uses a Chinese New Year's parade, with its crackers and shouts of *Goong hai fot choy*, as the occasion for Dirigible's appropriately rain-soaked remembrance of an early Chinatown love, the evangelical Buddhism of certain family members, dragon and other festivals, and a kaleidoscope of Charlie Chan images. Each has been the making of his Chinese but, again, never other than American boyhood. "A Chinese Lady Dies," within a narrative of childhood flashback, movie images, ah-Pete, family, restaurant ownership and more Chinese New Year festivity, has Dirigible confronting with repulsion yet love and guilt the fact of his mother's illness and pending death. His own local ambiguities so play into the larger ambiguities of Chinese entry into American life.

With "The Sons of Chan" Chin re-enters his most familiar polemical terrain, that of "Charlie Chan, my movie father, God's gift to Chinamans . . . from Earl Derr Biggers" (131). For the narrator, the Chinese American actor who will make his re-appearance as Longman Kwan in *Gunga Din Highway* (1994), "My life as a specimen Hollywood Chinaman began early" (134).[17] He envisions himself, according to requirement, as having played every version of screen Asian, orphan child, monosyllabic and dying "Jap" or "Chink," house-servant and soldier at arms. His ironic apogee, he suggests, lies in contrastive roles, on the one hand that of oriental spy-fiend, "a genius of violence and intrigue by night" (138), and on the other, that of Chan's "meek" and "comic lovably asshole son" (138). Hawai'i is summoned as "Hillbilly Heaven" (132) with Biggers himself its "antebellum southern cracker overseer" (132) whose dire, if white-comforting, and always profitable, Charlie Chan heads each singsong confection of page and screen.

In memory Longman re-enacts his life: the hotel boyhood where he first encountered Tempest Storm as the burlesque queen and stripper and whose white sexual amplitude denied, even as it tempted, a repressed 1950s American manhood; the Las Vegas sex-encounters with a young Chinese woman and then the older Janet and her 12-year old daughter; and the attempted reunion with the worn but still on-stage Storm. These episodes lie deftly situated inside the phantasmagora of an ongoing dialogue with the "white" Charlie Chan of the more than forty movies, and amid which, obsessively, the narrator repeats his own contradictory vow to kill off this Chan while negotiating to become the first ever Chinese American actor in the role. Life, even so, denies him. "I'm still in a Charlie Chan movie" (164), he ends, live "Chinaman," for sure, yet at the same time for the rest of America, he insists, never other than more shadow than substance, still one of Chan's "Gee whiz, Pop" numbered sons.

Chin's feat in "The Sons of Chan," with its borderline surrealism, is to write quite one of the best honed and wittiest of what might be called his memory-soliloquies. Each run of consciousness, whether in first or third voice, gives off immediacy, a persuasive sense of present. But he also, and assiduously, wraps the story in the remembrance of how American popular culture has imaged its Chinese in a continuum of radio, stage, movies, TV and comic-book. The story's deftly paced mix of black humor and sadness, offense and defense, could not speak better to Chin's call for the unmaking of all fantasy as against actual Chinese Americans.

* * *

"Donald Duk does not want to laugh about his name forever. There has to be an end to this" (1).[18] So, with understandable resolve, the 11-year old boy protagonist of *Donald Duk* begins the rite-of-passage which will free him of the burden of his cartoon name over the course of a San Francisco 15-day Chinese New Year. Steeped in both Cantonese and Chinatown lore, yet full of its own eventfulness, *Donald Duk* offers perhaps the most affecting, even poignant, of Chin's fictions.

Donald's transcendence of his Disneyland nomenclature, and of his initial resistance to being a Chinatown boy, does not come without price. A litany of false steps presides, not least his obsessive dream of becoming the Chinese Fred Astaire, an emulated debonair whiteness replete with top hat and tails and perfectly choreographed dance routines. Astaire's screen persona from his 1930s debut in *Dancing Lady*, and through each MGM and RKO film musical with Ginger Rogers, affords Donald his model: no matter for him, any more than for Astaire, the Depression or World War II, 1882 Exclusion laws or Angel Island. This is to dance through an America given only to white romance and as seemingly cleansed of historical time and politics as of unwanted Chinese legacy.

So overwhelming an internal assimilation gives Chin his opportunity to bring into focus the cultural availability carried from China into America. A formidable complexity of allusion enters, and shapes, the story. Kwan Kung warrior and avian myth in the form of the family's collection of the 108 model toy planes once again features, notably in the father's highly symbolic plan to "fly them off of Angel Island on the fifteenth day of the Chinese New Year" (108). For King Duk this will be the re-enactment of the outlaw Lee Kuey's derring-do at the head of his 108 soldiers as recorded in *The Water Margin*, known as *Shui hu zhuan*, the epic novel of thirteenth-century Northern Song dynasty, likely authored by Shi Nai-an. The Robin Hood ethos, and struggle against an unfair regime, involves Chinese manhood as warrior-heroic swordsmanship, a way of being which also supplies a link to King Duk's earlier life as former Southern Pacific Railroad brakeman, actor-star impersonator of Kwan Kung, and present-day Chinatown restaurateur.

The 12-year Chinese life-solar calendar, each with its animal icon, operates alongside an American chronology of Christmas and Thanksgiving. Donald's family embodies both, King Duk as both Chinese and American father, Daisy Duk as both US and Chinatown mother, the self-staging twin sisters, Venus and Penny, as both China girls and US girl-youth, and always, for each, the shared touchstones of Kwan ancestralism and San Francisco contemporaneity. Chinatown dragon-parade festivity bears the footfalls of dynastic China, all mask and firecracker, gong and color. School, freeways, US city life, in turn, each act as counterparts, America as a modernity, new against old order. The closing launch of the family's model airplanes bespeaks nothing if not the Duks's flight of celebration of both, the Chinese of America, the America of the Chinese. Alongside, appropriately, Donald has his white school chum, Arnold Azalea, the one and other kind of China-apprentices.

But it is the China within American history which most counts. Food-ways take on busiest embodiment in King Duk's restaurant-and-kitchen virtuosity. Opera, Cantonese and Shanghaihese, lavishly summoned by Chin for its music and plot-line, costuming and acrobatics, takes on yet more live reality in the person of Uncle Donald as "Cantonese opera entrepreneur" (8). This same opera, in turn, plays into Donald's dream references to the California sierras as western mother-lode, together with all the other connecting railroad and track-laying histories. The emphasis, thus, is America more than China, the "Chinese" life of the American west.

"Chinatown life lies against Donald Duk's cheek like a purring cat" (15). Yet for the boy it seems anything but feline, rather, initially, an unwanted cultural maze, alien code, street threat, or prison-house, and to be stepped free of, precisely, by resort to the beckoning ease of an Astaire routine. American private school, his Uncle Donald tells him, has "turned you into some kind of engineer of hate for everything Chinese" (22), adding "You hate your name. You blame every Chinese who ever lived, everything Chinese you ever heard of for the way white kids act like fools when they heard your name" (23). King Duk contributes his own measure—"I think Donald Duk may be the very last American-born Chinese-American boy to believe you have to give up being Chinese to be American" (42). The novel take its cue from both observations as a chronicle of China to US life-bridging, the America to have emerged out of China.

Chin tells Donald's life as a magic of transformation, the once wannabe Fred Astaire hoofer brought inexorably into his own dance of identity. The way-stations en route, accordingly, build into a pattern. Between Donald's initial hatred of his name and exuberant final celebration of the Black Tornado warrior-myth, his dream of the 12,000 Chinese railway tracklayers and the *Water Margin* soldiery, his theft of the one model plane and then subsequent ritual release of them all, he experiences more than just a call to consciousness. The effect is one of transformation, self-rebirth. To this end King Duk's kitchen also serves. A "Chinese kitchen in a Chinese restaurant" (8) as may be, yet which can offer American as much as Cantonese and other Chinese cuisine, it becomes the very fusion of family, hearthstone, *gong gu tsai* or talk-story, archive, a live China-America customhouse.

Taken by his father to a Chinatown herbalist to purge him of his whiteness, the echo that of Ben Loy's search for a cure to his impotence in Louis Chu's *Eat A Bowl of Tea*, Donald once again veers off into a dream of railroads. It acts as his subconscious rebellion against the whitewash of his conscious awake-time.[19] Uncle Donald fills out this railway history in the memory of the family's great-great-grandfather migrant lineage. But it is Donald's own obsessive western and mythic-locomotive dreams which most take possession. He fantasizes himself a tracklayer, one of the erased figures in the Promontory Point photograph in which Irish labor is celebrated but no "heathen" Chinese. He imagines a Kwan Kung figure as Central Pacific Chinese foreman set against Charles Crocker as Irish foreman, with their respective work-gangs, the Chinese the winners in a battle of muscle to lay more track than the other. These dreams he comes to envision as "true" (138), Chinese American history recovered from its near removal in most long standard official versions of the west.

Donald's Chinese, alongside, or in parallel with, his American education, increasingly becomes one of a diasporic China of history, culture and art, along with opera lore, dragon roles, ginseng and other remedy, as against Charlie Chan and Suzie Wong/John Chinaman shadow. These come to him slowly, and against his own shows of reluctance, the gradual recognition of how the Chinese have indeed been erased from the record of US history in the interests of "White men. . . .White dreams. White brains and white brawn" (130). In company with Arnold he goes on to explore a Chinatown bookshop whose shelves contain classics from Luo Guan Zhong's *The Three Kingdoms* to Wu Cheng'en's *Journey to the West*.[20] But this living archive, and its preservations of cultural memory, has to compete against still another, that of the high school curriculum and the Chinese American narrative it seeks to perpetuate.

The boys find themselves moved to contest the version of their history teacher, Mr. Meanwright, and his demeaning "passive philosophy and noncompetitive" image (149) of the Chinese. Donald's rejoinder, the echo of Chin's own, serves as corrective, his declaration of independence from formula. He berates his own teacher for ignorance of Chinese tracklayers, blasters of Summit Tunnel in the High Sierras and strikers for due pay (150). By the fifteenth day Donald's re-incarnation, shared cross-culturally with Arnold, becomes complete, the dragon a huge illuminating lantern, the parade a passage into Chinese time-space, the planes his flight into liberation and self-meaning. It makes for an ending both believably actual and yet emblematic, Donald Duk as modern American and his own version of Kwan Kung.

Cavils undoubtedly have arisen from first publication of *Donald Duk*. Does railway history, it continues to be asked, convey a sufficient lodestone for the history of Chinese America? Has not Chin, notoriously, failed to engage seriously with women characters, in the immediate case Daisy Duk as mere silhouette, Venus and Penny as clever-cute voices or rather voices-over, and the Frog Twins, so-called, as fussed, cranky Chinatown siblings? Ideology, especially Asian American feminist ideology, inevitably comes into contention, not inappropriately given Chin's own repeated insistences upon a "masculinist" version of Chinese and Chinese American history. But none of this denies the novel its achievement as portrait, boyhood grail.

*　*　*

With *Gunga Din Highway* Chin attempts his largest canvas to date, an American kaleidoscope-satire of Longman Kwan and his China-US family genealogy, Charlie Chan movies, San Francisco's Chinatown, and Hawai'i as Chinese Pacific.[21] The novel locates each within the egg and axe, brother-sister, Chinese creation myth of Poon Goo and Nur Waw and its tierings of *The Creation, The World, The Underworld* and *Home.* These, not unlike those in play throughout LeRoi Jones/Imamu Baraka's Newark ghetto novel, *The System of Dante's Hell* (1965), allows Chin to frame America's modern complexity within China's ancient complexity, a refiguring yet also transformation.[22] From the spoof Kipling title on, and in a sustained show of bravura, *Gunga Din Highway* can be thought a novel which plies family scroll into movie archive, Chinese into American history. As Longman observes, synoptically, this is both "A-M-E-L-I-C-A" and "A-M-E-R-I-C-A" (9), a story of American generational language, American generational history.

Chin as usual writes densely, and at pace, a China-in-America of evolving time-spans. The 1860s of Chinese migrancy, be it bachelor or rail-track memory, links to the 1960s of American counterculture, be it Oakland-Berkeley protest, hippiedom, sex and drugs, or the call for an Asian version of Black Power. Screen Asia spans each Charlie Chan movie ("Charlie Chan is the Chinese Gospel of the New Testament," [14]) to Vietnam-era films like John Wayne's *The Green Berets* (1968), with its Special Forces triumphalism, and Jane Fonda's *Coming Home* (1978), with its anti-war ethos. The novel's 1960s, if a California of time-now excitation, becomes also a California-then of nostalgia, to be seen from the 1980s of college Asian American Studies departments in which Kingston-like authorship (Chin rarely misses his chance) carries the banner of Chinese America. *Gunga Din Highway* subjects all of these flows and contraflows to Chin's reflexive imagining.

Each of the four story-panels gives confirmation. In *The Creation,* Longman Kwan, Chan's supposed one-time Number Four son, aspires to be the first actual Chinese American actor to take on the part. In Hawai'i for a typical guest-spot on TV's longest running detective series, *Hawaii Five-O,* he seeks out Anlauf Lorane, "six-foot-four-Belgian, five years my junior, and the fourth white man to play Charlie Chan" (15). Both know role-play to a fault. Longman has acted virtually every Hollywood Asian part of warlord, criminal, convert, Japanese spy, and above all, in Chin's memorable formulation, "the Chinaman Who Dies." Lorane, in his turn, has segued into the obese, fugitive pornographer living in a shoreline Quonset hut under the name Henly Hornbrook with Milagro, his "fat blobular fifth wife" (21). Movie father to Longman, he also serves as the novel's version of Dorian Gray, the "Charlie Chan" of screen formula revealed in life as a grotesque, haunting voracity of white flesh.

Amid the haze of Maui Wowie as marijuana of choice, a vat of simmering chili con carne, and the one after another screen snippet, Longman's colloquy with Lorane becomes a memorial, and often lavishly funny, roll-call of the whole Charlie Chan ethos and the China fantasy behind it. Key names, whether Warner Oland, Sidney Toler or each other white-acted Chan, Anna May Wong as both Los Angeles Chinatown actress and the name inscribed in a World War II B-47, and the cinematographer James Wong Howe, all enter together with a plethora of movie and TV lore. Longman's own Hollywood roles, from fiend to dying retainer, are recalled as always the specific, and yet collective, supporting role to white action heroes, whether John Wayne in *Genghis Khan*, Steve McQueen in *The Sand Pebbles*, or a list to include Gary Cooper, Frank Sinatra and Spencer Tracy. No role, however, anything like rivals the begetting figure of Earl Derr Biggers's lieutenant of detectives, Charlie Chan as embodied pornographic caricature, the cartoon, as it were, of an already off-color cartoon.

Longman Kwan's progeny and their generation, in the three succeeding parts, pursue different, but connecting lives from their "Cantonese opera heartthrob-turned-Hollywood-star" absentee father (56). Ulysses Kwan, younger son, negotiates the turns and pivots of being "an American of Chinese descent" even as, in childhood, he is wrong-Asianly taken for "a Jap kid" (52). His will be the life of Seattle newsman, 1960s radical, movie reviewer, stage director, scriptwriter of *Night of the Living Third World Dead*, and who will speak recurrently of living in America's "movie about me" (146). Longman Kwan Jr, older brother, wartime Technical Sergeant, and known as "Hollywood Junior," finds a life away outside the paternal glitz both as brakeman and mixed-fare family man. Ulysses's student-era gallery numbers Diego Chang as musician-guitarist, one time Hawaiian drop-out and sidekick; Benedict Mo as the playwright of *Fu Manchu Plays Flamenco* who becomes a San Francisco college teacher; and Pandora Toy as woman-about-town journalist and pastiche Kingston-Tan conflation.

Within this cast of Kwan family and friendship, Chin unfurls his aggregate fact-fiction history with matching élan and detail. The coverage runs from Ulysses's adoptive childhood with a white vaudeville couple and youth ("pubescent kids in the early Eisenhower '50s," [93]) to the death of Longman Kwan, from marriages and divorces to hidden incest, from Chinese language school to Berkeley, and as timelines and social geographies from Chinatown to Oakland, New York to Maui. "Everyone is in the wrong movie" (151) Chin has Ulysses say at one point. Given a novel steeped in film reference and memorabilia it makes for self-referring textual commentary as pertinent as any.

Chin, for sure, exhibits all his usual signature concerns, whether America's "wrong" China, the continued exotica and stereotype, or the west's assault on Asian masculinity as he sees it. He risks longueurs, the one or another over-insistence. But that is not to miss the encompassing resource of vision or wit. Jane Fonda can be "a long overdue Pocahontas in reverse" (145). Beat America, un-sacrosanctly, contains "Kerouac's wracked and cultish homosexuality in Zen disguise" (201). Hawai'i takes on status as "where the walking wounded of the Third World come to recover from the '60s" (239). Each eases any tendency towards solemnity, the novel as too relentless a case-study.

Inevitably, perhaps, Chin has *Gunga Din Highway* close with yet another fantasy, the undermining, funeral invocation: "In the name of Charlie Chan the Father, Charlie Chan the Son, Charlie Chan the Ghostly Host" (393). In these obsequies, ostensibly for Longman Kwan but in fact for all Charlie Chan figuration, recall is made of Hollywood's Cary Grant-Douglas Fairbanks Jr. version of *Gunga Din*. The irony is hardly to be missed that it has been "Pa's favorite movie" (395). A due extract from Kipling's poem is given but as though recited by Sam Jaffe in his film role of subaltern and brown-face ghost. The implications need little underlining: Chin's own novel of the would-be real as against fake, Raj-Indian, and by analogy US-Chinese, travesty itself duly counter-travestied.

* * *

Chin will likely continue to sit uncomfortably both in Asian America's literary canon and beyond. Has he always been right to think China wrongly charged with oppression, and especially misogyny? If, indeed, Chinese and Chinese American men have been feminized in the west is Kwan-style masculinism the appropriate redress? Have the myths been betrayed or, in fact, renewed by Kingston, Tan or Hwang, not to say by the yet further different adaptations in Ruthanne Lum McCunn, Sky Lee, Fae Myenne Ng and their literary generation? Opinion continues to linger and stir, and certainly as to Chin's own insistence upon the one seeming writ, or to doubters his own seeming reified fiction, for the Chinese diaspora and the China and US histories it has entailed.

Yet like other writers known for the one or another contentious lifeview, D.H. Lawrence, say, or a Céline, any truly judicious account of Chin cannot simply be allowed to stay there. For beyond his particular disturbances of the peace, the censoriousness often associated with him, too rarely has he been allowed the larger imagination of his plays, his essays and, at especial risk of under-estimation, his storytelling. Bad Boy or Godfather, and albeit at times quite despite himself, it is this power of imaginative width and fashioning to his China fictions which long has invited the fuller estimation.

14 Manila Tropics
Jessica Hagedorn

Manila I was born here. Manila, I will die here.
—Jessica Hagedorn, "Kundiman," *Dogeaters* (1990)[1]

Manila, our dazzling tropical city of memory
—Jessica Hagedorn, *The Gangster of Love* (1996)[2]

The cabbie drove past swamplands and crumbling colonial ruins, past jazzy discotheques, grand hotels, and haunted cathedrals.
—Jessica Hagedorn, *Dream Jungle* (2003)[3]

Manila-born, raised a teenager in the San Francisco of the 1950s where she subsequently trained at the American Conservatory Theatre, and based since 1978 in New York City, Jessica Tarahata Hagedorn has come to feature as one of the proverbial Bad Girls of the American arts. It has been a reputation, however, achieved not without ambiguity. On the one hand her anthology *Charlie Chan Is Dead* (1993) could be taken for exemplary fighting talk, a raised flag against all Asian (and Asian American) stereotype.[4] On the other hand, and for all their assault on the rafts of exploitation and condescension built into Spanish and US colonial history from Magellan to Rizal to Marcos, her novels and other writings could also attract opprobrium for their supposed spilling of Filipino family secrets.

How, moreover, best to accommodate not only the anthologist and novelist but the performance artist who has long served as lead singer-writer for the band *The Gangster Choir*, or the poetry-and-prose collagist of early work like *Chiquita Banana* (1972), *Pet Foods & Tropical Apparitions* (1975) and the stories of *Dangerous Music* (1975), or the text-and music playwright of *Mango Tango* (1977) and screenplays like *Kiss Kiss Kill Kill* (1992) and *Fresh Kill* (1994), or the creator of first-hand documentary poetry to accompany the photography of Marissa Roth in *Burning Heart: A Portrait of The Philippines* (1999)?[5] So various a creative biography inevitably, if unfairly, has invited charges of having spread herself too thin, versatility edging into slickness. But for those who look to keystones in her work, both of vision and design, no better source is to be found than her fiction. There, in all three novels, she brings her savviest powers to bear, whether the lowered eye as to what the Philippines and the US have meant to each other across eras from Magellan's arrival to the Spanish-American

War to the Arroyo presidency, or whether storytelling as full of sharpest deflationary wit and riff as it is given to postmodern textuality.

Dogeaters, set in the Marcos-era of the New Society, manages to up-end any amount of Manila foible—Americanization, religiosity, the graft of military and government elites, the sway of TV chat-show culture and radio soaps, and, if inevitably then with quite fresh virtuosity, Imelda as both operatic self-invention and symptom. *The Gangster of Love*, its span Manila, San Francisco, Los Angeles and New York, brings to bear not only the music-culture of sex, drugs 'n' rock and roll, it dares to make diaspora as much American black comedy as Filipino economic and cultural dispersion. *Dream Jungle* updates both American colonization of Filipino identity and the Philippines's own interlocking corruptions, a novel to stalk Manila's contradictory wealth and poverty, the Mindanao of a hidden mountain tribe, and the implications of a Hollywood-dispatched film crew making yet one more Vietnam war-movie.

Detractors no doubt will go on insisting Hagedorn to be the all-rounder as maybe but somehow always too facile, even a cartoonist. Other opinion, however, joins with Ishmael Reed in thinking her quite the exemplary vanguard artist, possessed throughout of rare compositional verve. In taking on the Manila of her fiction, and the Philippines and Filipino-America it bespeaks, it would be unobservant if nothing else not to recognize this achievement. Manila, or rather the "Manila" Hagedorn makes of it, gives a pathway into her singular imagining of Filipino worlds both at home and abroad and summoned in intimate fondness yet always as through a glass darkly.

* * *

Nothing is impossible, I suppose, with that crazy imagination of yours . . . but if I were you, *prima*, I'd leave well enough alone. (249)

So Pucha, homegirl cousin to Rio Gonzaga, the main first-person narrator along with the Manila rent-boy Joey Sands of *Dogeaters*, writes a letter from 1970s Manila to America. It supplies just the right comic-reflexive touch. Hagedorn's own text could not more act as a species of playfield, *film noir*, each of its near-fifty increments contributing to the overall simulacrum. For however seamed in history—what more so than a Manila of Marcos-like dictatorship, an Aquino-like assassination and the New People's Army—the Philippines chronicled by Rio and Joey might equally well be thought to edge into the fantastical. The effect, certainly, is one of urban tropic, Manila, and the world for which it serves as the focus, told under magic-realist auspices, Hagedorn's own true lies.

In this respect *Dogeaters* uses various kinds of frame to locate "our tropical archipelago of 7100 known islands" replete with its "eighty languages and dialects," "loyal believers," "blood feuds", "torrid green world" and "legacy of colonialism" (100). However recognizable actual timelines or place, this Philippines reads as though chimerical, wondrous. When Daisy Consuelo Avila, former Manila Beauty Queen, flees to her guerilla lover in the hills, Hagedorn conjures up the following terrain:

> We are serenaded by mournful gecko lizards, preyed on by vampire bats and other auswangs . . . enchanted by malevolent spirits living in caves and termite-dwellings . . . causing hallucinations, insanity, or death. (100)

Auswang. Kapre. The Tagalog terms add exactly to the sense of mythic heraldry, Nature's warning omens. Avian or reptile, nightmare insect or un-seeable mosquito, each presages Manila—the metropolis as danger-zone, cell, feeding ground. Hagedorn can be said to make the whole novel, in fact, a city-as-text: a mural of family, politics, dream. Contradiction abounds, whether the spectacular private wealth yet ground-zero poverty, the fervent Catholicism yet military torture, ostensible respectability yet the drugs and brothels. This is Manila as Gothic, the city indeed under the rule of reptile and insect spirits.

Another frame put to shared imaginative purpose is to be met with in the Preface. In citing literally from *Les Philippines* (1846) by Jean Mallat, the nineteenth-century French Jesuit and explorer, Hagedorn indicates an anthropology as selective as it is patronizing: *"They have the greatest respect for sleeping persons, and the greatest curse they can pronounce against anybody is to wish that he die in his sleep."*[6] The pitch is effortlessly orientalist, a selective local superstition made over into some supposed general fact. People and climate, the Filipino Pacific, manifest a wholly un-western languor, almost a call to narcolepsy. Sleep, infantilism, preside. *Tristes tropiques* indeed.

History, or at least a self-deriding version of it, supplies *Dogeaters* with yet another frame in the person of President William McKinley and his address to Methodist Churchmen in 1898. "I thought first we would take only Manila; then Luzon; then other islands, perhaps, also" (71) he is quoted as saying. It is a speech in which McKinley invokes God as guiding him not to return the Philippines to Spain, or Germany or France as interested parties, and sets out his resolve to "uplift and Christianize" the population. So decided upon "I went to bed, and went to sleep and slept soundly" (71). McKinley's voice, in line with Mallat's, would hardly be out of place were it written by the Mark Twain of *Pudd'nhead Wilson* or "The Man Who Corrupted Hadleyburg." The colonial double-speak, the lavish sanctimony, give an aptest ironic gloss to the passage of the Philippines into US suzerainty in the wake of the Spanish-American War.

These frames, mythic, anthropological, historical, along with a number of others in *Dogeaters*, could hardly better set up the overall imaginative play of Hagedorn's narrative. The novel works in contrasting but always connected panels, whether offered in the voice of Rio or Joey. To this end the novel resorts to girl-talk, intimacies and love letters, politics-speak, bar exchanges, movie dialogue, TV soaps, interviews and press reports, diary extracts, and always, the unceasing buzz of *tsismis*. The upshot, in English, Tagalog, Spanish, or their hybrids, is a portrait of Manila only marginally more surreal than its actuality, the vying exaggerations, the revolving heteroglossia.

"Love Letters," the opening chapter of *Dogeaters*, leaves little doubt that Manila will be as figural as actual. With 1956 as memory the text invokes the Avenue Theater, its "sugary chocolates, cigarette smoke, and sweat" with "*All That Heaven Allows* . . . playing in cinemascope and Technicolor" (3). As Rio and Pucha settle in for screen romance this quite literal *camera obscura* yields two worlds, the WASP New England of *All That Heaven Allows* ("perfect picture-book American tableau" [3]) as against the boxed heat and fervor of Manila. The Jane Wyman, Rock Hudson and Agnes Morehead characters, and the liaison of older woman and young gardener (the latter played by a straight Hudson) offer one kind of reality against the background of the cinema's own "furtive lovers stealing noisy kisses" (3). Afterwards, during *merienda* at the Café España, the precociously bosomed Pucha will add her own transfer from screen to life as she preens shamelessly for Boomboom Alacran. Love, Hollywood-style, finds its shadow in the early-adolescent flirtation of a Manila eatery.

The portrait of the Gonzagas follows in suit: the split of Rio's mother and father, she all recrimination, he with his Beauty Queen mistress; Freddie Gonzaga's boastful pride in his Spanish heritage yet *mestizaje* and hustle ("He believes in dual citizenships, dual passports, as many allegiances . . . as possible" [7]); the grandmother Lola Narcisa's obsession with the radio serial *Love Letters* playing on DZRK RADIOMANILA, which will be filmed in yet fuller extravagance at Mabuhay Studios starring Nestor Noralez and Barbara Villanueva, and which she listens to with the servants and Rio under "the tormented face of Christ rendered in bloody, loving detail" (10); and the illness of her American husband George Whitman Logan dying either of malaria or the fantasy "nightmare sickness" of *bangungot* (14). Each, amid the family rounds of talk and eating, the dutybound if uncertain Catholicism, makes ever more baroque yet immediate the warring love-hate of the Gonzagas.

Pucha, back in the cinema with Rio (her recurrent judgment "Que corny!") and chaperoned by Cousin Mikey, is in love with the Montgomery Clift of *A Place in The Sun*, the 1951 film based on Dreiser's *An American Tragedy*. Yet again screen transposed into life, Pucha can say of the Shelley Winters role, "She deserves to die" (15). This real-unreal nexus also again connects into the Gonzaga home. Buzz and static have emanated like some eerie other-world siren from the radio. Outside the typhoon rages and "the air is crackling, electric" (17). A "speckled lizard" (17) slithers the walls of the house. Hagedorn's Manila in *Dogeaters*, fiction of fact, could not be better indicated.

Manila, reality and image, extends and amplifies. The tinsel and rigged ballots of the beauty competitions, Young Miss Philippines or Miss Universal Universe, outbid their American originals. Jeepneys with names like "Guilty Mother" navigate the speed and exhaust fumes of the highways. Each costume-romance put out by Mahubay Studios might be Filipino Hollywood, the world of actor celebrity yearned for by the would-be star Romeo (or Orlando) Rosales—yet, almost as if in screen farce, this restaurant waiter will be killed by a stray bullet at the assassination of Senator Domingo Avila. TV delivers daytime soaps like *Love Letters* and *Maid of The Philippines*, along with its celebrity interviewer in the person of Cora Camacho (her *Celebrity Pinoy* column titled "Dateline: Manila") even as national politics provide their own soap-opera. Radio and the discos belt out Afro-pop and reggae, the hotels and stores "piped-in Muzak" (159), even as respectable Manila vaunts manners, the Latin mass, Spanish antiquity. The news as served up by the government-fearing *Metro Manila Daily* replaces journalism with pseudo-journalism. Tabloid glossies like *Celebrity Pinoy* echo US gossip columns. If Manila conducts its cultural life inside the wrap, the skin, of its American counterpart, it also retains a lavish hispanism in names like Boomboom and Girlie Alacran, Cherry Pie Lozano, the Alacran family dentist Dr. Benita Zamora, the soothsayer La Sultana who lives in an abandoned Mercedes-Benz near to Paco Cemetery, the ex-star Lolita Luna, or the bar-owner Andres Alacran, "the Queen of Mabini" (32) whose only one true love has been the hermaphrodite Eugenio/Eugenia.

Corporate Manila looks to its patron in Severo "Chuchi" Luis Alacran, "The King of Coconuts" (18). His writ as entrepreneur, sybarite, womanizer, dancer, art-collector, and hemorrhoid sufferer, Hagedorn guys in a description hinged to the word "because he owns." The list of possessions, and the power that accompanies, includes *The Metro Manila Daily* and other newspapers, the Mahubay recording studios, Apollo Records, the Monte Vista Golf and Country club and "SPORTEX, futuristic department store in the suburb of Makati" (18). Monte Vita Golf Club comes under the text's satiric purview as the icon of First World affluence amid Third World poverty. The club's claim to genteel exclusivity (MEMBERS & GUESTS ONLY) is mocked by the accompanying sign PLEASE DEPOSIT ALL FIREARMS HERE. The Sportex supermarket mall, well out of reach for most of Manila's citizenry, in name and goods pits gaudy consumer plentitude against Filipino make-do and indigency.

The vision of Manila as precisely host and virus holds throughout. Senator Avila, opposition politician, is gunned down by government apparatchiks even as presidential oratory bleats of Filipino patriotism. General Nicasio Ledesma parodies Marcos and other US-sponsored authority as would-be guardian to the nation while revealing himself the sadist, torturing, exquisitely, with *Love Letters* playing on television. His dalliance with the drug-addled, beauteous mistress, Lolita Luna, is engaged in even as his wife, a reclusive pathology in her own right, acts the role of model Catholic penitent. The ten or so First Families, each with their own power interests, feature alongside the Church under the righteous but unfortunately true-named Cardinal Sin. The liberal-Jewish Goldenbergs, he the US Consul, are rewarded with the irony of a new posting to Saudi Arabia. The Manila of the novel so becomes a species of antic map, the cartography of a city given to the revels both of quotidian life and chance yet also lethal interest-group conspiracy.

Joey Sands might be thought the very embodiment of street Manila, the son of a black GI and Zenaida, Manila streetwalker, whose bloated corpse is found in a sewer. Rent boy, DJ, druggie, a fan of US glitz, the love-object of Ranier Werner Fassbinder in town for Imelda's Manila International Film Festival—itself show-time amid poverty—he carries the city's mix and darkness in his very bones. "I'm on display"(131) he says of himself as he beguiles the German cinematographer. This is the Joey, self-named for Las Vegas show-time and once the urchin raised to steal and hustle in order to survive by his "father confessor " (190), the Manila Fagin-figure of Uncle. It is also the Joey who will be the un-intending and at-risk witness to the murder of Senator Avila which obliges him to flee and, farcically, perforce to join a New People's Army opposition group, the pastiche guerilla fighter. "The matter-of-fact brutality of the murder," he thinks, "seemed unreal, like a gangster movie" (189), with himself one of the cast, yet another of *Dogeaters*'s screen-and-life Manila players.

Madame Galactica. Miss Manila. Pacific Rim Regina from her beauty-competition days. Mother of Asia. The Iron Butterfly. How, allowing for Hagedorn's own nomenclature for her, to invent an Imelda beyond her own exquisite self-invention as the Filipina Eva Peron or Hollywood's Rita Hayworth? In one sense Imelda serves as Manila's all-too-literal mistress of Malacañang Palace, Marcos consort, *fashionista*. In Hagedorn's version she transitions into American holograph. Interviewed by an American reporter she is to be seen as "Queen of the Beauty Queens," "coiffed and complacent" in her "custom-made peau-de-soie pumps" and given to the ritual warning "God save us from the day my husband steps down from this glorious country" (221). She laments, explicitly, not having become a movie actor ("I was going to call myself Rose Tacloban" [224]). Instead, coyness itself, she sees herself called to a higher mission. "I am simply here," she avers, "to carry out our Lord's wishes" (224). She becomes Hagedorn's perfect satiric invention, whether her "respect for Oscar de la Renta" (217), the celebrated shoe cellars, the coiffure, the singing, her insouciance at the deaths of Orlando Rosales (for her a communist with a gun) and Senator Avila ("We warned Senator Avila to stop cavorting with the left" [222]), and even her explanation that the President is off on "one of his golf days" (224). In a fantasy-dream she imagines herself at a party in New York's Waldorf Astoria, without shoes, and in the company variously of Pope

John XXIII and George Hamilton, It makes for the perfect skewering, the Imelda of the novel the very fantasy of a fantasy.

The Manila of *Dogeaters*, in turn, becomes the sign, the cryptogram, for all these interacting components, and in a novel whose careful disjunctures parallel the culture it most seeks to en-capture. When, in "Kundiman," the Filipino terms for prayer or dirge, the voice enunciates "*Manila I was born here. Manila I will die here* "(250), the appeal is to a process of healing, a better energy than the abuses, the wealth gaps, the cronyism, the sheer bad faith in the face of the people's good-faith needs. Far from doing ill by Manila and the Philippines the very point of Hagedorn's dexterous storytelling in *Dogeaters* has the altogether better purpose of creating a necessary pathway into any number of Filipino truths both at home and away.

*   *   *

"News from Manila—that's what she lived for" (15). As *The Gangster of Love* reveals at the outset, the "she" is Milagros Rivera, newly decamped from Manila to San Francisco, and whose husband Francisco Rivera will bigamously marry Baby Gonzalez two years later. The date is September 21 1972, the same day Marcos imposes martial law on the Philippines. Ever a vital presence in her own right she acts as luminary, the spirit of Manila in exile, to her three offspring, Rocky (Raquel), Voltaire and Luz. Her story, even so, and that of her dynasty, has passed into the narrative custodianship of Rocky. Grand-daughter of the Filipino inventor who created the yo-yo as weapon and toy (Grandfather Baby) yet also eventual punk-songwriter and front-woman for the group *The Gangster of Love*, Rocky's story yields precisely the shared drama—contemporary American picaresque seamed in ancestral Filipino footfall.

Rocky's American life, as daughter to the Milagros of the Lumpia X-press business, involves a complex track—love affair with the Chinese American musician Elvis Chang and their fractious gigs and road life, watch over Voltaire as Hendrix-fixated and at times near-catatonic brother, sister-lover intimacy with Keiko Van Keller as exotic shaman photographer, and itinerary to New York and birth-giving to Venus Rivera Montano. This rite of passage from twelve-year old Filipina girlhood into Filipino-American womanhood is also interstitially given in Elvis's voice, double-witness as befits a tale of two generations, two geographies. "I have made it a point to try and remember everything" (14) Rocky says at the outset. Well she might, for the upshot eventuates in Hagedorn's own second novel of Manila as family culture, America as pop culture.

This double-ply works to great advantage in *The Gangster of Love*, Milagros with her Manila etiquette ("[she] can't believe her daughter lives the way she does. They'd be better off in a shack in Manila" [190]) and Rocky in her fascination with America as anything-goes style ("This is New York, after all. Capital of pain and desire" [143]). In her vignette of the Carabao Kid, "Pinoy poet from Watsonville . . . a man totally obsessed with the Philippines who'd never been there" (198), hero to Voltaire who craves little more than return to Manila, Rocky gives the push-and-pull of her two competing yet always overlapping worlds precise formulation. "America was here," she imagines him saying, "vast, inhospitable, and harsh. The Philippines was there: distant, lush, soulful, and sexy" (199).

Rocky's own different amours, male and female, Elvis and then Jake as father of Venus, play against the spectacle of her mother's many American suitors yet none of whom can take the sting out of the Filipino betrayal by her husband ("It was a source of painful and juicy *tsismis* in Manila" [211]). Her Uncle Marlon (for Brando), kindly gay actor-chef, can contemplate a last return to the Philippines, his once and long-ago domicile for his peripheral Hollywood. The novel's overall trajectory works at pace and in detail as the one and the other cross-over, whether the Rivera and Rocky-Elvis-Jake-Sly-Keiko extended and nuclear families, or the domains, respectively, of Milagros as mother and Rocky as mother, or the music-scene and road alternative America as against its straight counterpart, or Tagalog and English as both languages and foodways, or above all, Manila and New York.

One key motif lies in the pattern of reference to the yo-yo. An opening citation speaks of it as a "spool-like toy" and in adjectival form as "fluctuating, variable" (3). In both respects it might serve as a reflexive index of the novel itself. In a last section and as Rocky makes her own long delayed visit to Manila she observes "I read somewhere that in Tagalog, *yo-yo* means 'to return.' I've also read that *yo-yo* comes from *yan-yan*, which means 'to cast out' " (285). If, accordingly, Manila is to signify home, it is also where her long-ago admirer Jose Mari will tell her "You sound so American" (301). *The Gangster of Love* makes busy and formidably plausible filigree of this past-within-present, Manila both always real yet always the mythic figuration and memory folded into the America of Hagedorn's encompassing larger story.

*   *   *

With *Dream Jungle* Hagedorn embarks on her likely most ambitiously conceived fiction to date, hugely adroit satire, a serious comedy of errors. Doubly located in Manila and Mindanao with California to follow, a smack both at the western romance of supposed Stone Age or jungle primitivism and at Francis Ford Coppola's *Apocalypse Now* as filmed in the Philippines, it exhibits all her signature speed and invention. The novel threads into one its two main story-lines, that of the Filipino-mestizo tycoon Zamora López de Legazpi as explorer-custodian of the Taobo people's Himal tribe and that of the making of an ultimate Coppola-style Vietnam film ("Napalm Sunset" [175] its main working title).

The upshot is an imagined Philippines as always fissured not only in its lavish discrepancies of power and wealth, be they business empire or street, but in its very sense of self-identity. Wealth taunts poverty. City north contrasts with island south. Nation state plays uneasily alongside culturally imperialized outpost. A Marcos presidency operates as "a legacy of lies, deceit, and delusion" (57). The novel's many lives, be they inside Zamora's gated mansion, in the street sex trade and bars, or in the Mindanao villages and tribal dwellings, set up different kinds of Filipino hierarchy each with its social and gender gaps. Throughout, and whatever the site, Manila, or rather "Manila," presides again as reference-point, the very spirit-of-the-place key.

A minor figure, Napoleon Padilla, chauffeur to Fritz Juan Pablo Magbantay, the mayor of Sultan Rammayah and nephew of the President, from where Zamora launches his "ethnic" expedition for the so-called lost tribe and where the film in all its star-celebrity and drug-addled confusion is being shot, at one point dreams of the capital. It is a city Nap "has never been to but often daydreamed about" and where he hopes to win a prize on a TV talent show "hosted by giddy starlets and cruel, has-been comedians" (253). The terms in play, daydream Manila, TV, stardom, even bad comedy, fit the spirit of the novel's geographies to a tee. There is no want of seemingly actual sites, Manila as Intramuros, Divisoria Market, or the Pasig River leading into Manila Bay, along with rich-poor residential Manila and its billboards of Camay, Kikkoman, *Aji-No-Moto* and the rest. In Mindanao the novel offers a wholly plausible Lake Ramayyah and surrounding mountains, jungle and herbage.

But whether locatable on any actual map, or seemingly so, Hagedorn again edges her novel's geography towards near-fantasy, a Philippines of literal coordinates but also, as it were, *tableau vivant*, its own stage-set of people, politics, sex, food, memory, and always Manila as energy and unabating urban text. "The whole country should see a doctor" (220) says Pepito Ponce de Leon, the exorbitantly named and gay would-be movie director who is cousin to the journalist Paz Marlowe. He is responding to her reprimand about the nation's chronic condition, its psychic illness, of which habitual lateness, she believes, is but one symptom.

Accordingly Zamora can live in a mansion called Casas Blancas in the Hollywood Hills, derive his family fortune in part from a rum called Flor de Manila, and after his death and cremation look back posthumously upon a Manila funeral "unsure of its final destination. Perhaps Rizal Park, perhaps Intramuros, perhaps Malacañang Palace" (290). Married to Ilse, his "knockout Teutonic goddess of a wife" (9), at once serial philanderer and the "Mister" of his dynastic estate, he seeks in the Himal people, and the adopted boy Bodabal, a kind of flamboyant restorative from the jaded excesses of flesh and dollar, his own hoped-for rejuvenation through earth, tribe, and always some elusive existential otherness (Kenneth Forbes, the Vietnam photographer, calls Mindanao "the Wild, Wild South" [83]). Zamora's sexual appetites—whether exercised on the servant Celia or on the Mindanao village girl Rizalina with whom the novel opens—are as little in the face of this grotesque Nietzschean urge for authenticity.

Whether indeed the "protector of the Stone Age Taobo tribe" (293) against mineral and logging interests, or in the words of the University of The Philippines anthropologist Amado G. Cabrera, "our very own mestizo trickster," "iconoclast playboy," and "gangster, poet, and an exploiter of our dreams" (306), in death as in life his is the consummate performance from within a Philippines itself taken up with its own performances of identity, religion and etiquette. Hagedorn's novel reads throughout in matching spirit.

The other focus, Tony Pierce's Conradian Vietnam film, yields further literal yet also metaphoric Asia. His film extravaganza, true to the Coppola heritage, uses one country for another, the 1960s Vietnam of Diem and US-Viet Cong battle re-seen—and re-set—against an adjusted landscape of 1970s Philippines. Off-screen, as Hagedorn leave no doubt, lies Marcos despotism, government and big business kleptomania, and Mindanao-Muslim bids for independence. The film screens the one conflict, Vietnam under American firepower, while shadowing the other, the Philippines under America-supported martial law. Not the least of *Dream Jungle*'s achievement is to work the changes on this interplay of screenings both inerasably historic and yet dazzlingly always fictional.

Not inappropriately given the cast and shambolic mise-en-scene, Pierce's script at one point is described as "boogie-woogie war epic" (194). He himself is termed "the genius auteur, the highbrow intellectual" (177) even as he wolfs down gourmet Italian cuisine. Scenes have "no scripted dialogue" (245) even as the ending is written and re-written. Given endless special effects explosions, helicopters borrowed yet withdrawn almost whimsically at intervals from the Philippine military as they go on national security missions, the catering and the groupies, both the film's players and performances might be said not to know quite which reality is being inhabited or created.

Vincent Moody, drunk, druggie, lover of Rizalina in her incarnation as the Manila sex-worker Jinx, drifts in and out of the filming like some lost California soul. Sebastian Claiborne, the Brando figure of Colonel Kurtz re-fashioned as Commander X, gives "his rambling analysis of the role he was to play" (245). Seen close-up his "bald head and massive girth added to the majesty" (246). The starlet Claire Jenks disappears. Janet Pierce, wife and would-be video artiste, films the filming—reflexivity itself mocked. Pierce himself veers into and out of nervous collapse even as he goes into cahoots with Mayor Fritz, murderer of his own abusive father, molester, and yet always genial eye-for-the-main-chance drugs and commodities entrepreneur. A Bengal tiger is flown in from India to complete the animal imagery. The upshot is newly minted Vanity Fair, America's Vietnam via Hollywood and Manila to Mindanao.

The novel's multi-voicing does apposite good service. Citations from the Jesuit-explorer Antonio Pigfatta's account of the Magellan expedition give a mythic cast to the events to hand. Amado Cabrera writes inside-out anthropology, half-right but shadowed in academic nit-picking. Janet Pierce, bruised, resentful, writes her own there-at-the-time diary. The voices of

Rizalina, the interpreter-guide Duan, Moody, Paz Marlowe, Fritz, Zamora both before and after his demise, and each of the plethora of subsidiary participant-witnesses, make for a vying consortium, a dialogic gathering of participant witness. These voices, for sure, all belong to Hagedorn's ebulliently imagined Philippines, Manila as "Manila," Asia as screen Asia. But no less than *Dogeaters* and *The Gangster of Love*, the mirror textuality of *Dream Jungle* also does exact further service: it holds up to the light, with quite virtuoso ironic flourish, the Philippines's own true fictions as historical narrative.

15 Black South, Black Europe
William Demby

He took the mirror down from the hall and held it so that when he
stood in front of the full length mirror in the hall he could see himself
from the back view.

—*Beetlecreek* (1957)[1]

Am I dreaming inside a dream?

—*The Catacombs* (1965)[2]

"You're a very gifted writer, you know. But, as with so many of our
older Black writers, there is a certain self-conscious apology for being
a writer . . ."

—*Love Story Black* (1978)[3]

"William Demby Has Not Left The Building."[4] The title of Jeff Biggers's
profile written in 2004 for Denver's *Bloomsbury Review* offers an apt tease.
For to say of Demby's published fiction that it has met with mixed critical
fortune heads towards understatement with a twist. To be sure he has not
wanted for selective high praise, the occasional strong review, honorable
but passing mention in most African American literary critique. But quite
as often he looks to have gone missing in action, the absentee in a span
more drawn to the Black Arts efflorescence of the 1960s and to offering the
greater plaudits, however deserved, to a Ralph Ellison or Toni Morrison,
Ishmael Reed or Alice Walker. This does genuine disservice to Demby's
slim but formidable body of authorship, blackness, albeit as he makes clear
but the one mode of being among others, a human filtering unique in its
own cross-ply of history, and to be met with in his fiction across geo-cul-
tural sites as distinct the one from the other as the West Virginia hill south,
a 1960s Rome, and upper and lower Manhattan. As each of heading quota-
tions indicates, it is also to underestimate Demby's awareness of his own
art, his sense of using but not being pinioned to any one category, racial or
otherwise.

Beetlecreek (1957) customarily is given the nod as vintage realist-nat-
uralist writ, its West Virginia cul-de-sac township the mirror of an Afro-
America hexed by both Dixie color-line and its own inward provincialism.
The Catacombs (1965), with Rome as fulcrum, for the most part wins only
niche readerships, subject and fashioning a case of the black postmodern

text *avant la lettre*. *Love Story Black* (1978) may well lower a sly satiric eye on schools and magazine fads within black writing but its offbeat love-affair, with a dip into Africa alongside New York, also elicits the charge of whimsy, too oblique a wit. Taken, however, with the as yet unpublished *Comus*—its compass, reportedly, the Congress of Vienna in 1815 as the remaking of Europe through to the race-inflected remaking of the international order as First and Third World, these novels can truly be said to map Demby's own Black Atlantic, America-Europe-America as a variorum in which US and allied black history assumes quite inerasable consequence.

To this end Demby brings to bear a curriculum vitae as apposite as it is singular, and exactly both American and European. First has to be his birth in Pittsburgh in 1922, his middle-class family's move across the state line to Clarksburg, West Virginia in 1941, study at West Virginia State College (where a young Margaret Walker was teaching and whose verse-collection *For My People* appeared in 1942) and from which he frequently absconded to play jazz trumpet in South Carolina nightspots, and after a two year stint in the American cavalry spent mainly in Italy, a transfer to Fisk in Nashville, Tennessee, from which he graduated in liberal arts in 1944.[5] In college he had also begun the story-writing carried over into his reportage and feature contributions to the army's *Stars and Stripes*.

Italy, to which he returned in 1947, yields his other life, one of ready and longstanding expatriation. He studied painting and music in Rome, immersed himself in Italian avant-guard art circles and became a not inconsiderable collector himself, married the author and translator Lucia Druidi, and found work as variously English-language translator, script-writer and even a once-off assistant director within the orbit of Cinecitta films and prime names like Antonioni, Fellini and Visconti. Their break with Italian screen realism in favor of altogether more subjectivist image would long be a key influence, even as he earned income from *Holiday Magazine* and advertising copy. In the late 1960s, after his divorce, he took up a two-decade teaching post in Staten Island with subsequent bases both in Sag Harbor and Rome. He has also been responsible for a small archive of essay-work and opinion columns. Throughout, to immediate purposes, he has continued work at his fiction, three published novels, various manuscripts still in progress (one titled *Blueboy*—in various blurbs announced as actually being in print but not in fact so), in all a commitment to the sustained invention of storytelling across each trans-Atlantic shift of locale.

*   *   *

Beetlecreek gives the hill south as racial *huis clos*, Demby's own Book of The Dead. Its West Virginia black world of the boy Johnny Johnson and his uncle David Diggs, together with Bill Trapp, the white ex-carnival loner who has fetched up in a shack between black and white small-town Beetlecreek, has usually been dubbed realist, time-and-place actuality.

Johnny's adolescence as The Pittsburgh Kid sent to Beetlecreek in the wake of his mother's sickness, the descent of David's marriage with Mary into formula and his delusionary would-be escape to Detroit with the playgirl returnee Edith Jones—once the love of his life, and Trapp's intending but fatally destined cross-racial kindliness, take on literal enough credibility, a version of the seemingly actual.

But without pitching for something quite opposite, or perverse, this truly falls short on the novel's best working seams and imagery. From start to finish it manages a subtler resonance, to be sure the depiction of the township black South of Tolley's barbershop and Telrico's tavern, Mary Johnson's church etiquette and the Nightrider boy gang, Johnny's friendship and betrayal of Bill Trapp, but also one whose very disequilibrium is equally given situating magnification through a narrative language always imagistic, purposely double.

Demby, initially, was much said to resemble Richard Wright on the assumption that both of them belonged in the standard protest-realist literary stable. But this, to a large extent, was to mis-read Wright as much as Demby. Rather the resemblance, if such it be, lies in the kinds of "inside narrative" on offer in story-collections like Wright's *Uncle Tom's Children* (1938) and *Eight Men* (1961).[6] This is symbolist Wright, close at times to the surreal, rarely more so than in "Big Boy Leaves Home" with its image-pattern of blues and the dozens, black boyhood life and white soldier death, bucolic swimming hole and hell-like kiln, snakes and mastiff, or "The Man Who Lived Underground" as Fred Daniels's sewer-eye view of America walled by hallucinatory whiteness and blackness, Afro-Bartlebyism as it were. Demby's Beetlecreek has much of the same refractive quality, the township and its drama summoned as though off-tilt, fissured, a distortion.

First, in this respect, has to be Beetlecreek as a sense of place. The town's own name just about hints of Kafka, insectoid, suspended, a South caught in a Dixie stasis of black and white and imagined as though existential ground-zero. Demby's imagery everywhere implies life whose energies have lost larger purpose. The creek itself is initially said to be subject to "a brisk, cold wind," to be beset with "candy wrappers," and to be presided over by "frantic," "screaming" birds (25). A "fat tomcat" (25), not unlike the sun-drenched and portentous cat "asleep and peaceful" at Dawson's Landing in Mark Twain's *Pudd'nhead Wilson*, hovers complacently on the barbershop steps. Death is actualized in the passing of Mrs. Johnson, Edith Johnson's unloved foster-mother, and in its wake the dense run of allusion to hearses, wakes, and the very rustle of the churchwomen's black-silk funeral garb. The gathering effect is stygian, a Gothic less of extravagant scene or act than ordinariness, the familiar as alien.

Johnny takes into himself this shadow, the passed-along boy at the threshold of life yet brought close to death-in-life. He sees Beetlecreek as though transmogrified into "Black Enamelled Death," a hell landscape where the streets have turned brilliant copper in the sunset, "birds swooped screeching on every perch," and he senses only "vague fear and shame" that augur yet more dislocation (79). Indeed power of shadow extends into the whole ecology of place, Beetlecreek as much moral as geographic axis. Johnny sees "boxes, tin cans, bottles" float down the creek, get caught in a whirlpool, and end up in "the deadly mud backwater in the reeds" (94). David Diggs is said to sit "in the corner against the white wall of the church . . . trapped in the village, arrested, closed in" (93), black against white, self against shadow. He envisages himself as "unable to move again," literally a "rusty can." (94). A sign-writer by profession, and as a life less than his college-educated mind warrants, the signs about him bespeak not life, vitality, but its opposite. Beetlecreek he thinks "suffocation" (94), "death-grip" (96), just as Johnny believes himself "entirely alone" (116). Bill Trapp, true to his name, a gargoyle at the margins, is initially said to be caught in "clammy silence" (8).

Not the least part of Demby's achievement is to make this stasis dynamic, a staging of the will to human connection against a south of historic borders of consciousness as much as skin and class. Each main figure in turn so undergoes a respective rite-of-passage, intense, inward, paradoxically animated by the very deadness that prevails. The upshot in *Beetlecreek* is an enactive fable, the capturing of the will-to-life even as the town reduces and encloses life. Demby can thereby be thought to have managed a considerable balancing-act: a narrative full of vitality, serious momentum, in the very process of depicting the latitude and longitude of severance or loss.

Quite another part of Demby's achievement is to play his black figures— Johnny, David, Edith, Tolley's barber's shop regulars and Bill his shoeshine boy, Mary Diggs and the churchwomen, the boy Nightrider gang—against Bill Trapp, pariah white man. If another "peckerwood" in off-duty black township speech, he is also to become Diggs's drinking and talking companion, be-friender of Johnny and the children, the wrongly dubbed molester and finally the likely burned-to-death scapegoat. As Johnny's price of entry into the Nightriders, in all its Lord of the Flies syndrome, requires the burning of Trapp's house, so Trapp himself is last to be seen as almost Christly and at once "sad" and "resigned" (202). This last vista, Trapp in silhouette, Demby offers with the same delicate touch of fantasticalism as in fact from the start, a footfall of "symbolist" Richard Wright, even it can be said, of Poe, the presiding *figura* of a south intimately local yet also transfigured.

For from the outset Trapp's portrait is given in terms that anticipate this iconic, almost heraldic destruction. The carefully pitched opening bears out Trapp as self-within-self, a kind of vernacular *Doppelgänger* set down in the Dixie of West Virginia implicitly as much dream-wasteland as literal map. He is said to look into a mirror only to find "unanswerable questions" and "the eyes of a dead man, jellied and blank" (7). The hint of Kafka is emphatic, Trapp as "a silent ugly man who could no longer tell whether he was inside the mirror or inside himself " (7). The ensuing detail amplifies the double self. His first encounter with Johnny, apple-owner to apple-thief, then with David Diggs ("a nervous, jerky flow of words" [12]), leads to more self-reflection at the broken mirror. Is he whole, part, ever divided, ever to be joined again? Drinking at Telrico's with Diggs his face is said to be "a gratework of wrinkles" (18), as if en-webbed in, and by, time. In his shack he hardly sleeps but when he does it is as though his actual life has become oneiric: the circus tent of Harry Simcoe's Continental Show; his orphan fostering-out with his sister Hilda; the Depression-era drift and illusory Retirement Plan Insurance; and his friendship with the Italian performer, the bequeathed stuffed dog, and his eventual role as circus hand dressed in shabby-cavalier uniform. For Trapp the outward life becomes interior, wakefulness the dream.

Mocked at first by Beetlecreek's black children he even so dreams on, a cut-price Gatsby, imagining the juncture of the two race-communities, pumpkin and dandelion wine picnics, children at play, and yet he does so perched in an apple tree "like some kind of vulture bird" (60). The omen weighs perfectly. The pumpkins, the picnic, the colloquies with Diggs, and his mentorship of Johnny all turn against him. He may well dream of "coming alive again" (170) but the dream ends in accusation of molestation and fire and death, Johnny's rite-of-initiation into the Nightrider gang his own end. Amid the flames of his small-holding—"his figure exaggerated by the light of the fire" (202)—he again becomes the fugitive double-self he has seen in the mirror, if for a moment the winner then finally the loser of his dream. In Demby's conception of him, both un-parented and unable to parent, Trapp finally serves as lost hope, a grown Huck disabled by Beetlecreek's bad faith, false witness.

Each of the other key players take their cue accordingly. Johnny alternates from one implicitly tranced state to the next. Initially he can be the boyhood reader, his chosen text *Doctor Zorro and The Dope Smugglers*. At night he can dream of his mother suffused in blood, in hospital and fighting consumption, a figure of helpless, drowning hemorrhage. In the barbershop he is the Pittsburgh boy outsider, subject to the quick-fire black josh and repartee of Tolley and the customers about his sideburns and witness to dismissive gossip about white men ("He *do* have funny eyes" Jim Anderson says of Trapp [29]). To the Nightriders he is the object of gang mockery yet also their self-desiring recruit, the appalled yet fascinated observer-participant as the Leader twists off the head of a baby pigeon with its blood splattered against the wall. With Trapp, as though in interlude, he can be both story-listener and co-spirit in the recognition of his own will to the power of word and narrative.

Left to his own devices he thinks of himself as locked in the specific time-and-place of his Aunt Mary's hostility and yet wondering if he is not resident in some other-world—"Everything he had done since he arrived in Beetlecreek had the feeling of being an episode in a dream" (118). This sense of displacement persists, the bus-station wrapped around in "quiet," his own index of "separation" (119), or the first encounters with the Nightriders and Bill Trapp which are described as suffused in "dream feeling" (119). In turn the sight of his uncle drinking with Trapp, the shack episode with the pigeon, the joshing he receives at the barbershop, his vision of his uncle as loner, and even his fantasies about girls become "dream scenes" (119), a litany of disconnection. "What if Beetlecreek were a ghost town and he were the only inhabitant" (123) he speculates, alterity as haunting. Finally, in himself becoming a Nightrider, the township's revenge-agent, he serves as Trapp's betrayer, and yet both like and unlike Trapp, his own secret sharer, the one self shadowed in the other.

Demby's portraiture of David Diggs carries the imprint of a life overwhelmingly driven to be the thing it is not. His marriage to Mary Phillips Diggs mocks their early passion, a life of deadly church-centered routine and gingerbread-baking for the Fall Festival country fair and anticipated in the stillbirth of their child and the pregnancy before marriage and for which he has given up Edith Johnson ("He came to Beetlecreek and did his duty" [97]). With Trapp he crosses the race-line, finds succor, drinks, for both a wary friendship, and yet intractably snared in a south which not only has made the mutuality of blackness and whiteness ancestral taboo but turned blackness into its own close-tied human knot. "Negro life," he thinks impossible to explain to Trapp, is "a fishnet, a mosquito net, lace, wrapped round and round, each little thread a pain . . . too complicated " (104).

His hope lies in Edith, city-savvy, feisty, a drinker on equal terms in Telrico's as against the gingerbread-baking Mary, with her rise to Chair of the Women's Missionary Guild and preening for the approval of the minister. Yet as Diggs awaits the late-to-arrive Edith, he finds himself listening to the addled patter of Doc, the bus depot shoeshine man with his dream of a magical numbers fortune. The voice is one of roulette, exactly the game and scale of chance Diggs is embarking on with Edith. She it is, whisky to hand, abrupt-irritable in speech, impatient with a cat that has crept on to the Detroit-bound bus, who duly embodies the sheer contingency of their action. Leaving as the fire engines race towards Trapp and his house theirs is no great romance but rather a dark, peevish and all too late extrication. Beetlecreek, black and white, south and north, for both Biggs and Edith, as for Johnny and Trapp, will travel with and inside them.

For all its Depression-era time or West Virginia specificity of black locale, in other words, the Trapp-Johnson-Diggs configuration affords its own kind of existential haunting. Each close-encounter, Johnny with Trapp, his aunt, the barbers and the Nightriders, Trapp with Diggs and the town, Diggs with both Mary and Edith, is given in terms that embed their shared force of disconnection in an idiom, an imagery, to match. Demby, on this measure, goes beyond simple point-for-point realism into infinitely more psychic territory, a south whose racialization operates at synaptic inner levels. The arising narrative served notice of consequential talent.

* * *

In this respect *Beetlecreek* can be also said to anticipate *The Catacombs*, however ostensibly different their fashioning. For Demby's second novel, a reflexive tour-de-force clearly as well out ahead as any in the then contemporary mid-1960s (the novel itself runs from March 1962 to March 1964), cannily situates blackness—again inevitably but not exclusively the axis of the novel—using almost all the levers of the postmodern repertoire.

To be sure it invites comparison with other African American landmarks kindred in compositional spirit, foremost Ellison's *Invisible Man* (1952) with its trope of black on white as both mythic rite-of-passage from enslavement to freedom and the inscription of black word on white page.[7] Further touchstones would include William Melvin Kelley's *dem* (1967), with its vision of Harlem and white suburbia as mutually refractive but disjunctive American realms, Ishmael Reed's *Mumbo Jumbo* (1972) as a reflexive primer in how Africa, Afro-America, lies at the very core of America's making, and Trey Ellis's *Platitudes* (1988) as a "new black aesthetic" novel-colloquium given over to what kind of art a post-Civil Rights black authorship might best deploy.[8] But, if so, it also acts on Demby's self-appointed imaginative parameters, a "narration" (223) set in "cubistic time" (40), as the text calls it, and pitched for its own tapestried runs-of-consciousness.

William Demby, "real" black writer-expatriate in Rome with Italian wife and son James, seeks to take the measure of his time in a relentless consumption of newspaper and TV. Yet he also enters his own story as "William Demby," friend, occasional lover, of "Doris," black extra cast as a handmaiden in the Elizabeth Taylor film-spectacular *Cleopatra* and the mistress to Count Raffaelle Della Porta, excecutive in a British airline company. Both authorial selves, at once actual and virtual, patrol each other, while they at the same time patrol a violent world of Cold War, the OAS and the Algerian War, the assassination of John Kennedy, the space race, local Rome suicides, and the "blackness" of each sorry race-death from Europe's colonial rape of Africa (the Count has a sister who serves as a nun in the Congo in reparation for their father's racism and plundering) to the US's Birmingham bombings, desegregation battles in Alabama and the DC Freedom March. Demby/"Demby" describes it as "truly . . . a Gothic age" (38), a "Year of the Plague" (38), a media glut of "poisons and strange and violent deaths" (38). This is modernity seen postmodernly, a global trauma narrative made up of each *petit récit* and yet played out against the novel's own referred-to bulwarks like Judaeo-Christianity, the Catholic calendar of Rome, and Greek tragedy.

The respective narratives, discrete yet braided into each other, could not be busier, full of allusion, dialogue, extract, dream. Robert Bone gives a useful cue when he invokes Gertrude Stein's notion of the world as "continuous present," the simultaneity of life and text, event and awareness.[9] The one narrative can be said to be utterly bound into the world, its power politics and ideologies, and the other into virtuality, self-aware as to its own formation and in which "Doris" can at once be her creator's creature yet also able to answer back and even accuse him of authorial vampirism. Both, in truth, are treated as parallel and operative fictions. Demby's tactic, certainly, is to elide the two, the novel as double-helix, moving tableau or mosaic, with the catacombs as enclosing life-and-death iconography. The upshot is a literary equivalent of the collagist art compositions by the Italian neo-realist installation artist Mimmo Rotella mentioned on the very opening page ("The sun has finally come out and my Rotella collages have begun to dance like gorgeous jungle flowers" [3]), the sustained energy of interactive facts and fiction, disclosure and speculation.

Demby/ "Demby" discusses his/their life, and his/their novel, with friends, with the reader, with himself. On a visit to the country with his family an old Marchesa tells him she prefers mystery novels to any other kind. The one or other author responds "I am beginning to feel trapped in a mystery novel myself" (172). Well he, or the both of them, might, for the world they seek to inscribe exists inside a McLuhan universe of medium as message, huge, unstoppable electronic fictions of fact. *The Catacombs*, an image to refract the novel's technique as much as its religious-ontological vision, acts wholly on this new media world-order, the instantaneousness of the modern. A diary entry by Demby/ "Demby" gives the novel's rules of the game, "a strict selection of the facts to write down, be they "fictional" facts or "true" facts. . ." (93).

As the narrative wheels round and forward this is added to, glossed, time and again—Doris's might-be pregnancy and uncertainty as to whether the Count or Demby is the father, her loss of the child, and the final revelation to the Count of life over death as he steps for the first time into the catacombs. "I am telling Alice how the novel shall end" (36) says the author early in the novel. He reports a literary session in which "One novelist even began to criticize the novel as though it had already been written, which is perfectly in harmony with the theory of cubistic time I am so recklessly fooling with" (40). The process of de-familiarizing the all too familiar, or familiarly constructed, world elicits the comment "I am beginning to have the strangest feeling that we are all nothing more than shadows, spirits, breathed into life and manipulated by Pirandello's fertile mind" (45). As the one story launches into the other, moreover, the accommodating author even slyly acknowledges "I return to the typewriter" (160).

Suitably, towards the close, a summary is ventured, the composite Demby of the novel as reflexive-conceptual writer bearing "the theory of this narration." (208). This he glosses as "everything and everybody, real or invented" mattering, each "news" as true as each other (209). The inter-connectedness of the world, in other words, however for its power-brokers apparently binary, however vicious the separation implied in its wars and murders, requires art, narrative, a metaphysics ("existence is sacred" [202]) in all its rich indeterminacy—its contestation of single meanings—to act as counter-acting force. To that end Demby suggests that as much as *The Catacombs* acts as tabulation, memory-record, a story conscious of its own storying, its play of self-reference aims always for the quite more consequential goal: the need to see humanity, the world, in its fuller, better kinetic whole, in essence the principle of life over death.

Commentary has understandably seized upon the novel's organizing narrative, the visual and sculptural art references, the religious schema. But it has not anything like sufficiently addressed the novel's seams and allusions to black life and history or the ends they serve. Demby avails himself of allusions to Isak Dinesen as Gothic prophet of the modern world; uses a letter from Steinbeck, newly a Nobel winner, to suggest language's moral duty; tacitly adverts to Marshall McLuhan as the semiotician of global media; and invokes names from Ezra Pound to James Baldwin, however in themselves contrary, in the quest for order out of disorder. His art-allusions run from Rotella to Michelangelo's *Pietà* to Losavio: each artists who have "made new" in their art but also in their call to reconfigure a humanity trapped in prior habits of ideology and practice. Teilard de Chardin supplies the key theology, a Catholic metaphysics, as the process of thought or action or belief whereby the world is coned or spiraled to rise above its fixities of either-or hatred, the lethal oppositeness of war.

It is in the context of these matrices, and actually a matrix of its own, that *The Catacombs* as the "black" story of Demby/"Demby," Doris, the Count, and Rome as at one and the same time ancient Holy City and modern international metropolis, offers imaginative sway. A complex serial of allusion builds within the unfolding narrative, Africa, Afro-America, Afro-Europe as pathways into understanding earliest civilization and yet also the contemporaneity of US Civil Rights or De Gaulle and Algeria. Pausing, as it seems, as he writes his section of the novel about Doris and her night with the Count, the author begins a letter to a black woman writer-friend in Alabama. Can she write her poetry beyond the battles of desegregation? Can her husband, Donald, imagine drawing cartoons of "the more grotesque aspects of being a Negro doctoring a small Alabama town, or about 'the Race Problem' " (6)? He is interrupted with word of a lecture by the Italian translator of *Beetlecreek* on "The White Whale and Other Myths" (7). He turns both to Whitman's Civil War diaries and newspaper reports of plastic bombs in Algeria. The Dixie of black and white, America and Europe, Europe and Africa: the spectrum is one of humanity absurdly, punitively, specified un-benignly into fissures of race, color, colonialism.

Doris herself, film extra as may be, flawed, a wine-bibber, the daughter of "Demby's" own early college love in the south, Barbara Havers, even so suggests the incipient black Madonna ("She breaks out laughing, and somehow her dream-secret Negro laughter seems sacrilegious here in this country trattoria on the ancient Appian way, and the Catacombs with their layers and layers of bone-powder death just across the street" [17]). Laura, a Creole Jamaican friend woman, kills herself, another female suicide adrift under male governance (she lives with a poet who has abandoned her) in the wake of Marilyn Monroe. The press gives reports of a crisis of bourgeois male self-identity, feminism as breaking inherited both black and white forms of patriarchy and the politics of phallicism. The Count, Doris reveals, is said to be "fascinated with the idea that there are gangsters in America and that one of them is my father" (102). Doris bills herself for "Demby" as "a fellow Nigra-American all alone in Rome" (113) as he, in turn, observes that "the (white) European world is cold" (121). The uncertainty as to the color of her baby, black, white, both, a new beginning, speaks perfectly to a world caught up in the zig-zag, the cat's cradle, of its own contradiction.

Which, both Dembys ponder, will best bring the world together, Vatican II (with its first African cardinal) or the Kruschev-Kennedy Vienna meeting about the bomb, the eucharist or contraception? The text imagines the Count in Doris's company believing himself to be a crocodile on the Nile, the exact locale of her role in *Cleopatra*. At RAI-TV Demby works on a documentary on Harlem starring Louis Armstrong, jazz's premier horn and voice at the very centre of Europe. On his visit to America Demby takes heed of the Birmingham bombing, a Cleveland race-beating, the Clay-Liston fight, the Black Muslims, the Freedom march ("Never in my life have I seen so many Negroes in one place" [177]), Oswald's shooting of a "New Frontier" Kennedy. If, however, this is a litany of injured blackness, blackness also reminds of a way forward.

The novel invokes Africa not simply as French-Algerian war but an example of a place and timeline possessed of culture-before-technology, an organic power of word, art, culture, the human nexus. In this it is the Count's sister, the nun, who bears witness—"She said the problem with Africa is that they speak there a *human* language the rest of humanity has almost forgotten" (195). The contrast is made with "machine" language in the First World, language reified, un-human, formulaic. This version of Africa as humanly inter-wired is to be set against the "squarish cadence" (196) of the west, the geometric logic of line as against the spontaneous logic of circle. That trope of circle acts to round out the novel—Doris in the catacombs. Her child is no more, she disappears, the Count is bereft, the fiction evaporates. What is left is the dance of life ("Voulez-vous danser avec moi?" is repeated several times as motif), the image of a shared global

Africa as the touchstone of a wholly interconnecting and contingent humanity and yet also lost womb. Demby's novel, itself life-filled even about death,
gives a reminder of transcending human possibility even as it writes its own
kind of requiem.

* * *

Looking to the experiences chronicled in *Love Story Black*, its narrator,
Professor Edwards, black, another longtime European novelist-expatriate
(sound familiar?), and currently teaching both African American literature
and *Beowulf* and the medieval literature of romance at a Staten Island
college, speaks of them as "strange journeys through time and reality"
(20). Commissioned by *New Black Woman Magazine* to do a series of
articles on Miss Mona Pariss, ancient *chanteuse*, blues queen, his emerging
account causes Gracie, the magazine's editor, Edwards's on-off lover and
an always sharp but foul-mouthed black Vassar graduate, to observe "I
know you're a novelist—and a fairly good one . . . But even *you* wouldn't
put a thing like this in a novel" (25). For this is Demby in lighter, at times
comic-fantastical vein, his novel a seriously clever, well-turned portrait of
south-to-north American cultural blackness and its linkage to Africa and
the wider world.

As Edwards reels in the life of Mona, well into her eighties, cranky,
anachronistically dressed, as ready with her whisky and pork chops and
collard greens as her Zora Neale Hurston down-home vernacular, he finds
himself obliged almost freakishly to co-exist both in his own 1970s and
the Jazz Age 1920s. For her part Mona has emerged from Orlando County
in an unspecified south, sung her way out of rural obscurity into international show-time, if a Josephine Baker then one at whom she takes any
number of gossipy slaps. Alongside in the same ghetto Manhattan tenancy
("crumbling brownstone" [21]) is the Reverend Grooms, "a light-skinned
Black man with . . . puffy jowls" (3), a speaker of "the word" and bibber
of jugs of Gallo red wine. Edwards, required to lay naked alongside Mona
in her boudoir as she speaks her history, is not only to tell her story but
actually to help it conclude, the perfect life-imitating-art parody of the
participant-observer.

Mona herself, just as much as her story, cuts across all manner of stereotype but in no respect more so than in keeping her virginity: a gift, an
honoring, of her early one-time love, Doc. He, the perfect lover-man, handsome, a legendary Pullman Porter, having vowed to protect her, is castrated
by the Klan. Grooms, in fact, turns out to be the same Doc, his own apartment meticulously recreated as a Pullman carriage. He also refers Edwards,
now accompanied by the beauteous Hortense Schiller, to the Halbrin Theatrical Storage Company where Mona's trunk has been assigned through
more than fifty years and ended up in Harlem. Its papers, starting with
newspaper cuttings about Cal Coolidge's election and not least about Doc,

the dresses and trinkets, open the one era of blackness to another, the one past south to a present north.

In the interim Edwards tries to keep his own life in balance. His college classes become their own mirror of the times, especially when Melinda Rodriguez, Puerto Rican radical Marxist, berates him as he teaches Richard Wright with the "you're an associate professor of English right?. . .If you ask me neither you nor Richard Wright know your ass from a hole in the ground—you're both a couple of jive turkey nigger cultural sell-outs. . .!" (31–2). As he moves from this to classes on courtly love the connection to Mona is inescapable: Chaucer pre-shadows Doc, *The Knight's Tale* pre-shadows Mona's biography. Gracie, PR virtuoso as much as editor, a TV presence, hosts a revolutionary poetess who believes in glorifying the pimp as true insurrectionist (the gathering held at Soul Conglomerates). Edwards's love-affair with Hortense takes them to Ghana on a scheme to have "African Liberation Movements" out-sourced to black businessmen and consumer marketing, where she abandons him for marriage in Zambia to the Catholic Marxist Georges Mantu, and where he comes down with food-poisoning, each the deflation of his mythic fantasy of Mother Africa.

Only in the final, and literal, consummation of his bed story-listening with Mona does he find scale, perspective, for his own turnings as to race, masculinity, blackness. With Grooms/Doc finally killed by his consumption of "Gallo wine communion wine" (136), the building under demolition, he re-enacts the love-making which by rights should have taken place decades earlier between Doc and Mona. Theirs is the south as mythic black ancestry, a "love story black" worthy of medievalism, its own unique, and enduring triumph of sorts even if scarred by pain, white cruelty. As Edwards stands in for Doc, and Mona dies euphorically in their sublime anachronistic one act of love, a happiest real or imagined de-flowering as she remembers herself down by the southern river of her young womanhood, so the story hitherto still to be told is finally able to have its own ending. In having his novel make life of art, and as equally art of life, Demby once again and in continuity with *Beetlecreek* and *The Catacombs* acts with exquisite imagination, his text a ranking counter-text.

16 Rearview Mirrors
Gerald Vizenor

native storiers
by tease
create. . .
circle of footprints
in the snow
—"Window Ice," *Almost Ashore:*
Selected Poems (2006)[1]

I was a crossblood on the natural margins of a cultural contradance.
—"Envoy to Haiku," *Shadow Distance:*
A Gerald Vizenor Reader (1994)[2]

Gerald Vizenor has rarely given the standard reference books much of a free ride. It would be easy, at least relatively easy, to say Ojibway-Chippewa Native American novelist, critic-theorist, essayist, short story writer, auto-biographer, dramatist, anthologist, interviewee, series editor, and infinitely to immediate purposes, poet. But what happens, amid this abundance of a literary career with its frequent spurs to controversy, when he himself plays neologist and creates registers like Native storier, Anishinaabe haiku-ist, crossblood trickster, and above all, his great orchestral signature phrasings—*postindian, survivance, shadow distance, fugitive pose, double other?* Do these two styles of register simply overlap, or are they better seen as caught up in a teasing equation wholly appropriate to a writer who has always fought against monochrome fixities or binaries of category, and whether in respect of Native Americans and their history, art and thought or indigenous cultures well beyond? Either way, and quite as much as fellow Native American poets, N. Scott Momaday to Simon Ortiz, Diane Glancy to Luci Tapahonso, he has mounted a verse-record full of his own kind of contradance.

Yet despite the fact that poetry represents his earliest creative bow and has continued throughout his considerable authorship, it tends to be accorded a kind of also-ran status, the less noted activity. To be sure it has to contend for attention within the voluminous context of the fiction from *Bearheart* (1978, 1990), with its story of visionary pilgrimage across America, to *Hiroshima Bugi: Atomu 57* (2003), his reflexive-trickster take on nuclear calamity, and *Father Meme* (2008), his subtly voiced revenge-novella of abuse of Native boys by reservation priests.[3] There has also been Vizenor's influential, and often fiercely contentious, discursive writing, from the essay-stories of *Wordarrows: Indians and Whites in the New Fur Trade* (1978, 2005) through to the monograph *Fugitive Poses: Native Scenes of Absence and Presence* (1998).[4] It would be remiss, equally, to leave un-noted *Interior Landscapes: Autobiographical Myths and Metaphors* (1990), his landmark self-narrative of Minneapolis boyhood, fractured White Earth family, army service in Japan, city activism and journalism, and eventual life as novelist and professor-writer from Bemidji to Berkeley to the University of New Mexico.[5]

But there the poetry has always been, beginning with *Two Wings The Butterfly* (1962) and *Raising The Moon Vines* (1964), and continued in both small-press and university-press publication as in *Summer in The Spring: Ojibwe Lyric Poems and Tribal Stories* (1965, revised 1993), together with journal and anthology publication, in all a keen, persistent output, and quite as full of imaginative swerve as his prose writings.[6] The appearance, accordingly, of *Almost Ashore: Selected Poems* (2006) and *Bear Island: The War at Sugar Point* (2006) could not be timelier: the former a compilation of past and continuing lyrics and haiku, the latter an epic-in-small of the 1898 Leech Lake battle between the Anishinaabe band of the Pillagers and the US army.[7] To come at this poetry through the contradance, the torque, of Vizenor's imagery, his "imagistic gaze" as he calls it in *Postindian Conversations* (1998), is inevitably to link it to the virtuosity of his prose writing.[8]

But it is also to recognize the poetry's necessary distinctiveness, the play of juncture and disjuncture, the oral inside the written, the voicings that run counter to easy cliché or mask about indigenous experience in America. *Almost Ashore* involves a span of White Earth, ravens, rivers, shadows, bears, cranes, crows, flies, Columbus, museums and the cities. *Bear Island*, for its part, looks to Leech Lake, Anishinaabe creation story, the great trickster-creator figure of Naanabozho, clan affiliation, army and tribal soldiery, guns and death. At the same time, and across both volumes, there can be no doubt of the shared import of *survivance* as working dynamic, the utter, ongoing creativity both personal and communal within Native life.

*   *   *

Four poems can serve as a departure-points for those gathered overall, and in some cases re-written, in *Almost Ashore*, a way of encountering, and centering, the contradance of imagination in play. The emphasis, of necessity, falls upon prisms of reflection, imagery challengingly given to seeing and mirroring the one and several ways at the same time. To this end "White Earth," in an earlier version appositely subtitled "Images and Agonies," especially counts—an opening longitude and latitude, a call to place and memory he calls "october sunrise" in which "native tricksters/roam in the shadows/ rearview mirrors" (10). It is a poem that then calls up colonial, religious and government intrusion, a people and land often made ruinously subject, and yet not quite, to the colonizing geometries of "soldiers and civilization" be the latter road, ledger, city or the movies. Yet, as equally, it gives remembrance, ongoingly and redemptively, to Anishinaabe pathways (those of a woodland people after all) of birch, cottonwood and pine, to the crane clan and shaman visions and practices, to wild rice, bears, beavers, moose, and to the ravens of trickster lore. This, precisely, is to hold up White Earth to "rearview mirrors," a watchful overlap of perception, the world to hand seen from an exterior perspective as linear, straight-ahead history, yet also, and of far greater import, seen interiorly as possessed of its own vast, kinetic habitation whose Native cultural resources of experience and story remain as alive in the present as in any time-past.

To this composite purpose the poem opens with an iconography of daybreak time and place ("october sunrise/shimmers in the birch/and cottonwoods" [10]), the curtain raised, a visionary season begun. The ensuing images contrast and vie. The "rearview mirrors" silhouette "colonial missions" and "government agents" (10), a litany of plunder, torture, and underestimation of "the woodland dead," but also a counter-legacy of "native tricksters," the "faces of shamans" (10). The former have logged the pine, sought to reduce crane culture, made "native ceremonies" into curiosity, turned beaver and muskrat pelt and eagle feathers into mere trapper accessory, and imposed a Catholic theology upon tribal belief-system ("jesuit dominion", "ghostly crossbones" [12]). Yet however against odds, tricksters indeed still "roam in the shadows" (10), "tricky stories" (11) continue to get told, meadowlarks sing, moose browse albeit "near the mission ruins" (13), and tribal life, against setback or snare, has managed to seize upon its own continuing existence.

Above all the "mighty ravens" (13), avian trickster virtuosi, wiseacres, and in this instance also Anishinaabe necromancers, serve as messengers for the restoration of a better human order. Their presence, and flight, inspire nick-naming, the playful intimacy of fellowship. As spirits they traffic easily between the dead and the living. As Nature's own "black beads" (13) they contrast tellingly with "the benedictory beads" (10) of missionary rosaries. Their pine residences serve perfectly as ambassadorial lodges between the mirrors of the one world and the other. The poem's language could not be more appropriate: might, inspiration, night, vision, trickery. In returning to their "embassies" (13) in the pine trees, a habitat at once actual yet also magical or spiritual, these ravens bear nothing less than both the force of ancient understanding and the call to new life, new language, new mirrors of reflection.

"Praise Ravens" offers a connecting, but distinctive, bead. The Native terrain to hand, under winter snow, is but one of many kinds made subject to waste, city leisure, recreational hunting, and again, the inhuming road. The run of lines, however, suggests song, euphony. The first lines themselves, "seven ravens praise winter," readily call up seven-maids-a-dancing or the seven pleiades. But these ravens possess their own status as Native icons, woodland deities. The note is celebratory ("praise the winter"), playful ("tease the distance"), tribal-specific ("shamans at white earth"), and as the stanzas to follow make yet more immediate a simultaneously both real and mirror landscape of "pale poplar/crowned by snow" (30), a "winter dance" (31).

The contradance could not be clearer. On the one hand, as though lost totems of modern American technology, are to be found "abandoned cars/half-buried/at the roadside" (30). Place, under frontier historic time, has become conquest, a form of extraneous custody ("native meadows marked by treaties" ([30]). On the other hand resides the natural order of fox run and beaver dam even if that finds itself marred by "rusted ploughs" (30). Quite as intrudingly, country sight and country sound give way to modern city sound, the rushing, dissonant "bay" of the snowmobile, a new "savagery" to mock, even outpace, that so readily once attributed to Native peoples. The echo continues in the lines "snared/their necks/on barbed wire" (30) as if the snowmobilers were caught by latter-day hunting devices. But imperturbably the ravens hold to their custodial watch and play. They "bounce in the poplar/ a winter dance," their festive gaiety a rebuke to "spent cultures/dead in the weeds" (31). It makes for imagery to savor, contradance as both subject and means in the poem's imagining.

In "Columbus Endures" (74–5) the High Admiral takes a further turn in Vizenor's imagining. In his *The Heirs of Columbus* (1991) the adventurer variously designated Cristoforo Colombo, Cristóbal Colón, Cristóvão Colón, Juan Colom, and his own messianic Greek-Latin amalgam Xρo FERENS, the Christ BEARER, became of all things a returnee mixedblood, an "Indian" himself as he ventured back from Europe to America. It was a more than engaging tease on the author's part.[9] This time around the hero-villain of American "discovery" becomes subject to a gender-switch, aging, and eventual bouts of fantasy and delirium. Initially he might be some manikin, a living clothes-rack or bag lady ("she wears robes/and smells wooly") with due preservative odors and adhesive ("moth balls/and gum" [74]). Each stanza adds to the fantasy-portrait. Columbus struggles against winter snow in her coat, pulls a bedspread over her mouth and shouts with maybe just a touch of the last paragraph in *Gatsby* "landfall ahead/on the green" (41); dreams surreally of some Dalí-like orchestra on a string of appaloosa horses; and finally, draws bathwater in hopes that the Atlantic might re-instate him/her into a place of honor in "the old world." Each image divests Columbus of standard heroism, the poem's anti-discovery, as it were, of man and legacy.

With "Museum Bound" (79–80) Vizenor brings into play quite one of the most vexed issues of Native-white cultural politics: the role of the museum. His own potshots, zany, serious, sexual, at the storing of Native bones are familiar from satiric campus fiction like *Chancers* (2000).[10] His poem, however, takes on more serious hue, a line of phrasal images and counter-images. The "bound" of the title nicely turns two ways, Native America bound down and bound for museumization. In the poem's vision tribal nations, in all their vitality of life, have become folded into "nonce" words, relegated to "stone" storage-places, and been obliged to exchange a food-way like "pemmican" for the drug world of "laudanum." Under museum rules rivers have turned concrete and the once seasonal food-gathering and harvests given way to "concrete fast foods." Yet as "Museum Bound" unfolds, and as often in Vizenor's poetry, Nature's own citizenry—squirrels, bears, crows—remind of counter-life. They "march at the treelines" even as the museum regime of "coin-returns" and "slot machines" betrays one-time natural intimacy. The concluding stanza contrasts a lyric, almost haiku landscape of willow and rain with the museum as seizure and misnaming ("noisy cultures"). Contradance again presides, the best of Native culture as always live over dead time.

*   *   *

Haiku has long been a Vizenor forte, dating from his student studies at the University of Minnesota, re-enforced by his service in the military in Japan, given early publication in *Seventeen Chirps: Haiku in English* (1964) and *Matsushima: Pine* Islands (1984), and reworked into the two small volumes entitled *Cranes Arise* (1999) and *Raising The Moon Vines* (1999).[11] To that end he has been an avid admirer of Bashō, Buson and Issa and written illuminatingly on the seventeen-syllable form as enactive scene and gaze, action and contemplation. "Haiku in the Attic," in *Interior Landscapes: Autobiographical Myths and Metaphors* (1990) speaks of "shadow words" and suggests a link to between the "haiku spirit" and "oral tribal literature."[12] "Fusions of Survivance: Haiku Sccnes and Native Dream Songs" (2000), more precisely still, associates haiku ("my first poetry") with "the dream songs and visionary images of the *anishinaabe*, or Chippewa."[13] The latter essay also sets out his own taxonomy of the imaginative workings of haiku, a form he terms "a tease of nature, a concise, imagic moment . . . a tricky fusion of nature, motion, and culture."[14]

"Haiku Scenes" in *Almost Ashore*, actually a sequence of haiku-threesomes, displays a rare acuity of eye and ear, scenes, usually of Nature, each offered as self-completing dynamic, another species of contradance. "Trumpeter Swans" (37) offers a key instance, its "three sparrows" bouncing in red tulips, its acacia, its silent and circling swans. The delicate tulip ceremony of the three sparrows might indeed suggest an end-of-the week holiday, a "sunday spectacle" or time-off during which to see, and relish, the small opera of bird, movement, color and flower. The shift to evening-time, to the sound of wind, and to the acacia as decorative shrub or plant implies a possible Sabbath, the "early service" of Nature's own Sunday. Meantime, the trumpet-like swans, curvilinear embodiments of Nature's statelier music, circle White Earth's Bad Medicine Lake. Their silence, the implied ballet of their movement, paradoxically but altogether credibly conveys its own species of soundless sound. The upshot is a Nature's panel at once kinetic, and contemplatively visual, a haiku triad as symphony-in-small. "Crow Dance" (38), with its further lake-and-shoreline vista, carries both the distant echo of Native ceremonial dance, and yet also of modern contradance, in its very title. The scene is a Sunday morning Leech Lake storm in which two plovers seem to run the waves, three children walk and dance with the blown sheets of a clothesline.

Taken together these sequential haiku align different kinds of movement, meteorological, avian, child and domestic. Sky joins water as the thunderclouds find an answering rhythm in the Leech Lake shore-waves. The plovers run as though apprehensive, storm or squall in the offing. A parallel scene invokes Sunday white-shoed children, off to church maybe or on a stroll, even as geese ride the riffs and stillness of the lake. The third haiku takes up the implications: a risen wind across the prairie, helter-skelter children, the sheets about their own encore of rise and fall flutter. Will the thunderclouds break, the children get home, the sheets be brought in before the rain? All align under the imaginative rubric of "crow dance," storm and plovers, children and geese, clothes line and sheets contra-held in the one panorama.

"Square Dance" (46), again in three parts, works similarly. Each holds a moment, an *entr'acte*, yet each contributes to the whole, the pinion boughs at the doorway, children chasing pencil boats in the thaw, and notably, the "fat green flies" square-dancing across a grapefruit. In the first the pinion that enters from Nature, seeming ecological neighbors, finds their voice precisely in a storm—an arriving scratch of sound, speaking branches. In the second the "sudden thaw" that releases the stream teasingly runs parallel with the children's play, the chased pencil boats as against the likely pencils in the classroom. Its closing "late for school" blends hints of fun, delicious possible truancy, with the call of the clock and possible admonishment. The third carries a touch of food-as-gothic, a kind of half-comic alimentary *danse macabre*. "Fat green flies" summons insects already seemingly well-fed, maybe on offal or carcass, a hint of threat, or at least unwanted intrusion, in the satiety and the ominousness of their shiny, almost all too visible wingspan green. Their "square dance," even so, might also be leisure-time, the grapefruit itself a dance-floor. "Honor your partner," call and bow, gives a suitably ironic formality to this juncture of pest and fruit that would irritate, if not disturb, almost any potential breakfaster, diner or grocery-shopper. This three-sequence haiku, in common with the others in *Almost Ashore*, does vintage service, contradance at once serious and antic.

*   *   *

Reading across the various landscapes of *Almost Ashore* a number especially come into view, perhaps most strikingly those of bird and animal life, place, and family. The different aviaries, bestiaries and insect kingdoms, for instance, play against the human world, Nature's citizenry alive and vivid in its own right but also a kind of chorus, the antiphonal presences to ourselves. One listing would look to "dragonflies . . . at sunrise" in "Crane Dance" (4), "kingfisher" and "sandhill cranes" in "Mission Road" (24), "moths at dusk" in "Safe Harbor" (36), "blue butterflies" in "Camp Grounds" (70), "red spider" and "cat tricksters" in "Trickster Cats" (93), "redwing blackbirds" in "Treuer Pond" (97), "noisy sparrows" in "Homewood Hospital" (99), and "seven flights/of canada geese" in "Whole Moon" (105). Each bespeaks a wonderfully animate natural order, reservation White Earth to city Minneapolis, Bemidji to Berkeley. For all that Vizenor has been associated with the postmodern turn, the trickster wit of his fiction and theory, there can be little doubt as these and his other poetry confirm of respect, a genuine relish, for Nature's live habitation.

The sense of place, both as geography and timeline, likewise acts as a call to attention. "Guthrie Theater" compares a contemporary "wounded Indian" with "movie mockery" of Native America, each screen mythology of Wounded Knee, the Seventh Cavalry and Buffalo Bill (15). "North Dakota," in three pairs of couplets, takes a car highway view of Fargo and surrounds: "*east*" invokes a full moon behind Jamestown (with its historic echo) with "seven wings of geese" on the ice; "*west*" moves into red morning sun, spring prairie flowers; and "*exit*," a nice implied ambiguity in the road-sign, links back to "feral shadows," untrammeled natural time and place before road or settlement and, once more appositely, held in the image of "fingerprints/on the rearview mirror" (66). "Camp Grounds" takes aim at how the onetime Native land of "birch" and "white pine" has become "fabricated" leisure site, a "postcard" of the original whose "native ghosts" stalk the campers (70–1). "Treuer Pond," caught shimmering at a moment of "late summer," and not unlike Thoreau's Walden Pond, is remembered as once "never owned" but now property of the state, an imperium of blackbird, geese, heron, along with "bright dragonflies," "noisy frogs" and a "crash of kingfishers" (97–8).

"Family traces," as Vizenor calls them in "Choir of Memory," are frequent in *Almost Ashore* (53). The title poem itself, "Almost Ashore," speaks memorially of "my traces/blood, bone stone" (3). "Crane Dance," with its refrain of "by song" as the echo of Anishinaabe song practice (a tradition early explored in *The People Named the Chippewa* [1984]), gives a link to his father's Crane clan and his own mixedblood heritage, the liberating "dance" of an identity derived less from some census-bureau blood quantum than "natural reason" and "continental liberty/among dragonflies/at sunrise" (4–5).[15] "Hand Prints" gives further imagistic expression to that legacy as though tribally reposed in Nature—"spider webs," "eagle feathers," "circles of the sun," and "bear claws," all inscribed "on stone/ pictomyths" under the custodianship of "silent ravens/balanced/in the white pine." (26).

Most affectingly of all, perhaps, is "Family Photograph," that of his White Earth father, "immigrant/in the city" and house painter murdered in Minneapolis during Vizenor's infancy (6). He is also remembered in the black-and-white image reprinted in *Interior Landscapes* with his child in arms and smile against the backdrop of city housing. The poem has him exist doubly as substance yet silhouette, one of the "family photographs/ washed ashore (7)," the latter a phrasing to refract the collection's title overall. For his son, Gerald Vizenor, not only art but life would become contradance—newly born at his father's death, Native descended yet passed around in the city, and if so abruptly un-fathered then destined to become his own father, his own self-author. That would hold not only for actual place and time but, eventually, for all the quite abundant word of his writing with *Almost Ashore* but a latest installment.

*   *   *

Both Jace Weaver in his Foreword, and Vizenor himself in his Introduction, usefully supply due historical bearings for *Bear Island: The War at Sugar Point*. In capsule the events to hand of October 5 1898 involve the Minnesota arrest and then summons to trial of Bugonaygeshig (*bagone giizhig*), literally Hole in The Day (and insultingly Old Bug to local whites), chief of the Anishinaabe Pillager Band, in Duluth, where he refused to testify about reservation liquor-sales. A second would-be arrest at Leech Lake's Onigum Agency followed, then his rescue by nineteen or twenty tribal supporters and flight and hide-out at Sugar Point. With or without Bugonaygeshig (whether he was hiding there was never actually ascertained) their action brought the Third Infantry into play, first at Bear Island, then Buginaygeshig's cabin and vegetable garden at Sugar Point after the authorities inflatedly had reported an "Indian Uprising" (later to be called the "Last Indian War in the United States") and requested military assistance. The shoot-out to follow, started by the accidental discharge of a rifle and despite the army's five-to-one superiority in numbers, led to six dead (Major Wilkinson and five soldiers) and eleven wounded. No Pillager was killed. It eventuated, even so, in a trial, a sentence, but in due course a pardon, for the Anishinaabe men involved.

As a war episode, maybe better designated a mini-war episode, it can be seen as at once symptomatic of longtime US racial policy towards the tribes, a last ridding of Native impediment in the forward surge of Manifest Destiny, and an unsought but heroic tribal stand, necessary resistance, on the part of the Pillagers. Either way, and however often overlooked in histories of the west, it amounted in truth to a mix of administrative misjudgment, racism, near-farce (the shoot-out took place in Bugonaygeshig's vegetable garden) and tragedy. Vizenor's feat is to blend each component into a six-part verse narrative, all lower-case and unimpeded by punctuation, his latest version of US-Native history as itself a species of contradance and told in requisite line and imagery. Two moments in the poem offer working summaries.

In "Bearwalkers: 5 October 1898," mindful of how the Wounded Knee Massacre of 1890 has usually been taken for the closing conflict between the US government and its indigenous peoples, the poem offers a synopsis. "A single shot" has "started by chance/the last war/between natives/and the united states" (63). The literal encounter becomes emblematic, statistics as iconography, a near symbolist reckoning, nineteen Bear Island pillagers who have defeated the eighty army soldiers in a battle fought "in a bloody garden" (72).

"Overture: Manidoo Creations" opens proceedings, the careful verse restatement of Anishinaabe creation story and the interacting myth-realities of *miigis, naanabozho*, the crane, bear, catfish, marten and loon clans, and *manidoo*. It is into this tribal homeland, alive and active, seasonal and ancestrally ceremonial, and as ever totemic, that "three centuries/of expatriates/sweaty newcomers" (15) enter in a latest manifestation as the army's heavily blue-uniformed soldiers. Genocide, no less, shadows their presence, a litany of Indian-hating, attributed savagism, disease, removal, "scorn" and "bounty." Yet the white world, and the power-structure for which the army soldiers serve as emissaries whether officers or farmboys, small-town or immigrant enlistees, for a one-time, maybe a last-time, finds itself "outgunned/at sugar point" and then memorialized "forever in the book." The poem's prelude acts not only to supply specific site and calendar, or simply to launch the action, but to establish a context of psychodrama, two Americas yet again unnecessarily but fatally snared by stereotype, shadow, the familiar mythology of savagist otherness.

In each of the sequences that follow Vizenor deploys two kinds of track. One is historic, a line of Anishinaabe past-into-present. That summons Leech Lake as reservation and Pillager leaders like Chief Flat Mouth at the time of US Independence, the Lac du Flambeau elder Keeshkemun, and Bugaunak or Bagwana as the sole survivor of a skirmish with the Dakotas and whose name can be translated as "by my heart"—a phrase repeated throughout—who in ancestry of spirit and seemingly magical escape links him to Bugonaygeshig. The poem equally widens its ambit to include "native survivance" as against Euro-America's "godly triumphalism," "continental liberty" as against "manifest manners." More exactly the net of allusion embraces the outbreak of Plains smallpox (1837), the Sand Creek Massacre (1864), Custer, Sitting Bull and Little Big Horn (1876) and the Allotment Act (1887). To these, in Vizenor's imagining, the Bear Island-Sugar Point conflict of 1898 is to be thought both historical footfall and continuance.

The other track derives from his unyielding landscape and animist imagery of raven, cedar, sumac, waxwing, "bear traces," silver birch and the like, as also a way to locate the Sugar Point and Bear Island happenings. Together with each Anishinaabe invocation of "midewiwin singers/under cedar boughs," "manidoo," "gichiziibi" (the Mississippi) or Bugonaygeshig as "midewiwin healer," the effect is to lift the 1898 Minnesota episode into iconographic history, history "real" as need be but also transposed into symbolic-visionary realm. "The red sumac/brightens memories," it is said at the outset, the battle not merely one of newspaper report but enseamed in Anishinaabe speech-remembrance in kind with communal "creation story," "sandy shallows," the lore and presence of woodland, fauna, flora, and the always all-present bird and animal life.

"Bagwana: The Pillagers of Liberty," the second sequence, having invoked "native rights" as against "treaty decadence," "cedar stands" as against "greed and guile," and with Leech Lake and the reservation in view, invites witness, memory (19–36). Six soldiers die, unnecessarily and near-farcically "over the turnips/cabbage and potatoes" in Bugonayshig's "ragged garden" (20). This might well be a drama to recall the earlier Dakotas fight ("for the wanton/unforgivable murder/of a pillager child") with its one Anishinaabe survivor in the person of Bugaunak. Even, too, amid the killing, there has been the "scent of cedar" and "summer colors." Past white-Native history, however, yields the far more accusing litany. Vizenor's phrasings might be the route-markers of a tapestry, a précis of sorts, for the so-called winning of the west: "crown agents," "weary traders," "miners," "mountain men," "missions of genocide," "deadly pathogens," Sand Creek's "colorado militia," "frontier treachery" and "prairie genocide." It is against this back-cloth, "the cruelty/of american creation," that "the war/that afternoon/in a vegetable garden" takes place. It derives further ironic gloss from Whitman's benchmark of "liberty" in *Leaves of Grass* as cited in the volume's prefatory extract ("Liberty relies upon itself, invites no one, promises nothing . . . is positive and composed, and knows no discouragement"), the contradance of one order of freedom at the expense of another.

"Hole in the Day/Grafters and Warrants," the third sequence, takes up the course of action with Bugonaygeshig ("bear island pillager/midewiwin healer/elusive warrior") as contrarily both present yet also absentee main player (39–50). In a setting of Walker Bay and the Onigum Agency, and a dark, storm-driven Leech Lake dockside, recollection is made of how "shady agents" have cheated the Anishinaabe Pillagers of treaty-guaranteed annuities. The upshot is "hungry children," a "bogus/bootleg trial" with Bugonaygeshsig commandeered for attendance in Duluth at the instigation of Colonel Tinker and Deputy Marshall Robert Morrison, his one-hundred-mile walk back after being "removed/from an empty boxcar," and the would-be subsequent arrest and escape with the aid of "twenty warriors."

This run of events Vizenor tells in his own synoptic image-play, typically "hole in the day/returned to the bears," "creases of abuse," "visions of resistance," "false warrants/ captured natives," and "sentiments of survivance." He also specifies the harassment of Bugonaygeshig with allusions to "federal legacies" and the overstatement "of a native menace/by telegram." But far from "straight" history, mere recitation of event, the verse continuingly calls up a tribal-animist context. As each installment happens a kind of counter-drama takes place. Ravens "bounce/and crack," "dream songs" are to be heard, "cedar and willow" supply a sightline, "tender fern" and "wild roses" grow, and "sacred otter," "redwinged blackbirds" and "mighty white pine" exert their dominion even as the timber and flour industries cut into the natural land and air (45–50). In the seizure, and then escape, of Bugonaygeshig, white jurisprudence plays against "natural reason," settler writ against an Anishinaabe tribal sense of life and order. Vizenor's imagery of contradance continues to keep pace.

"Bearwalkers: 5 October 1898," the fourth sequence, gives portraits of the duelists involved (51–73). General Bacon, of the Texas Indian wars, Major Melville Wilkinson, veteran of wars against the Nez Perce, Colonel Sheehan and Lieutenant Ross who respectively will command the left and right flank, take off to Bear Island aboard a Walker Timber Company streamer at the head of seventy-seven "wary soldiers." The Pillager warriors "at the tree line," in contrast, are to be thought "bearwalkers/ spirits of the night," "a natural presence." The scene transposes into no epic battleground, however, but "a spacious garden/turnips and potatoes/ cabbage and cucumbers." This is by the book officer-and-soldier army versus "native warriors," "fugitive warriors." The former, "blue immigrants," "blue soldiers," find themselves pitted against a tribal people of "birch bark houses" and "cedar smoke," each one of them "circle dancers" even as they carry their own Winchesters.

The encounter, as the poem in choric vein observes, is to become "capital news," headlines of "troops battle savages" and "rumored massacre/ of one hundred men." Wilkinson will die of wounds. The stray bullet that causes the exchange of fire has come from a "krag jorgensen/a new norwegian/magazine rifle." Camouflage, "a native garden," army recruits pitched against the Pillagers, Sergeant Butler the first dead of a bullet to the head, shouts of "give 'em hell" as against a "boy warrior" dancing and shouting in Anishinaabe in taunt of the army soldiers, and bullets striking arm, thigh and belly, all fuse into the day's drama. A "bloody garden" is one of Vizenor's concluding expressions in the sequence, the paradoxically perfect literal metaphor, both implicitly Adamic and postlapsarian, for what has just occurred.

"Gatling Gun: 6 October" 1898 (77–82) and "War Necklace: 9 October 1898" (85–93), the two brief closing sequences, act as elegy, two acts of rumination. In "Gatling Gun" four presences are invoked: Lieutenant Colonel Abram Horbach, with two hundred infantry and a gatling gun brought to end for ever Native resistance; German-born Daniel Schallenstocker, "the last casualty," dead at twenty-nine amid the potatoes; Schallenstocker's "native warrior" killer; and Chief White Cloud, would-be last peace emissary and intermediary. Each has been embroiled in an action accidental yet also willed into being by massive, not to say ritual, error. It is says the poems, "a chance war," one "provoked by arrogance" at the hands of federal agents and "mercenaries/of the white pine" (81).

"War Necklace," the allusion to the necklace made by Bugonaygeshig from the left-over cartridges, takes on its own symbolism: the whole affray a war necklace, men on both sides caught in the brute historical circle of killing. No triumphalism holds. Pillager land has been "stolen and stained," "trickster creations" have been "corrupted" (85). Yet as the serial of short biographies of the Third Infantry soldier participants reveals Vizenor also extends necessary sympathy to those called to act out, at cost of life or injury, the government's anachronistic last "indian war," its vestigial colonialism. Each is afforded recognition, to include Privates Wicker, Burkhard, Antonelli, Brown, Daly, Jensen, Turner, Boucher, Onsted, Schallenstocker, Ziebel and Lowe, Sergeants Ayers and Butler, Dr. Harris and Brevet Major Wilkinson. But whatever the sympathy his poem at the same time gives rebuke for the underlying arrogance of power, the actions of a consortium of civil authority, Indian agent and the army officers and men.

For "military conceit" has led to funerals, "a last salute" at Fort Snelling and "military ceremonies," and for the living, wounds of flesh, bone, teeth and leg, together with a crippling of "mind and body" (87–93). Wicker would steal ceremonial eagle feathers, Burkhard a sacred drum, Dr. Harris, against his medical calling, "a sacred/birch bark scroll/songs of the anishinaabe/midewiwin ceremonies/the absolute savagery of a combat healer"(88). Their thefts, however, merely underline the larger theft of sovereignty, land, governance, and above all liberty. It cannot be thought less than history's mixed report-card, two bodies of warriordom, Native and non-Native America, caught out by "treacherous/emissary war" (93). The summary final lines, nevertheless, leave no doubt where the preponderance of moral judgment lies. Vizenor calls attention to the betrayal of "treaty rights/and continental liberty" along with "constitutional trickery" (93).

The verse-epic of *Bear Island: The War at Sugar Point*, as the lyric and haiku writing of *Almost Ashore*, works to imaginative good purpose. Each bespeaks contradance, the rear-view mirror. The upshot is genuinely singular verse, postindian flourish, a display of local craft in the service of wholly larger imagining.

Notes

NOTES TO THE INTRODUCTION

1. Herman Melville, Letter to Evert A. Duyckinck, 3 March 1849. *The Letters of Herman Melville*, eds., Merrell R. Davis and William H. Gilman, New Haven: Yale University Press, 1969, 78.
2. Lorna Sage, "Angela Carter." *The Guardian*, February 17, 1992.
3. *The Wild One* (1953). Directed by Lázló Benedek. Produced by Stanley Kramer, Columbia Pictures.
4. Walter Lippmann, *Public Opinion*, New York: Harcourt, Brace & Company, 1922. The term is notably taken up by Noam Chomsky and Edward S. Herman, *Manufactured Consent: The Political Economy of the Media*, New York: Pantheon Books, 1988.
5. Herman Melville, *The Confidence-Man: His Masquerade*, New York: Dix, Edwards, & Co., 1857; Mark Twain, *What is Man?*, London: Watts & Co., 1906; Ambrose Bierce, "An Occurrence at Owl Creek Ridge," reprinted in *An Occurrence at Owl Creek Ridge and Other Stories*, Mineola, New York: Dover Publications, 2008, and *The Devil's Dictionary*, originally published as *The Cynic's Word Book*, New York: Doubleday, Page & Co., 1906, subsequently as *The Devil's Dictionary* in Vol. 7, *The Collected Works of Ambrose Bierce*, New York: Neale Pub. Co., 1909–11; and Nathanael West, *Miss Lonelyhearts*, New York: Liveright, Inc., 1933 and *The Day of the Locust*, New York: Random House, 1939.
6. Randolph Bourne, "Trans-National America," *Atlantic Monthly*, 118, July 1916.
7. Arthur M. Schlesinger Jr., *The Disuniting of America: Reflections on a Multicultural Society*, New York: W.W. Norton, 1992; Lawrence W. Levine, *The Opening of the American Mind: Canons, Culture, and History*, Boston: Beacon Press, 1996; and Ronald T. Takaki, *A Different Mirror: A History of Multicultural America*, Boston: Little, Brown and Co., 1993.
8. Allen Ginsberg, letter to Richard Eberhardt. Reprinted in *Eberhardt to Ginsberg: A Letter about HOWL*, Lincoln, Massachusetts: Pennean, 1976; Jack Kerouac, *On The Road*, New York: Viking, 1957; Gregory Corso, *The Vestal Lady of Brattle and Other Poems*, Cambridge, Massachusetts: Richard Brukenfeld, 1955, and San Francisco: City Lights Books, 1968, *Gasoline*, San Francisco: City Lights Books, 1958, subsequently reprinted as *Gasoline/ The Vestal Lady of Brattle*, San Francisco: City Lights Books, 1968; William Burroughs, *The Naked Lunch*, Paris: Olympia Press, 1959, *Naked Lunch*, New York: Grove Press, 1962; and Lawrence Ferlinghetti, *Pictures of the gone world*, San Francisco: City Lights Book, 1955, and *A Coney Island of the Mind*, New York: New Directions, 1958.

9. John Clellon Holmes, *Go*, New York: Scribner's 1952, reprinted with Introduction, New York: Thunder's Mouth Press, 1988; Joyce Johnson, *Door Wide Open: A Beat Affair in Letters, 1957–1958*, New York: Viking, 2000; LeRoi Jones/Imamu Amiri Baraka, *Preface to a Twenty Volume Suicide Note*, New York: Token Press/Corinth, 1961; and Herbert Huncke, *Guilty of Everything*, Madras, New York: Hanuman Press, 1987, New York: Paragon House, 1990.

10. Hunter Thompson, *Hell's Angels: A Strange and Terrible Saga*, New York: Random House, 1967, and *Fear and Loathing in Las Vegas: A Savage Journey to the Heart of the American Dream*, New York: Random House, 1972.

11. Joan Didion, *Slouching Towards Bethlehem*, New York: Farrar, Straus & Giroux, 1968, and *The White Album*, New York: Simon and Schuster, 1979.

12. Kathy Acker, *Politics*, New York: Papyrus Press, 1972, and *The Childlike Life of the Black Tarantula: Some Lives of Murderesses*, San Francisco: Community Congress Press, 1973. Expanded edition, *The Childlike Life of the Black Tarantula by the Black Tarantula*, New York: TVRT Press, 1975, also in *Portrait of an Eye: Three Novels*, New York: Pantheon, 1992.

13. Frank Chin, *The Chinaman Pacific & Frisco R.R.Co.*, Minneapolis: Coffee House Press, 1988, *Donald Duk*, Minneapolis: Coffee House Press, 1991, *Gunga Din Highway*, Minneapolis: Coffee House Press, 1994, and *Bulletproof Buddhists and Other Essays*, Honolulu: University of Hawai'i Press, in association with UCLA Asian American Studies Center, 1998.

14. Jessica Hagedorn, ed. *Charlie Chan is Dead: An Anthology of Asian American Fiction*, New York: Penguin Books, 1993.

15. Jessica Hagedorn, *Dogeaters*, New York: Random House/Penguin, 1990, *The Gangster of Love*, New York: Pantheon, 1996, and *Dream Jungle*, New York: Viking, 2003.

16. William Demby, *Beetlecreek*, New York: Rinehart, 1950, *The Catacombs*, New York: Random House, 1965, and *Love Story Black*, New York: E.P. Dutton, 1978.

17. Gerald Vizenor, *Almost Ashore: Selected Poems*, Cambridge, UK: Salt Publishing, 2006, and *Bear Island: The War at Sugar Point*, Minneapolis: University of Minnesota Press, 2006.

NOTES TO CHAPTER 1

1. "Notes on The Beat Generation" was initially published by Snyder in 1960 in Japan with the journal *Chuo-koron*, 1960. Snyder republished it in *American Poetry*, Vol. 2, No. 1, Fall 1984, and in *A Place in Space: Ethics, Aesthetics, Watersheds*, Washington DC: Counterpoint, 1995.

2. Allen Ginsberg, "Poetry, Violence, and The Trembling Lambs," *San Francisco Chronicle*, July 26, 1959.

3. Allen Ginsberg, *Howl and Other Poems*, San Francisco: City Lights Books, 1956; Jack Kerouac, *On The Road*, New York: Viking, 1957; Gregory Corso, *The Vestal Lady on Brattle and Other Poems* Cambridge, Massachusetts: Richard Brukenfeld, 1955, and San Francisco: City Lights Books, 1968, *Gasoline*. San Francisco: City Lights Books, 1958, reprinted 1973, *Gasoline/The Vestal Lady on Brattle*, San Francisco: City Lights Books, 1968; William Burroughs, *The Naked Lunch*, Paris: Olympia Press, 1959, *Naked Lunch*, New York: Grove Press, 1962; Lawrence Ferlinghetti, *Pictures of the gone world*, San Francisco: City Lights Books, 1955, and *A Coney Island of the Mind*, New York: New Directions, 1958.

4. Were one attempting yet fuller coverage the roster would include, among still others, Gary Snyder, Jack Micheline, David Meltzer, Andy Clausen, Sy Perkhoff, Philomene Lang, and Albert Saijo.

5. Cited by Joyce Johnson in *Door Wide Open: A Beat Love Affair in Letters, 1857–1958*, New York: Viking Penguin, 2000, xxii.

6. William Burroughs, "Remembering Jack Kerouac," 1985, 1986. Reprinted in William Burroughs, *Word Virus: The William S. Burroughs Reader*, New York: Grove Press, 2000.

7. A typical recent European conference would be "Cultural Icons: City Lights and The Pocket Book," held at the University of Rome (Roma Tre) in December 2002. This led to the collection: Maria Anita Stefanelli, ed. *City Lights and Pocket Books*, Ila Palma: Mazzone Editori, 2004.

8. Ed Sanders, *Tales of Beatnik Glory*, New York: Stonehill Publishing, 1975, 2. This volume became Vol. I of the two-volume *Tales of Beatnik Glory*, New York: Citadel Underground, 1998. A third version was published as *Tales of Beatnik Glory*, New York: Thunder's Mouth Press, 2004.

9. Norman Podhoretz, "The Know-Nothing Bohemians," *Partisan Review*, XXV: 2, Spring 1958, 305–11, 313–16, 318. Republished in Norman Podhoretz, *Doings and Undoings: The Fifties and After in American Writing*, New York: Farrar, Straus and Company, 1964.

10. Robert Brustein, "The Cult of Unthink," *Horizon*, Vol. 1, No. 1, 1958, 38–45, 134–5.

11. For a valuable synopsis of the literary and popular culture impact of the Beats see John Tytell. "The Beat Legacy," in Cornelis A. van Minnen, Jaap van der Bent and Mel van Elteren eds. *Beat Culture: The 1950s and Beyond*, Amsterdam: VU University Press, 1999, 269–74.

12. David Halberstam, *The Fifties*, New York: Villard Books, 1993.

13. Cited in Barry Miles, *Jack Kerouac: King of The Beats, A Portrait*, New York: Henry Holt & Co., 1998, 263.

14. Jack Kerouac: *Road Novels 1957–1960 (On The Road, The Dharma Bums, The Subterraneans, Tristessa, Lonesome Traveler)*, New York: Library of America, 2007; David Gates, "Road Rules," *Newsweek*, August 13, 2007, 51–2; Walter Salles, *On The Road*, script and film currently in progress.

15. Allen Ginsberg, *Death and Fame: Poems 1993–1995*, New York: Harper-Flamingo, 1999, xv.

16. Allen Ginsberg to Eberhardt, 1956. Reprinted *To Eberhardt from Ginsberg: A Letter About HOWL*, Lincoln, Massachusetts: Pennean Press, 1976.

17. Richard Eberhardt, "West Coast Rhythms," *New York Times Book Review*, September 6 1956. Eberhardt speaks of "Howl" as "the most remarkable poem of the young group."

18. *To Eberhardt from Ginsberg: A Letter About HOWL*, 1976.

19. Hollander's review and Ginsberg's letter of September 7 1958 to him are also reprinted in Matt Theado, ed. *The Beats: A Literary Reference*, New York: Carroll and Graf, 2001, 250–52. Also: Bill Morgan and Nancy J. Peters, eds. *Howl on Trial: The Battle for Free Expression*, San Francisco: City Lights, 2006, 84–101. Ginsberg speaks emphatically of his interest in "poetry techniques," his impatience with being berated for "juvenile delinquency, vulgarity, lack of basic education, bad taste, etc, etc, no form etc." He then sets out, much along the lines of the letter to Eberhardt how the envisioned structure of "Howl." Part I "uses repeated base *who*, as a sort of kithara BLANG, Homeric (in my imagination) to mark off each statement, each rhythmic unit. So that's experiment with longer & shorter variations on a fixed base— the principle being, that each line has to be contained within the elastic of one breath . . ." In Part II "the basic repeated word is Moloch. The long line

is now broken up into component with "rhythmical punctuation." Part III , "perhaps an original invention," amounts to "a sort of free verse prose poem STANZA form invented or used here." "Footnote to Howl" he describes as "too lovely & serious a joke to try to explain. The built-in rhythmic exercise should be clear, it's basically a repeat of the Moloch section. It's dedicated to my mother who died in the madhouse and it says I loved her anyway & that even in the worst conditions life is holy."

20. Ginsberg's interest in poetics was always considerable. See, for instance, his considerations of reflexivity in *Indian Journals March 1962-May 1963*, New York: Grove Press, 1970. He writes "Poetry XX Century like all arts and science is devolving into examination-experimentation on the very material of which it's made." 38.

21. Gregory Corso, "Elegaic Feelings American: *for the dear memory of Jack Kerouac*," *Elegaic Feelings American*, New Directions 1970, 3–12.

22. For a careful consideration of Sal's role and voice see, for instance, R. J. Ellis, *Liar! Liar! Jack Kerouac Novelist*, London: Greenwich Exchange, 1999, 67–86.

23. Gilbert Millstein, *The New York Times*, September 5, 1957.

24. Jack Kerouac, "Bath Tub Thought," *Pomes All Sizes*, San Francisco: City Lights Books, 1992. Interestingly Allen Ginsberg uses this notion of word-as-Buddha in his *Allen Verbatim*, New York: McGraw Hill Book Company, 1974. Speaking of Kerouac's response to a suggestion by Malcolm Cowley that he "write a sort of nice, simple-sentenced book so people can understand your ideas" Ginsberg observes "So Kerouac took it as a challenge and did write a great little classic called *Dharma Bums*, with short sentences, like haikus, actually."

25. These terms are to be found in Kerouac's Introduction to *Lonesome Traveler*, Drawings by Larry Rivers, New York: McGraw-Hill, 1960. The relevant paragraph reads: "Had own mind.—Am known as "madman bum and angel" with "naked endless head" of "prose."—Also a verse poet, *Mexico City Blues* (Grove, 1959.—Always considered writing my duty on earth. Also the preachment of universal kindness, which hysterical critics have failed to notice beneath frenetic activity of my true-story novels about the 'beat' generation.—Am actually not 'beat' but strange solitary crazy Catholic mystic . . ."

26. Jack Kerouac to Allen Ginsberg, May 10 1952. Anne Charters ed. *Jack Kerouac: Selected Letters, 1940–1956*, New York: Viking Penguin, 1955, 353.

27. Lawrence Ferlinghetti, *Woodstock Journal*, Vol. 6, September 2000.

28. Cover notes, reprint of Gregory Corso, *Gasoline/The Vestal Lady on Brattle*, San Francisco: City Lights, 1969.

29. Gregory Corso, *Mindfield: New and Selected Poems*, New York: Thunder's Mouth Press, 1989.

30. Ann Douglass, " 'Punching a hole in the big lie': The Achievement of William Burroughs," Introduction, James Grauerholz and Ira Silverberg, eds. *Word Virus: The William Burroughs Reader*, New York: Grove Press/Atlantic, 1998, xv.

31. Mary McCarthy, "Burroughs' *Naked Lunch*," *Encounter*, April 1963, 92–8

32. J.G. Ballard, "Introduction," *Naked Lunch*, London: Flamingo Modern Classic, 1993.

33. Burroughs speaks explicitly and helpfully on the word as virus in Robert Palmer, "The 1972 Rolling Stone Interview: William S. Burroughs," Holly George-Warren, ed. *Book of The Beats: The Beat Generation and American Culture*, New York: Hyperion, 1999, 182.

34. For an informed perspective on Burroughs's debts to Korzybski and his views on language as authority see David Ingram "William Burroughs and Language," in A. Robert Lee, ed. *The Beat Generation Writers*, London and East Haven, Connecticut: Pluto Press, 1996, 95–113.

35. Anne Waldman to A. Robert Lee, personal communication.

36. John Clellon Holmes, *Go*, New York: Scribner's, 1952; reissued New York: Thunder's Mouth Press, 1976, 1988, Introduction, xvii- xxiii.

37. John Clellon Holmes, *Go*, New York: Scribner's, 1952.

38. LeRoi Jones/Amiri Baraka, *The Autobiography of LeRoi Jones/Amiri Baraka*, New York: Freundlich Books, 1984. Revised edition, New York: Thunder's Mouth Press, 1991, 156.

39. LeRoi Jones, "How Do You Sound?," Donald Allen, ed. *The New American Poetry*, 1960, 424.

40. Arthur and Kit Knights, eds. *The Beat Vision: A Primary Sourcebook*, New York: Paragon House Publishers, 1987, 131.

41. Amiri Baraka, *The LeRoi Jones/Amiri Baraka Reader*, ed. William J. Harris, New York: Paragon House Publishers, 1991.

42. LeRoi Jones, *Preface to a Twenty Volume Suicide Note*, New York: Totem Press/Corinth, 1961.

43. Barbara Probst Solomon, *The Beat of Life*, New York: J. B. Lippincott, 1960. Reissued New York: Great Marsh Press, 1999, "Forward," i.

44. Michael McClure, *Lighting the Corners: On Art, Nature, and The Visionary*, Albuquerque: University of New Mexico Arts and Sciences, 1993, 283.

45. Michael McClure, *The Beard*, New York: Grove Press, 1965.

46. Michael McClure, "Painting Beat by Numbers," Holly George-Warren, ed. *The Rolling Stone Book Of The Beats: The Beat Generation and American Culture*, New York: Hyperion, 1999, 32.

47. Diane di Prima, *Memoirs of a Beatnik*, New York and Paris: Olympia Press, 1969. Reprinted San Francisco: Last Gasp Press, and New York: Penguin Books, 1998, 191–93.

48. Ira Cohen, "Interview," *Goodie Magazine*, No. 1, 1999.

49. Irving Rosenthal, *Sheeper*, New York: Grove Press, 1967.

50. William Burroughs, cover-note, *Sheeper*, 1967.

51. "Bonnie Bremser (Brenda Frazer)," in Nancy M. Grace and Ronna C. Johnson, eds. *Breaking The Rule of Cool: Interviewing and Reading Women Beat Writers*, Jackson, Mississippi: University Press Of Mississippi, 2004, 112.

52. Bonnie Bremser, *Troia: Mexican Memoirs*, New York: Croton Press, 1969, reprinted as *For Love of Ray*, London: Tandem Press, London Magazine Editions, 1971.

53. William Burroughs, Foreword, Harold Norse, *Beat Hotel*, San Diego: Atticus Press, 1983, i.

54. Harold Norse, *Beat Hotel*, San Diego: Atticus Press, 1983.

55. Harold Norse, *Memoirs of a Bastard Angel: A Fifty-Year Literary and Erotic Odyssey*, New York: Thunder's Mouth Press, 1989.

56. *Memoirs of A Bastard Angel: A Fifty-Year Literary and Erotic Odyssey*, 349.

57. Herbert Huncke, *The Herbert Huncke Reader*, ed. Ron Schafer, New York: William S. Morrow, 1997. Foreword un-numbered.

58. Herbert Huncke, *Guilty of Everything*, Madras, New York: Hanuman Books, New York: Paragon House, 1990.

59. Herbert Huncke, *Huncke's Journal*, New York: Poets Press, 1965, and *The Evening Sun Turns Crimson*, Cherry Valley, New York: Cherry Valley Editions, 1980.

60. Joyce Johnson, "Beat Queens: Women in Flux," in Holly George-Warren, ed. *The Rolling Stone Book of The Beats: The Beat Generation and American Culture*, New York: Hyperion, 1999, 45.

61. Joyce Johnson, *Minor Characters: A Memoir of a Young Woman of the 1950s in the Beat Orbit of Jack Kerouac*, Boston: Houghton, Mifflin Company, 1953.

62. Joyce Johnson, *Door Wide Open: A Beat Love Affair in Letters, 1957–1958*, New York: Viking, 2000.

NOTES TO CHAPTER 2

1. Diane di Prima, "Anne Waldman Talks With Diane di Prima," Arthur and Kit Knight, eds. *The Beat Vision: A Primary Sourcebook*, New York: Paragon House Publishers, 1987, 143.

2. Joanne Kyger, *About Now*, Orono, Maine: National Poetry Foundation, 2007, 618.

3. Anne Waldman, Fast Speaking Woman," Interview, Nancy M. Grace and Ronna C. Johnson, eds. *Breaking The Rule of Cool: Interviewing and Reading Women Beat Writers*, Jackson, Mississippi: University Press of Mississippi, 2004, 259

4. For contributions to the scholarship see Helen McNeil, "The Archaeology of Gender in the Beat Movement," 178–99, and Amy L. Friedman, " 'I Say My New Name': Women Writers of the Beat Movement," 200–16, in A. Robert Lee, ed. *The Beat Generation Writers*, London and East Haven, Connecticut: Pluto Press, 1996, and the relevant essays in Jennie Skerl, ed. *Reconstructing The Beats*, New York: Palgrave, 2004.

5. Brenda Knight, ed. *Women of the Beat Generation: the Writers, Artists, and Muses at the Heart of a Revolution*, Berkeley: Conari Press, 1996.

6. Richard Peabody, ed. (1997), *A Different Beat: Women of The Beat Generation*, New York: Serpent's Tail, 1997.

7. Ronna C. Johnson and Nancy M. Grace, eds. *Girls Who Wore Black: Women Writing The Beat Generation*, New Brunswick, New Jersey: Rutgers University Press, 2002; Nancy M. Grace and Ronna C. Johnson, eds. *Breaking the Rule Of Cool: Interviewing and Reading Women Beat Writers*, Jackson, Mississippi: University Press of Mississippi, 2004.

8. Diane di Prima, *Recollections of My Life as a Woman: The New York Years, a Memoir*. New York: Viking, 2001; Joanne Kyger, *The Japan and India Journals 1960–1964*, Berkeley: North Atlantic Books, 1981; and Anne Waldman, *Vow to Poetry: Essays, Interviews and Manifestos*, Minneapolis: Coffee House Press, 2001.

9. Carolyn Cassady, *Heart Beat, My Life with Jack and Neal*, Berkeley: Creative Arts, 1976; and *Off The Road, My Years with Cassady, Kerouac and Ginsberg*, New York: William Morrow and Company, 1990.

10. Bonnie Bremser (Bonnie Frazer), *Troia: Mexican Memoirs*, New York: Croton Press,1969, reprinted as *For Love of Ray*, London: Tandem Press, London magazine Editions, 1971; Joyce Johnson, *Minor Characters: A Memoir of a Young Woman of the 1950s in the Beat Orbit of Jack Kerouac*, Boston: Houghton Mifflin Company, 1983; and Hettie Jones, *How I Became Hettie Jones*, New York: E.P. Dutton, 1988.

11. Joan Haverty Kerouac, *Nobody's Wife: The Smart Aleck and The King of the Beats*, Berkeley: Creative Arts Books,. 2000. Edie Parker Kerouac, *You'll Be OK: My Life with Jack Kerouac*, San Francisco: City Lights Books, 2007.

12. Ellen Kaufman, "Laughter Sounds Orange at Night," in Arthur and Kit Knight, eds. *The Beat Vision: A Primary Sourcebook*, New York: Paragon House Publishers, 1986, 259–67.

13. Joanna McClure, *Wolf Eyes*, San Francisco: Bearthm Press, 1974.

14. Anne Charters, *Beats and Company: A Portrait of a Literary Generation*, Garden City: Doubleday Company, 1986; ed. *The Portable Beat Reader*, New York: Viking-Penguin, 1992; and ed. *Beat Down To Your Soul: What Was The Beat Generation?*, New York: Penguin, 2001.

15. Camlle Paglia, *Vamps and Tramps: New Essays*, New York: Vintage Books, 1994.

16. Denise Levertov, *Here and Now*, San Francisco: City Lights Books, 1957.

17. A first-ever selection of Cowen's poems is published in *Women of the Beat Generation*, 158–65.

18. Ruth Weiss, *Desert Journal*, Boston: Good Day Poets, 1977.

19. Janine Pommy Vega, *Poems to Fernando*, San Francisco: City Lights Books, 1968; *Tracking The Serpent: Journeys to Four Continents*, San Francisco: City Lights Books, 1997.

20. Joanna McClure, *Wolf Eyes*, San Francisco: Bearthm Press, 1974; *Extended Love Poems*, Berkeley: Arif Press, 1978; and *Hard Edge*, Minneapolis: Coffee House Press, 1987.

21. Lenore Kandel, *The Love Book*, San Francisco: Stolen Paper Review Edition, 1966.

22. Mary Norbert Körte, *Beginnings of Lines: Responses to Albion Moonlight*, Berkeley: Oyez Press, 1968; *The Generation of Love*, New York: Bruce Publications, 1969; and *The Midnight Bridge*, Berkeley: Oyez Press, 1970.

23. Mary Fabilli, *Aurora Bligh and Early Poems*, Berkeley: Oyez Press, 1968; *The Animal Kingdom: Poems 1964–1974*, Berkeley: Oyez Press, 1975; and *Poems 1976–1981*, Murray, Kentucky, 1981.

24. Patti Smith, *Seventh Heaven*, Berkeley: Telegraph Books, 1972.

25. Patti Smith, "Introduction," *Gregory Corso: An Accidental Autobiography: the Selected Letters of Gregory Corso*, New York: New Directions, 2003.

26. Allen Ginsberg, *Daily Camera Magazine*, Boulder, Colorado, July 1989.

27. The Amram quotation is from publicity for di Prima's writing.

28. Anthony Libby's "Diane di Prima: 'Nothing Is Lost; It Shines in Our Eyes', *Girls Who Wore Black*, 2004, gives a well-taken account of her "career path," 45–68.

29. Diane di Prima, *This Kind of Bird Flies Backward*, New York: Totem Press, 1958; *Loba: Part I*, Santa Barbara, Capra Press, 1973, *Loba, Part* II, Point Reyes: Eidolon Editions, 1974, *Loba, Parts I-VII*, Berkeley: Wingbow Press, 1978. *Loba, Parts I-XVI*, Books 1 and 2, New York: Penguin Books, 1998; *The New Handbook of Heaven*, San Francisco: Auerhahn Press, 1962, 1965; *New Mexico Poems*, New York: Poets Press, 1967; *Earthsong: Poems 1957–1959*, New York: Poets Press, 1968; *L.A. Odyssey*, New York: Poets Press, 1969; and *The Calculus of Variation*, San Francisco: City Lights Books, 1972.

30. Diane di Prima, *Dinners and Nightmares*, New York: Corinth Books, 1961.

31. Diane di Prima, *Murder Cafe*, New York: Living Theater, 1960.

32. Diane di Prima, *Memoirs of a Beatnik*, Paris: Olympia Press, 1969, reprinted New York: Last Gasp Press, 1969, and New York: Penguin Books, 1988; *Selected Poems, 1956–1975*, Plainfield: North Atlantic Books, 1975.

33. Ron Silliman to Linda Russo, April 18 1998. EPC/Kyger Author Web Page. epc.buffalo.edu/authors/kyger. Also used as a cover quotation for Joanne Kyger, *Again: Poems 1989–2000*, Albuquerque: La Alameda Press, 2001.

34. Joanne Kyger, All poems cited are to be found variously in Joanne Kyger, *Going On: Selected Poems 1958–80*, New York: Dutton, 1983; *Again: Poems 1989–2000*, Albuquerque, La Alameda Press, 2001; and *As Ever: Selected Poems*, New York: Penguin, and *About Now: Selected Poems*, New York: Dutton, 2006.
35. Joanne Kyger, *The Tapestry and The Web*, San Francisco: Four Seasons Foundation, 1965; *About Now: Collected Poems*, Orono: The National Poetry Foundation, 2006.
36. Joanne Kyger, *Some Sketches From the Life of Helena Petrovna Blavasky*, Boulder: Rodent Press & Erudite Fangs, 1996.
37. H.D., *Helen in Egypt*, New York: Grove Press, 1961; Anne Waldman, *Iovis: All is Full of Jove*, Vol. 1, Minneapolis: Coffee House Press, 1993, and *Iovis: All is Full of Jove*, Vol., II, Coffee House Press, 2003.
38. Joanne Kyger, "Place To Go," Nancy M. Grace and Ronna C. Johnson, eds. *Breaking The Rule of Cool: Interviewing and Reading Women Beat Writers*, 2004, 166.
39. Anne Waldman, "Grasping The Broom more Tightly Now," Interview with Eric Lorberer, *Rain Taxi Review of Books*, June 1998. Reprinted in Anne Waldman, *Vow To Poetry: Essays, Interviews, & Manifestos*, Minneapolis: Coffee House Press, 2001, 292.
40. Anne Waldman, *Helping The Dreamer: New and Selected Poems, 1966–1990*, Minneapolis: Coffee House Press, 1987; and *In The Room of Never Grieve: New and Selected Poems 1985–2003*, Minneapolis: Coffee House Press, 2003.
41. Ann Waldman, *Contemporary Autobiography Series*, Detroit, Michigan: Gale Research, 1993, 271.
42. William Burroughs, *My Education*, New York: Viking, 1995, 26.
43. Anne Waldman, *Structure of the World Compared to a Bubble*, New York and London: Penguin Books, 2004.
44. Anne Waldman, *Fast Speaking Woman*, San Francisco: City Lights Books, 1985. *Fast Speaking Woman*, 20th Anniversary Edition, San Francisco: City Lights Books, 1996.
45. Nancy M. Grace and Ronna C. Johnson, eds. *Breaking The Rule of Cool: Interviewing and Reading Women Beat Writers*, 2004, 269.

NOTES TO CHAPTER 3

1. Ted Joans, "Je Me Vois (I See Myself)," in Shelley Andrews, ed. *Contemporary Authors Autobiography Series*, Detroit: Gale, 1996, Vol. 25, 242.
2. Ted Joans, "Je Me Vois (I See Myself)," 227.
3. Ted Joans, *Beat Poems*, New York: Derection, 1957; *Beat Funky Jazz Poems*, New York: Nuderection Press, 1959; *All of Ted Joans and No More: Poems and Collages*, New York: Excelsior Press, 1960; *Black Pow-Wow: Jazz Poems*, New York: Hill and Wang, 1969; *Afrodisia: Old and New Poems*, New York: Hill and Wang, 1970; and *Teducation: Selected Poems 1949–1999*, Saint Paul, Minnesota: Coffee House Press, 1999.
4. The Bancroft Library at the University of California at Berkeley has acquired a collection of Joans's manuscripts and out of print early writings.
5. *Teducation: Selected Poems 1949–1999*, Saint Paul, Minnesota: Coffee House Press, 1999. "Sanctified Rhino" 72–3.
6. Ted Joans, *Teducation*, "Jazz Anatomy," 170, "The Statue of 1713," 220–23.
7. *Teducation*, "The Ladder of Basquiat," 83–88.

8. *Teducation*, "Harlem to Picasso," 31. Like "Sanctified Rhino" "Harlem to Picasso" was first published in *Afrodisia: Old & New Poems*, New York: Hill, 1969.
9. *Teducation*, "The Sax Bit," 92.
10. The canvas has now been acquired by the De Young Museum.
11. *Teducation*, "They Forget Too Fast," 98, and "Ice Freezes Red," 39–41.
12. *Black Pow-Wow: Jazz Poems*, New York: Hill, 1969. "Jazz Must Be a Woman," 76–77.
13. *Teducation*, "Jazz is . . .," 48.
14. *Teducation*, "Long Gone Lover Blues," 57, and "Commonplace Bulues," 142–43.
15. *Teducation*, "Jazz Me Surreally Do," 173.
16. *Teducation*, "Happy 78 Hughes Blues," 28.
17. *Teducation*, "Another Dream Deferred?," 7.
18. *Teducation*, "Promised Land," 69.
19. *Teducation*, "Passed on Blues: Homage to a Poet," 65–67.
20. "Ted Joans on Langston Hughes," Interview by St. Clair Bourne. *Langston Hughes Review*, 15:2, 1997, 71–77.
21. "Je Me Vois," 225.
22. *Teducation*, "Laughter you've gone and . . ." 178–79.
23. Joans within this African American context I explore in A. Robert Lee, "The Black Beats: The Signifying Poetry of LeRoi Jones/Amiri Baraka, Bob Kaufman and Ted Joans," in A. Robert Lee ed. *The Beat Generation Writers*, London and East Haven, Connecticut: Pluto Press, 1995. This is revised and expanded as Chapter 7, 133–51, of my *Designs of Blackness: Mappings in The Literature and Culture of Afro-America*, London and East Haven, Connecticut: Pluto Press, 1999, and in turn reprinted in Anne Charters, ed. *Beat Down to Your Soul: What Was The Beat Generation?*, New York: Penguin, 2001, 303–28.
24. *Teducation*, "The Sermon," 94.
25. "Gerald Nicosia Talks with Ted Joans," Arthur Winfield Knight and Kit Knight, eds. *Beat Vision: A Primary Sourcebook*, New York: Paragon, 1987, 271–83.
26. Joans has long made a distinction between Beat and Beatnik. In "Je Me Vois" he cites a college newspaper report of one of his 1950s readings. "Unlike most poets of the beat generation, Ted Joans who spoke here Thursday, refuses to be called a beatnik. He is a "jazz poet of the beat generation." (235). In his poem "Don't let The Minute Spoil The Hour," republished in *Afrodisia*, he makes the point yet more emphatic in the lines:
    HE IS A BEATNIK
    AND THUS THE lovesick ARTIST IS DEAD!
27. Ted Joans, "The Beat Generation and Afro-American Cultures," *Beat Scene Magazine*, December 1991, 22–3.
28. Nicosia, 274.
29. *Teducation*, "the Wild Spirit of Kicks," 97.
30. *Teducation*, "Dead Serious," 99.
31. "Je Me Vois," 220.
32. Further detail can be found in Fred McDarrah, *Kerouac & Friends: A Beat Generation Album*, New York: William Morrow, 1985. Shaping other affiliations and friendships include Hoyt Fuller, Black Aesthetic luminary and the journalist and critic who, as Editor, turned *Negro Digest* into *Black World* and was early to publish Joans's poetry; Harold Cruse, the tough, savvy author of a diagnostic classic like *The Crisis of The Black Intellectual*, New York: Morrow, 1967; Seymour Krim, Jewish Manhattanite and

key anthologist of *The Beats*, Greenwich, Connecticut: Fawcet, 1960; Joyce Mansour, Anglo-Egyptian collector of surrealist art; Jayne Cortez, poet, dramatist, founder of Bola Press and a 1960s Black Arts figure whom Joans, in a making-over of the name for the band in which her son by Ornette Coleman was drummer, calls "a fierce fire-spitter of the truth"; and Alan Ansen, Manhattan literary expatriate, poet, Auden scholar, and promoter of the New York Poets. These, too, need to be given place alongside Joans's Beat connections, co-presences in a life nothing if not always various.

33. "Je Me Vois," 223.
34. *Teducation*, "Him the Bird," 167.
35. *Teducation*, "My Ace of Spades," 59.
36. Ted Joans, *Black Pow-Wow*, " No mo' Kneegrow," 26, "TWO WORDS" 20.
37. David Applefield, Richard Hallward and T. Wignesan eds. *Fire Readings: A Collection of Contemporary Writing From the Shakespeare & Company Fire Benefit Reading*, Vincennes, France: Frank, SARL,1991
38. *Fire Readings*, "Good Morning," 39.
39. *Fire Readings*, "To—*bailer* or not to *éternuer*," 39–40.
40. *Afrodisia*, 64.
41. *Afrodisa*, "Afrique Accidentale," 4–8.
42. Nicosia, Interview, 1987.
43. *Afrodisia*, "Afrique Accidentale," 8.
44. "Je Me Vois," 230.
45. *Afrodisia*, "Afrodisia," 71.
46. *Teducation*, "Eternal Lamp of Lam," 152–55.
47. *Teducation*, "Do Not Walk outside This Area," 52–55.
48. *Teducation*, "*Sor Juana con Bessie Smith*," 153.
49. "Je Me Vois," 219–58.
50. *Teducation*, "A Powerful Black Starmichael," 8.
51. *Black Pow-Wow*, "Nadja Rendezvous," 113.
52. For what has become his posthumous work, see Ted Joans and Laura Corsiglia, *Our Thang*, Victoria, British Columbia, Ekstasis Press, 2001.
53. "Je Me Vois," 253.
54. *Teducation*, "Alphabetical Love You," 125, "Collected & Selected Family Groupings," 139–41, "I Am The Lover," 168–9, "And None Other," 126.
55. *Teducation*, "How Do You Want Yours," 35–38.
56. *Afrodisia*, "God Blame America!!," 79
57. *Afrodisia*, "Dear Miss America," 100.
58. *Teducation*, "Uh Huh," 107
59. *Teducation*, "The Nice Colored Man," 90
60. *Teducation*, "Why Try," 115
61. *Teducation*, "Sanctified Rhino," 72–3.
62. *Teducation*, "Him the Bird," 167.
63. Gerald Nicosia, "Introduction," *Teducation*, ii.
64. "Je Me Vois," 242.

NOTES TO CHAPTER 4

1. "Lamb, No Lion" was first published in *Pageant*, February 1958.
2. Anne Waldman, "Lineages and Legacies." In Ann Charters, ed. *Beat Down To Your Soul: What Was The Beat Generation?*, New York: Penguin, 2001, 590.
3. Allen Ginsberg, *Kaddish and Other Poems: 1958–1960*, San Francisco: City Lights Books, 1961.

4. Harold Norse, *Beat Hotel*, San Diego: Atticus Press, 1983. Prior German edition, *Beat Hotel*, Carl Weismer, Augsburg: Maro Verlag, 1975. Barry Miles, *The Beat Hotel: Ginsberg, Burroughs and Corso in Paris 1957–1963*, New York: Grove Press, 2000.

5. Brion Gysin and William Burroughs, "The 1972 Rolling Stone Interview: William S. Burroughs," Holly George-Warren, ed. *The Rolling Stone of The Beats: The Beat Generation and American Culture*, 183.

6. Kay Johnson, ". . . in Heaven at 9-Git-le-Coeur," reprinted in Richard Peabody, ed. *A Different Beat: Writings by Women of the Beat Generation*, London: Serpent's Tail, 1997, 85–87.

7. Jack Kerouac, *Mexico City Blues*, New York: Grove Press, 1959.

8. William Burroughs and Allen Ginsberg, *The Yage Letters*, San Francisco: City Lights Books, 1963.

9. Paul Bowles, *The Sheltering Sky*, New York: New Directions, 1949, *A Hundred Camels in the Camels in the Courtyard*, San Francisco: City Lights Books, 1962.

10. Jane Bowles, *The Collected Works of Jane Bowles*, New York: Farrar, Straus & Giroux, 1966.

11. *Penguin Modern Poets 5, Gregory Corso, Lawrence Ferlinghetti, Allen Ginsberg*, Harmondsworth, Middlesex: Penguin Books, 1963, 1970.

12. Lawrence Ferlinghetti, *Starting From San Francisco*, Norfolk, Connecticut: New Directions, 1961. Enlarged edition, 1967.

13. *Wholly Communion: International Poetry Reading at the Royal Albert Hall*, London: Lorrimer Films/Publications, New York: Grove Press, 1965.

14. Lawrence Ferlinghetti, "After the Cries of Birds," *The Secret Meaning of Things*, New York: New Directions, 1968, 32–9.

15. See Graham Caveney, *Screaming with Joy: The Life of Allen Ginsberg*, New York: Broadway Books, 1999, 120.

16. Jeff Nuttall, *Bomb Culture*, London: McGibbon and Kee, 1968.

17. Adrian Mitchell, "The Man Who Set Me On Fire—Poet Allen Ginsberg," *New Statesman*, April 1997.

18. Alexander Trocchi, *Cain's Book*, New York: Grove Press, 1960, and *Young Adam* , London: Heineman, 1961.

19. See, for instance, Kurt Hemmer, ed. *Encyclopedia of Beat Literature*, New York: Facts on File, 2007.

20. Iain Sinclair, *The Kodak Mantra Diaries, October 1966 to June 1971*, London: Albion Village Press, 1971. Brian Docherty, *Armchair Theatre*, London: Hearing Eye, 1999.

21. Eric Mottram, "Introduction," Jack Kerouac, *The Scripture of The Golden Eternity*, New York: Corinth Books, 1960. Reprinted San Francisco: City Lights, 1994, *William Burroughs: The Algebra of Need*, Buffalo, New York: Intrepid Press, 1970; 1970, and *Allen Ginsberg in The Sixties*, Brighton, England: Unicorn Press, 1971.

22. Royston Ellis, *Jiving to Gyp*, Northwood: Scorpion Press, 1959, *Rave*, Northwood: Scorpion Press, 1960, *The Big Beat Scene*, London: Four Square, 1961, and *Myself to Face*, London: Consul Books, 1964.

23. Toby Litt, *Beatniks: An English Road Movie*, London: Secker and Warburg, 1997.

24. Wolf Wondratscek, *Menshen. Orte. Fäuste*, Zurich: Diogenese, 1987. I owe the quotation to the excellent account given by Anthony Waine and Jonathan Woolley in " 'Blissful, Torn, Intoxicated': Brinkmann, Fauser, Wondratscek and The Beats," in Jennie Skerl, ed. *College Literature*, 27:1, Winter 200, 177–98. Special issue: Teaching The Beats.

25. Jan Cremer, *I Jan Cremer*, New York: Shorecrest, 1965.

26. Simon Vinkenoog, *Hoogseizoen/High Season*, Amsterdam: De Bezige Bij, 1962. For a greatly informed Dutch response to The Beats see two articles by Jaap van der Bent, " 'Holy Amsterdam Holy Paris': The Beat Generation in Europe," in Cornelius A. van Minnen, Jaap van der Bent and Mel van Elteren, eds. *Beat Culture: The 1950s and Beyond*, Amsterdam: VU Press, 1959, 49–60, and "'O Fellow travelers I write you a poem in Amsterdam': Allen Ginsberg, Simon Vinkenoog, and The Dutch Beat connection," in Jennie Skerl, ed. *College Literature*, 27:1, Winter 2000, 199–121. Special Issue: Teaching The Beats.

27. Michael Dransfield, *Streets of the Long Voyage*, Brisbane and St. Lucia: University of Queensland Press, 1970, *The Inspector of Tides*, Brisbane and St. Lucia: University of Queensland Press, 1972, and *Drug Poems*, Melbourne: Sun Books, 1972.

28. Michael Dransfield, *Collected Poems*, Brisbane and St. Lucia: University of Queensland Press, 1987.

29. Robert Adamson, *Canticles on The Skin*, Sydney: Illumination Press, 1970, and *Inside Out*, Melbourne: Text Publications, 2004.

30. Robert Adamson, *The Rumour*, Sydney: New Press, 1971.

31. Andrew Burke, *Let's Face The Music and Dance*, Subiaco, Western Australia: Peter Jeffery, 1975.

32. Richard Neville, *Hippie, hippie shake: the dreams, the trips, the trials, the love-ins, the screw-ups . . . the Sixties*, London: Bloomsbury, 1995.

33. Kaoru Shoji, *Akazukin-chan Ki Wo Tsukete/Be Careful Little Red Riding Hood*, Tokyo: Kotansha, 1969.

34. Ryu Murakami, *Kagiranaku Tomei Chikai Buru/Almost Transparent Blue*, Tokyo and New York: Kodansha International, 1997.

35. Haruki Murakami, *Noruwei No Mori/Norwegian Wood*, Tokyo: Kodansha International Corporation, 1987. Trans. Jay Rubin, New York: Vintage International, 2000.

36. Nanao Sakaki, *Bellyfulls*, Eugene, Oregon: Toad Press, 1966, *Break The Mirror*, San Francisco: North Point Press, 1996.

37. Kazuko Shiraishi, *Seinaru Inja No Kisetsu/Seasons of Sacred Lust*, New York: New Directions, 1970, 1978.

38. Michael Horovitz, ed. *Children of Albion: Poetry of the Underground in Britain*, Harmondsworth, Middlesex: Penguin Books, 1969.

39. Michael Horovitz, *Wordsounds and Sightlines: New and Selected Poems*, London: Sinclair-Stevenson, 1994.

40. See, in this connection, Chris Challis, *Quest for Kerouac*, London: Faber and Faber, 1984.

41. Michael Horovitz, *Growing Up: Selected Poems and Pictures*, London: Alison and Busby, 1979.

42. Michael Horvitz, *Bank Holiday*, London: Latimer Press, 1967.

43. *Red Cats*, San Francisco: City Lights Books, 1962.

44. Anselm Hollo, "*Red Cats* Revisited," *Ahoe And How on Earth*, Erie, Colorado: Smokeproof Press, 1997. Reprinted in *Notes on the Possibilities and Attractions of Existence: Selected Poems 1965–2000*, Minneapolis: Coffee House Press, 2001, 277.

45. Andrei Voznesensky, *Dogalypse: San Francisco Poetry Reading*, San Francisco: City Lights Books, 1972.

46. Andrei Voznesenky, *Antiworlds, and the Fifth Ace*, Lonodn and Oxford: Oxford University Press, 1967

47. Kazuko Shiraishi, *Tamago No Furu Machi/Falling Egg City*, Tokyo: Kyoritsu Shoten Co., 1951.

48. Kazuko Shiraishi, *Little Planet and Other Poems*, Tokyo: Shichigatsudo Publishing Corporation, 1982, reprinted 1994.

49. Kazuko Shiraishi, *Araweru mnotachi o shite/ Let Those Who Appear*, New York: New Directions, 2002.
50. Kazuko Shiraishi, *Seinaru Inja No Kisetsu/Seasons of Sacred Lust*, New York: New Directions, 1970, 1978.

NOTES TO CHAPTER 5

1. Hunter Thompson, "Jacket Copy for Fear & Loathing in Las Vegas: A Savage Journey to the Heart of the American Dream" (previously unpublished), *The Great Shark Hunt: Strange Tales from a Strange Time*, New York: Summit Books, 1979. Reprinted New York: Simon & Schuster, Gonzo Papers, Volume 1, New York: 2003, 106. Hunter Thomson, *Fear and Loathing in Las Vegas: A Savage Journey to the Heart of the American Dream*, New York: Random House, 1972.
2. Hunter Thompson, *Fear and Loathing: On The Campaign Trail '72*, New York: Random House, 1972. Reprinted New York: Warner Books, 1983, 2006, 33.
3. *Kingdom of Fear: Loathsome Secrets of a Star-Crossed Child in the Final Days of the American Century.* New York: Simon & Schuster, 2003, xxi.
4. *Macbeth*, 1, 4, 7–8.
5. Hunter Thompson, *Hell's Angels: A Strange and Terrible Saga*, New York: Random House, 1967, reprinted New York: Random House/Modern Library Edition, 1999.
6. The latter is used as a prefatory quotation under the name of "Raoul Duke" in *The Great Shark Hunt*.
7. The phrase is taken from the Introduction to the Modern Library edition of *Hell's Angels*, v. All page references are to this edition.
8. Norman Mailer, *Advertisements for Myself*, New York: Putnam, 1959; Truman Capote, *In Cold Blood*, New York: Random House, 1966; and Tom Wolfe, *The Kandy-Colored Tangerine-Flake Streamline Baby*, New York: Farrar, Straus and Girard, 1965, and *Electric Kool-Aid Acid Test*, New York: Farrar, Straus and Girard, 1968.
9. Hunter Thompson, *The Curse of Lomo*, New York: Bantam 1983, reprinted Cologne: Taschen, 2005; *Screwjack and Other Stories*, New York: Simon & Schuster, 1991; and *The Rum Diary: The Long Lost Novel*, New York: Simon & Schuster, 1998.
10. Hunter Thompson, *The Proud Highway: The Saga of a Desperate Southern Gentleman 1955–1967*, New York: Simon & Schuster, 1997, *Fear and Loathing in America: The Brutal Odyssey of an Outlaw Journalist 1968–1976*, New York: Simon & Schuster, 2000, *The Kingdom of Fear: Loathsome Secrets of a Star-Crossed Child in the Final Days of the American Century*, New York: Simon & Schuster, 2003, and *Hey Rube: Blood Sport. The Bush Doctrine, and The Downward Spiral of Dumbness: Modern History from the Sports Desk*, New York: Simon and Schuster, 2004.
11. *Hell's Angels*, 43.
12. "Jacket Copy for Fear and Loathing in Las Vegas," 106.
13. I offer an account of Acosta as writer and activist in A. Robert Lee, "*Chicanismo*'s Beat Outsider? The Texts and Contexts of Oscar Zeta Acosta," in *College Literature*, 27:1, 158–76, Winter 2000, Teaching Beat Literature special edition, ed. Jennie Skerl. Reprinted in Kostas Myrsiades, ed. *The Beat Generation: Critical Essays*, New York: Peter Lang Publishing, 2002, 259–80.

14. *Fear and Loathing in Las Vegas,* 6.
15. *Fear and Loathing: The Campaign Trail '72,* 7.
16. Nixon clearly obsessed Thompson, rarely better or more graphically expressed in his obituary "He Was a Crook," Given in full in *Better Than Sex: Confessions of a Political Junkie,* Gonzo Papers, Volume 4, New York: Random House/Ballantine, 1994: "Richard Nixon is gone now, and I am the poorer for it. He was the real thing—a political monster straight out of Grendel and a very dangerous enemy . . . He has poisoned our water for ever. Nixon will be remembered as a classic case of a smart man shitting in his own nest. But he also shit in our nests, and that was the crime that will burn on his memory like a brand. By disgracing and degrading the presidency of the United States, by fleeing the White House like a diseased cur, Richard Nixon broke the heart of the American Dream." 239–46.
17. Hunter Thompson, *The Great Shark Hunt: Strange Tales from a Strange Time,* New York: Summit Books, 1979, Reprinted New York: Simon and Schuster, Gonzo Papers, Volume 1, 2003, *Generation of Swine: Tales of Shame and Degradation in The '80s,* New York: Summit Books, 1988, reprinted New York: Simon & Schuster, Gonzo Papers, Volume 2, 2003, *Songs of The Doomed: The Death of The American Dream,* New York: Simon & Schuster, 1990, reprinted Simon & Schuster, Gonzo Papers, Volume 3, 2002, and *Better Than Sex: Confessions of a Political Junkie,* New York: Random House/Ballantine, Gonzo Papers, Volume 4, 1994.
18. *Better Than Sex,* 7.
19. As given in *Loathsome Secrets of a Star-Crossed Child in the Final Days of the American Century.*
20. *Songs of the Doomed,* 193.
21. *Kingdom of Fear,* 282.
22. *Kingdom of Fear,* 51.

NOTES TO CHAPTER 6

1. Joan Didion, "On Keeping a Notebook," reprinted in *Slouching Towards Bethlehem* New York: Farrar, Straus & Giroux, 1968,131–41, 136.
2. Joan Didion, "Why I Write," initially published in the *New York Review of Books,* 5 December, 1976, and reprinted in Ellen G. Friedman, ed. *Essays and Conversations,* Princeton, New Jersey: Ontario Review Press, 1984, 6.
3. Joan Didion, "The White Album," reprinted in *The White Album,* New York: Simon and Schuster, 1979, 11.
4. Joan Didion, *Slouching Towards Bethlehem,* Op. Cit., *The White Album,* Op. Cit.
5. Joan Didion, *Salvador,* New York: Simon & Schuster, 1982, *Miami,* New York: Simon & Schuster, 1987, *After Henry,* New York: Simon & Schuster, 1992, *Political Fictions,* New York: A.A. Knopf, 2001.
6. Joan Didion, *Where I Was From,* New York: Knopf, 2003, *The Year of Magical Thinking,* New York: Knopf, 2005.
7. Joan Didion, *Run River,* New York: I. Obolensky, 1963, *Play It As It Lays,* New York: Farrar, Straus & Giroux, 1970, *Telling Stories,* Berkeley: University of California Press,1978, *A Book of Common Prayer,* New York: Simon and Schuster, 1977, *Democracy,* New York: Simon and Schuster, 1984, *The Last Thing He Wanted,* New York: Alfred A. Knopf, 1996.
8. Joan Didion, "The Women's Movement," reprinted in *The White Album,* 113.
9. Joan Didion, "Some Dreamers of the Golden Dream," reprinted in *Slouching Towards Bethlehem,* 20.

10. Joan Didion, "The White Album," *The White Album*, 13
11. Joan Didion, "Fixed Opinions, Or the Hinge of History," delivered as a lecture at the New York Public Library in November 2002, and reprinted in *Vintage Didion*, New York: Vintage, 2004, 173–96.
12. Joan Didion, "The White Album," *The White Album*, 11
13. *Salvador*, 13.
14. *Miami*, 31.
15. Joan Didion, *The Year of Magical Thinking*, New York: Knopf, 2005, 7.

NOTES TO CHAPTER 7

1. Kathy Acker, "Seeing Gender," *Bodies of Work*, London: Serpent's Tail, 1997, 159.
2. Kathy Acker, *Empire of the Senseless*, New York: Grove Press, 1988.
3. Amy Scholder, "Preface," in Amy Scholder, Carla Harryman, and Avital Ronell, eds. *Lust for Life: On The Writings of Kathy Acker*, London and New York: Verso, 2006, VII.
4. Jeanette Winterson, "Introduction," Amy Scholder, ed. *Essential Acker: The Selected Writings of Kathy Acker* New York: Grove Press, 2002. Jeanette Winterson, *Oranges Are Not The Only Fruit*, London: Pandora Press, 1985.
5. Kathy Acker, *The Childlike Life of the Black Tarantula*, New York: Viper's Tongue Books, 1973, reprinted New York: TVRT Press, 1975, reprinted in *Portrait of an Eye: Three Novels*, New York: Grove Press, 1992; *Kathy Goes to Haiti*, New York: Grove Press, 1978, reprinted in *Literal Madness: Three Novels*, New York: Grove Press, 1988; *Blood and Guts in High School*, New York: Grove Press, 1978; *Empire of the Senseless*, New York: Grove Press, 1988; *In Memory of Identity*, New York: Grove Press, 1990; *Portrait of an Eye: Three Novels*, New York: Grove Press, 1992; and *Eurydice in the Underworld*, London: Arcadia, 1997.
6. Kathy Acker, "A Conversation with Ellen G. Friedman," http://www.centerforbookculture.org/interviews/interview-acker.html Accessed July 2009.
7. Kathy Acker, *Great Expectations*, New York: Grove Press, 1983; *Don Quixote, which was a dream*, New York: Grove Press, 1988; and *Pussy, King of the Pirates*, New York: Grove Press, 1996.
8. Kathy Acker, *My Mother: Demonology*, New York: Pantheon, 1993.
9. Kathy Acker, *The Childlike Life of the Black Tarantula by the Black Tarantula*. Text cited is that of *Portrait of an Eye* (1992).
10. Kathy Acker, *Kathy Goes to Haiti*, reprinted in *Literal Madness*, 1988. 8.
11. Kathy Acker, *Blood and Guts in High School*, 1978, 20.
12. *Great Expectations*, 16.
13. *Don Quixote*, 9.
14. The phrase belongs to one of the many elucidatory essays in Michael Hardin, ed. *Enduring Institutions: The Life Work of Kathy Acker*, San Diego: San Diego State Press, 2004. See Jan Corbett, "Words hurt! Acker's appropriation of myth in *Don Quixote*," 167–88.
15. Kathy Acker, *Hannibal Lecter, My Father*, New York: Semiotext(e), 1991.
16. Kathy Acker, *In Memoriam to Identity*, New York: Grove, 1990, 50

NOTES TO CHAPTER 8

1. "How It Feels to Be Colored Me" first appeared in *World Tomorrow*, No. 11, May 1928.

2. Zora Neale Hurston, *Their Eyes Were Watching God*, Philadelphia and London: J.B. Lippincott, 1937; *Dust Tracks on a Road*, Philadelphia: J.B. Lippincott, 1942.
3. George Schuyler, *Black No More: Being An Account of the Strange and Wonderful Workings of Science in the Land of the Free, A.D. 1933–1944*, New York: MaCauley Co., 1931.
4. Wallace Thurman, *Infants of The Spring*, New York: MaCauley Co., 1932; Alain Locke, ed. *The New Negro: An Interpretation*, New York: Alfred Knopf, 1925.
5. Chester Himes, *Pinktoes*, Paris: Olympia Press, 1961.
6. Ishmael Reed, *The Free-Lance Pallbearers: An Irreverent Novel*, New York: Doubleday, 1967; *Yellow Back Radio Broke-Down*, New York: Doubleday, 1969; *Mumbo Jumbo*, Garden City, New York: Random House, 1972; *Flight To Canada*, New York: Random House, 1976.
7. Carlene Hatcher Polite, *Sister X and The Victims of Foul Play*, New York: Doubleday, 1975.
8. Trey Ellis, *Platitudes*, New York: Vintage, 1988; *Home Repairs*, New York: Simon and Schuster, 1993.
9. Darryl Pinkney, *High Cotton*, New York: Farrar, Straus and Giroux, 1992.
10. James Weldon Johnson, *The Autobiography of an Ex-Colored Man*, Boston, Massachusetts: Sherman French, 1912.
11. Zora Neale Hurston, *Jonah's Gourd Vine*, Philadelphia and London: J.B. Lippincott, 1935.
12. Zora Neale Hurston, *I Love Myself When I Am Laughing . . . and Then Again When I Am Looking Mean and Impressive: A Zora Neale Hurston Reader*, ed. Alice Walker, Old Westbury, New York: Feminist Press, 1979.
13. Ralph Ellison, *Invisible Man*, New York: Random House, 1952, 1982.
14. Henry Louis Gates, Jr., "Zora Neale Hurston: 'A Negro Way of Saying Things,'" Afterword to Zora Neale Hurston, *Dust Tracks On a Road*, The Restored Text Established by the Library of America, New York: Harper Perennial, 1992.
15. Zora Neale Hurston, *Dust Tracks on a Road*, Philadelphia: J.B. Lippincott, 1942. *Dust Tracks on a Road*, reprinted, with additional original chapters and Introduction by Robert Hemenway, Urbana, Illinois: University of Illinois Press, 1984. Page references are to this edition, 1984.
16. Zora Neale Hurston, *Mules & Men*, Philadelphia and London: J.B. Lippincott, 1935.
17. Gerald Vizenor, *Crossbloods: Bone Courts, Bingo, and Other Reports*, Minneapolis, Minnesota: University of Minneapolis Press, 1990.
18. Gerald Vizenor, *Interior Landscapes: Autobiographical Myths and Metaphors*, Minneapolis, Minnesota: University of Minnesota Press, 1990.
19. Neal Bowers and Charles Silet, "An Interview with Gerald Vizenor," MELUS, 8:1, 1981, 41–9.
20. Gerald Vizenor, "Visions, Scares, and Stories," *Contemporary Authors Autobiography Series*, Vol. 22, Detroit, Michigan: Gale Research Company, 1995, 3.
21. Gerald Vizenor, *Darkness in Saint Louis Bearheart*, Minneapolis, Minnesota: Truck Press, 1978, revised as *Bearheart: The Heirship Chronicles*, Minneapolis, Minnesota: University of Minnesota Press, 1990; *Griever: An American Monkey King in China*, Normal, Illinois: Illinois State University/Fiction Collective, 1987, *The Trickster of Liberty: Tribal Heirs to a Wild Baronage at Petronia*, Minneapolis, Minnesota: University of Minnesota Press, 1988, *The Heirs of Columbus*, Hanover, New Hampshire: Wesleyan University Press/University Press of New England, 1991, *Dead Voices: Natural Agonies in the New World*, Norman, Oklahoma: University of Oklahoma Press, 1992,

Hotline Healers: An Almost Browne Novel, Hanover, New Hampshire: Wesleyan University Press/University Press of New England, 1997, and *Chancers,* Norman, Oklahoma: University of Oklahoma Press, 2000.

22. *Hiroshima Bugi: Atomu 57,* Lincoln, Nebraska: University of Nebraska Press, 2003, and *Father Meme,* Albuquerque: University of New Mexico Press, 2008.

23. Gerald Vizenor, *Manifest Manners: Postindian Warriors of Survivance,* Hanover, New Hampshire: Wesleyan University Press/University Press of New England, 1994, and *Fugitive Poses: Native American Indian Scenes of Absence and Presence,* Nebraska: University of Nebraska Press, 1998.

24. *Wordarrows: Indians and Whites in the New Fur Trade,* Minneapolis, Minnesota: University of Minnesota Press, 1978; *Earthdivers: Tribal Narratives on Mixed Descent,* Minneapolis, Minnesota: University of Minnesota Press, 1981, and *Crossbloods: Bone Courts, Bingo, and Other Reports,* Minneapolis, Minnesota: University of Minnesota Press, 1990,

25. *Interior Landscapes: Autobiographical Myths and Metaphors,* Minneapolis, Minnesota: University of Minnesota Press, 1990, and Gerald Vizenor and A. Robert Lee, *Postindian Conversations,* Lincoln, Nebraska: University of Nebraska Press, 1999.

26. Michel Foucault, *Ceci n'est pas une pipe,* Montpellier: Fata Morgana, 1973. Trans. James Harness, *This Is Not a Pipe,* Berkeley: University of California Press, 1983.

27. Ellen L. Arnold, "Listening to the Spirits: An Interview with Leslie Marmon Silko," *Studies in American Indian Literatures,* 10: 3, 1998, 1–33. Reprinted in Ellen L. Arnold, *Conversations with Leslie Marmon Silko,* Jackson, Mississippi: University Press of Mississippi, 2000, 165.

28. Leslie Marmon Silko, *Ceremony,* New York: Viking Press, 1981, *Almanac of The Dead,* New York: Simon and Schuster, 1991, and *Gardens in the Dunes,* New York: Simon and Schuster, 1999.

29. Leslie Marmon Silko, *Storyteller,* New York: Little Brown/Arcade, in arrangement with Seaver Books, 1981.

30. Vine Deloria Jr., *Custer Died For Your Sins: An Indian Manifesto,* New York: Macmillan, 1969, and *We Talk, You Listen: New Tribes, New Turf,* New York: Macmillan, 1970.

31. Elizabeth Cook-Lynn, *Why I Can't Read Wallace Stegner and Other Essays: A Tribal Voice,* Madison, Wisconsin: University of Wisconsin Press, 1996.

32. Craig Womack, *Red on Red: Native American Literary Separatism,* Minneapolis: University of Minnesota Press, 1993.

33. Sherman Alexie, *The Lone Ranger and Tonto Fistfight in Heaven,* New York: Atlantic Monthly Press, 1993.

34. Louis Owens, *Mixedblood Messages: Literature, Film, Family, Place,* Norman, Oklahoma: University of Oklahoma Press, 1998.

35. Rodolfo González , *I Am Joaquín/I Am Joaquín,* New York: Bantam Books, 1972.

36. Tomás Rivera , *". . . y n lo tragó la tierra/And The Earth Did Not Part,* Berkeley, California: Quinto Sol Publications, 1971; Rudolfo Anaya, *Bless Me, Ultima,* Berkeley, California: Quinto Sol Publications, 1972; and Rolando Hinojosa, *Klail City y sus alrededores,* Havana, Cuba: Casa de las Americas, 1976, and *Klail City,* Houston, Texas: Arte Público Press, 1987.

37. Cherrié Moraga, *Loving in the War Years: lo que nunca pasó por sus labios,* Boston, Massachusetts: South End Press, 1983; Ana Castillo, *The Mixquiahuala Letters,* Binghamton, New York: Bilingual Press/Editorial Bilingüe, 1986; Sandra Cisneros, *Woman Hollering Creek and Other Stories,* New York: Random House, 1991. These texts are given close analysis in my *Multicultural*

American Literature: Comparative Black, Native, Latino/a and Asian American Fictions, Edinburgh: Edinburgh University Press, 2003, Jackson, Mississippi: University Press of Mississippi, 2003, especially Chapter 5.

38. Luis Valdez, *Zoot Suit and Other Plays*, Houston: Arte Público Press, 1992; Guillermo Gómez-Peña, *Warrior for Gringostroika*, St. Paul, Minnesota: Graywolf Press, 1993.

39. Guillermo Gómez-Peña, *Warrior for Gringostroika*, St. Paul: Graywolf Press, 1993.

40. Hunter Thompson, *Fear and Loathing in Las Vegas: A Savage Journey to the Heart of the American Dream*, New York: Random House, 1972.

41. Hunter S. Thompson, *Fear & Loathing in America: The Brutal Odyssey of an Outlaw Journalist 1968- 1970*, New York: Simon & Schuster, 2001, 36.

42. Hunter S. Thompson, *Fear & Loathing in America: The Brutal Odyssey of an Outlaw Journalist 1968- 1970*, New York: Simon & Schuster, 2001, 52.

43. Oscar Zeta Acosta, *The Autobiography of a Brown Buffalo*,San Francisco: Straight Arrow, 1972, reprinted New York: Vintage, 1989, and *The Revolt of the Cockroach People*, San Francisco: Straight Arrow, 1973, reprinted New York: Vintage, 1989.

44. Richard Rodriguez, *A Hunger of Memory: The Education of Richard Rodriguez*, Boston, Massachusetts: Codine, 1982.

45. Linda Chavez, *Out of The Barrio: Towards a New Politics of Hispanic Assimilation*, New York: Basic Books, 1991.

46. Richard Rodriguez, *Days of Obligation: An Argument with My Mexican Father*, New York: Viking Penguin, 1992.

47. Richard Rodriguez, *Brown: The Last Discovery of America*, New York: Viking, 2002.

48. Frank Chin, Jeffery Paul Chan, Lawson Fusao Inada and Shawn Wong, eds. *The Big Aiiieeeee! An Anthology of Chinese American and Japanese American Literature*, New York: Meridian/Penguin, 1991.

49. David Mura, *A Male Grief: Notes on Pornography and Addiction*, Minneapolis, Minnesota: Milkweed Editions, 1989, *The Colors of Desire*, New York: Anchor-Doubleday, 1995, and *Turning Japanese: Memoirs of a Sansei*, New York: Atlantic Monthly, 1991.

50. Maxine Hong Kingston, *The Woman Warrior: Memoirs of a Girlhood Among Ghosts*, New York: Vintage, 1977; Theresa Hak Kyung Cha, *DICTEE*, New York: Tanam Press, 1982; Jessica Hagedorn, *Dogeaters*, New York: Random House/Penguin, 1990; and Meena Alexander, *The Shock of Arrival: Reflections on Postcolonial Experience*, Boston, Massachusetts: South End Press, 1996.

51. Epifanio San Juan Jr., *Racism and Cultural Studies: Critiques of Multiculturalist Ideology in the United States*, Durham, North Carolina: Duke University Press, 2002.

52. Monica Sone, *Nisei Daughter*, Boston: Little Brown 1945, reprinted Seattle: University of Washington Press, 1979.

53. Amy Tan, *The Joy Luck Club*, New York: Putnam, 1989, and *Saving Fish from Drowning*, New York: Putnam, 2005; and Lan Cao, *Monkey Bridge*, New York: Viking, 1997.

54. Chang-rae Lee, *Native Speaker*, New York: Riverhead Books, 1995.

55. Max Yeh ,*The Beginning of The East*, Boulder, Colorado: Fiction Collective Two, 1992.

56. Ed Morales, "Rebirth of a New Rican," in Miguel Algarín and Bob Holman, eds. *Aloud: Voices from the Nuyorican Café*, New York: Henry Holt, 1994, 98–99, and Ed Morales, *Living in Spanglish: The Search for Latino Identity in America* , New York: St. Martin's Press, 2002.

57. Carter Revard, *Winning The Dust Bowl* , Tucson, Arizona: The University of Arizona Press, 2001.
58. Carter Revard, "Herbs of Healing: American Values in American Indian Literature," in Brian Swann and Arnold Krupat, ed. *I Tell You Now: Autobiographical Essays by Native American Writers*, Lincoln, Nebraska: University of Nebraska Press, 1987, 172–192.
59. Sherman Alexie, Interview with Robert Capriccioso, *identitytheory.com*, a literary website, 2003.
60. Meena Alexander, *The Shock of Arrival: Reflections on Postcolonial Experience*, Boston: South End Press, 1996, 128.
61. Both these phrases are to be found in "In Opposition—Which State?," first delivered as a speech at the 48ᵗʰ International PEN Congress in New York City, 16 January 1986, and reprinted in Ishmael Reed, *Writin' Is Fightin'*, New York: Atheneum, 1988, 113–20.
62. "America: the Multinational Society," December 1983, *San Francisco Focus*, reprinted in Ishmael Reed, *Writin' Is Fightin'*, New York: Atheneum, 1988, 54.

NOTES TO CHAPTER 9

1. Robert Lowell, "The Fourth of July in Maine," *Near The Ocean*, New York: Farrar, Straus & Giroux, 1967, 27.
2. Russell Leong, "The Country of Dreams and Dust," *The Country of Dreams and Dust*, Albuquerque, New Mexico: West End Press, 1993, 24.
3. Lorna Dee Cervantes, "Visions of Mexico While at a Writing Symposium in Port Townsend, Washington," *Emplumada*, Pittsburgh, Pennsylvania: University of Pittsburgh Press, 1981, 45–7.
4. Toni Morrison, *Jazz*, New York: Alfred A. Knopf, 1992, 33.
5. Luis Omar Salinas, "Ode to Mexican Experience," *Afternoon of The Unreal*, Fresno, California: Abramás Publications, 1980, 23–4.
6. Wing Tek Lum, "Minority Poem," *Expounding The Doubtful Points*, Honolulu: Bamboo Ridge Press, 1987, 69.
7. Charles Simic, "The Wind," *The Silence*, New York: Braziller, 1974, 4.
8. Mark Pawlak, *The Buffalo Sequence*, Port Townsend, Washington: Copper Canyon Press, 1978.
9. Hamod, Sam, ed. *Grapeleaves: A Century of Arab-American Poetry*, Salt Lake City, Utah: University of Utah Press, 1988; Akash, Munir and Mattawa, Khaled, eds. *Post-Gibran Anthology of Arab American Writing*, West Bethesda, Maryland: Kitab, Syracuse, New York: Distributed by Syracuse University Press, 1999.
10. Naomi Shihab Nye, "Steps," *Fuel: Poems by Naomi Shihab Nye*, New York: BOA Editions, 1998, 79.
11. Duane Niatum, ed. *Harper's Anthology of 20ᵗʰ Century Native American Poetry*, San Francisco: Harper, 1988; Nicolás Kanellos, ed. *Herencia: The Anthology of Hispanic American Literature of the United States*, New York: Oxford University Press, 2002.
12. Mark Him Lai, Genny Lim and Judy Yung, eds. *Island: Poetry and History of Chinese Immigration on Angel Island, 1910–1940*, Seattle, Washington: University of Washington Press, 1980.
13. Frank Chin, Jeffery Paul Chan, Lawson Fusao Inada and Shawn Wong, eds. *AIIIEEEEE! An Anthology Of Asian-American Writers*, Washington DC: Howard University Press, 1974; *The Big Aiiieeeee! An Anthology of Chinese American and Japanese American Literature*, New York: Meridian/Penguin, 1991.

14. Shirley Geok-lin Lim, Mayumi Tsutukawa and Margarita Donnelly, eds. *The Forbidden Stitch: An Asian American Women's Anthology*, Corvallis, Oregon: Calyx Books, 1989; Sunaina Maira and Rajini Srikanth, eds. *Contours of the Heart: South Asians Map North America*, New York: Asian American Writers' Workshop, 1996.

15. Victor Hernández Cruz, "Loisida," *Rhythm, Content, and Flavor*, Houston, Texas: Arte Público Press, 1981, 160–64.

16. Carl Sandburg, *The Complete Poems of Carl Sandburg*, San Diego and New York: Harcourt Brace Jovanovitch, 1970. Revised and expanded edition.

17. Robert Penn Warren, "Audubon: A Vision," *Audubon: A Vision*, New York: Random House, 1969; James Dickey, *Deliverance*, Boston: Houghton Mifflin, 1970, *Buckdancer's Choice*, Middletown, Connecticut: Wesleyan University Press, 1965.

18. Langston Hughes, "The Negro Speaks of Rivers," *The Collected Works of Langston Hughes, Vol. 1: The Poems 1921–1940*, ed. Arnold Rampersad, Columbia and London: University of Missouri Press, 2001, 36.

19. Jimmy Santiago Baca, *Immigrants in Our Own Land*, Baton Rouge, Louisiana: Louisiana State University Press, 1979.

20. Lawrence Ferlinghetti, "Starting From San Francisco," *Starting From San Francisco*, New York: New Directions, 1961.

21. Eric Chock and Darrell H. Y. Lum, eds. *The Best of Bamboo Ridge: The Hawaii Writers' Quarterly*, Honolulu: Bamboo Ridge Press, 1986.

22. Walt Whitman, "Song of Myself," *Leaves of Grass*, Variorum Edition, Vol. 1, eds. Sculley Bradley, Harold W. Blodgett, Arthur Golden, and William White, New York: New York University Press, 1980, 17 .

23. Allen Ginsberg, "Howl," *Howl and other Poems*, San Francisco: City Lights, 1956, 26.

24. Robert Frost, "The Land Was Ours Before We Were the Land's"/"The Gift Outright," *The Collected Poems of Robert Frost*, New York: Holt, Rinehart and Winston, 1964, 467.

25. Hart Crane, "The Bridge," *The Bridge, The Complete Poems of Hart Crane*, New York: Liveright, 1986, 56.

26. Sylvia Plath, "Daddy," *Ariel*, London: Faber and Faber, 1965, 56.

27. Sylvia Plath, "Lady Lazarus, *Ariel*, London: Faber and Faber, 1965, 16, 19.

28. William Heyen, *The Swastika Poems*, New York: Vanguard Press, 1977.

29. Theodore Roethke, *The Collected Poems of Theodore Roethke*, New York: Doubleday, 1966, 44.

30. Charles Bukowski, "Near Hollywood," Web, uncollected.

31. Susan Howe, *The Europe of Trusts*, Los Angeles: Sun and Moon, 1990, 97; John Norton, "Com-plaint," *The Light at the End of The Bog*, San Francisco: Black Star Series, 1989, 1992. Republished in J.J. Phillips, Ishmael Reed, Gundars Strads, and Shawn Wong, eds. *The Before Columbus Foundation Poetry Anthology*, New York: W.W. Norton, 1992, 272.

32. Terence Winch, "The Irish Riviera," *Irish Musicians/American Friends*, Minneapolis, Minnesota: Coffee House Press, 1985; Susan Firer, "God Sightings," *The Lives of The Saints and Everything*, Cleveland, Ohio: Cleveland State University Poetry Center, 1993; and Eamonn Wall, " Immigrants," *Iron Mountain Road*, Cliffs of Moher, Ireland: Salmon Publishing, 1997.

33. John Ciardi, "Firsts" (1971), *For Instance*, New York: W.W. Norton, 1979, 61.

34. Lawrence Ferlinghetti, "The Old Italians Dying," *Landscapes of Living and Dying*, New York: New Directions, 1979, 4; Diane di Prima, " Backyard," *Pieces of a Song*, San Francisco: City Lights Books, 1990, 114.

35. Felix Stefanile, "The Americanization of the Immigrant," *The Country of Absence*, West Lafayette, Indiana: Bordighera, 2000, 59.

36. Denise Levertov, "Illustrious Ancestors," *Collected Early Poems, 1940– 1960*, New York: New Directions, 1979, 77; "A Map of the Western Part of the County of Essex in England," *Poems 1960–1967*, New York: New Directions, 1983, 21.

37. Philip Levine, "I Was Born in Lucerne," *One For The Rose*, New York: Atheneum, 1981, 12–13; Gerald Stern, "Soap," reprinted in *This Time: New and Selected Poems*, 1982, 49–51; and Samuel Menashe, *The Niche Narrows: New and Selected Poems*, New Jersey: Talisman House, 2000, 53.

38. Hilton Obenzinger, " This Passover or the Next I Will Never Be in Jerusalem" and "The X of 1492" are both reprinted in J.J. Phillips, Ishmael Reed, Gundars Strads and Shawn Wong, eds. *The Before Columbus Foundation Poetry Anthology*, New York: W.W. Norton, 1992. Respectively 294 and 291–4.

39. Marilyn Chin, "How I Got That Name," *The Phoenix Gone, The Terrace Empty*, Minneapolis: Milkweed Editions, 1994, 17.

40. Wing Tek Lum, "At A Chinaman's Grave," reprinted in *The Before Columbus Foundation Poetry Anthology*, 1992, 209–10.

41. Li-Young Lee, "The Cleaving," *The City in Which I Love You*, Brockport, New York: BOA Editions, 1990, 87.

42. Kimiko Hahn, "Resistance: A Poem on Ikat Cloth," *Air Pocket*, New York: Hanging Loose Press, 1989.

43. Lawson Fusao Inada, "Legends From the Camp," reprinted in *The Before Columbus Foundation Poetry Anthology*, 1992, 7–15.

44. Cathy Song, "Easter: Wahiawa, 1959," *Picture Bride*, New Haven, Connecticut: Yale University Press, 1983, 7–9.

45. Myung Mi Kim, "Into Such Assembly," *Under Flag*, Berkeley, California: Kelsey St. Press, 1997, 29–31; Jessica Hagedorn, "Souvenirs," *Danger and Beauty*, San Francisco: City Lights, 2002; 26–29; Thuong Vuong-Riddick, "Seeds," Barbara Tran, Monique T.D. Truong, and Luu Truong Khoi, eds. *Watermark: Vietnamese American Poetry and Prose*, New York: Asian American Women's Workshop, 1998; and S. Shankar, "Passage to North America," reprinted in *Contours of the Heart: South Asians Map North America*, 1996, 107–14.

46. Rodolfo Gonzalez, ""I Am Joaquín/Yo Soy Joaquín," *I Am Joaquín/Yo Soy Joaquín*, New York: Bantam Books, 1972, 98.

47. Carlos Cumpián, "Cuento," *Coyote Sun*, Chicago: MARCH/Abrazo Press, 1990, 62–3.

48. Pat Mora, "Immigrants," *Borders*, Houston, Arte Público, 1986, 15.

49. Jimmy Santiago Baca, *Martín and Meditations on the South Valley*, New York: New Directions, 1987.

50. Tato Laviera, *AmeRícan*, Houston, Texas: Arte Público Press, 1985, 94.

51. Pablo Medina, "Madame America," reprinted in Nicolás Kanellos, ed. *Herencia*, 2002.

52. Gina Valdés, "English Con Salsa," *Bridges and Borders*, Tempe, Arizona: Bilingual Press, 1996.

53. Robert Hayden, "Middle Passage," *Robert Hayden: Collected Poems*, ed. Frederick Glaysher. New York: Liveright, 54, 48, 50, 51, 54.

54. Countee Cullen, "Heritage," *My Soul's High Song: The Collected Writings of Countee Cullen, Voice of the Harlem Renaissance*, ed. Gerald Early, New York: Doubleday, 104–8.

55. Gwendolyn Brooks, "To The Diaspora," *Blacks*, Chicago: David Company, 1987, 99.

56. Rita Dove, *Thomas and Beulah*, Pittsburgh: Carnegie-Mellon University Press, 1986.
57. Jayne Cortez, "For The Poets (Christopher Okigbo & Henry Dumas)," reprinted in *The Before Columbus Foundation Poetry Anthology*, 1992, 60–2.
58. Ted Joans, "No mo' Kneegrow," *Black Pow-Wow: Jazz Poems*, New York: Hill, 1969, 26.
59. Ted Joans, "Afrique Accidentale," *Afrodisia: Old & New Poems*, New York: Hill, 1969, 4–8.
60. Jimmy Durham, "Columbus Day," reprinted in Duane Niatum, ed. *Harper's Anthology of 20ᵗʰ Century Native American Poetry*, San Francisco: Harper, 1988, 129.
61. Gail Tremblay, "Indian Singing in Twentieth Century America," reprinted in Duane Niatum, ed. *Harper's Anthology of 20ᵗʰ Century American Poetry*, 193–4.
62. Simon Ortiz, "Wind and Glacier Voices," *Woven Stone*, Tucson, Arizona: University of Arizona Press, 1992, 114.
63. Joseph Bruchac, "Ellis Island," *Entering Onondaga*, Austin, Texas: Cold Mountain Press, 1978, 34.

NOTES TO CHAPTER 10

1. Gloria Anzaldúa, *Borderlands/La Frontera, The New Mestiza*, 1987, San Francisco: Aunt Lute Books, 3.
2. Victor Hernández Cruz, *Red Beans*, Minneapolis, Minnesota: Coffee House Press, 1991, 9.
3. Gustavo Pérez Firmat, *Life on The Hyphen: The Cuban-American Way*, Austin, Texas: University of Texas Press, 1994, 4.
4. General historical studies include Joan Moore and Harry Pacton, *Hispanics in the United States*, Englewood Cliffs, New Jersey: Prentice Hall, 1985; Earl Shorris, *Latinos: A Biography of the People*, New York: Avon Books, 1992; Francisco H. Vásquez, and Rodolfo D. Torres, *Latino/a Thought: Culture, Politics, and Society*, Langham, Maryland: Rowman and Littlefield, 2003; and Hector Tobar, *Translation Nation: Defining a New American Identity in the Spanish Speaking United States*, New York: Riverhead., 2006. For Chicano history see Rodolfo Acuña, *Occupied America: The Chicano's Struggle Towards Liberation*, San Francisco: Canfield Press, 1972; Stanly R. Ross, ed. *Views Across The Border: the United States and Mexico*, Albuquerque, New Mexico: University of New Mexico Press, 1978; Tom Miller, *America's Southwestern Frontier*, Tucson, Arizona: The University of Arizona Press, 1981; Raul A. Fernández, *United States-Mexico Border Region: Issues and Trends*, Notre Dame, Indiana: University of Notre Dame Press, 1989; Andrew Grant Wood, ed. *On the Border: Society and Culture Between the United States and Mexico*: Lanham, Maryland: SR Books. For Puerto Rican-American history see Juan Flores, *Divided Borders: Essays on Puerto RicanIdentity*, Houston, Texas: Arte Público Press, 1984. For Cuban American history see Thomas D. Boswell, and James R. Curtis, *The Cuban-American Experience: Culture, Images and Perspectives*, Montclair, New Jersey: Rowman Allanheld, 1983; Felix Roberto Masud-Piloto, *With Open Arms: Cuban Migration to the United States*, Totowa, New Jersey: Rowman and Littlefield, 1988; James S. Olsen and Judith E. Olsen, *Cuban-Americans: From Trauma to Triumph*, New York: Twayne, 1995. Dominican-American

history is given in Sherri Grasmuck and Patricia R. Pessar, *Between Two Islands: Dominican International Migration*, Berkeley: University of California Press, 1991; and Silvio Torres-Saillant and Ramona Hernández, Ramona, *The Dominican Americans*, Westport, Connecticut: Greenwood Publishing, 1998.

5. Literary-cultural discussion of this achievement has been steadily augmenting since the 1960s. Relevant overall accounts includes José David Saldívar, *The Dialectics of Our America: Genealogy, Cultural Critique, and Literary History*, Durham, North Carolina: Duke University Press, 1991; Nicolás. Kanellos, *The Hispanic Almanac: From Columbus to Corporate America*, Detroit: Visible Ink Press, 1994; Francisco A. Lomelí, ed. *Handbook of Hispanic Cultures in the US: Literature and Art*, Houston, Texas: Arte Público Press, 1993; José David Saldívar, *Border Matters: Remapping American Cultural Studies*, Berkeley, California: University of California Press, 1997; and Raphael Dalleo and Elena Machado Saéz, *The Latino/a Canon and The Emergence of Post-Sixties Literature* New York: Palgrave Macmillan, 2007.

6. Rudolfo Anaya, *Bless Me, Ultima*, Berkeley, California: Quinto Sol Publications, 1972. Tomás Rivera, *". . . y no se lo tragó la tierra/And The Earth Did Not Part*, Houston, Texas: Arte Público Press, [1971] 1987. For critical assessments of overall Chicano literary achievement, see Julio A. Martinez and Francisco Lomelí, eds. *Chicano Literature: A Reference Guide*, Westport, Connecticut: Greenwood Press (1985); Juan Bruce-Novoa, *Retrospace: Collected Essays on Chicano Literature, Theory and History*, Houston, Texas: Arte Público, 1990; Ramón Saldívar, *Chicano Narrative: The Dialectics of Difference*, Madison: University of Wisconsin Press, 1990. Héctor Calderón and José David Saldívar, eds. *Criticism in the Borderlands: Studies in Chicano Literature, Culture and Ideology*, Durham, North Carolina: Duke University Press, 1991; Diana Tey Robolledo, *Women Singing in the Snow: A Cultural Analysis of Chicana Literature*, Tucson, Arizona: University of Arizona Press, 1995; Deborah Madsen, *Understanding Contemporary Chicana Literature*, Columbia, South Carolina: University of South Carolina Press, 2000; and Raúl Homero Villa, *Barrio-Logos: Space and Place in Urban Chicano Literature and Culture*, Austin, Texas: University of Texas Press, 2000.

7. Rudolfo Anaya, *Zia Summer*, New York: Warner Books, 1995; *Rio Grande fall*, New York: Warner Books, 1996; *Shaman Winter*, New York: Warner Books, 1999.

8. Rudolfo Anaya, *Alburquerque*, Albuquerque, New Mexico: University of New Mexico Press, 1992.

9. Rolando Hinojosa, *Klail City y sus alrededores*, Havana: Casas de las Americas, 1976 and *Klail City*, Houston, Texas: Arte Público Press, 1987.

10. Rolando Hinojosa, *Ask A Policeman*, Houston, Texas: Arte Público Press, 1998.

11. Sandra Cisneros, *Woman Hollering Creek*, New York: Random House, 1991.

12. Roberta Fernández, *Intaglio: A Novel in Six Stories*, Houston, Texas: Arte Público Press, 1990.

13. Ana Castillo, *The Mixquiahuala Letters*, Binghamton, New York: Bilingual Press/Editorial Bilingüe Press, 1986; *Sopogonia*, Houston, Texas: Bilingual Press/Editorial Bilingüe, 1990; and *So Far From God*, New York: W.W. Norton, 1993.

14. Denise Chávez, *The Face of an Angel*, New York: Farrar, Straus & Giroux, 1994.

15. Denise Chávez, *The Last of the Menu Girls*, Houston, Texas: Arte Público Press, 1986.
16. Alejandro Morales, *The Rag Doll Plagues*, Houston, Texas: Arte Público Press, 1992.
17. Daniel Cano, *Pepe Ríos*, Houston, Texas: Arte Público Press, 1991.
18. Arturo Islas, *Migrant Souls*, New York: William Morrow, 1991.
19. Demetria Martínez, *Mother Tongue*, New York: Random House/Ballantine, 1994.
20. Helena María Viramontes, *Under The Feet of Jesus*, New York: Dutton, 1995.
21. John Rechy, *City of Night*, New York: Grove Press, 1963.
22. John Rechy, *The Miraculous Day of Amalia Gómez*, New York: Little, Brown & Company, 1991.
23. Piri Thomas, *Down These Mean Streets*, New York: Knopf, 1967; Edward Rivera, *Family Installments: Memories of Growing Up Hispanic*, Harmondsworth and New York: Penguin Books; Judith Cofer Ortiz, *Silent Dancing: A Partial Remembrance of a Puerto Rican Childhood*, Houston, Texas: Arte Público Press, 1990. For overall interpretation of the tradition, see Faythe Turner, *US Puerto Rican Writers on the Mainland: The Neoricans*, Amherst, Massachusetts: University of Massachusetts Press, 1978, and *Puerto Rican Writers at Home in the USA*, Seattle, Washington: Open Hand Publishing Company, 1991; Lisa Sánchez Gonzalez, *Boricua Literature: A Literary History of the Puerto Rican Diaspora*, New York: New York University Press, 2001; and Carmen S. Rivera, *Kissing the Mango Tree: Puerto Rican Women Rewriting American Literature*, Houston, Texas: Arte Público Press, 2002.
24. Nicholasa Mohr, *Nilda*, New York: Harper, 1970; *Growing Up Inside The Sanctuary Of My Imagination*, New York: J. Messner, 1994; *The Magic Shell*, New York: Scholastic, 1995; *A Matter of Pride and other stories*, Houston, Texas: Arte Público Press, 1997.
25. Judith Ortiz Cofer, *The Latin Del: Prose and Poetry*, Athens, Georgia: the University of Georgia Press, 1993; and *An Island Like You*, New York: Orchard Press, 1995.
26. Ed Vega, *The Comeback*, Houston, Texas: Arte Público Press, 1985.
27. Ed Vega, *Casualty Report*, Houston, Texas: Arte Público Press, 1991.
28. Oscar Hijuelos, *The Mambo Kings Play Songs of Love*, New York: Farrar, Straus & Giroux, 1989. Useful sightlines for Cuban American writing include: Gustavo Pérez Firmat, *Life on The Hyphen: The Cuban-American Way*, Austin, Texas: The University of Texas Press, 1994, and *Tongue Ties: Logo-Eroticism in Anglo-Hispanic Literature*, New York: Palgrave MacMillan, 2003; Virgil Suárez and Delia Poey, *Little Havana Blues: A Cuban-American Literature*, Houston, Texas: Arte Público Press, 1996; Isabel Alvarez Borland, *Cuban-American Literature of Exile: From Person to Persona*, Charlottesville, Virginia: University of Virginia Press, 1998; and Andrea O'Reilly Herrera, ed. *ReMembering Cuba: Legacy of a Diaspora*, Austin, Texas: University of Texas Press, 2001.
29. Oscar Hijuelos, *The Fourteen Sisters of Emilio Montez O'Brien*, New York: Farrar, Straus & Giroux, 1993.
30. Cristina Garcia, *Dreaming in Cuban*, New York: Alfred A. Knopf, 1992.
31. Virgil Suárez, *Havana Thursdays*, Houston, Texas: Arte Público Press, 1995.
32. Roberto Fernández, *Holy Radishes!*, Houston, Texas: Arte Público Press, 1995.
33. Achy Obejas, *We Came All the Way From Cuba So You Could Dress Like This?*, San Francisco, California: Cleis Press, 1994; *Memory Mambo*, San Francisco: Cleis Press, 1996.

34. Julia Alvarez, "Las Mariposas," Interview with Ilan Stavans, *Nation*, November 7, 1994, 552–6. Quotation, 553.
35. Julia Alvarez, *How The García Girls Lost their Accents*, Chapel Hill, North Carolina: Algonquin Books, 1991; ¡*Yo!*, New York: Plume, 1997; *In the Time of Butterflies*, 1994.
36. Junot Díaz, *Drown*, New York: Riverhead, 1996.
37. Loida Maritz Pérez, *Geographies of Home*, New York: Viking, 1999.
38. Lauro Flores, ed. *The Floating Borderlands: Twenty-Five Years of US Hispanic Literature*, Seattle, Washington: University of Washington Press, 1998.
39. Francisco Goldman, *The Long Night of White Chickens*, New York: The Atlantic Monthly Press, 1992.
40. Guillermo Gómez-Peña, *Warrior for Gringostroika*, St. Paul, Minnesota: Graywolf Press, 1993.

NOTES TO CHAPTER 11

1. Marilyn Chin, "We Are Americans Now, We Live in the Tundra," *Dwarf Bamboo*, Greenfield Center, New York: Greenfield Review Press, 1987, 28.
2. Gish Jen, *Typical American*, Boston: Houghton Mifflin/Seymour Lawrence, 1991, 85.
3. Nellie Wong, "Where is my Country?", reprinted in L. Ling-chi Wang and Henry Yiheng Zhao, eds. *Chinese American Poetry: An Anthology*, Santa Barbara: Asian American Voices, 1991, distributed Seattle and London: University of Washington Press, 1991.
4. Frank Chin, *Bulletproof Buddhists and Other Essays*, Honolulu: University of Hawai'i Press, in Association with UCLA Asian American Studies Center, 1998, and *Gunga Din Highway*, Minneapolis, Minnesota: Coffee House Press, 1994.
5. These issues are addressed in my edited essay-collection, A. Robert Lee, ed. *China Fictions/English Language: Literary Essays in Diaspora, Memory, Story*, Amsterdam and New York: Rodopi, 2008.
6. Max Yeh, *The Beginning of the East*, Boulder, Colorado: Fiction Collection Two, 1992.
7. Marilyn Chin, *Dwarf Bamboo*, Greenfield Center, New York: Greenfield Review Press, 1987; *The Phoenix Gone, The Terrace Empty*, Minneapolis: Milkweed Editions, 1994; and *Rhapsody in Plain Yellow*, New York: W.W. Norton, 2003.
8. "We Are Americans Now, We Live in The Tundra," *Dwarf Bamboo*, 28.
9. "The End of a Beginning," *Dwarf Bamboo*, 3.
10. "The End of a Beginning," *Dwarf Bamboo*, 3.
11. "How I Got That Name," *The Phoenix Gone, The Terrace Empty*, 18.
12. "How I Got That Name," *The Phoenix Gone, The Terrace Empty*, 18.
13. "Child," *Dwarf Bamboo*, 24.
14. "Repulse Bay," *Dwarf Bamboo*, 63.
15. "Barbarian Suite," *The Phoenix Gone, The Terrace Empty*, 22–23.
16. "How I Got That Name," *The Phoenix Gone, The Terrace Empty*, 17.
17. Russell Leong, *The Country of Dreams and Dust*, Albuquerque, New Mexico: West End Press, 1993; *Phoenix Eyes and Other Stories*, Seattle: University of Washington Press, 2000.
18. "Aerogrammes," *The Country of Dreams and Dust*, 5.
19. John Yau, *Crossing Canal Street*, Binghampton, New York: Bellevue Press, 1976, *The Sleepless Night of Eugene Delacroix*, Brooklyn, New York: Release Press, 1980, *Corpse and Mirror*, New York: Holt, Rinehart, and

Winston, 1983, *Notarikon*, New York: Jordan Davis, 1981, *Dragon's Blood*, Colombes, France: Collectif Genération, 1989, and *Postcards from Trakl*, New York: ULAE, 1994.

20. John Yau, *Radiant Silhouette: New and Selected Work, 1974–1988*, Santa Rosa, California: Black Sparrow Press, 1989.
21. John Yau, *Edificio Sayonara*, Santa Rosa: Black Sparrow Press, 1992, *Forbidden Entries*, Santa Rosa: Black Sparrow Press, 1996.
22. "Genghis Chan: Private Eye," *Radiant Silhouette*, 189.
23. "Genghis Chan: Private Eye," *Radiant Silhouette*, 190.
24. "Genghis Chan: Private Eye," *Radiant Silhouette*, 191.
25. "Genghis Chan: Private Eye," *Radiant Silhouette*, 194.
26. "Genghis Chan: Private Eye," *Radiant Silhouette*, 195.
27. "Translations," *Expounding The Doubtful Points*, 71–72.
28. Wing Tek Lum. "Translations," *Expounding The Doubtful Points*, Honolulu, Hawaii: Bamboo Ridge Press, 1987, 71–72.
29. "The Return of Charlie Chan," *Expounding The Doubtful Points*, 66.
30. "Translations," *Expounding The Doubtful Points*, 72.
31. "A Moon Festival Picnic at Kahala Beach Park," *Expounding The Doubtful Points*, 99–102.
32. "A Moon Festival at Kahala Park," *Expounding The Doubtful Points*, 101.
33. "Chinese Hot Pot," *Expounding The Doubtful Points*, 105.

NOTES TO CHAPTER 12

1. Lafcadio Hearn, "Bits of Life and Death," *Out of The East* (1895). Reprinted in Francis King, ed. Lafcadio Hearn, *Writings From Japan*, Harmondworth, Middlesex: Penguin Books, 1984, 135.
2. Quoted in *New America Media*, September 19 2005.
3. Michael Crichton, *Rising Sun*, New York: Ballantine, 1992.
4. Shintaro Ishihara and Akio Morita, *The Japan That Can Say No: Why Japan Will Be First Among Equals*, Trans. New York: Simon and Schuster, 1991.
5. Masahiko Fujiwara, *Kokka no Hinkaku/ The Dignity of a State*, Tokyo: Shincho-sya, 2005.
6. Arthur Golden, *Memoirs of a Geisha*, New York: Alfred A, Knopf, 1997.
7. Yukio Mishima, "Patriotism," in *Death in Midsummer and other stories*, Trans. Edward G. Seidensticker, New York: New Directions, 1966; *Confessions of a Mask*, 1948, trans. Meredith Weatherby, 1958; *The Sea of Fertility* (tetralogy): 1. *Spring Snow*, Trans. Michael Gallagher, 1972, 2: *Runaway Horses*, Trans. Michael Gallagher, 3: *The Temple of Dawn*, Trans. E. Dale Saunders and Cecilia S. Seigle, 1973, 4: *The Decay of the Angel*, Trans. Edward Seidensticker, 1974.
8. Kenzaburo Oe, *The Day He Himself Shall Wipe Away the Tears*, 1972. Trans. 1977.
9. Kenzaburo Oe, "Japan, the Ambiguous, and Myself," Nobel Prize Address, Stockholm 1994. Reprinted in Kenzaburo Oe, *Japan, the Ambiguous and Myself*, Trans. Kunioki Yanashita, Tokyo: Kodansha International, 1995.
10. Kazuo Ishiguro, *Remains of The Day*, London: Faber and Faber, 1989, and *A Pale View of The Hills*, London: Faber and Faber, 1982.
11. Yone Noguchi, *The American Diary of a Japanese Girl*, 1902. Reprinted Philadelphia: Temple University Press, 2006, eds. Edward Marx and Laura E. Franly.

12. Garrett Hongo, *Volcano: A Memoir of Hawai'i*, New York: Alfred A. Knopf, 1995. David Mura, *Turning Japanese: Memoirs of a Sansei*, New York: Atlantic Monthly, 1991.
13. Garrett Hongo, *Yellow Light*, Middletown, Connecticut: Wesleyan University Press, 1982.
14. Toshio Mori, *Yokohama. California*, Caldwell, Idaho: Caxton Printers, 1949. Reprinted Seattle: University of Washington Press, 1985.
15. John Okada, *No-No Boy*, Rutherford, Vermont: Charles Tuttle, 1957. Reprinted Seattle: University of Washington Press, 1979.
16. Milton Murayama, *All I Asking For Is My Body*, San Francisco: Supa Press, 1975.
17. Joy Kogawa, *Obasan*, Boston: David R. Godine, 1981.
18. Joy Kadohata, *The Floating World*, New York: Viking, 1989.
19. Jessica Saiki, *From the Lanai and other Hawaii stories*, Minneapolis: New Rivers Press, 1991.
20. Hisaye Yamamoto, *Seventeen Syllables and other stories*, Latham New Jersey: Kitchen Table/Women of Color Press, 1988.
21. David Mura, *Turning Japanese: Memoirs of a Sansei*, New York: Atlantic Monthly, 1991.
22. Karen Tei Yamashita, *Through The Arc of the Rain Forest*, Minneapolis and St. Paul: Coffee House Press, 1990.

NOTES TO CHAPTER 13

1. Frank Chin, "Afterword," John Okada, *No-No Boy*, Seattle, Washington: University of Washington Press, 1979, 254.
2. Frank Chin, "Confessions of a Chinatown Cowboy," *Bulletproof Buddhists and Other Essays*, Honolulu: University of Hawai'i Press, in association with UCLA Asian American Studies Center, 1998, 71.
3. Frank Chin, *USA Ni Umerete, Born in the USA: A Story of Japanese America, 1889–1947*, ed. Lanham, Maryland: Rowman & Littlefield Publishers Inc., 2002, xvii.
4. Ishmael Reed, *Writin' is Fightin': Thirty-Seven Years of Boxing on Paper*, New York: Athenaeum, 1988.
5. Frank Chin, *AIIIEEEEE! An Anthology of Asian-American Writers*, ed. with Jeffery Paul Chan, Lawson Fusao Inada and Shawn Wong, Washington D.C.: University of Washington Press, 1972, and *The Big Aiiieeeee! An Anthology of Chinese American and Japanese American Literature*, ed. with Jeffery Paul Chan, Lawson Fusao Inada and Shawn Wong, New York: Meridian/Penguin, 1991.
6. Pardee Lowe, *Father and Glorious Descendant*, Boston: Little Brown, 1943, and Jade Snow Wong, *Fifth Chinese Daughter*, New York: Harper, 1950.
7. David Henry Hwang, *M. Butterfly*, New York: New American Library, 1988.
8. Maxine Hong Kingston, *The Woman Warrior: Memoirs of a Girlhood Among Ghosts*, New York: Vintage Books, 1977.
9. Frank Chin, *Donald Duk*, Minneapolis: Coffee House Press, 1991.
10. Frank Chin, *The Chickencoop Chinaman/The Year of The Dragon*, Seattle: University of Washington Press, 1971, 1974.
11. Shawn Wong, *Homebase*, New York: I. Reed Books, 1979.
12. Maxine Hong Kingston, *China Men*, New York: Knopf, 1980.

13. Ruthanne Lum McCunn, *Thousand Pieces of Gold*, San Francisco: Design Enterprises, 1981, Sky Lee, *Disappearing Moon Café*, Seattle: Seal Press, 1991, Gish Jen, *Typical American*, Boston: Houghton Mifflin/Seymour Lawrence, 1991.
14. Maxine Hong Kingston, *Tripmaster Monkey: His Fake Book*, New York: Knopf, 1989.
15. For a fuller version of the story told in Kingston's novel see Lo Kuan-Chung, *The Three Kingdoms*, Trans. Moss Roberts, Berkeley: University of California Press, 1994.
16. Frank Chin, *The Chinaman Pacific & Frisco R.R. Co: Short Stories*, Minneapolis: Coffee House Press, 1988.
17. Frank Chin, *Gunga Din Highway*, Minneapolis: Coffee House Press, 1994.
18. Frank Chin, *Donald Duk*, Op. Cit.
19. Louis Chu, *Eat A Bowl of Tea*, New York: Lyle Stuart, 1961.
20. Lo Kuan-Chung, *The Three Kingdoms*, Op. Cit, Wu Cheng'en, *Journey to the West*, Trans. Arthur Waley, New York: Grove Press, 1984.
21. Frank Chin, *Gunga Din Highway*, Op. Cit.
22. LeRoi Jones/Imamu Amiri Baraka, *The System of Dante's Hell*, New York: Grove Press, 1965.

NOTES TO CHAPTER 14

1. Jessica Hagedorn, *Dogeaters*, New York: Random House/Penguin, 1990, 250.
2. Jessica Hagedorn, *The Gangster of Love*, New York: Pantheon, 1996, 57.
3. Jessica Hagedorn, *Dream Jungle*, New York: Viking, 2003, 134.
4. Jessica Hagedorn, ed. *Charlie Chan is Dead: An Anthology of Contemporary Asian American Fiction*, New York: Penguin Books, 1993.
5. Jessica Hagedorn, *Chiquita Banana*, in *Third World Women*, San Francisco: Third World Communications, 1972; *Pet Foods and Tropical Apparitions*, San Francisco: Momo's Press, 1975; *Dangerous Music*, St. Momo's Press, 1975, *Mango Tango*, Y'bird Magazine, 1977, *Kiss Kiss Kill Kill*, The Airways Project, 1992; *Fresh Kill*, The Airways Project, 1994; *Burning Heart: A Portrait of the Philippines*, with photography by Marissa Roth, New York: Rizzoli International Publications, 1999.
6. Originally published as Jean Mallat, *Les Philippines: histoire, géographie, moeurs, agriculture et commerce des colonies espagnoles dans l'Océanie*. Paris: A. Bertrand, 1846.

NOTES TO CHAPTER 15

1. William Demby, *Beetlecreek*, New York; Rinehart, 1950. Reprinted Jackson, Mississippi: University Press of Mississippi, 1998, 131. All page references are to this edition.
2. William Demby, *The Catacombs*, New York: Random House, 1965, reprinted New York: Harper & Row/Perennial Library, 1970, 230. All page references are to this edition.
3. William Demby, *Love Story Black*, New York: E. P. Dutton, 1978, 57.
4. Jeff Biggers, "William Demby Has Not Left the Building," *The Bloomsbury Review*, 24:1, 2004.

5. Margaret Walker, *For My People*, New Haven: Yale University Press, 1942.
6. Richard Wright, *Uncle Tom's Children*, New York and London: Harper and Bros, 1938, and *Eight Men*, Cleveland, Ohio: World Publishing, 1961. "Inside Narrative" is Herman Melville's half-title for *Billy Budd*. I use it in the following study of Wright—A. Robert Lee, "Richard Wright's Inside Narratives," in Richard Gray, ed. *American Fiction: New Readings*, London: Vision Press, 1983, 200–21.
7. Ralph Ellison, *Invisible Man*, New York: Random House, 1952.
8. William Melvin Kelley, *dem*, Garden City: Doubleday 1967; Ishmael Reed, *Mumbo Jumbo*, Garden City: Doubleday, 1972; Trey Ellis, *Platitudes*, New York: Vintage, 1982.
9. Robert Bone, "William Demby's Dance of Life," *Triquarterly* 15, Spring, 127–41

NOTES TO CHAPTER 16

1. Gerald Vizenor, *Almost Ashore*, Cambridge, UK: Salt Publishing, 2006, 28.
2. "Envoy to Haiku," in A. Robert Lee, ed. *Shadow Distance: A Gerald Vizenor Reader*, Hanover: Wesleyan University Press/University Press of New England, 1994, 25.
3. Gerald Vizenor, *Bearheart*, originally published as *Darkness in Saint Louis Bearheart*, Saint Paul: Truck Press, 1978, revised edition, *Bearheart: The Heirship Chronicles*, Minneapolis: The University of Minnesota Press, 1990; *Hiroshima Bugi: Atomu 57*, Lincoln: University of Nebraska Press, 2003, *Father Meme*, Albuquerque: University of New Mexico Press, 2008.
4. Gerald Vizenor, *Wordarrows: Indians and Whites in the Fur Trade*, Minneapolis: University of Minnesota Press, 1978. Revised new edition, Minneapolis: University of Minnesota Press, 2005; *Fugitive Poses: Native American Scenes of Absence and Presence*, Lincoln: University of Nebraska Press, 1998.
5. Gerald Vizenor, *Interior Landscapes: Autobiographical Myths and Metaphors*, Minneapolis: University of Minnesota Press, 1990. A fuller version of Vizenor's literary output is given in Chapter 8, "Ethnics Behaving Badly: Texts and Contexts."
6. Gerald Vizenor, *Two Wings The Butterfly*, St. Cloud: Privately Printed, 1962; *Raising The Moon Vines*, Minneapolis: Callimach Publishing Company, 1965; and *Summer in the Spring: Ojibwe Lyric Poems and Tribal Stories*, Minneapolis: Nodin Press, 1965, revised edition *Summer in the Spring: Anishinaabe Lyric Poems and Tribal Stories*, Norman: University of Oklahoma Press, 1993.
7. Gerald Vizenor, *Almost Ashore*, Cambridge, UK: Salt Publishing, 2006; and *Bear Island: The War at Sugar Point*, Minneapolis: University of Minnesota Press, 2006.
8. Gerald Vizenor and A. Robert Lee, *Postindian Conversations*, Lincoln: University of Nebraska Press, 1999, 65.
9. Gerald Vizenor, *The Heirs of Columbus*, Hanover: Wesleyan University Press/University Press of New England, 1991.
10. Gerald Vizenor, *Chancers*, Norman: University of Oklahoma Press, 2000.
11. Gerald Vizenor, *Seventeen Chirps: Haiku in English*, Minneapolis: Nodin Press, 1964; *Matsushima: Pine Islands*, Minneapolis: Nodin Press, 1984; *Cranes Arise*, Minneapolis: Nodin Press, 1999; and *Raising The Moon Vines*, Minneapolis: Nodin Press, 1999.

12. "Haiku in the Attic," *Interior Landscapes: Autobiographical Myths and Metaphors*, 171–84.
13. Gerald Vizenor, "Fusions of Survivance: Haiku Scenes and Native Songs," *Modern Haiku*, XXXI: I, Winter-Spring, 2000, 37–47.
14. Gerald Vizenor, "Fusions of Survivance," 39.
15. Gerald Vizenor, *The People Named The Chippewa: Narrative Histories*, Minneapolis: University of Minnesota Press, 1983.

Index

A

Abella, Alex, 173
  Killing of The Saints, The, 173
Abdulla, Mohammed ben, 35
Acker, Kathy, 3, 22, 111–22
  Birth of The Poet, The (libretto),
    112; *Blood and Guts in High
    School*, 113, 116–17; *Bodies of
    Work: Essays*, 111, 114; *Child-
    like Life of the Black Tarantula,
    The*, 3, 113, 114–15; *Don Quix-
    ote which was a dream*, 113,
    117, 118, 119–20; *Empire of
    the Senseless, The*, 3, 111, 113,
    120; *Eurydice in Underworld*,
    113; *Great Expectations*, 117,
    118–19; *In Memoriam to Iden-
    tity*, 113, 114, 120–21; *Kathy
    Goes to Haiti*, 113, 115–16,
    Politics, 3; *Portrait of an Eye*,
    113; *Pussy, King of the Pirates*,
    113; *Variety* (screenplay), 112
    "Seeing Gender," 111,
Acosta, Oscar Zeta, 4, 90, 91, 93,
    136–40
  *Autobiography of a Brown Buffalo,
    The*, 137–8, *Revolt of the Cock-
    roach People, The*, 138–40
Adam, Helen, 44, 46
Adams, Joan Vollmer, 40, 46, 71
Adamson, Robert, 76
  Canticles on The Skin, 76; *Inside
    Out*, 76; *Rumour, The*, 76
Agnew, Spiro, 92
*AIIIEEEEE! An Anthology of Asian-
    American Writers*, 151, 198,
    199
Albert Hall Poetry Reading/ Wholly
    Communion, 73

Alcott, Louisa May, 116
  Little Women, 116
Alexander, Meena, 146
  *Shock of Arrival: Reflections on Post-
    colonial Experience, The*, 146
Alexie, Sherman, 135, 145
  *Lone Ranger and Tonto Fistfight in
    Heaven, The*, 135
Ali, Muhammad, 93, 198
All That Heaven Allows (film), 215
All The King's Men (film), 93
Allen, Donald, 29, 42, 55
  ed. *New American Poetry, The*, 29
Allen, Paula Gunn, 131
Allotment Act (1887), 243
al-Qaeda, 103
Alvarez, Julia, 170–1
  *How The García Girls Lost Their
    Accents*, 170–1; *In The Time of
    Butterflies*, 170–1; *¡Yo!*, 170
Amerasia Journal, 148, 177
American Indian Movement (AIM),
    130
American Me (film), 163
American Scholar, 141
Americas Review, 173
Amran, David, 48
Anaya, Rudolfo, 135, 163–4
  Alburquerque, 164, *Bless Me,
    Ultima*, 135, 163; *Rio Grande
    Fall*, 163; *Shaman Winter*, 163;
    Zia Summer, 163
Anderson, Sherwood, 189
  Winesburg, Ohio, 189
Angel Hair (magazine), 56
Angel Hair (anthology), 56
Angel Island, 151
Anger, Kenneth, 34
Ansen, Alan, 35

Antin, David, 111
Anzaldúa, Gloria, 161, 198
  Borderlands/La Frontera, 161
Apollinaire, Guillaume, 15
Armstrong, Louis, 59, 232
Arnold, Matthew, 12, 78
  Culture and Anarchy, 12
Artaud, Antonin, 111
Ashbery, John, 179
Aso, Taro, 184
Astaire, Fred, 206
Atsumi, Ikuko, 82
Aubuisson, Roberto d', 108
Aztlán, 135

B
Baca, Jimmy Santiago, 152, 158
  Immigrants in Out Own Land, 152,
  *Martín and Meditations on the
  South Valley*, 158
Bad Subjects, 1
Baez, Joan, 105
Baker, Josephine, 233
Bakker, Jim, 95
Baldwin, James, 231
Ballard, J.G., 22
Bamboo Ridge, 153
  *Best of Bamboo Ridge: The Hawaii
  Writers Quarterly*, eds. Chock,
  Eric and Lum, Darrell H.Y., 153
Banks, Dennis, 130, 131
Baraka, Imamu Amiri, 3, 10, 29–30,
  40, 42, 48, 49, 61
  Dutchman, 32, LeRoi Jones/Amiri
  Baraka Reader, 29; Preface to a
  Twenty Volume Suicide Note, 3,
  29–30
Barker, Diane, 71
Barth, John, 113
Barthelme, Donald, 113
Bashō, Matsuo, 194, 239
Basquiat, Jean-Michel, 59
Bataille, Georges, 111, 114
Baudelaire, Charles, 34
Bearden, Romare, 59, 66
Beat Hotel, 70–1,
Beat Review, The, 11
Beat Scene, 75
Beatles, The, 74, 75, 76
Beatniks, 10,
Beckett, Samuel, 32
  En Attendant Godot, 32
Bellecourt, Clyde, 131
Berman, Shirley, 48

Berman, Wallace, 48
Berkeley, 10,
Bernstein, Carl, 94
Bierce, Ambrose, 2, 90
  Devil's Dictionary, The, 2 "Occurrence
  at Owl Creek Bridge, An," 2,
*Big Aiiieeeee!, An Anthology of Asian-
  American Writers, The*, 151, 198
Biggers, Erle Derr, 174
Biggers, Jeff, 223
  "William Demby Has Not Left the
  Building," 223
Black Mask (magazine), 175
Black Mountain, 52, 54
Black Mountain Review, 22
Black Panthers, 94
Blake, Mike, 71
Blake, William, 3, 72, 77
Blitzer, Wolf, 110
Blunden, Edmund, 183
Borges, Jorge Luis, 113
Born on the Fourth of July (novel), 175
Born on the Fourth of July (film), 175
Bourne, Randolph, 153
Bowes, Ed, 56
Bowles, Jane, 44, 63, 72
  "East Side: North Africa," 72,
  "Everything is Nice," 72
Bowles, Paul, 63, 72
  Hundred Camels in the Courtyard,
  72, *Sheltering Sky, The*, 72
Bradley, Tom, 109
Bradstreet, Anne, 150
Brakhage, Stan, 34
Brando, Marlon, 1, 90
  The Wild One (film), 1, 90
Brecht, Berthold, 34
Bremser, Bonnie (Brenda Frazer), 3, 10,
  36–7, 40, 45
  Troia: Mexican Memoirs, 36–7, 45
Bremser, Ray, 36–7, 40
Breton, André, 58, 59, 66
Brodsky, Joseph, 150
Bronte sisters, 114
Bronte, Charlotte, 116
  Jayne Eyre, 116
Brooke, Rupert, 78
Brooks, Gwendolyn, 53, 159
  "To The Diaspora," 159
Brooks, Mel, 126
  Dir. *Blazing Saddles* (film), 126
Brown, Pete, 73, 74, 77
Bruchac, Joseph, 160
  "Ellis Island," 160

Brustein, Robert, 12
Buchanan, Pat, 94
Buck, Pearl, 174
  Good Earth, The, 174
Buddhism, 13, 50
Bukowski, Charles, 155,
  "Grand Central Market," 155,
  "Near Hollywood," 155
Buena Vista Social Club, 163
Bueys, Joseph, 111
Bunyan, John, 153
Burgess, Anthony, 120
  Clockwork Orange, 120
Burke, Andrew, 76
  Let's Face The Music and Dance, 76
Burroughs, William, 2, 11, 13, 15, 22–4,
  28, 35, 37, 38, 39, 46, 49, 63,
  70, 72, 73, 74, 75, 93; *Dead
  Fingers Talk*, 22; *Junkie*, 40;
  My Education, 56; *The Naked
  Lunch/Naked Lunch*, 3, 9, 22–4,
  35, 36, 40, 47, 71, 73, 120; *Nova
  Express*, 22; *Soft Machine, The*,
  22; *Ticket That Exploded, The*,
  22; *Yage Letters, The*, 22, 71
Bush, George W. Jr., 11, 88, 97, 109
Bush, George, H.W. Sr., 11, 88
Buson, Yosa, 239
Byrne, Edward, 156
  ed. *Valparaiso Poetry Review*, 156
Byrne, Johnny, 73

C
Cage, John, 111
Cain, James M., 104
Caligula (film), 93
Calle Ocho, 162
Camus, Albert, 166
  La Peste, 166
Caney, Mary, 46
Cannastra, Bill, 28
Cano, Daniel, 167
  Pepe Rios, 167
Cao, Lan, 144
  Monkey Bridge, 144
Capote, Truman, 12, 19, 89
  In Cold Blood, 89
Carmichael, Stokely, 66
Carter, Angela, 1, 22
Carter, Jimmy, 11, 88, 95
Carr, Lucien, 40
Carr, Vicki, 140
Casey, William, 95
Cassady, Carolyn, 45

*Heart Beat: My Life with Jack and
  Neal*, 45; *Off The Road: My
  Years with Cassady, Kerouac,
  and Ginsberg*, 45
Cassady, Neal, 13, 25, 28, 46
Castillo, Ana, 165
  Mixquiahuala Letters, The, 165,
  Sapogonia, 165; *So Far From
  God*, 165–6
Castro, Fidel, 71
Céline, Louis-Ferdinand, 117, 211
Cervantes, Lorna Dee, 147, 148, 149,
  158
  "Visions of Mexico While at a
  Writing Symposium in Port
  Townsend, Washington," 147,
  158
Cézanne, Paul, 15
Cha, Theresa Hak Kyung, 143
  Dictée, 143
Chagall, Marc, 27
Challis, Chris, 78
  "The Rhythms of My Own Voice: A
  Brit on the Beats," 78
Chan, Charlie, 143
Chapman, Abraham, 68
  Black Voices, 68, *New Black Voices*,
  68
Chapman, Harold, 71
Chardin, Teilard de, 231
Charlie Chan, 5, 174
Charters, Ann, 45
  ed, *Beat Down to Your Soul: What
  Was The Beat Generation?*, 45;
  *Beats and Company: A Portrait
  of a Literary Generation*, 45;
  Portable Beat Reader, The,
  45, 68
Chase, Hal, 40
Chaucer, Geoffrey, 234
  Knight's Tale, The, 234
Chávez, César, 135, 139, 140, 151, 167
Chavez, Linda, 141
  *Out of the Barrio: Towards a New
  Politics of Hispanic Assimila-
  tion*, 141
Chávez, Denise, 166
  Face of an Angel, 166; *Last of the
  Menu Girls, The*, 166
Cheney, Bill, 71
Chen'en, Wu, 208
  Journey to the West, 208
Chicago Review, 22
Chin, Frank. 4, 143, 175, 198–211

co-ed. *AIIIEEEEE! An Anthology of Asian-American Writers*, 151, 198, 199; *Big Aiiieeeee! An Anthology of Chinese American and Japanese American Literature, The*, 143, 198,198, 199; *Bulletproof Buddhists and Other Essays*, 5, 175, 198, 200–1, 202; *Chickencoop Chinaman, The*, 200; *Donald Duk*, 5, 199–200, 205–8; *Chinaman Pacific & Frisco R.R. Co., The*, 5, 202–5; *Gunga Din Highway*, 5, 175, 205, 208–11; *Ni Umarete, Born in the USA: A Story of Japanese America, 1889–1947*, 198; *Year of the Dragon, The*, 200
"Bulletproof Buddhists," 202, "Chinaman in Singapore, A," 202; "Chinatown Kid, The," 204; "Chinese Lady Dies, A, 204–5; "Come All Ye Asian American Writers of the Real and the Fake," 143–4; "Confessions of a Chinatown Cowboy," 175, 198, 200; "Eat and Run People," 203–4; "Give The Enemy Sweet Sissies and Women," 204; "I Am Talking to The Strategist Sun Tzu About Life When The Subject of War Comes up," 201; "In Search of John Okada," 198; "Lowe Howe and The Three-Legged Toad," 202; "Only Real Day, The," 204; "Railway Standard Time," 202; "Sons of Chan, The, 205; "Yes, Young Daddy," 204
Chin, Marilyn, 4, 157, 174, 175, 176–7
Dwarf Bamboo, 176; *Phoenix Gone, The Terrace Empty, The*, 176; *Rhapsody in Plain Yellow*, 176
"Barbarian Suite," 177; "Child," 177; "End of the Beginning, The," 176; "How I Got That Name, 157, 176–7; "Repulse Bay," 177; "We Are Americans Now, We Live in the Tundra," 174, 176
Chinaman, John, 143
Chinatown (film), 175
Christie, Agatha, 114
Chu, Louis, 207
Eat A Bowl of Tea, 207

Ciardi, John, 156
Birds of Pompeii, The, 156; *Homeward to America*, 156
"Firsts," 156
Cisneros, Sandra, 164–5
Woman Hollering Creek and Other Stories, 164–5
"*Bien* Pretty," 165, "Mericans," 165; "My Lucy Friend Who Smells Like Corn," 165; "Never Marry an American," 165; "Woman Hollering Creek," 165
City Lights Bookstore, 25, 47
City Lights Journal, 11, 64
Cleaver, Eldridge, 108
Cleaver. Katherine, 106
Cleopatra (film), 229, 232
Clift, Montgomery, 215
A Place in The Sun (film), 215
Clinton, Bill, 11, 88, 97, 109
Clinton, Chelsea, 110
Clinton, Hilary, 110
CNN, 110
Cobbing, Bob, 74
Cocteau, Jean, 34
Cofer, Judith Ortiz, 162,167
Island Like You, An, 168; *Latin Deli, The*, 168; *Silent Dancing: A Partial Remembrance of a Puerto Rican Childhood*, 167
"American History," 168; "Corazon's Café," 168; "El Building," 162; "Letter from a Caribbean Island," 168; "Twist and Shout," 168; "Witch's Husband, The," 168
Cohen, Ira, 35
ed. *GNAOUA*, 35
Coleman, Ornette, 72
Colson, Ted, 94
Coltrane, John, 59, 106
Commager, Henry Steele, 189
Conrad, Joseph, 101, 221
Cook-Lynn, Elizabeth, 131, 134,
Why I Can't Read Wallace Stegner and Other Essays: A Tribal Voice, 134; *Contours of The Heart South Asians Map North America*, eds. Sunaima, Maira and Srikanth, Raijini, 151
Coppola, Francis Ford, 219
Apocalypse Now (film), 219
Coppola, Roman, 13

Coppola, Sofia, 186
Lost in Translation, 186
Corman, Cid, 55, 72, 183
ed. *Origin*, 72, 183
Corsiglia, Laura, 66
Corso, Belle Carpenter, 46
Corso, Gregory, 2, 13, 19–21, 34, 40, 43, 50, 56, 61, 70, 71,72, 73, 74, 76, 78, 83, 156
Gasoline, 3, 9, *Mindfield: New and Selected Poems*, 19; *Vestal Lady of Brattle, The*, 3, 9
"America Politica Historia, In Spontaneity," 20; "Bomb," 19, 70, "Cambridge, First Impressions, 20; "Columbia U. Poesy Reading—1975," 20; "For Miles," 21; "Greenwich Village Suicide," 20; " I Am 25," 21; "In The Tunnel-Bone of Cambridge," 20; "Mad Yak, The" 21; "Marriage," 19; "My Hands are a City," 20; "Ode to Coit Tower, 20–21; "Paris," 21; "Requiem for 'Bird' Parker, 20; "Thoughts on a Japanese Movie," 20; "Uccello,"21; "Vestal Lady on Brattle, The" 20; "Vision of Rotterdam, 20–21
Corso, Paula, 156
Corso, Sally November, 46
Cortázar, Julio, 165
Rayuela, 165
Cortés, Hernán, 150
Cortez, Jayne, 159–60
"For The Poets (Christopher Okigbo & Henry Dumas," 159
Cowen, Elise, 35, 40, 41, 42, 43, 46
"Emily," 46
Crane, Hart, 15, 154
The Bridge, 154
Crazy Horse, 155
Creeley, Robert, 13, 15, 46, 52, 72
Cremer, Jan, 75
I Jan Cremer, 75
Crichton, Michael, 185
Rising Sun, 185
Cruz, Victor, Hernández, 151
Red Beans, 161
"Loisaida," 151–2
Cullen, Countee, 159
"Heritage," 159
Cumpián, Carlos, 158
"Cuento," 158

Custer, George Armstrong, 243

D
Daley, Richard, 93
Dalí, Salvador, 59, 82
Dances With Wolves (film), 131
Dancing Lady (film), 206
Davis, Miles, 59
Dawson, Fielding, 42
Dean, James, 67
Dean, John, 94
De Gaulle, Charles, 231
De Quincey, Thomas, 35
De Sade, Marquis de, 37, 93, 111, 114
Juliette, 37
Deleuze, Gilles, 111
Deloria, Vine, 134
Custer Died For Your Sins: An Indian Manifesto, 134; *We Talk, You Listen: New Tribes, New Turf*, 134
Demby, William, 5, 223–34
Beetlecreek, 5, 223, 224–9, 234, *Catacombs, The*; 5, 223–4, 229–33, 234; *Love Song Black*, 5, 223, 224, 233–4
Depp, Johnny, 87
Díaz, Junot, 171, 172
Drown, 171
"Aurora," 172; "Drown," 172; "Fiesta, 1980," 172; "Ysrael," 172
Dickens, Charles, 113
Great Expectations, 113
Dickey, James, 152
Buckdancer's Choice, 152, *Deliverance*, 152
"Slave Quarters," 152
Dickinson, Emily, 52
Dinesen, Isak, 231
Di Prima, Diane, 3, 10, 13, 28, 33–5, 40, 44, 46, 47–51, 57
Calculus of Variation, The, 49; *Dinners & Nightmares*, 49; *Earthsong: poems 1957–1959*, 49; *L.A. Odyssey*, 49; *Loba*, 53; *Memoirs of a Beatnik*, 33–5; *Murder Café*, 49; *New Handbook of Heaven, The*, 49; *New Mexico Poems*, 49; *Recollections of My Life as a Woman: The New York Years*, 33, 45, 48–9, *This Kind of Bird Flies Backward*, 33, 48, 49
"Backyard," 156; "Book of Days," 50; "Brass Furnace Going

Out," 48; "Conversations,"
49; "Elephant Power," 51; "I'll
Always Remember the Maltese
Falcon," 51; "Memories of
Childhood," 49; "More or Less
Love Poems," 49, 50; "New
Mexico Poem," 51; "No Problem
Party Poem," 50; "Passionate
Hipster to His Chick, The"
50; "Poetics," 51; "Practice of
Magical Evocation, The" 51;
"Traveling Again," 51; "Wings-
of-Speech," 51
Didion, Joan, 3, 99–110
   After Henry, 99, 109; *Book of Com-*
      mon Prayer, A, 99; *Democracy*,
      99; *Last Thing That He Wanted,*
      The, 99; *Miami*, 99, 107, 108–9;
      Play It As It Lays, 99; *Political*
      Opinions, 102, 109; *Salvador*,
      99, 107–8; *Slouching Towards*
      Bethlehem, 3, 99, 103–5, 107;
      Telling Stories, 99; *Where I Was*
      From, 99; *White Album, The*,
      3, 99, 105–7; *Year of Magical*
      Thinking, The, 99, 110
   "Clinton Agonistes," 109, "Fixed
      Opinion, Or The Hinge of His-
      tory," 101–3; "Goodbye to All
      That, "105; "Morning After the
      Sixties, The," 105; "On Keep-
      ing a Notebook," 99, 105, 110;
      "Seven Places of Mind," 105;
      "Slouching Towards Bethle-
      hem," 103–4; "Some Dreamers
      of the Golden Dream," 101,
      104; "White Album, The," 99,
      106–7; "Why I Write," 99;
      "Women's Movement, The,"
      100, 106
Docherty, Brian, 74
   Armchair Theatre, 74
Doonesbury, 87
Doors, The, 11, 108
Dove, Rita, 159
   Thomas and Beulah, 159
Dransfield, Michael, 76
   Collected Poems, 76; *Drug Poems*,
      76; *Inspector of Tides, The*, 76;
      Streets of the Long Voyage, 76
Dreiser, Theodore, 215
   American Tragedy, An, 215
Duchamp, Marcel, 58, 63
Duncan, Robert, 26, 52, 76

Duras, Marguerite, 111
Durham, Jimmy, 160
   "Columbus Day," 160
Dworkin, Andrea, 113
Dylan, Bob, 25, 49, 56, 75
   Renaldo and Clara (film), 56

E
Eagleton, Tom, 93
Eastman, Charles Alexander (Ohiyesa).
   131
Easy Rider, 11
Eat a Bowl of Tea, 207
Eberhardt, Richard, 14
   "West Coast Rhythms," 14–15
Eel, Roberta, 6
Ehrlichman, John, 95
Eliot, T.S., 15
   "The Waste Land," 15
Ellington, Duke, 59
Ellis, Royston, 75
   Big Beat Scene, 75, *Jiving to Gyp*, 75,
      Myself to Face, 75, *Rave*, 75
Ellis, Trey, 126, 229
   Home Repairs, 126, *Platitudes*,
      126–5, 229
   "Guess Who's Coming to Seder," 126
Ellison, Ralph, 128, 223, 229
   Invisible Man, 128, 229
Eluard, Paul, 25
Erdrich, Louise, 145
Ernest, Max, 58
Esquire, 88
Estefan, Gloria, 163
Evers, Medgar, 63
Everson, William (Brother Antoninus),
   47
Exclusion Act (1882), 149, 151, 173
Executive Order 9066, 153, 189, 195

F
Fabilli, Mary, 47
   Animal Kingdom: Poems 1964–1974,
      The, 47; *Aurora Bligh and Early*
      Poems, 47; *Poems 1976–1991*,
      47
Fainlight, Harry, 73
   "Spider, The" 73
Fassbinder, Ranier Werner, 217
Faulkner, William, 97, 113, 120–21
   Absalom, Absalom!, 120–21; *Wild*
      Palms, The, 121
Fauser, Jörg, 75
Fenollosa, Ernest, 15

Ferlinghetti, Lawrence, 2, 13, 24–7, 46, 48, 55, 61, 63, 73, 74, 76, 79, 83, 156
  A Coney Island of the Mind, 3, 10, 26–7; *Pictures of the gone world*, 3, 10, 24–6; *Secret Meaning of Things, The*, 73; *Starting From San Francisco*, 73
  "Adieu à Charlot," 25; "After the Cry of Birds," 73; "Autobiography," 25; "Fireword," 63; "I Am Waiting," 25; "Old Italians Dying," 156; "Situation in the West Followed by a Holy Proposal, The," 73; "Starting From San Francisco," 152; "Tentative Description of a Dinner Given to Promote the Impeachment of President Eisenhower," 25
Fernández, Robert, 139, 140
Fernández, Roberto, 170
  Holy Radishes!, 170
Fernández, Roberta, 165
  Intaglio: A Novel in Six Stories, 165
Fire Readings, 63
Firer, Susan, 155, 155
  Lives of Saints and Everything, The, 155
  "God Sightings," 155
Firmat, Gustavo Pérez, 161
  Life on the Hyphen: The Cuban-American Way, 161
Fitzgerald, Scott, 34, 238
  Great Gatsby, The, 238
Floating Bear, The, 48
Flores, Lauro, 172
  ed. *Floating Borderlands: Twenty-Five Years of U.S Hispanic Literature*, 172
Flowers, Gennifer, 97
Fluxus Movement, 111
Fonda, Jane, 209, 210
  Coming Home (film), 209
Ford, Gerald, 88
Forrest, Lee, 71
Fouquet, Betty Lansdown, 101
Foucault, Michel, 111, 130
  This Is Not a Pipe, 130
Frank, Mary, 41, 42
Frank, Robert, 43
Free Speech Movement, 10
Fritsch, William, 47
Frost, Robert, 145, 154
  "The Gift Outright," 154

Fu Manchu, 5, 143, 174, 210
Fugs, The, 11
Fujiwara, Masahiko, 185
  Kokka no Hinkaku/The Dignity of the State, 185
Fuller, Margaret, 1

G
Gallup, Dick, 50
Garcia, Cristina, 169
  Dreaming in Cuban, 169–70
Garcia, Jerry, 138
Gasgoyne, David, 58
Gaudí, Antoni, 82
Genet, Jean, 111, 117
Geok-Lin Lim, Shirley, 151
  co-ed. *Forbidden Stitch, The*, 151
Genji, Tale of, 194, 197
Gillepsie, Dizzie, 59
Gilliam, Terry, 87
  Fear and Loathing (film), 87
Gingrich, New, 100, 109
Ginsberg, Allen, 2, 11, 12, 13, 21, 22, 25, 27, 30, 35, 39, 40, 41, 42, 43, 44, 46, 47, 49, 50, 55, 56, 58, 61, 64, 66,70, 71, 72, 73, 74, 75, 76, 78, 79, 80, 81, 82, 83, 103, 154
  Howl and Other Poems, 9, 10, 61, *Kaddish*, 70
  "America," 66, "Howl" 2, 12, 13–16, 22, 33, 48, 75, "Poetry, Violence, and The Trembling Lambs," 9
Ginsberg, Naomi, 46
Gioseffi, Daniela, 156
Girodias, Maurice, 22, 33
  Olympia Press, 22, 33
Golden, Arthur, 186
  Memoirs of a Geisha, 186
Goldman, Francisco, 173
  Long Night of the White Chickens, The, 173
Goldwater, Barry, 92, 100
Gómez-Peña, Guillermo, 135, 173
  Warrior for Gringostroika, 135, 173
Gonzalez, Babs, 62
Gonzalez, Corky, 135, 139, 140, 158
  I Am Joaquín/Yo Soy Joaquín, 135
  "I Am Joaquín, Yo Soy Joaquín," 158
González, Elian, 162
Goon Show, The, 77

Gordon, Dexter, 59
Gore, Al, 109
Goya, Francisco, 27
Grace, Nancy (and Ronna C. Johnson),
    45
    *Girls Who Wore Black: Women
    Writing The Beat Generation*,
    45; *Breaking The Rule of Cool:
    Interviewing and Reading Beat
    Women Writers*, 45; *Grapeleaves:
    A Century of Arab-American
    Writing*, ed. Hamod, Sam, 150
Grateful Dead, The, 138
Gray, Thomas, 78
Greenwich Village, 10, 41, 48, 56
Greer, Germaine, 76
Grolmes, Samuel, 82
Grove Press, 35
Guevara, Che, 13
Guggenheim Museum, 62
Gunga Din (film), 211
Guthrie, William, 71
Gutiérrez, José Angel, 135
Gysin, Brion, 37, 39, 63, 70, 72
    Last Museum, The, 70

H
Hagedorn, Jessica, 5, 143, 158, 212–22
    ed. *Charlie Chan is Dead*, 5; *Chiquita
    Banana*, 212; *Dangerous Music*,
    212; *Dogeaters*, 5, 143, 212,
    213–18, 222; *Dream Jungle*,
    5, 212, 213, 219–22; *Gangster
    Choir, The* (group), 212; *Gang-
    ster of Love, The*, 5, 212, 213,
    218–19, 222; *Mango Tango*,
    212; *Pet Foods & Tropical
    Apparitions*, 212
    "Kundiman," 212, "Souvenirs," 158
Hagedorn, Jessica, and Roth, Marissa,
    *Burning Heart: A Portrait of The
    Philippines*, 212
Hahn, Kimiko, 157
    "Resistance: A Poem on Ikat Cloth,"
    157
Haight-Ashbury, 10, 88, 100, 103
Halberstam, David, 12
    Fifties, The, 12
Haldeman, H.R., 95
Hammett, Dashiell, 175
    Continental Op, The, 175
Handy, John, 82
Harris, William, 29
    ed. *LeRoi Jones/Amiri Baraka
    Reader*, 29

Hart, Gary, 92
Harte, Bret (and Mark Twain),
    174
    Ah Sin, 174
Harwood, Lee, 74
Havel, Vaclav, 71
Hawaii Five-O (TV series), 209
Hawkins, Coleman, 59
Hawkins, Spike, 73
Hawthorne, Nathaniel, 113, 116
    Scarlet Letter, The, 116, 117
H.D., 52, 53
    Helen in Egypt, 53
Hayden, Robert, 159
    "Middle Passage," 159
Heaney, Seamus, 156
Hearn, Lafcadio, 183
    "Bits of Life and Death," 183
Hearst, Pattie, 109
Heliczer, Piero, 77
Heller, Joseph, 108
    Catch-22, 108
Hemingway, Ernest, 138
Henderson, Lu-Anne, 46
Hendrix, Jimi, 10
Henri, Adrian, 74, 78
Herr, Michael, 175
    Dispatches, 175
Hesse, Hermann, 34
Hijuelos, Oscar, 169
    *Fourteen Sisters of Emilio Montez
    O'Brien, The*, 169; *Mambo
    Kings Play Songs of Love, The*,
    169
Himes, Chester, 70, 126
    Pinktoes, 126
Hinckle, Helen, 46
Hinojosa, Rolando, 135, 164
    Ask a Policeman, 164; *Klail City y
    sus alrededores/Klail City*, 135,
    164
Hinton, Deane, 108
Hippies, 10, 103–4
Hiroshige, Utagawa, 184
Hochman, Sandra, 45
Hogg, James, 35
Hoggart, Richard, 142
Holiday Magazine, 224
Hollander, John, 15
Hollo, Anselm, 73, 79
    ed. *Jazz Poems*, 79
    "*Red Cats* Revisited," 79
Holmes, John Clellon, 3, 10, 13, 27–9,
    40, 41, 43
    Go, 3, 27–9, 40

"This is the Beat Generation," 41
Hongo, Garrett, 188, 189, 194–5, 197
  Volcano, 188, 194–5, *Yellow Light*, 189
  "Stepchild," 189
hooks, bell, 198
Horloff, Guy, 71
Horovitz, Frances, 78
Horovitz, Michael, 3, 70, 72, 73, 74, 77–9, 83
  Bank Holiday, 78; ed. *Children of Albion: Poetry of The Under-ground in Britain*, 77; *Growing Up: Selected Poems and Pictures, 1951–'79*, 78; *Wordsounds and Sightlines*, 78
  "For Leon Bismarck Beiderbeck," 78; "Glad Day," 78; "Homages & Updates," 78; "Jazz Poems," 78; "Soho Awakening," 77; "Spring Welcomes You To London," 77; "Thelonius," 78
Howe, James Wong, 209
Howe, Susan, 155
  Europe of Trusts, The, 155
  "Speeches at the Barriers," 155
Hughes, Langston, 60, 65, 152
  "Harlem," 60; "Negro Speaks of Rivers, The," 60, 152; "Weary Blues, The," 60
Humphrey, Hubert, 93
Huncke, Herbert, 15, 27, 28, 35, 39–41, 42, 46
  Guilty of Everything, 39–41; *Evening Sun Turned Crimson, The*, 39, 40; *Huncke's Journal*, 39
Hunt, Howard, 95
Hurston, Zora Neale, 3, 125, 127–8, 233
  Dust Tracks on a Road, 125, 127, 128; *I Love Myself When I Am Laughing . . . And Then Again When I Am Being Mean and Impressive: A Zora Neale Hurston Reader*, 127–8, 127; *Jonah's Gourd Vine*, 127; *Mules & Men*, 128; *Their Eyes Were Watching God*, 125, 127
  "How It Feels to Be Colored Me," 125
Hutchinson, Anne, 1
Hwang, David, 5, 143, 199, 211
  M. Butterfly, 199

I

I Love Lucy, 194
Ignatow, David, 157
Iliad, 194
Immigration Act (1924), 175
In The Empire of the Senses (film), 120
Inada, Lawson Fusao, 157–8
  "Legends From The Camp," 157–8
Indian Removal Act (1830), 149
Ino, Nobuyoshi, 82
International Times, 75
Ishiguro, Kazuo, 183, 187–8
  Pale View of the Hills, A, 187–8; *Remains of the Day, The*, 187
Ishihara, Shintaro, and Morita, Akio, 185
  Japan That Can Say No: Why Japan Will Be First Among Equals, The, 185
Islas, Arturo, 167
  Migrant Souls, 167
Issa, Kobayashi, 239

J

James, Henry, 34, 101, 105
Jandl, Ernst, 73
Januszczak, Waldemar, 81
Jen, Gish, 174, 200
  Typical American, 174, 200
Joans, Ted, 3, 58–69
  Afrodisia: Old and New Poems, 58; *All of Ted Joans and No More: Poems and Collages*, 58; *Beat Funky Jazz Poems*, 58; *Beat Poems*, 58; *Black Pow-Wow: Jazz Poems*, 58; *Niggers From Outer Space*, 68; *Teducation: Selected Poems 1949–1999*, 58, 66
  "Africa," 64; "Afrique Acciden-tale," 63; "Alphabetical Love You," 66; "Another Dream Deferred?," 60; "Collected & Selected Groupings," 66; "Commonplace Bulues," 60; "Dead Serious," 60; "Dear Miss America," 67; "Do Not Walk Outside This Area," 65; "Good Morning," 63; "Happy 78 Hughes Blues," 60; "Harlem to Picasso," 59; "Him The Bird," 62, 67; "How Do You Want Yours?," 66; "I, Too, At

the Beginning," 56; "I Am The Lover," 66; "Ice Freezes Red," 59; "Jazz Anatomy," 59; "Jazz Must be a Woman," 59; "Je Me Vois (I See Myself)," 56; 60, 64, 65, 66, 69; "Ladder of Basquiat, The," 59; "Long Gone Lover Blues," 59; "My Ace of Spades," 63; "My Trip," 64; "Nice Colored Man, The," 67; "No Mo' Kneegrow," 63, 160; "Powerful Black Starmichael," A, 66; "Sanctified Rhino," 59, 67; "Sax Bit, The," 59; "Sermon, The," 61; "Statue of 1713, The," 59; "They Forget Too Fast," 59; "Uh, Huh," 67; "Why Try," 67; "Wild Spirit of Kicks, The," 62

Johns, Jasper, 179

Johnson, James Weldon, 127
Autobiography of an Ex-Colored Man, The, 127

Johnson, Joyce, 3, 10, 41–3, 45, 46
Door Wide Open: A Beat Love Affair in Letters, 3, 41–2; *Minor Characters: A Beat Memoir,* 41, 42–3, 45

Johnson, Kay, 71

Johnson, Lyndon, 88

Johnson, Ronna C. (and Nancy M. Grace), 45
Breaking The Rule of Cool: Interviewing and Reading Beat Women Writers, 45; *Girls Who Wore Black: Women Writing The Beat Generation,* 45

Jones, Brian, 72

Jones, Hettie, 41, 42, 45, 49
How I Became Hettie Jones, 45

Jones, LeRoi, see Baraka

Joplin, Janis, 10, 106, 194

Journey to the West, 208

K

Kadohata, Cynthia, 192–3, 197
Floating World, The, 192–3

Kahlo, Frida, 65

Kafka, Franz, 24, 35, 82, 194

Kaja, 71

Kandel, Lenore, 47
The Love Book, 47

Kanellos, Nicolás, 151
Herencia: The Anthology of Hispanic Literature in the United States, 151

Kasabian, Linda, 107

Kaufman, Bob, 3, 45.61

Kaufman, Eileen, 45
"Laughter Sounds Orange at Night," 45

Keats, John. 48

Keene, Donald, 80

Kelley, John, 155

Kelley, William Melvin, 229
dem, 229

Kennedy, Edward, 92

Kennedy, John F., 49, 63, 153, 229, 232

Kennedy, Robert, 101,140

Kerouac, Edie Parker 45, 46
You'll Be OK: My Life with Jack Kerouac, 45

Kerouac, Gabrielle (Mémère), 46

Kerouac, Jack, 2, 3, 10, 13, 15, 16–19, 22, 27, 28, 30, 34, 39, 40, 41, 42, 43, 44, 62, 64, 67, 70, 75, 83
Dharma Bums, The, 3; *Mexico City Blues,* 62, 71; *On the Road,* 2, 9, 10, 12, 13, 16–19, 29, 61; *On The Road* manuscript, 12; *Pomes of all Sizes,* 19; *Subterraneans, The,* 55; *Scripture of the Golden Eternity, The,* 75 "Bath Tub Thought," 19; "Letter to Myself," 10

Kerouac, Joan Haverty, 45
Nobody's Wife: The Smart Aleck and The King of the Beats, 45

Kerouac, Stella Stampas, 46

Kesey, Ken, 75, 96

Killy, Jean-Claude, 94

Kim, Myung Mi, 158
"Into Such Assembly," 158

King, Charles, 131

King, Martin Luther, 161

Kingston, Maxine Hong, 5, 143, 199, 202, 210, 211
China Men, 200, *Tripmaster Monkey: His Fake Book,* 202; *Woman Warrior: Memoirs of a Girlhood Among Ghosts, The,* 143, 199

Kinnell, Galway, 155

Kinsey, Alfred, 28, 40

Kirsanov, Semyon, 79

Kitazono, Katsue, 81

Klein, Joe, 110

Kline, Franz, 25, 59

Knight, Brenda, 44
Women of the Beat Generation: The Writers, Artists and Muses at the Heart of the Revolution, 44
Koch, Kenneth, 179
Kogawa, Joy, 192, 197
Obasan, 192
Koizumi, Junichiro, 184
Kooning, Willem de, 59
Körte, Mary Nobert, 47
Beginnings of Lines: Response to Albion Moonlight, 47; *Midnight Bridge*, 47
Korzybski, Alfred, 23
Kovic, Ron, 175
Born on The Fourth of July, 175
Kropotkin, Peter, 34
Kunitz, Stanley, 157
Kurosawa, Akira, 184, 195
Rashomon, 184
Kyger, Joanne, 3, 44, 45, 46, 51–5, 57, 72, 183
About Now: Collected Poems, 52; *All This Every Day*, 52, 53; *Going On: Selected Poems 1958–1980*, 52; *Just Space*, 54; *Places To Go*, 53; *Some Sketches from the Life of Helena Petrovna Blavasky*, 53; *Japan and India Journals 1960–1964, The*, 45, 52, 54–5, reissued as *Strange Moon: Japan and India Journals*, 52; *Tapestry and The Web, The*, 52, 53; *Wonderful Focus of You, The*, 53
"A Brisk Wind in Blowing Thoughts to Philip on the Phone," 54; "All Members of the Dharma Committee Are Cool," 53; "At The Purple Gate Tent Bolinas, My Memoirs," 53; "I'm going to be a poet. I can put it together too," 53; "Is This the Buddha?," 53; "July '92 at Naropa," 52; "Just Space," 54; "Life of Naropa, The," 53; "October 29, Wednesday," 52; "The Odyssey," 53; "Philip Whalen's Hat," 53; "Thank You. It's Me," 53; "Pigs for Circe in May, The" 53; "12.29 & 30," 53; "Snapshot for Lew Welch 25 Years Later," 53; "Tapestry," 52; "Town Hall Reading with Beat Poets," 54

L
La Malinche, 150
LaFemina, Gerry, 156
Lam, Wilfredo, 65
L-A-N-G-U-A-G-E poets, 54
Larson, Charles R., 131
American Indian Fiction, 131
Laski, Michael, 105
Last of the Mohicans (film), 131
Lautrec, Toulouse, 114
Laviera, Tato, 158
AmerRícan, 158
Lawrence, D.H., 211
Leary, Timothy, 49, 138
Leduc, Violette, 114
Lee, Chang-rae, 144
Native Speaker 144
Lee, Li-Young, 157
City in Which I Love You, The, 157
"Cleaving, The" 157
Lee, Sky, 200, 211
Disappearing Moon Café, 200
Lennon, John, 186
Leong, Russell, 4, 147, 148, 149, 157, 175, 177–9
Phoenix Eyes and Other Stories, 178; *Country of Dreams and Dust, The*, 178
"Aerogrammes," 178–9; "In the Country of Dreams and Dust," 157
Lero, Etienne, 59
Levertov, Denise, 46, 52, 156
Here and Now, 46
"Illustrious Ancestors," 156
Levine, Lawrence W., 2
Opening of the American Mind: Canons, Culture, and History, The, 2
Levine, Philip, 156
"I Was Born in Lucerne," 156
Lewinsky, Monica, 109
Lewis and Clarke Expedition, 152
Lieberman, Joseph, 109
Lincoln, Abby, 82
Litt, Toby, 75
Beatniks: An English Road Movie, 75
Little Big Horn, 243
Locke, Alain, 126
ed. *New Negro: An Interpretation, The*, 126
Logue, Christopher, 73, 78
London, Jack, 174
Daughter of the Snows, A, 174

"Unparalleled Invasion, The," 174
Lone Star (film), 173
Lorca, Frederico, 15, 25, 34
Los Angeles Times, 106
Los Lobos, 163
Losavio, Francesco, 231
Lowe, Pardee, 199
  Father and Glorious Descendant, 199
Lowell, Amy, 154
Lowell, James Russell, 154
Lowell, Robert, 79, 147, 148, 149, 154, 160
  "Fourth of July in Maine," 147, 160
Lucie-Smith, Edward, 74
Lum, Wing Tek, 4, 149, 157, 175, 180–2
  Expounding The Doubtful Points, 181
  "At a Chinaman's Grave," 157;
  "Chinese Hot Pot, 182; "Minority Poem," 149; "Moon Festival at Kahala Beach park," 181–2;
  "Translations," 181

M
Macbeth, George, 74
  "Owl," 74
Maciunas, George, 111
Mad Magazine, 61
Magritte, Réné, 58, 59, 130
Mailer, Norman, 32, 34, 89, 198
  Advertisements for Myself, 89; *White Negro, The*, 61
Malcolm X, 49, 63, 64, 161
Mallat, Jean, 214
  Les Philippines, 214
Manchurian Candidate, The (film), 175
Manson, Charles, 106, 107, 140
Marcos, Ferdinand, 95
Marcuse, Herbert, 111
Mariel Boatlift, 162
Marin, Cheech, 135
Marlowe, Alan, 49
Martin, Peter, 25
Martinez, Demetria, 167
  Mother Tongue, 167
Mason, Bonnie Ann, 175
  In Country, 175
Masvidal, Raul, 108
Matrix trilogy, 22
Mayakovski, Vladimir, 79
McClure, Joanna, 45, 47, 48
  Extended Love Poem, 47; *Hard Edge*, 47; *Wolf Eyes*, 45, 47, 48

McClure, Michael, 3, 10, 32–3, 45
  Beard, The, 32–3
  "Writing *The Beard, Lighting The Corners*," 32
McCarthy, Gene, 140
McCarthy, Mary, 22,
McCarthyism, 10
McCunn, Ruthanne Lum, 200, 211
  Thousand Pieces of Gold, 200
McDarrah, Fred, 62
McGough, Roger, 74, 78
McGovern, George, 92, 93
McGrath, Tom, 73, 155
  Crazy Horse, 155
McKay, David, 82
McLuhan, Marshall, 230, 231
McQueen, Steve, 210
  Sand Pebbles, The (film), 210
Means, Russell, 130, 131
Meany, George, 93
Medina, Pablo, 159
  "Madame America," 158
Meese, Ed, 95
Melville, Herman, 1, 2, 97, 174
  Confidence-Man, The, 2, 152, 174;
  Letter to Evert Duyckinck, 1
Menache, Samuel, 156
  Niche Narrows: New and Selected Poems, The, 156
  "Promised Land, The," 156
Mencken, H.L., 93, 125
Metropolitan Museum, 62
Michelangelo, 231
  Pietà, 231
Milagro Beanfield War, The (film), 173
Milagro Beanfield War, The (novel), 173
Miles, Barry, 70, 74
  Beat Hotel: Ginsberg, Burroughs and Corso in Paris 1957–1963, The, 70
Miller, Henry, 26
  Into the Night Life, 26
Millstein, Gilbert, 18–19
  New York Times review of *On The Road*, 18–19
Milton, John, 145
Minneapolis Tribune, 129
Mirja, 71
Miró, Jean, 58, 82
Mishima, Yukio, 186, 194
  Confessions of a Mask, 186; *Sea of Fertility, The*, 186; *Temple of the Golden Pavilion, The*, 186

"Patriotism," 186
Miskievicz, Adam, 150
Mitchell, Adrian, 73, 74, 78
"To Whom It May Concern," 73,
  74
Mitchell, John, 95
Mo, Timothy, 187
Mohamed, Hamri, 72
Mohr, Nicholasa, 168
  Growing Up Inside The Sanctuary of
    My Imagination, 168; *In Nueva*
    York, 168; *Magic Shell, The*,
    168; *Matter of Pride, A*, 168;
    Nilda, 168
Momaday, N. Scott, 149
Monk, Thelonius, 59
Monroe, Marilyn, 49, 232
Moore, Alan, 22
Moore, Robin, 175
  Dir. *Green Berets, The* (film), 175
Mora, Pat, 158
  "Immigrants," 158
Morales, Alejandro, 166
  Rag Doll Plagues, The, 166
Morales, Ed, 145
  "Rebirth of a New Rican," 145
Moraga, Cherrié, 135
  Loving in the War Years: lo que
    nunca pasó or sus labios,
    135
Morgan, Frank, 82
Mori, Toshio, 189–90
  Yokohama, California, 189–90
  "Lil' Yokohama," 190; "Say It With
    Flowers," 190; "Slant-Eyed
    Americans," 190; "Tomorrow
    is Coming Children," 189–90;
    "Woman Who Makes Swell
    Doughnuts, The," 190
Morris, William, 71
Morrison, Jim, 106
Morrison, Toni, 148, 228
  Jazz, 148
Mortola, Sandra, 156
Mottram, Eric, 74–5
  ed. *Poetry Review*, 74
Mura, David, 143, 188, 195–7
  Colors of Desire, The, 143; *Male*
    Grief: Notes on Pornography
    and Addiction, A, 143; *Turning*
    Japanese: Memoirs of a Sansei,
    143, 188, 195–7
Murasaki, Shikibu, 197
  Tale of Genji, The, 197

Murakami, Haruki, 76
  Noruwei No Mori/Norwegian Wood,
    76
Murakami, Ryu, 76
  Kagirinaku Tomeu ni Chikai Buru/
    Almost Transparent Blue, 76
Murayama, Milton, 191–2, 197
  All I Asking For Is My Body, 191–2
Murphy, Ann, 46
Murnaghan, Brigid, 45
Museum of Modern Art (MOMA), 62
Muskie, Ed, 93
My Lai, 101

N
Naguchi, Thomas A., 140
Naipaul, V.S., 194
Nakasone, Yasuhiro, 184
Naropa, Jack Kerouac School of Disem-
  bodied Poetics, 3, 11, 56
Nash, Thomas, 35
  Unfortunate Traveller, The, 35
Nation, The, 88
National Observer, 88
Nemerov, Howard, 56, 157
Neville, Richard, 76
  Hippie, hippie shake; the dreams, the
    trips, the trials, the love-ins, the
    screw-ups . . . the sixties, 76
New Departures, 77
New Journalism, 1
New Moon Poetry Festival, 77
News Hour (PBS), 141
Newton, Huey, 106
New York Review of Books, 99, 100
New York Times Magazine, 88
Ng, Fae Myenne, 211
Niatum, Duane, 151
  ed. *Harper's Anthology of 20th*
    Century Native American
    Poetry, 151
Nichols, John, 173
  Milagro Beanfield War, The, 173
Nicosia, Gerald, 61, 68
Nimmo, Dixie, 71
Nixon, Richard, 11, 88, 92,93, 94,
  97
Noguchi, Yone, 188
  American Diary of a Japanese Girl,
    The, 188
North American Free Trade Agreement
  (NAFTA), 162
Norton Anthology of African American
  Literature, 68

Norse, Harold, 3, 10, 37–9, 70,
    Beat Hotel, 37–9, 70, *Memoirs of a
    Bastard Angel*, 38
North, Oliver, 95
    North to Alaska (film), 204
Norton, John, 155
    Light at the End of the Bog, The, 155
    "Com-plaint," 155
Novarro, Ramon, 106
Nuttall, Jeff, 73, 78
    Bomb Culture, 73, 78
Nye, Naomi Shihab. 150
    "Steps," 150

O

Obama, Barack, 11
Obenzinger, Hilton, 157
    "This Passover or the Next I Will
    Never Be in Jerusalem," 157;
    "X of 1492, The," 157
Obejas, Achy, 170
    Memory Mambo, 170; *We Have
    Come All This Way From Cuba
    So You Could Dress Like This?*,
    170
Oe, Kenzaburo, 186–7, 194
    *Day He Himself Shall Wipe My Tears
    Away, The*, 187
    "Japan, the Ambiguous and Myself"
    (Nobel Prize Address), 187
O'Hara, Frank, 51, 62, 179
Okada, John, 190–1, 197
    No-No Boy, 190–1
Oki, Itaru, 82
Oland, Warner, 209
Olisevich, Alik, 71
Olmos, Edward James, 135, 163
    Zoot Suit (film), 163, *American Me*
    (film), 163
Olson, Charles, 2, 15, 26, 46, 52, 55,
    72
Olympia Press, 22, 33
O'Neill, Eugene, 150
    Long Day's Journey Into Night, 150
Ono, Yoko, 112, 186
Oppenheimer, Joel, 48
Orbison, Roy, 194
Oregon Trail, The, 152
Origin, 72
Orlovsky, Lafcadio, 40, 41
Orlovsky, Peter, 40, 41, 55, 61, 70, 71,
    72
Ortiz, Simon, 145, 149, 160
    "Wind and Glacier Voices," 160

Orwell, George, 101, 103
Osborne, John, 72
Oshima, Nagisa, Dir. 120
    In the Empire of the Senses (film), 120
Ovid, 35
Owens, Louis, 135
    *Mixedblood Messages: Literature,
    Film, Family, Place*, 135
Oz Magazine, 75

P

Page, Robin, 71
Paglia, Camille, 46
    Vamps and Tramps: New Essays, 46
Palmer, Gail, 96
Paris Review, 98
Parker, Charlie, 3, 11, 20, 67
Parker, Edie, 40, 46
Pasolini, Pier Paolo, 114
Pasternak, Boris, 79
Patten, Brian, 73, 74, 78
Paz, Octavio, 65
Peabody, Richard, 44
    ed. *Different Beat: Writings by
    Women of the Beat Generation,
    A*, 44–5
Partisan Review, 15, 43
Penrose, Roland, 58
Pérez, Loida Maritz, 171, 172
    Geographies of Home, 171, 172
Perry, Matthew, 153, 188
Picasso, Pablo, 27
Pickard, Tom, 74, 78
Pike, Bishop James, 107
Pinckney, Darryl, 4, 139
    High Cotton, 127
Plath, Sylvia, 154
    Daddy," 155, "Lady Lazarus," 154
Playboy, 88
Plimpton, George, 98
    ed. *Paris Review*, 98
Plotinus, 15
Podhoretz, Norman, 12
    "Know-Nothing Barbarians, The,"
    12
*Post-Gibran: Anthology of New Arab
    American Writing*, eds. Akash,
    Munir and Mattawa, Khaled,
    150
Poe, Edgar Allan, 15, 25, 61
Poetry Review, 74
Poets Press, 40
Polanski, Roman, 106, 175
    Dir. *Chinatown* (film), 175

Polite, Carlene Hatcher, 126
Sister X and The Victims of Foul Play, 126
Pollock. Jackson, 25, 62
Pound, Ezra, 15, 34, 48, 49, 55, 81, 174, 231
Cantos, The, 174
Powlak, Mark, 150
"The Buffalo Sequence," 150
Prévert, Jacques, 25
Paroles, 25
Puente, Tito, 163
Pulitzer, Herbert, "Pete," and Pulitzer, Roxanne, 96
Pull My Daisy (film), 11
Pushkin, Alexander, 79
Pynchon, Thomas, 22

Q
Quinn, Anthony, 140

R
Rand, Ayn, 34
Rawls, Lou, 83
Raworth, Tom. 74
Ray, Man, 58
Raza Unida, La, 135, 136
Réage, Pauline, 118
L'Histoire d'O, 118
Reagan, Ronald, 11, 88, 95, 97, 109
Rechy, John, 167
City of Night, 167, *Miraculous Day of Amalia Gómez*, 167
Redford, Robert, 173
Dir. *Milagro Beanfield War, The*, 173
Redgrave, Peter, 74
Reed, Ishmael, 3, 66, 126, 146, 156, 228, 229
Flight to Canada, 126; *Free-Lance Pallbearers: An Irreverent Novel, The*, 126; *Mumbo Jumbo*, 126, 229; *Writin' is Fightin'*, 198; *Yellow Back Radio Broke-Down*, 126
"America: The Multinational Society," 146
Reich, Wilhelm, 28
Reiner, Bob, 62, 67
Resnais, Alain, 186
Dir. *Hiroshima Mon Amour* (film), 186
Rexroth, Kenneth, 48, 80, 82
Revard, Carter, 145
Winning The Dust Bowl, 145

"Herbs of Healing: American Values in American Indian Literature," 145
Revista Chicana-Riqueña, 172
Rimbaud, Arthur, 15, 25, 64, 76, 111, 113, 114. 120, 121
Le Bateau Ivre, 76, *Une Saison en Enfer*, 76
Ring, Kevin, 75
ed. *Beat Scene*, 75
Rivera, Diego, 65
Rivera, Edward, 167
Family Installments: Memories of Growing Up Hispanic, 167
Rivera, Tomás, 135, 163
"*. . . y no se tragó la tierra/And the Earth Did Not Part*, 135, 163
Rivers, Sam. 82
Robbe-Grillet, Alain, 111
Roberts, Cokie, 110
Roberts, Oral, 95
Robertson, Pat, 93
Rodriguez, Richard, 4, 136, 140–3, 198
Brown: The Last Discovery of America, 142–3; *Days of Obligation: An Argument With My Mexican Father*, 142; *Hunger of Memory: The Education of Richard Rodriguez, A*, 140–2
Roethke, Theodore, 155
"Cuttings," 154; "Frau Bauman, Frau Schmidt, and Frau Schwartz," 155; "Root Cellar," 155
Rogers, Ginger, 206
Rohmer, Sax, 174
Rolling Stone, 88, 94, 95
Rolling Stones, The, 72
Rollins, Sonny, 59
Rose, Wendy, 145
Rosenthal, Irving, 3, 10, 35–6, 40, 46
Sheeper, 35–6, 40
Rotella, Mimmo, 231
Ruby, Jack, 49
Rukeyser, Muriel, 157
Russell, Vickie, 40, 46

S
Sadat, Anwar, 118
Sage, Lorna, 1
"Obituary for Angela Carter," 1
Saiki, Jessica, 193
From the Lanai and Other Hawaii Stories, 193

"From the Lanai," 193; "Hermit, The," 193; "Oribu," 193
Salazar, Reuben, 139
Salerno Beach (film), 204
Salinas, Luis, 149
"Ode to Mexican Experience," 149
Salles, Walter, 13
Dir. Motorcycle Diaries, The (film), 13
San Francisco Examiner, 88
San Juan, Epifanio, 143
Racism and Cultural Studies: Critiques of Multiculturalist Ideology and the Politics of Difference, 143
Sand Creek Massacre, 243
Sandburg, Carl, 152
"Chicago," 152; "Hog Butcher," 152; "Freight Handler to the Nation," 152; "Stacker of Wheat," 152
Sanders, Ed, 11
Tales of Beatnik Glory, 11
Sartre, Jean-Paul, 32, 34, 66
Huis Clos, 32
Sasaki, Nanao, 76
Allen Ginsberg Meets Nanao Sakaki (video), 76; Bellyfuls, 76; Break The Mirror, 76
Saturday Evening Post, 99
Sayles, John, 173
Dir. Lone Star (film), 173
Scaffold, The, 74
Scanlon's Monthly, 88
Schwartz, Delmore, 157
Schlesinger, Arthur, 2
Disuniting of America; Reflections on a Multicultural Society, The, 2
Schomburg Library, 63
Schuyler, George, 125
Black No More, 125
Schule für Dictung, 71
Selby, Hubert, 48
Shakespeare, William, 87, 194
Shankar, S., 158
"Passage to North America," 158
Shapiro, Karl, 157
Shelley, Patrick, 71
Shepp, Archie, 59, 66
Shiraishi, Kazuko, 3, 70, 76–7, 80–3
Little Planet and Other Poems, 81; Sei-naru Inja No Kisetsu/Seasons of Sacred Lust, 77, 82; Tomago No Furu Machi/Falling Egg City, 81

"I and I," 81; "Dedicated to John Coltrane," 83; "Little Planet," 81; "Man Root, The," 81; "My America," 82–3; "My Tokyo," 82–3; "Once Again, The Season of the Sacred Lecher," 81, 82; "Phallic Root," 81; "Phallus," 81; "Spring," 81
Shoji, Kaoru, 76
Akazukin-chan Ki Wo Tsukete/ Be Careful Little Red Riding Hood, 76
Shumsky, Thelma, 71
Silko, Leslie Marmon, 4, 132–4
Almanac of The Dead, 132–4
Silliman, Ron, 51
Sillitoe, Alan, 72
Simic, Charles, 150
"Wind, The," 150
Simpson, O.J., 97
Sinatra, Frank, 51
Sinclair, Iain, 74, 78
Kodak Mantra Diaries, October 1966 to June 1971, 74
Sirhan, Sirhan, 140
Sitting Bull, 243
Skir, Leo, 35
Smart, Verta Kali, 71
Smith, Ali, 187
Smith, Leo, 82
Smith, Bessie, 51
Smith, Patti, 47
Horses, 47, Seventh Heaven, 47
"Introduction," An Accidental Autobiography: The Selected Letters Gregory Corso, 47; "Piss Factory/Hey Joe," 47
Snyder, Gary 1, 13, 15, 30, 54, 72, 183, 195
"Notes on the Beat Generation," 9
Soderbergh, Steven, 173
Dir. Traffic (film), 173
Solomon, Barbara Probst, 10, 13, 30–2
Beat of Life, The, 30–2
Solomon, Carl, 14, 46
Solt, John, 82
Sommerville, Ian, 70
Sone, Monica, 4, 143, 197
Nisei Daughter, 143–4
Song, Cathy, 158
"Easter: Wahiawa, 1959," 158
Sontag, Susan, 101, 118
Spellman, A.B., 3, 48, 61

Spicer, Jack, 52
Spider Magazine, 88
St. John of the Cross, 15
St. Marks's Poetry Project, 3, 56
Stand and Deliver (film), 135
Star Trek, 194
Starr, Kenneth, 110
Stars and Stripes, 224
Steadman, Ralph, 94
Stefanile, Felix, 156
"Americanization of the Immigrant,
   The," 156
Stein, Gertrude, 52
Steinbeck, John, 231
Stern, Gerald, 156
"Soap," 156
Stevens, Wallace, 145
Stevenson, Adlai, 49
Stevenson, Robert Louis, 113
Suárez, Virgil, 170
Havana Thursdays, 170
Summer of Love (1967), 10
Susskind, David, 12
Open End, 12
Swaggart, Jimmy, 95
Switters, Kurt, 73

T

TallMountain, Mary, 149
Tan, Amy, 143, 144, 199, 210
Joy Luck Club, The, 144; *Saving Fish
   From Drowning*, 144
Tanizaki, Junichiro, 195
Tate, Sharon, 106
Taylor, Edward, 150
Telemundo (TV)
Thomas, Edward, 78
Thomas, Piri, 167
Down These Mean Streets, 167
Thompson, Hunter, 3, 87–98
Better Than Sex, 97; *Curse of Lomo,
   The*, 89; *Fear and Loathing in
   America: The Brutal Odyssey of
   an Outlaw Journalist 1968–
   1976*, 89; *Fear and Loathing in
   Las Vegas: A Savage Journey
   to the Heart of the American
   Dream*, 3, 90–2, 136; *Fear and
   Loathing on the Campaign
   Trail '72*, 92–3; *Generation of
   Swine*, 95; *Great Shark Hunt,
   The*, 93–5; *Hell's Angels: The
   Strange and Terrible Saga of the
   Outlaw Motorcycle Gangs*, 3,

88, 89–90, 96; *Hey Rube: Blood
   Sport, the Bush Doctrine, and
   the Downward Spiral of Dumb-
   ness: Modern History from the
   Sports Desk*, 89, 97; *Kingdom
   of Fear: Loathsome Secrets of a
   Star-Crossed Child in the Final
   Days of the American Century*,
   89, 97; *Prince Jellyfish*, 93;
   *Proud Highway: The Saga of
   a Desperate Southern Gentle-
   man 1955–1967, The*, 89; *Rum
   Diary*, 89, 93; *Screwjack*, 89;
   Songs of the Doomed, 93–7
Thoreau, Henry David, 1, 241
Walden, 241
Thurman, Wallace, 125–6
Infants of The Spring, 125–6
Time, 88, 110, 141
Times Literary Supplement, 74
Tindall, Tim, 71
Tokyo Rose, 143, 184
Toler, Sidney, 209
Torah, The, 12, 15
Traffic (film), 173
Trail of Tears (1838), 149
Transit, 75
Tremblay, Gail, 149, 160
"Indian Singing in 20th Century
   America," 160
Tripp, Linda, 109
Trocchi, Alexander, 35, 40, 73, 74, 78,
   114
Cain's Book, 74; *Young Adam*, 74
Trudeau, Gary, 87
Doonesbury, 87
Tsumura, Yumiko, 82
Twain, Mark, 2, 152, 174
Huckleberry Finn, 152; *Pudd'nhead
   Wilson*, 225
"What is Man?," 2
Twain, Mark (and Harte, Bret), 174
Ah Sin, 174

U

Ulewicz, Laura, 45
Umezu, Kazutoki, 82
Univision (TV)

V

Valdés, Valda, 159
"English Con Salsa," 159
Valdez, Luis, 135
Zoot Suit, 135

Valparaiso Poetry Review, 156
Vedas, The, 12
Vega, Ed., 168–9
  Casualty Report, 168–9; *Comeback,
    The*, 168
  "Casualty Report," 169; "Kite, The,"
    169; "Revenge and Prelude to
    a Well Deserved Suicide," 169;
    "Spanish Roulette," 169
Vega, Janine Pommy, 40, 47
  Poems for Fernando, 47; *Tracking
    The Serpent: Journeys to Four
    Continents*, 47
Verlaine, Paul, 76
Vietnam, 88, 95–6,
Village Voice, The, 43, 61
Vinkenoog, Simon, 73, 75
  Hoogseizoen/High Season, 75
Viramontes, Helena, 167
  Under the Feet of Jesus, 167
Vizenor, Gerald, 4, 5, 128–32, 235–46
  Almost Ashore: Selected Poems, 5,
    235, 236–42, 246; *Bear Island:
    The War at Sugar Point*, 5, 236,
    242–6; *Bearheart*, 129, 235,
    Chancers, 130, 238; *Cross-
    bloods: Bone Courts, Bingo,
    and Other Reports*, 128, 130;
    *Dead Voices: Natural Agonies in
    The New World*, 129; *Earthdiv-
    ers: Tribal Narratives on Mixed
    Descent*, 130; *Father Meme*,
    130, 235; *Fugitive Poses: Native
    American Scenes of Absence and
    Presence*, 130, 131–2; *Griever:
    An American Monkey King in
    China*, 129; *Heirs of Colum-
    bus, The*, 129; *Hiroshima Bugi:
    Atomu 57*, 130, 235; *Hotline
    Healers: An Almost Browne
    Novel*, 129–30; *Interior Land-
    scapes: Autobiographical Myths
    and Metaphors*, 129, 236, 239,
    242; *Manifest Manners: Postin-
    dian Warriors of Survivance*,
    130–31; *People Named The
    Chippewa, The*, 241; *Raising
    The Moon Vines*, 239; *Seventeen
    Chirps: Haiku in English*, 239;
    *Shadow Distance: A Gerald
    Vizenor Reader*, 235; *Summer in
    The Spring: Ojibwe Lyric Poems
    and Tribal Stories*, 236; *Trickster
    of Liberty: Tribal Heirs to Wild

Baronage, The, 129, 235; *Two
    Wings The Butterfly*, 236; *Word-
    arrows: Indians and Whites in
    The New Fur Trade*, 130, 236
  "Camp Grounds," 241; "Choir
    of Memory," 241; "Colum-
    bus Endures," 238; "Crane
    Dance," 241; "Crow Dance,"
    240; "Envoy to Haiku," 235;
    "Family Photograph," 241–2;
    "Guthrie Theater," 241; "Haiku
    in the Attic," 239; "Haiku
    Scenes," 239; "Hand Prints,"
    241; "Homewood Hospital,"
    241; "Mission Road," 241;
    "Museum Bound," 238–9;
    "North Dakota," 241; "Praise
    Ravens," 237–8; "Safe Har-
    bor," 241; "Square Dance,"
    240; "Treuer Pond," "Trickster
    Cats," 241; "Trumpeter Swans,"
    239; "White Earth," 236–7;
    "Whole Moon," 241; "Window
    Ice," 234
Vollmer, Joan, see Adams, Joan Vollmer
Voznesensky, Andrei, 3, 70, 75–6, 78,
    79–80, 82, 83
  Antiworlds, 80, *Dogalypse: San Fran-
    cisco Poetry Reading*, 79–80;
    Red Cats, 79
  "American Buttons," 80; "Anti-
    worlds," 79; "Beatnik's Lament,
    A," 80; "Dogalypse," 79–80; "I
    Am Goya," 79; "Story Under
    Full Sail," 79; "Striptease on
    Strike," 80
Vuong-Riddick, Thuong, 158
  "Seeds," 158

W
Waldman, Anne, 3, 11, 22, 44, 45, 46,
    55–7, 70, 75, 80
  Fast Speaking Woman, 56–7;
    *Fast Speaking Woman: Chants
    and Essays*, 56–7; *Helping
    The Dreamer: New and
    Selected Poems, 1966–1990*,
    56; *Iovis*, 53; *Room of Never
    Grieve: New and Selected Poems
    1985–1990, The*, 56; *Structure
    of the World Compared to a
    Bubble*, 56; *Vow to Poetry:
    Essays, Interviews and Manifes-
    tos*, 45

"Billy Work Peyote," 57; "Fast
Speaking Woman," 57; "Lines
to a Celebrated Friend," 56;
"Musical Garden," 56–7
Walker, Alice, 127, 228
Walker, Margaret, 224
For My People, 224
Wall, Eamonn, 155–6
"Immigrants," 155–6
Wall Street, 10
Wallace, George, 93
Warhol, Andy, 130, 179
Warren, Robert Penn, 152
"Audubon: A Vision," 152
Warsh, Lewis, 56
Washington Post, 94
Water Margin, The, 206, 207
Watergate, 11, 94, 110
Waters, Muddy, 83
Wayne, John, 105, 135, 209
Green Berets, The (film), 209;
Genghis Kahn (film), 210
Weegee, 67
Weiss, Ruth, 46
Brink, The, 47, *Desert Journal*, 46.
Welch, Lew, 53, 55
West, Nathanael, 2, 90
Day of the Locust, The, 2; *Miss
Lonelyhearts*, 2
Whalen, Philip, 48, 53, 54
Wharton, Edith, 105
Whitman, George, 63
Shakespeare & Company (book-
store), 63
Whitman, Walt, 12, 15, 25, 61, 78,
154, 174, 231
"Passage to India," 174; "Song of
Myself,"154
Whitehead, Peter, 73
Dir. *Wholly Communion* (film), 73
Wieners, John, 40, 48
Wigglesworth, Michael, 1
Wild One, The, 1
Will, George, 110
Williams, William Carlos, 2, 15, 46,
147, 153
Winch, Terence, 155
Irish Musicians American Friends, 155
"Irish Riviera, The," 155
Winterson, Jeannette, 112
Oranges Are Not The Only Fruit, 112
Wirshup, David S. 68
*Beat Generation & Other Avant-
Garde (sic) Writers, The*, 68

Wolfe, Tom, 89
*Kandy-Colored Tangerine-Flak
Streamline Baby, The*, 89
Womack, Craig, 135
*Red on Red: Native American Sepa-
ratism*, 135
Wondratschek, Wolf, 75
Wong, Anna May, 209
Wong, Nellie, 174
"Where is My Country?," 174
Wong, Jade Snow, 199
Fifth Chinese Daughter, 199
Wong, Shane, 200
Homebase, 200
Woodstock, 10
Woodward, Bob, 94
Wordsworth, William, 78
Wounded Knee, 131
Wright, Richard, 225, 234
Uncle Tom's Children, 225
"Big Boy Leaves Home," 225; "Man
Who Lived Underground, The,"
225

Y
Yamamoto, Hisaye, 193–4
*Seventeen Syllables and Other Sto-
ries*, 193–4
"Day in Little Tokyo," 194; "Legend
of Miss Sasagawara, The," 194;
"Life Among The Oilfields, A,"
194; "Seventeen Syllables," 193–4
Yamashita, Karen Tei, 197
Through the Arc of the Rain Forest,
197
Yamauchi, Wakako, 194
And The Soul Shall Dance, 194
Yau, John, 175, 179–80
Corpse and Mirror, 179; *Crossing
Canal Street*, 179; *Dragon's
Blood*, 179–80; *Edificio Sayo-
nara*, 180, *Forbidden Entries*,
180, *Notarikon*, 179; *Post-
cards from Trakl*, 180; *Radiant
Silhouette: New and Selected
Poems, 1974–1988*, 180; *Sleep-
less Nights of Eugene Delac-
roix*, 179
"Cameo of a Chinese Woman on
Mulberry Street," 180; "Genghis
Chan: Private Eye," 180; "Suite
of Imitations After Reading
Translations of Poems by Li He
and Li Shang-yin," 180

Yeats, W.B., 114
Yeh, Max, 144, 175
  Beginning of the East, The, 144–5,
  175
Yevtuschenko, Yevgeni, 79
Yorty, Sam, 140
Yugen, 22

Z
Zen, 12
Zhong, Luo Guan, 208
  Three Kingdoms, The, 208
Ziegler, Ron, 95
Zoot Suit (film), 163
Zukofsky, Louis, 157